A BEGINNER'S BOOK
OF
OFF-LOOM WEAVING

Books in this Series

A BEGINNER'S BOOK
OF
OFF-LOOM WEAVING

Xenia Ley Parker

Illustrated with diagrams and photographs

DODD, MEAD & COMPANY · NEW YORK

Photographs courtesy of:
Renie Breskin Adams, 76 (bottom), 90, 169; Vince Adesso, 204; Bernadyne Antin, 77, 99; Pat Banakus, 14 (right), 27, 35, 55, 70, 118 (left), 165 (top); Tadek Beutlich, 20; Joyce Cross, 60 (left), 73; Polly C. DeVito, 76 (top); Katherine Dickerson, 14 (left); Ruth Geneslaw, 17; Jan Knutson, 21, 144, 173, 174 (top), 185, 187, 206; Betty Lovejoy, 57, 111, 115, 191; Kathleen McFarlane, 174 (bottom), 186; Martin Parker, 79, 136 (top and center), 138, 196, 200 (bottom), 201, 208, 215; Scott Chase Parker, 16, 136 (bottom), 137, 147, 153, 165 (bottom); Xenia Ley Parker, 23, 25, 108 (bottom), 155, 211, 212; U. S. Department of the Interior Indian Arts and Crafts Board, 121, 141, 200 (top); Laureen Vlaisavljevich, 8, 108 (top); Margaret B. Windeknecht, 60 (right), 118 (right).

All drawings are by the author.

1   2   3   4   5   6   7   8   9   10

Library of Congress Cataloging in Publication Data

Parker, Xenia Ley.
A beginner's book of off-loom weaving.

Includes index.
SUMMARY: Introduces various off-loom weaving techniques including macramé, fingerweaving, braiding, and coiling.
1. Hand weaving—Juvenile literature. [1. Hand weaving. 2. Weaving. 3. Handicraft] I. Title.
TT848.P34   746.4   77-16880
ISBN 0-396-07558-4

CONTENTS

A BEGINNER'S BOOK
OF
OFF-LOOM WEAVING

Top view of Basket for Three Shells by Laureen Vlaisavljevich. Crocheted basket form of handspun wool: chain crochet of wool and linen plus shells embellishing inside of basket, 11″ x 24″ x 3″.

INTRODUCTION

Off-loom weaving is one of the most satisfying and creative means of expressing yourself. The possibilities are endless, as you learn just how many things you can do with the most basic of materials. The pleasure of off-loom weaving is that you work with fibers, textures, and color in a very personal way. There's great freedom of choice in the pattern and direction your weaving will take. This fiber art form consists of a group of techniques, related in that they all depend on the relationship of the yarns and threads themselves, as you work them by hand. You can blend the methods, change techniques, mix hues and fibers as you wish in order to produce the effects you want.

The techniques of off-loom weaving appear to be somewhat diverse, yet they all form shapes and patterns from the way in which you move the strands. As you become familiar with them, you'll enjoy the simplicity of the basic procedures and will love how soon you'll be able to do them yourself. You'll have fun creating all kinds of off-loom weavings. For most, you'll need little more in the way of equipment than the yarn plus the imagination inherent in each of us. If you want to discover how to use your own inspiration, to make articles that are both attractive and functional, off-loom weaving is for you.

1

OFF-LOOM WEAVING

Off-loom weaving is a creative *combination* of techniques. In its broadest sense, off-loom weaving is done with free or loose-ended threads. The threads are often held in a group by a knot, cord, or rod, or are supported by a basic construction or foundation. Many of the knotting and interlacing methods are worked from the top down. When you weave on a loom, you work with a tightly strung network of vertical threads called the *warp*. The filling or *weft* yarn is added from the bottom up, or on many looms from the front toward the back. In off-loom weaving, these threads can be worked in many ways, since they are not restricted by the loom. Weaving off loom allows great flexibility in changing direction, shape, color, and pattern because the strands are free to move and are not as formally structured.

The various techniques, related now in that they are all a part of the repertory of versatile off-loom artists, have developed throughout history in many diverse areas of the world. These methods include free-style weaving, which employs standard weaving textures, or "weaves," as they are called; weaving on supporting forms that aren't actual looms, with the same weaves; knotting or macrame, which is an ornamental method of knotting many strands; netting, a basically knotted technique of making the well-known diamond-shaped openings in threads to form nets; knotless netting, or *sprang*, which is a twisting version of netting; bobbin lace making, which is another variation of netting, using small wooden spindles to hold the threads as they are worked; plaiting, braiding, and finger-weaving, which are multithread variations of the three-strand braiding that is so familiar; twining and coiling, two methods which developed in

11

Egyptian weaving, rope sling for pot, coarse fiber, XI Dynasty, Province: Thebes, Deir el Bahri. *Courtesy, Metropolitan Museum of Art, Rogers Fund, 1922.*

12

basketry; and crochet, using the familiar hook and a single continuous strand of yarn to make the well-known stitches in new ways, far removed from the clothing that automatically comes to mind. Although these techniques are all distinctly different from each other, they work together so well that they are all a part of the off-loom weaver's background. You'll find that they are fun to do and easy to learn, so that you'll want to use them, alone or in combination, in many ways.

Off-loom weaving is perhaps one of the most ancient art forms, originating in the earliest days as people learned that they could make the things that they needed, rather than making do with whatever they happened to find. Well before there were loomlike structures, people learned to make knots and interlace natural fibers and grasses, using their own ingenuity to form them into functional articles. The basic principles of weaving were probably well established and extensively used before looms existed at all. As expertise in creating shapes and constructions grew, people began to enlarge on the simple methods, adding decorative beauty to their works. Just about any technique of interlocking fibers that could be devised could also be improved, so that the form and function of articles made were enhanced by the added dimension of design for its own sake.

Mats, nets, and simple baskets were most likely the first things that were fashioned by using off-loom weaving techniques. It is known that the first pottery was made on a base of woven basketry. As time went on, the individual methods of off-loom weaving came to stand on their own, while fabric weaving moved in another direction in which a standard system of supports and procedures was created.

In loom weaving, there are two sets of threads, called the *warp* and the *weft*. The warp threads are held in a parallel position, running up and down next to each other. They are set out together and then are woven with the weft threads, also called the *filling*, worked into the warp one at a time. The weft threads are taken into and between the warp threads from one side to the other, so that they are horizontal and cross the warp at right angles to it, creating a fabric or web. At first, the horizontal branch of a tree or a stick was used to hang the warp from, so that it could be woven more easily. Rudimentary shuttles, around which the weft was wrapped, made the weft less cumbersome to handle. Then, the warp threads were

 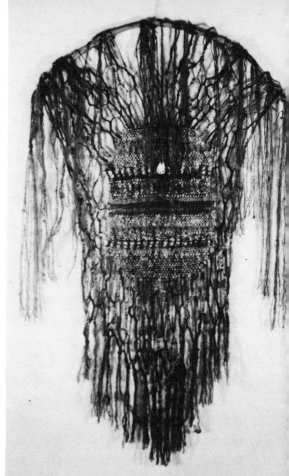

Left: Haystack Summer by Katherine Dickerson. Double weave, 24″ x 60″, plain weave background with fringed bottom, overhand knotted above the fringe to secure the weave. Striped double weave tubular sections in brown, tan, and deep gray on white are stuffed and fringed. Right: Curved top hanging by Pat Banakus. Central woven area with Greek knotting and plain weave in white on dark warp; top of warp is knotted to arched stick and then falls forward. Knotted and knotless netting and wrapping between warp fringe and central woven area.

often hung with stones or other weights to hold them taut. Simple looms, shaped like frames, were developed to hold the warp threads even tighter and more parallel, with regular spacing of the warp threads. As time passed, looms became more sophisticated, with *heddles*, which could lift groups of warp threads at one time, so that the weft could be moved more quickly from one side to the other. As more refinements were added, speeding up and easing the weaving process on a loom, the off-loom techniques became more separate and distinct. The off-loom methods depended more upon the manner in which the weaver held and worked the materials, with much less in the way of supports and equipment than loom weaving.

As the off-loom techniques developed along their own lines, they became more specialized, distinguished by the eventual use for which the article was being made and by the geographic location of the people doing the weaving. As the goal of creating finer fabrics with patterns and designs woven in was attained by loom weavers, off-loom methods developed for other, more specific purposes. Netting and knotting were naturally within the sphere of people who lived near seas, lakes, and rivers, since they depended upon their seines and large nets to help catch their food, the fish and shellfish that were readily found nearby. Seafaring peoples practiced netting and knotting—or macrame—on long voyages. The basic techniques served for everyday use on ships, but the mere fascination of variety led to the creation of more intricate knots and patterns in netting, to pass the time enjoyably.

Native American Indians created characteristic off-loom methods that differed greatly from one group to the next. Among these distinctive techniques that are familiar to us today are those which most often were related to basketry. Coiling, wrapping, and weaving in the round—now applied to off-loom works of many sorts—were developed primarily for use in baskets. Fingerweaving, a form of complex braiding, came into its own under the skilled fingers of Cherokee weavers, whose wide braids and sashes were also worked together upon completion of several parts to form a larger finished unit. Twining, worked with detailed designs and patterns, is seen in the distinctive pouches and flat bags formed by the Nez Percé of central North America. South American groups also continued to refine many off-loom methods, including the colorful netting of multistrand hammocks and bags in bright hues.

The techniques of basketry, in twining, coiling, plaiting, and blends of the three basics, are known and used throughout the world. Variations in pattern, application, and design developed in Europe, Africa, and the Orient. Along with the differences—which you will note as you begin to look at the works of off-loom weavers everywhere—you'll discover fascinating similarities in motif, method, and style from widely distant parts of

15

Chair, India, wrapped with rope. Rope seat in double-weft twill weave on narrow diameter bamboo. On Chinese straw mat. Macrame plant hanger in spiral sennits and single square knots.

Right: Ruth Geneslaw, Soft Birthday Cake. Stuffed plain weave in white with candle bases of single crochet stitch, wrapped yarns forming candles, flames in orange with wrapping in red and purple.

the globe. The weavers of many countries, working techniques that they have learned from their kin, carry on the traditions of centuries. Whenever you see a piece, notice how the design or pattern is created, how color is used, which types of materials are employed—in short, all of the parts that have made an attractive whole. Even the most basic flower basket, or patterned bag, or woven sash can provide you with an invaluable source of inspiration for your own off-loom works. The contributions of many diverse cultural backgrounds will enrich your own design vocabulary.

The connecting factor between all of these methods is that they are worked without a formal loom. Often, the strands of yarn are held together at the top, by a rod or knot, and worked in a downward progression. As the direction of the work is basically the same, you can thus combine weaving, knotting, netting, looping, twining, and crochet in one work. Of course, you'll select those that best suit the project at hand, and the possibilities are limitless. In most cases, the strands of yarn hang freely, so that you can manipulate them according to the technique you want to use for the desired effect. In other works, the strands are somewhat more controlled, as in weaving on a supporting form, but there is still the same great freedom to choose among techniques of working into and around the base yarns.

As you can see, there are countless styles and means of creating them that have come down to us through the centuries. Today's off-loom weavers have learned how to create with all of these techniques, combining and

experimenting to find the ones that are most personally satisfying and interesting. The rich and varied sources from which methods and designs can be drawn have produced a confederated style that is quite unlike the separate, singular forms in themselves. The freedom with which the different working patterns can be tried and employed is part of the challenge and creativity of off-loom weaving.

As you make your own off-loom weavings, you'll soon appreciate and understand their popularity. This type of weaving has the added appeal of portability. You won't find yourself limited to one work area by the demands of equipment, as these methods allow you to take them with you. For all but the largest works, you'll be able to weave off loom anywhere, using spare moments to advantage.

If you are new to this form, perhaps the most logical way to introduce yourself to off-loom weaving is to read about each technique and see which ones appeal to you most. As the methods do vary, you will need different articles to work with for some of them. However, all of these weavings are based on the simplest of materials, which you'll often find are already in your own house, or that you can make them easily. The few things that you may want to buy are quite inexpensive and are readily obtained from weaving or craft supply houses. If you can't find a local source, mail-order suppliers are available. (See Sources of Supplies list on page 220.) The simplicity of materials and equipment is one of the reasons that many off-loom weavers find that they become involved with each technique, familiarizing themselves with all of them. Once you have a background in all of them yourself, you'll have a firm foundation upon which all sorts of imaginative weavings can be built.

Along with the basic instructions in each method, study the works of fine weavers who are well versed in these styles. Their works will show you how great the design possibilities really are, providing a view of the fascinating world of off-loom weaving. At the end of this book, projects in each technique, and some which combine methods, will give you a working knowledge of just how they are done.

2

YARNS, THREADS, AND FIBERS

One of the most important aspects of off-loom weaving is the choice of the yarn, cord, or other material with which you create your work. The selection is rather crucial because the way in which the strands are moved and relate to the process being used is the basis of the weaving itself. The suitability of a certain yarn will greatly affect the outcome, helping you to achieve just the desired appearance that you have in mind. But since there are so many wonderful choices within each category, you'll find that you'll have no problems at all in making a choice within the right group. Once you know about the qualities of each type of fiber, and the yarn or cord made from those fibers, you'll be amazed at the range of colors and textures that will go well with the off-loom process you're going to use.

Fibers are the basic material out of which yarns and threads are made. They are found in nature and created by machines in the synthetics. The qualities of the fibers themselves make it possible for them to be spun into yarns of all sorts. Fibers, be they natural or synthetic, are varying lengths of substances which will hold the shape imparted to them by the spinning process. Their texture is such that when the relatively short lengths of fiber, known as the *staple*, are worked together, they hold their position and remain that way after they are twisted or spun. In natural fibers, the staple length is decided by the fiber itself, as it is found in nature. In synthetics, the staple can be as long as desired, since it is created by a machine which squeezes out chemical substances to create a fiber. When shorter fibers are needed, the machines simply cut them off as they are made and, conversely, when a longer fiber is needed—usually to add strength to the finished yarn—the fiber created is cut longer. The long strands of fiber

19

Cascade II by Tadek Beutlich. Warp of camel hair; weft of camel hair, jute, and sisal.

created by machines are known as *filaments*. The only filaments which occur in nature are those created by silkworms as they spin their cocoons.

Synthetic fibers were developed over a period of years, starting in the middle of the last century when the first one, rayon, was developed. The earliest synthetic fibers were created to meet the demand for fibers that looked like their counterparts in nature. Although they were often not successful in this attempt, successive chemists perfected new and different types of synthetic fiber until today's synthetics are useful, attractive, and strong. There are many kinds, too numerous to list, since the companies all have their own names for their particular products. The generic, basic, types of synthetic fibers most widely used are rayon, nylon, acetate, acrylic, and polyester. These are made in literally thousands of textures and colors and are given trademarked names such as Dacron, Orlon, or Acrilan. As you look for synthetic fiber yarns for off-loom weaving, you'll see just how many there are. Your choice can be made according to the qualities of a particular one that appeals to you. Synthetics are usually strong, easy to care for in articles which will be worn, and widely available. You'll also find synthetics blended with natural fibers, so that the resulting yarn has the benefits of both.

The most widely used natural fibers are wool, cotton, and linen. Although well known, silk is less used, perhaps due to its expense. Wool, spun out of the fleece of sheep, is made up into two kinds of yarn. The first, called *worsted*, is spun using the longer staple lengths of wool, so that the yarn is stronger than the second, the *woolens*. Woolen yarns, being made up of shorter lengths of fiber, are softer and a bit less durable than worsteds. In off-loom weaving, the relative strength of the yarn is most important for the supporting threads of the work. The interwoven threads, in works that have a distinct weft filling, can be much less strong, and even unspun wool fleece that has merely been cleaned and combed may be used.

Cotton is the most widely produced fiber, grown on plants which produce

Indoor Hammock by Jan Knutson. Detail showing textures of mixed fibers, wools, linens, handspun wool, and dog hair.

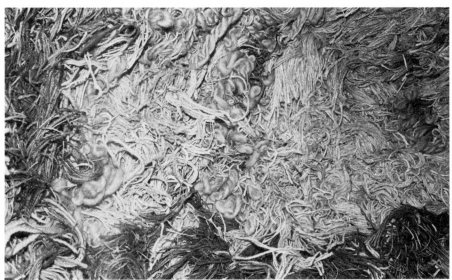

the soft fiber inside bolls, or seedpods, which burst open. Once the cotton is picked, the seeds are separated out and the fiber can then be spun into yarns and threads. The strength and sheen of cotton are often enhanced by a process known as *mercerization.*

Linen comes from the flax plant. Its fibers are found in the stems and are extremely strong and long. Once they are separated from the plant and spun, the resulting yarns are strong and durable. For fine quality and strength, linen has great appeal.

Jute and hemp are two natural fibers with much the same qualities. You'll find that they are often employed in off-loom weavings, because they are widely used to make rope and other thinner cords of similar nature. Jute is found more readily than hemp, although hemp is somewhat stronger and less coarse. Sisal is another fiber with qualities like hemp that is used for making cords and ropes.

Natural fibers often used in basketry are reeds, flexible split woods, bamboo, raffia, cane, and many types of tall grasslike plants. Imaginative weavings are also made using leather strips of various widths and lengths, bits of branches, feathers, and all sorts of found objects that can be worked into the weaving.

For softer, more exotic textures, the natural fibers which come from the coats of many different animals can be used. Among these are the fine softness of cashmere, gathered from the Far Eastern goats; fluffy angora, from rabbits grown especially for their fur in France; camel hair, from the Bactrian, or two-humped camel; alpaca, from the South American animal of the same name; and mohair, from the angora goat, which is the most widely used and usually least expensive of these fine hair fibers.

Yarns, Cords, and Threads

All of the fibers which are spun for use in weaving go through many steps in preparation for spinning. They are gathered, according to which type is being used, then cleaned or separated out from their source, combed or aligned so that they can be spun, and then spun up into yarn or thread. The various steps are performed differently, according to the type of fiber being used, but the basic procedures are similar. The fibers are often

Yarns, cords, and twines used in off-loom weaving

loosely spun prior to the actual spinning into a soft-textured fluffy sort of yarn called *roving*. For the special effect it can impart, roving is sometimes used as is for the weft or nonsupporting yarns in a weaving. For supporting, warp, or knotting techniques, roving isn't of sufficient strength.

The basic spun yarn, whether it has been spun by a machine or by hand on a spinning wheel or drop spindle (a simple but effective small wooden-weighted spindle with which you can spin your own yarns if you don't have a spinning wheel), is a twisted-together, continuous strand called a *singles* in weaving. The singles yarn doesn't look very twisted and it is fairly weak. The fibers are aligned and have been spun, but the strength of a plied yarn is not there, with the exception of some types of worsted wools and wet-spun linen. A *plied* yarn is one in which two or more singles are spun together. The singles are also called *ply*, so that you can tell how many singles were used to make up a yarn by its name. For example, a four-ply yarn has four individual strands—the single plies—which are clearly seen if you untwist the end of the yarn a bit. If you untwist the end of a singles, you'll see the tiny strands of the fibers that make up the yarn, rather than clearly defined plies.

To create yarns of different weights and textures, many means can be employed. The number of twists in one meter or inch of a certain yarn is carefully planned and controlled as the yarn is made. The amount of twists per inch changes the qualities of a yarn. Even when made from the same fiber, a yarn with many twists, sometimes called hard-twisted, is stronger, less elastic, and harder to the touch, a quality called the *hand* of a yarn. A soft-twisted yarn, with fewer twists, is more smooth to the hand, less durable, and stretches much more easily. For this reason, yarns which will undergo a lot of tension in an off-loom process should be hard-twisted.

The number of ply can also affect your choice of yarns, since the greater the number, usually the stronger the yarn. This is the case for yarns made out of the same fiber, not all yarns of the same number of ply made in different fibers. As the singles are twisted together to form a plied yarn, the spinning is done in the opposite direction than the ply themselves were spun, or they would unspin. The direction in which the yarn was spun can be seen in the finished yarn. On the whole, singles yarns are spun to the right, in what is known as an S twist, so that the plied yarns made out of these singles are spun to the left, in a Z twist. You can see why these names are given to the twist if you look at the direction in the yarn, held vertically. The S twist looks like a series of S-shaped curves, moving down toward the bottom of the yarn, and a left-twisted yarn looks like a series of Z's.

To form a cord, two or more plied yarns are spun together, adding great strength to the cord yarn formed. Just as a three-ply yarn is stronger than the three individual singles, even if held together, a cord is stronger than the plied yarns that make it up. That's why cords are so often used in off-loom works which require great strength, particularly in many knotting techniques.

In off-loom weaving techniques which are worked with yarns, you'll find that the most widely used are the yarns made in three- or four-ply. They are strong and have a good, smooth texture which makes them easy to work with as you learn the different methods. Singles and two-ply yarns are often used for lighter effects, and cords are good supporting threads.

Yarn sample cards. The larger ones show different types and weights of yarn; the smallest one shows shades of a rya yarn. A color card is usually available for each type of yarn on the yarn sample card. There is a small, hand-wrapped yarn butterfly in four-ply worsted wool on the cards.

As you look at yarns for your own weavings, you'll see that the number of ply does not always indicate the thickness. There are fine linen threads with many ply, and heavy-weight wools with only two. The medium weights, in any type of yarn, are usually best to start out with. You'll find that the number of plied yarns available is quite large in all thicknesses and fibers. The best way to discover just how many varieties of yarn there are is to visit a good craft or weaving supply store. If you don't have a large local source, a sample yarn card, available by mail from mail-order suppliers, is a good investment. There is a small charge for a yarn sample card, but you receive snippets of each kind of yarn, and often of each color in the group, attached to a card with descriptive names, fiber content, and price. In this way you can familiarize yourself with the yarns themselves.

When you look at the yarns you can use, you'll see that there are many with textures quite unlike the basic ply yarns. These are called *novelty* yarns, produced by adding new fiber elements to a yarn as it is spun or plied, or by using the plies in different ways as they are spun together. These yarns vary greatly in strength and texture, adding a new depth to your weavings. Experimentation with small amounts in sample works will show you just how they work and whether they are strong enough to be used for supporting or warp threads. They are always appropriate for the methods which don't require great strength, and as weft or filling in any work.

The names of novelty yarns are not necessarily interchangeable, so you should see the actual yarn before you make a selection. Sometimes, one kind of yarn will have the same name as another, entirely different, kind. In other cases, the same kind of yarn from two sources will have two different names. There are general categories, and most novelty yarns do fall within these groups. Descriptive names, such as loop, spiral, knot, corkscrew, and curl yarns, indicate what the yarn looks like. Other novelty yarns are named according to the process by which they are spun: flake yarn, which has small flecks of unspun fiber added into the yarn as it is plied; slub yarn, which is left deliberately unspun at specific intervals so that the yarn has tightly spun and unspun areas along its length, giving it an irregular thickness; and nub, knot, and knop yarns, all of which have similar tightly spun bumps along a thinner yarn strand, sometimes in an added hue. Bouclé, ratiné, and chenille are French names that have come to be used in English. The first two are types of curling or corkscrew yarns with added loops for greater surface texture, and the third is a yarn that is actually a woven fabric, cut into separate strands to form a soft, pipe cleaner-like appearance. The shine of metallic novelty yarns is now found

Hanging on a branch by Pat Banakus, made of softly textured novelty yarns. Narrow woven strips are wrapped at the center, with feathers added into the wrapped column. Fringe of wrapped and unwrapped yarns.

in several varieties, as the newer ones are made out of a flexible plastic with a central foil core which can be added to a ply yarn or used on its own. The original metallics are just that—metals—difficult to work with in many instances and sometimes likely to tarnish, lessening their sparkling effect.

As you choose yarns for your off-loom weavings, don't confine yourself to those which are specifically manufactured for weaving purposes. Yarns made for knitting, such as knitting worsted wool, are easy to find and work well. For smaller articles and bright effects, use wool needlepoint yarns such as three-ply Persian, which is actually made up of three strands of two-ply yarn which can be separated for use individually. The tapestry yarn, which is now sold for needlepoint, is a fairly lightweight four-ply yarn which is quite useful, as it is strong and durable. Both of the above are available almost everywhere in a huge selection of colors. For larger works, or bulky effects, rug-weight and quickpoint yarns are good choices. The rug yarns come in pure wool, wool and synthetic blends, synthetics and cotton, while the quickpoint yarns are usually made out of wool. If you're anxious to begin your adventure, it's nice to know that there are many suitable yarns which you will be able to buy nearby. For the cords and twines, widely used in off-loom weavings, you can look in hardware stores, stationers, and other seemingly unlikely places. There are so many different possibilities that you can look around with the idea of finding an attractive string or cord of any sort, as long as it has enough flexibility to be worked. Among the ones you should keep an eye out for are: seine twine, a natural for knotting and netting; plain rope, available in many widths, with a nice sheen and incredible strength; navy cord; heavy kite string, in cotton or synthetics; jute twine and rope; rattail, a shiny synthetic with a tubular shape, formed over an unseen base, often used for macrame but suited to many applications; soutache, a sort of double core covered by braiding; thin braided ribbons; wrapping strings and twine of all sorts. Alone or in combination with yarns and other threads, these basic materials yield such terrific results that you'll be surprised and pleased at how many new ideas occur to you.

Color

Color is naturally an essential factor. In yarns, there is a rainbow of varieties already on hand. You may find that the number of shades is limited in some types of fiber, such as the more unusual hair fibers like alpaca, which is used in its natural shades of browns, beiges, white, and black. Jute is also used in its natural brown hue, but there are bleached hues, ranging down toward beige and off-white. The sort of found object twines, like plain rope and string, are most often white, but you can dye them yourself with fine results. You can also dye, or overdye, adding new color to an existing shade, yarns that you have in large quantities in a single color. In fact, many weavers prefer to buy only the pale natural shades of wool and other yarns and dye them to produce precisely the colors that they have in mind. You can use ready-made synthetic dyes, which come in all hues, or experiment with dyestuffs made out of natural substances such as leaves and berries for soft, more muted yarn colors. Another interesting possibility is the space-dyed yarns, which come with several shades along the strand. These work up into attractive designs in themselves, with the pattern created by the varying colors unpredictably exciting.

In choosing the colors for your weavings, at first you may prefer to stay with basic color schemes, such as related colors in which you choose several shades within the same family. An example would be using lime, olive, and forest green in one composition. Another standard color scheme is called dominance and subordination. Pick two colors which go well together for the major part of the weaving, the dominant colors, and one color to be used in smaller amounts for accent, the subordinate color. Also, you can choose a single color that you really like and then change the textures of the yarns, or work with the one yarn shade in different techniques. The choice of colors and plans is so personal that it's really hard to say that any one plan is better than another. As you select the yarns you want to work with, hold them together and see how they look to you. It's your weaving, so your own opinion is by far the best guide in color schemes.

Buying Yarn

Yarn is usually sold by weight. If you are getting packaged yarn, it will usually be marked with the number of ounces or grams. Some helpful labels will also give you the yardage, but this is not often the case with yarns other than those made especially for weaving. When you come across a yarn sold by the gram, and you aren't familiar with the system, the approximate conversion rate is as follows:

1 ounce — 28 grams
2 ounces — 56 grams
4 ounces — 112 grams
8 ounces — 224 grams
1 pound — 448 grams

To convert in the other direction, when you buy yarn that is packaged by the gram, the usual approximations are:

25 grams   — just under 1 ounce
50 grams   — just under 2 ounces
100 grams — just under 4 ounces, or ¼ pound
250 grams — just under 9 ounces, or ½ pound +
1 kilogram — 2 pounds, 2 ounces

When buying yarns and cords for off-loom weaving, the most important consideration is the number of yards in a package or pound. Just knowing the weight of a skein doesn't give you this information. Often, it is marked on the label. For weaving yarns, the length is given indirectly by a number on the label which indicates the count, or number of yards per pound that can be spun out of a certain thickness of yarn. This is a fairly complex system and is used mainly for weaving yarns. It only applies to those made out of the natural fibers of wool, cotton, and linen, and not to novelty yarns, blends, or synthetics. As even seasoned weavers can become confused with the mathematics of figuring out yardage with the count system, most yarns are now labeled with the yardage as well. If you come across a yarn marked only with the count number, the salesperson in a good weaving supply house will be able to tell you the yardage. Other yarns, such as the novelties, synthetics, blends, and those sold for nonweaving purposes are usually sold by weight, with yardage added on some helpful labels. If you aren't sure how much yarn you'll need, make a sampler as described at the end of this chapter. You can also shop in good craft stores, where informed personnel can be of assistance.

Cords and twines made for knotting are usually sold by the yard, instead of by weight, so that they present no particular problem. Basketry materials are sold in bundles called *hanks* and sometimes by weight. They're most widely available in natural tones and can be used for many projects, so that it can be worthwhile to buy what may seem at first to be a lot in one hank. You'll always find a new way to use it.

Dye lot is the name used to describe yarn dyed in a particular batch. Each batch, or dye lot, is very slightly different than the next, even in yarns made by the same manufacturer in the same color. For this reason, the lot is indicated on the label by a number, letter, or combination of the two. If you are doing something which requires that areas in the work are blocks of the same color, be sure to buy all of the yarn or cord from the same dye lot. Yarns from two different lots will often form a streak in the weaving where they meet. In many off-loom works, there is a mixture of yarns, in color and texture, so that the dye lots aren't quite as important. However, when you know just what you plan to make, it's best to buy all of the yarn at one time so that you can be sure it's uniform throughout.

Choosing Yarns and Threads

For techniques such as free-style weaving, weaving on supporting forms, and fingerweaving, a medium-weight, firmly textured, four-ply yarn with a fairly hard twist is a good first choice. Cotton weaving yarns are fine to learn with, as they don't tend to stick together as wool or fuzzy yarns might. For knotting, macrame, and netting, you can use many different cords. Medium-weight, flexible, braided cord made for knotting is good, as are any well-made twines or heavy strings which don't unply easily. You should avoid slippery feeling synthetics, like nylon string, which is very strong but doesn't hold a knot. For traditional baskets in twining and coiling, wide raffia and flexible caning are used. For off-loom works in these techniques that aren't baskets per se, you can use light- to medium-weight rope and medium- to heavy-weight wool or wool-type yarns. For knotless netting or sprang, and bobbin lace, choose a lightweight durable cord, tightly spun mercerized cotton, or pearl cotton. All work well. To learn the basic crochet stitches, if you don't know them, pick any standard medium-weight, three- or four-ply knitting yarn, such as knitting worsted.

Samplers

Just as stitch samplers are made to learn embroidery stitches, you'll find that making a sampler for all of the off-loom techniques is always a good idea. You can use the same type of yarn or cord and technique that you want to learn to try out for a project you have in mind. You'll be in a good

Peruvian woven panel, unfinished, wool double cloth, length 14½″, width 5⅜″, X-XIV Century, Period: Pre-Inca. *Courtesy, Metropolitan Museum of Art, Rogers Fund, 1963.*

Weave sampler hanging by Pat Banakus. Techniques of plain weave, rya knots, wrapped warp, Greek knottings. Interesting changing weave patterns, and many textures and colors of yarn with warp fringe bottom. Hung from short dowel with warp fringe falling forward.

over the threads it went under and under the ones it went over on the previous row. The warp threads are the supporting threads, so that they must be quite strong. The weft can be almost anything that you can interlace with the warp, since it does not need great strength. For your first sampler, the weft and warp can both be medium-weight yarn, or a combination of medium-weight yarn or string warp with another yarn for the weft. Just choose yarns that are smooth and easy to work with.

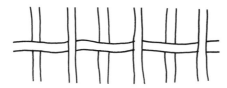

Basic weft movement—under one warp and over the next

35

Shed

Shed is the name of the opening formed between the warp threads as you lift specific sets of ends. You pass the weft thread into the open shed and work it into place in the warp to create your weaving. In free-style weaving, you create the sheds by hand as you go. There are two shed openings for the basic weave. The first lifts all of the odd-numbered threads and leaves the even ones underneath, so that the weft goes over the even threads and under the odd threads. The second shed, which is made by taking the weft yarn back through the warp threads in the opposite direction, lifts all of the even threads and leaves the odd threads underneath, so that the weft goes over the odd threads and under the even ones. To create the lifted openings in free-style weaving, you pick up the threads by hand and pass the weft into the opening. Or you can use a large blunt-tipped needle or other device to hold the weft yarn and work it in between the warp threads.

Shuttle

A *shuttle* is a notched wooden stick which holds the weft yarn as you weave with it. For this type of off-loom weaving, you can use the shuttle to create the sheds. The yarn is wound around the shuttle and fits onto it; the notches at either end hold it wrapped in place until you need it.

Row

As you pass the weft from one side of the warp to the other, moving from right to left on the first shed and left to right on the second shed, each movement is called one row. Rows are also referred to as *picks, shots,* or *throws.*

Selvedges

Sometimes spelled selvages, these are the side edges of the weaving that form as the weft is taken around and back from one side to the other. In basic weaving, the selvedges run up and down along the right and left sides of the work. To maintain the shape of your weaving—particularly in free-style works which depend on how you move the yarns to create the shapes—it's important to make a good selvedge at each side. When you begin the next row in your weaving, be sure to leave enough yarn so that it doesn't pull on the warp and cause it to tighten inward. It takes a bit of practice to make an even selvedge. When they are too loose they look loopy and somewhat uneven. That's just what your sampler is for—to try out the techniques and see how they work in actual weaving.

Beating

Beating is the pushing into place of the weft yarn after each pass of the weft. As you beat the weft, it interlaces with the warp. In order to have enough weft to move in between the warp evenly, you weave the weft at an angle or on a curved arc, in relation to the previous row. Then, as you beat it in, there is sufficient ease, or give, in the extra length of yarn created by the arc so that the weaving surface stays flat and smooth. If you find that the selvedges are pulling inward, check to see that you're allowing enough ease in the weft. In free-style weaving, the weft is put in place working from the top down, so that it is often beat quite strongly. As the weft is pushed into and between the warp threads in a weft-faced weave, the warp does not show in the finished weaving. This type of weave is used in making tapestries, which are often figurative designs that work well in a pattern where only the weft is visible. When the weft is beat more loosely, both sets of threads are seen in the finished weaving. For free-style weaving, the looser beaten weft can be used if the yarns are somewhat textured and stick together more, thereby combating the natural downward pull of gravity. In this type of work, the actual beating is done with any comblike device which will allow the warp ends to slip between the teeth as you push upward, firming the weft into place. You beat the weft after each pass of a row, holding all of the warp threads together in what is called the *closed shed* or "at rest" position. A tapestry beater is a wooden comb made for this purpose, but you can use a regular wide-toothed comb or a house-hold fork with equally good results.

As free-style weaving is an off-loom process, easy to do and simple in

Tapesty-type beater

mechanical terms, many of the words associated with on-loom weaving referring to specific loom parts and functions aren't used. This method is basic and direct, allowing you to weave with a minimum of equipment. It's sometimes recommended that you begin free weaving by practicing with the warp threaded around a piece of heavy cardboard or on a frame, but these then become looms, no matter what they are to begin with. It's best to weave your sampler in the real free style, just as you will your off-loom weavings on a larger scale.

Assembling the Materials

To make a sampler and learn the weaves, get a 12-inch long wooden dowel, from ½ to ¾ of an inch in diameter, for the top of the warp. If you can, drill two holes into it, ½ to ¾ of an inch in from each end, parallel to each other. Any rod, wooden bar, or a broom handle can be used if you don't have a dowel. A strong cord tied to a board is another top attachment that you can use, but a dowel gives better support as you weave and can be left in place when you're finished, making your sampler into an attractive wall hanging. You'll also need: a strong cord, about 18 inches long, to thread through the holes or tie tightly around the ends of your dowel; 25 yards of jute or similarly textured light- to medium-weight cord for the warp—smooth cords are harder to weave with at first as the weft tends to slip, even after it is beaten into place; an equal amount of weft yarn, such as a medium-weight wool worsted; a tapestry beater, comb, or fork; and twenty-four small weights of any sort, to hold the warp under a little tension. Optional equipment includes a shuttle or two for the weft yarn or a large blunt-tipped needle, either of the sort used in needlepoint for rug-weight yarns, or a special weaver's needle, which comes in lengths up to 12 inches. Looking like it was made from wire the thickness of a coat hanger, it helps to hold the warp yarns in an open shed, due to its length. Also, two C clamps, to help in making the warp.

Making the Warp

It is easier to make the warp in one step, before placing it on the dowel, so that all the threads are the same length. For this sampler, you're going to use warp threads that are folded in half as they are attached to the dowel. Each is one yard long, becoming two warp ends of approximately 16 inches in length when in place on the dowel. As you're using weights, add 6 inches to each length of warp thread, so that they are 42 inches each, folding to about 19 inches per warp end, leaving room for you to make the knots when you tie on the weights.

So that all of the warp threads are the same length on the dowel, wind them out beforehand between two stationary rods or poles of any sort, which you can place a known distance apart. The C clamps can be used

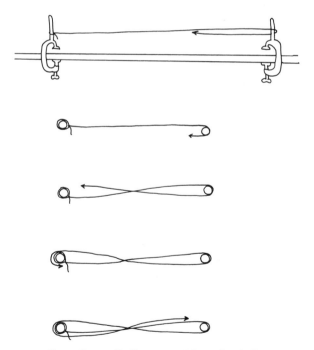

Winding out the warp threads on C clamps with rods, following the figure eight shape to form a cross in the threads.

39

to hold two smooth sticks or rulers on a table or workbench. There are also special clamps made for weavers which have a projecting rod on top and are merely screwed into place. You can also use the back of a chair, if it's the right size, or two sticks stuck into the ground, or two stout nails driven into a board. As each thread is made in a doubled position, place the winding rods 18 inches apart, or 21 inches for a weighted warp.

Start by tying the end of your warp thread onto one rod. Wind between the rods and up around the other one, then back to the first rod, crossing over the first half of the thread. Continue to wind in this fashion, creating a narrow flat figure eight of yarn, with the threads crossing in the middle until you have twelve complete ends and are back at the first rod on which the end is tied. Count the ends on the other rod to be sure that there are

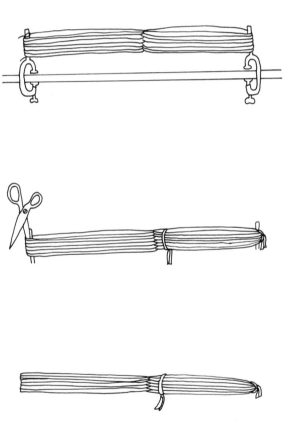

Completed warp. Cutting off the left rod after placing an extra cord next to the center cross, and the cut warp, ready to place on the dowel.

twelve. Then cut the warp and tie the end loosely to the first rod. Use an extra piece of yarn or cord, about 10 inches long, and slip one end into the warp threads as they go around the second rod. Slide the extra piece around so that it surrounds the ends and is at the top of them as they go around the rod, which is the exact center of the warp. Tie the ends of the piece of yarn together to hold the warp, then take another piece of yarn and tie it around all of the threads just above the cross in between the two rods. Take a sharp scissor, unknot the first and last warp end and cut it at each end so that the cut piece on each end is the same length as the wound warp. Then hold the warp near the first rod with one hand, slip the scissors into the warp at the edge of the rod, where it just goes around it, and cut through all of the ends. Place to one side and do the same thing again for a total of twenty-four lengths of warp. For larger works, the warp is usually done ten at a time instead of twelve. The cross in the center is placed there to help keep the threads evenly spaced as they're wound and to allow you to count them out and make sure that you've made the right number before you cut them off the rods. When using thinner yarns, you can also wind more at a time, such as all twenty-four in this case, but it seems simpler to work in two or more steps.

Placing the Warp

Take the dowel and, if there are holes drilled in the ends, thread one end of the 18-inch cord into one hole and tie a couple of knots in the end. Thread the other end into the other hole, making sure that the cord isn't twisted on the dowel and that both knots are on what is now considered the bottom of the dowel and a large open loop goes across the top. If your dowel has no holes, wrap the ends of the cord tightly around the dowel, ¾ of an inch in from the end and knot them well, so that the knots and loop are both on the top of the dowel. Suspend the dowel by the cord loop so that it is at a convenient height to reach while you are sitting down. If you have a place in a basement or workroom where you can put two hooks into the wall, use two heavy open hooks with screws at their ends and screw them in about 1½ feet above your waist while seated, at an equal height, about 12 inches apart from each other. Catch each side of the cord loop on a hook. If this is not possible, suspend the cord, using C clamps, on a bureau or other object, protecting the wood with heavy cardboard or padding between each side of the clamp and the object. You can also attach the cord to the top of a large sheet of heavy cardboard or thin plywood, about 18 inches in width and 22 inches in height. Prop the board against a table, with the end in your lap. In any case, the dowel should be hung so that it is parallel to the ground and easy to reach.

Take the first group of warp ends and carefully untie the two strings that are holding the ends together, placing them flat on a table or work surface with the folded loop ends toward you. Using a ruler, measure and mark the exact center of the dowel rod. Draw out the first looped warp cord from the rest, holding it folded and realigning it if necessary so that the two ends are even. Hold the warp by the loop and bring it up behind the dowel. Bring the loop over to the front and draw the two ends of the warp through the loop all the way. Pull lightly to tighten. This method of attachment is called a reverse lark's head knot and is used extensively in off-loom weaving. (If you bring the loop over the dowel to the back and then draw through the ends, you get a lark's head knot, which is equally effective, as long as you use the same one throughout the warp attachment.) Move the warp on the dowel so that it is just to the left of the center mark. Repeat the same motion, placing the next warp thread just to the right.

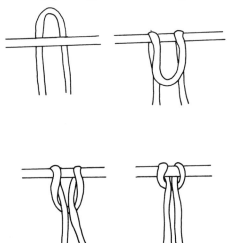

Making a reverse lark's head knot attachment

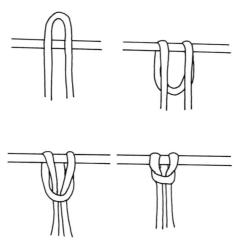

Making a lark's head knot

Continue, alternating sides so that the warp threads are evenly spaced along the bar and are equidistant from each other. In this sampler, they will be fairly close together along the dowel. When you've used up the first group of warp ends, do the same with the second, until all are in place. As you're using weights, tie one on each warp end, using whichever knotting is needed, according to the type of weights you have. Heavy metal washers and small fishing sinkers are particularly good here, as they have holes

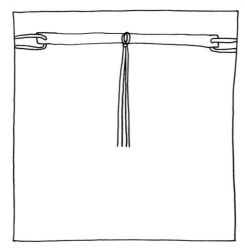

Placing the first warp on the dowel. Others are added from the center out in sequence.

which are easy to put the warp through. Their shapes are also interesting and can be left on your finished work as a decorative touch. Small, nicely colored stones tied around with the warp ends are another fine choice.

Winding the Weft

Now that the warp is ready to go, you prepare the weft so that it is easy to weave with. If you're using a shuttle, there is often a small notch within the larger one, or a small hole just below, on one side. If so, thread the end of the weft into the smaller notch or hole and wind the weft onto the shuttle. On a 12-inch shuttle, 4 yards of medium-weight yarn will fit well.

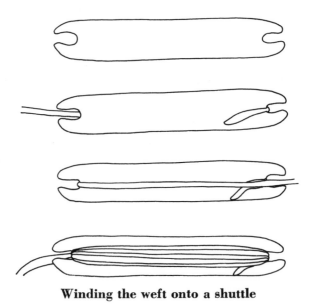

Winding the weft onto a shuttle

A shuttle wound too full is harder to weave with. Many shuttles are the same on both sides, in which case you merely hold the end of the weft in place near one notched side and wrap the weft around the shuttle. After a couple of turns, you can let go of the end of the yarn as it will be held in place by the newly wound yarn. With a blunt-tipped needle, you weave using only a yard or two at a time, cut and threaded through the eye of the needle. To weave without either, wind the weft into small skeins called

Making a yarn butterfly

butterflies. These hold the yarn as you use it.

To wind a butterfly, hold the weft yarn in one hand and place the other hand so that your palm faces you. Begin by placing the end of the weft in your palm and wrap the yarn up and then down around your thumb, across your palm and then up around your pinky. Continue to wind the yarn in this manner so that an X forms in the center of your palm, using about a yard or so of yarn. Cut the yarn and wind the end around the crossed center of the butterfly. Find the beginning end of the yarn and pull lightly on it. You'll see that the weft now unwinds from the center and doesn't tangle.

Beginning to Weave

If you're using a shuttle, unwind about 15 inches of yarn, or draw out that much from your butterfly. The needles are ready, once threaded. Start at the top outer right edge of the warp. Loosely tie the end of the weft around the first warp end, leaving about a 4-inch end that is woven in later. As you get used to weaving, you'll never tie on the weft unless for a special effect or technique, but it simplifies things at first. Using your fingers to lift the warp ends if you're using a butterfly, or the tip of the shuttle or needle, take the weft under and around the first end, to the front between the first and second warp ends, go over the second, under the third, over the fourth, and so on until you reach the left side. When using a shuttle or long needle, bring the front tip in and out between the warp ends, working right near the dowel, and draw the weft across through the warp when you reach the left side. Allow the weft to arc downward toward the left for ease. With a butterfly, it's easiest to pick up and hold several odd-numbered warp ends in sequence and pass the weft through the opening created by your lifting of the warp.

Using the beater and working from right to left, beat the weft into place by holding the warp ends in one hand and beating upward with the other. When beating a butterfly-woven weft, beat each small area just after you've passed the butterfly through the hand-manipulated shed. Again, you leave the weft at a slight arc-shaped angle for the necessary ease.

At the beginning of a weaving attached to a dowel, the first few shots or rows of weft serve to help hold the warp ends even and parallel, so they should be beaten in place fairly strongly. (Sometimes heavy cord or yarn is used for the first rows and is called a *heading*, which is removed or folded to the back of the weaving upon completion.)

For the second movement of the weft, you'll be going from left to right, taking the weft *under* the threads you went over and *over* the threads you went under in the previous row. The rest of the weaving is done in the same manner. If you stop after a row and don't remember which type you just did, you can tell by looking carefully at the weaving already finished. Also, you know that when moving from right to left on the first shed, you go under all the odd-numbered warp ends, and from left to right on the second shed, you go under all of the even ends.

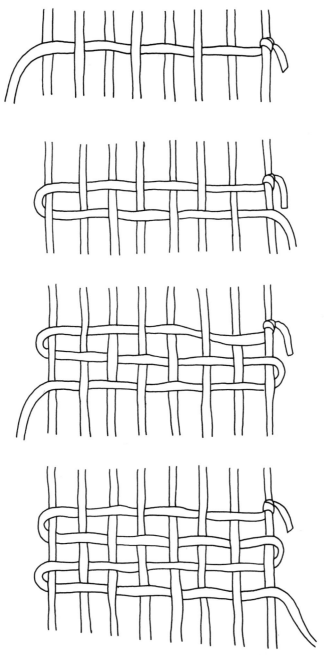

Weaving with the weft following the plain weave sequence, in the first, second, third, and fourth shots or passes of the weft through the warp ends. All odd-numbered rows are done as the first one and all even-numbered rows as the second.

Adding new weft yarn into the weaving in the middle of a row

All odd-numbered shots of the weft are done just as you did the first one, and all even-numbered ones are done as you did the second. These two basic motions across the warp create the plain or tabby weave. Weave several inches to see how it works.

If you use up the weft in the middle of a row, weave the end of the weft as usual. Then, take the tail end of the weft, unweave it for about an inch and push it to the back of the weaving between the two nearest warp ends. Take the new weft and begin to weave it into the same row, just before the last woven bit of the previous weft, so that the new weft overlaps for about 1½ inches. Stick the end of the new weft between two warp ends to the back as you begin to weave with it. Beat tightly where the two threads run next to each other.

Upon completion of the weaving, the loose weft ends are woven into the back of the weaving with a smaller blunt-tipped yarn needle. In a tightly beaten weft-faced weave, they can be cut at the back, about ½ inch long, and left as is. The first weft end is always unknotted and woven in. After your first weaving, try to begin the weft on future projects by wrapping it around the selvedge warp end once and leaving it at the back, as you don't need to rely on knotting it in place once you know how to weave.

After each pass of the weft, check the warp ends and comb them out with your fingers if they are beginning to wrap around each other. As you are using a free-hanging support and the weft is weighted, you'll probably find that the warp stays in place pretty well without tangling. However, it's always a good idea to check, since it is easier to shake or comb it out each time than to wait until it has become hard to weave.

As you weave, try beating some rows or *picks* more loosely to see how the effect changes. Get used to the feeling of how the yarns work together as the weaving proceeds. You can weave an entire work in only the tabby weave, changing the texture by changing the rhythm of your beating or just seeing how it turns out plain.

There are also many variations that you can experiment with, such as changing the basic weave, the texture or direction of the weave, the texture of the yarn, the color of the yarn, or any combination of these methods.

Basketweave

The basketweave is a weave which covers more than one warp end at a time, usually in a balanced progression, such as two over, two under, or three over, three under, all the way across the row. To balance the weave pattern, you repeat the shed for as many times going down as you went over, or under, a set of warp ends. For example, the basic basketweave is two over, two under, two over, and so on across one row of weft. At the end of the row, you wrap the weft yarn once around the selvedge or last warp thread and then beat. Repeat the same row moving from left to right.

The basketweave, in a balanced two-thread pattern

In this manner, you move down two weft shots, to balance the over two, under two weave. If there were three over, three under, you would repeat the same motion for three passes of weft yarn, wrapping it around the end warp each time. If you forget to wrap the weft around the selvedge warp, when you pass the weft through the same shed for the second or third time, you will merely unweave the previous row.

49

Twill weave, in a balanced two-thread sequence

Twill Weave

The twill weave is slightly more difficult than the basketweave, since you must keep track of four shed sequences. Once you see how the weave is done, however, you'll be able to do it just by following the pattern of threads in the previous row. There are three types of twill weave: the balanced, the weft faced, and the warp faced. What they all have in common is that the finished weaving shows a textural pattern of unbroken diagonal lines.

For a balanced twill, which is one in which the weft goes over and under the same number of warp threads, do the first row by going under two and over two all the way across. If you're doing the weave on the sampler, or any even-numbered warp, you start the second row according to the way in which the first one ended. When the first row ends with an under pass of the weft, start the next by going over the end warp, under the next two, over the next two, all the way across. At the end of the second shot, which moved from left to right, the last warp will be one over. On the third row, moving from right to left, go under the first two, over the second, and so on, ending with an over two. For the fourth shot, moving from the left, go over two, under two, across the row, ending on an under two. The illustration shows the sequence to be followed at the selvedges so that the weft does not pull back into the weaving. The sequence is then begun again, weaving the fifth row as you did the first, the sixth as you did the second, and so on. To make a reverse twill, or series of zigzagging lines, reverse the sequence, repeating row 3 on row 5, row 2 on row 6, row 1 on row 7, and row 4 on row 8. Start again with row 1 on row 9.

When your first row ends on an over pass of the weft, on row 2, moving from the left, go under one and then over two, under two across the row, ending with an over one. For row 3 go under two, over two across, ending with an under two; row 4, go over one, under two, over two across, ending on an under one. The sequence is repeated as above to form a twill.

As you learn to do the pattern weaves, you'll notice that the precise sequence is not always followed at the last or selvedge warp end. This is done to compensate for the weft, forming an even selvedge and maintaining the sturdiness of the weave. This adjustment is made whenever the last pass of the weft on the just completed row is the same as the first pass for the next row. For example, if one row ends on an under pass and the next row begins with an under pass to follow the exact pattern sequence, you have to make one over instead or the weft will merely pull back into the weaving, since nothing is holding it at the edge. The same occurs when two over passes meet in this manner and you correct it, for the selvedge only, with one under. The rest of the rows in all cases continue to suit the pattern, not the compensating pass of the weft at the selvedge. In weaves where there is a group of under passes on one row followed by a group of under passes on the next row, as in a basketweave, you wrap the weft once around the selvedge warp to secure it and maintain the pattern. The same holds true for a meeting of a group of over passes. In some weavings that don't need great strength or that don't have to be perfectly even along the selvedges for effect or a planned design, you can follow the pattern exactly and leave the areas of exposed edge warp as is. In general, it's best to keep a smooth selvedge for a well-woven article and use the compensating weft passes as needed, or make a narrow tabby section at each side.

For a weft-faced twill, you follow a four-row sequence, going under one warp and over three, under one, over three, and so on across each row. On the next row, you move one warp to the left and go under one, over three, all the way across, so that the "under one" thread is one warp over, moving toward the left. You do the same on rows 3 and 4, always moving the "under one" warp one warp to the left so that the diagonal forms in the weave. To do the zigzag herringbone weave, follow the sequence of row 1, 2, 3, 4, 3, 2, 1, 2, 3, and so on.

For the warp-faced twill, the same procedure is done with the exception

A. Weft-faced twill weave

B. Warp-faced twill weave

that the weft is taken over one and under three across so that the warp is seen in the finished weave.

Drafts

In weaving, the way in which the weft is taken over and under the warp and the sequence to follow in the rows or shots are shown in a graph. The graph is a diagrammatic representation of the threads themselves. Weaving drafts are the way in which the threads are lifted—or gone over and under —on each row, and the pattern is shown by filled-in squares on the graph. For most basic weaves, the graphs are four squares across by four up and down. In loom weaving, the four squares are numbered across the bottom from right to left and along the side, from the bottom to the top. In this

52

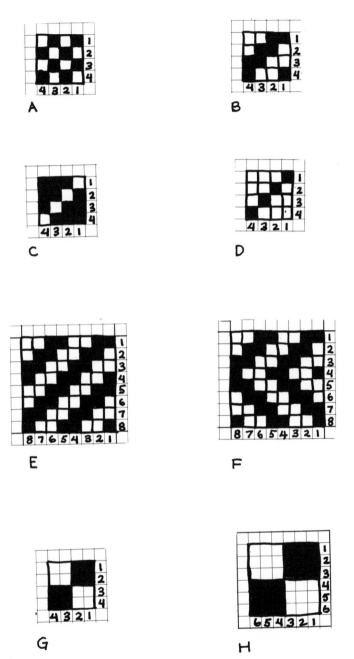

Weaving drafts on graph paper: A. Plain weave, B. Balanced two-thread twill, C. Weft-faced twill, D. Warp-faced twill, E. Eight-square balanced twill, F. Herringbone, G. Two-thread basketweave, H. Three-thread basketweave

application, it shows you how to thread the loom and weave the pattern. In free-style weaving, it shows how to lift the threads, by hand or by shuttle, and how to begin the next row. For off-loom weaving, the graph is numbered along the sides from the top down, since the weaving progresses from the top down.

For example, the plain weave on the graph, as shown, has every other square blacked in on the first row. The filled-in squares show you that one warp thread is lifted, or gone *under*, and the blank squares show that one is lowered, or gone *over*, as you move the weft across. The squares are numbered from right to left as the first shot moves from right to left. On the second row, you see that the opposite warp ends are lifted for this basic weave. Row 3, reading down along the side, is just like row 1, and row 4 is just like row 2. The graphic versions of the twill weaves show you how to work with rows that have different lifting plans for rows 1, 2, 3, and 4. To follow the twill, you start again with row 1. Just remember that as you read the draft on the even passes of weft, you read from left to right. The larger eight-square graphs show how the sequences work alongside the graph for both the twill and herringbone variations. Just as you repeat the row sequence, you repeat the warp-lifting sequence, starting again at 1 when you have lifted or lowered the threads as shown, either from 1 to 4 or 1 to 8. The two- and three-warp basketweaves show how the graph looks when the shed is repeated on the next row.

Variations in the Plain Weave

There are many ways to change the texture and shape of the plain weave according to the way in which you move the weft. As the weft does not have to be continued all the way across a row, you can vary your weaving by employing some tapestry techniques.

Slits

Slits are tapestry derived methods, which form up-and-down openings in the weaving. You make a slit by using two separate bundles of weft yarn. To do it, merely weave one section in the plain weave with one weft yarn,

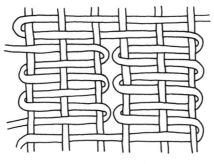

Weaving a slit

using the standard weave but not going all the way across the row. Turn back anywhere you like in the weaving and complete the second row as usual. Do several shots of weft over the same number of threads. Then, take the second bundle of weft and weave the remaining threads in the usual way, starting at the next empty warp thread to the left of the woven section. Go to the end and back using the same shedding sequence. When the same number of shots has been done on each side of the slit, end off the second yarn and go straight across with the first for a few rows, closing the bottom of the slit. You can make slits anywhere in the weaving. In tapestry making, they are often done with two or more colors of yarn on separate shuttles. They can be left open or sewn closed from the wrong side with regular thread and a needle when the weaving is finished.

Pat Banakus, hanging on white warp in plain weave with slits and color changes. Vertical edge along central square shows dovetailing. Fringe of unspun wool rya knotted onto bottoms of slit weave sections.

Other Tapestry Weaves

The different weaves in tapestries are often for the effect of changing colors within the weaving, but they also add texture to a solid color weaving, and can be done on your sampler. They allow you to move the weft over different areas of the weaving, making shapes and forms. For all of these techniques, you weave the standard plain weave, with two sheds. The change is the fact that the weft is not taken over the entire set of warp threads, but worked within them, with two or more bundles.

Dovetailing is a weave where the two wefts are worked in sequence. For the first side, you weave up to a warp thread, go around it, and head back to the right. For the second weft you weave from the left, go around the same warp thread, and back to the left. Each is done in turn so that the two weft threads meet and go around the same warp in sequence. Where the two threads meet along the same warp, the effect is like the meshing of the teeth on two gears.

Interlocking is done with two wefts, in the same manner as dovetailing, except that you bring the yarns together in the meeting space between two warp ends. At the point where the weft yarns meet in the space, you twist them together once. Then each is taken back in the opposite direction.

The *diagonal weave* is also done with two bundles of weft, but you can work the sections independently of each other. Weave the first section so that the weft doesn't cross the warp entirely. When you reach the same spot on the third row, stop weaving one warp end sooner. Repeat on the fifth row and you'll see the diagonal developing. You can continue it for

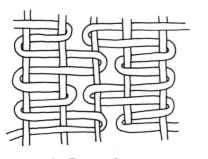

A. Dovetailing

B. Interlocking

Detail of Trees by Betty Lovejoy. Woven on a Masonite board (see Chapter Five), mostly wools and other yarns on linen warp, trunks show slit weave; ground, sky, and leafy areas in tapestry technique of diagonal weave and looped weft in golds, browns, olive greens, orange, tan, beige, and light blues.

C. Diagonal

as large a section as you wish. Then weave in the other half of the diagonal with the second weft yarn.

Another effect you can create with the plain weave is to weave a small section over the same number of warp ends, beating the outer edges of the weft section firmly so that they form a point at each end. The center of the section is beat more lightly, to form a curving upward arc shape. This is called a *pointed weave*, as you can work several sections, with a meeting over the same warp end of the outer pointed weft sections.

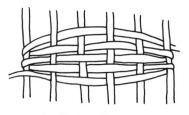

A. Pointed weave

Inlay is another technique with which you can form an arc shape within your weaving. To do it, you weave a background of fairly loosely beaten weft. Then, using the tip of your beater, shuttle, or needle, carefully open out a section of warp ends by beating upward and downward in between two weft threads. This creates an open area, which you can weave with the same yarn, or with another, lighter weft, perhaps in a different shade. Use a smaller blunt-tipped needle to weave into the opening in the same weave.

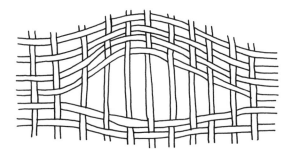

B. Making an opening in the woven weft for an inlay

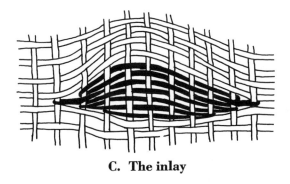

C. The inlay

Exposed warp ends are areas of your weaving which are left unwoven as part of the design. You can make a random weft pattern, going over some warp ends and not others, or skip entire areas, so that the warp becomes a vertical design element. In a finished weaving, the unworked sections of warp are held in place and remain in their visible up-and-down position. For this reason, the last several shots of weft are often taken all the way across the weaving, as at the beginning, to create a firm bottom edge. The exposed warp, if continued over too great an area, can weaken a weaving, and make it difficult to weave, since the warp ends aren't being held in position by the weft. Start weaving exposed areas in small sections to see how the technique works. In a weave that isn't dense, or tightly beaten, you can expose the warp threads after the weft is in place, by carefully separating two weft shots. Then beat up and or down, as you wish, just as you did to expose threads for an inlay.

59

Joyce Cross, detail, left, showing exposed white warp thread area with black rya knotted yarns ending in natural wooden beads. Upper area in beige, brown, and black shows free-hanging weft ends forming textural areas along each section as the weft ends hang down. Batik on hand-weaving, right, with rows of twisted thread leno worked with groups of warp ends in each twist, by Margaret B. Windeknecht.

Leno is a twisted warp thread technique, which works best in this type of weaving when you do one twist, weaving within an area framed by sides of plain weave. Weave one side first, with three shots of weft over six warp ends. Then, move to the next two warp ends toward the left, after weaving the first six as usual. Reach between the just woven section and the next end, to the back, take the second end under and then up around the first end, making a loop just large enough for the weft and pass it through. Then move to the next set, bring the left end under the right and up, pass the weft through the loop, continue across six pairs in all, stopping at the last six ends. Weave them in plain weave in three shots to match the

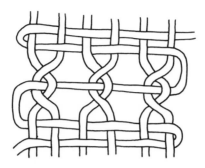

Twisted thread leno technique

other side. Beat the twisted area lightly, if at all. The warp remains in the twisted position beneath the crossing weft, as well as above it, as you begin to weave the next row which is a shot of plain weave from left to right. If you plan another row of leno, weave several shots of plain weave and beat them firmly. Because the leno twists the warp ends, you need the rows of plain weave in between rows of leno to realign and hold the warp in its parallel position.

Ghiordes knots add the texture of a pile, or set of standing threads, to your weaving. They also work best in a frame of plain weave, worked over, along the sides, and then under the knots. If you want to add several rows of knots for a dense pile effect, weave the plain weave beforehand, leaving an exposed warp area to be filled with knots. This is done so that you can knot from the bottom of the area upward, as it's almost impossible to make a row of knots under one that has already been done. For one row or

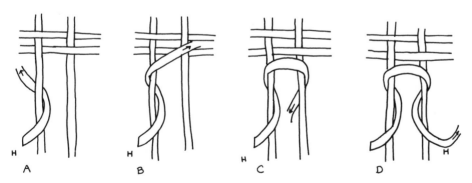

Making a ghiordes knot with a continuous strand. Hold at H, begin a new knot at the end of the first one, holding at H in step D.

61

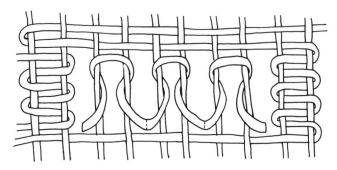

Completed series of knots within a plain weave outline. Clip for pile on dotted lines; leave uncut for loops.

many, each is done in the same way.

Work from left to right, over pairs of warp ends. Wrap the yarn around a small shuttle or thread it into a blunt-tipped yarn needle, using about 18 inches of yarn at a time. Bring the weft just to the right of the first exposed end on the left. Slip it in between the first and second end, to the back, holding the end of the weft with your other hand, at the height you want the pile to be. Bring the weft behind the first end, up and to the front at its left. Then bring it up and around to the right side of the second end, put it in to the back between it and the third end. Then, bring it down and around the second thread, out to the front between it and the first one where you're holding the end of the yarn. Pull lightly on the end of the yarn and the rest of the weft to tighten the knot. Let go of the end of the yarn and move your hand over the knot just completed. Place your thumb on the weft leading from the knot and make a loop of the yarn on your thumb, the same height as you made the end of the weft at the beginning of the first knot. Then bring the weft over between the next pair of warp ends to the right and make another knot as you did the first one. At the end of the area, or row, you simply cut the weft, leading from the last knot, to the same length as the loops. The loops are then cut, pulling lightly with the scissor so that the two sides are the same length, forming the pile. If you like, you can leave the loops uncut, for a more rounded textural pattern. The beginning and end of each area will naturally have one cut end, but you can tuck it to the back of the weaving if you want a completely loopy appearance.

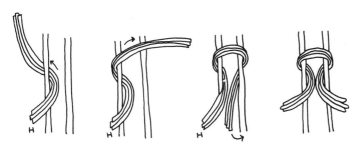

Making a rya knot with cut lengths of yarn, hold at H

This kind of knot is called a *rya knot*, as it is widely used in Scandinavian rug making. It can be varied by using several wefts in each knot, or by using precut lengths of yarn, alone or in small bunches. For the true rya look, use the hard-twisted, two-ply, rya wool yarn, several strands at a time. You can also use lengths of the weft you've been using, or any other yarn that appeals to you. The yarn is cut into lengths of 3 to 4 inches, giving a pile of from 1¼ to 1¾ inches, as part of the length is taken up by the knot and you work with the strands folded in half. Take one length of yarn, or up to four at a time—the knot is made in the same way. Work from either the right or the left, over pairs of ends. Hold one end of the yarn just above a pair of ends, at the length of the pile. Wrap the other end into the pair, under the left one, up and around the top, over to the right, over it and under it to the space between the ends. Bring it out where you're holding the beginning end of the yarn. Pull upward on both ends of the knot at once to tighten it in place.

Knots worked with precut lengths of yarn are often faster to make and are better for multistrand knots than a continuous weft. For small areas where the warp ends are harder to reach through, as in the exposed thread areas, which can be opened up for knotting as they are for inlay, you'll probably find it easiest to work with a continuous strand, or several, threaded into a blunt-tipped yarn needle. Then you make the knots as in the first technique. You can trim finished knots for a shorter pile, or deliberately make them uneven, for a shaggier look.

Dense pile, worked with several strands over a large warp area, will become quite heavy. Be sure to weave several rows of plain weave to support the knots between rows. The length of the pile will cover the areas of plain weave completely, so that you'll have a pile surface that's strong and well made. As a free-hanging weaving needs a certain lightness to weave well, make small sections of dense knotting, or place them in individual rows with plain weave supporting them for best results.

Changing Yarns for Texture

When you change the kind of weft yarn you are using, the texture and appearance of the weaving will change as well. Each yarn weaves up into a different surface. Experiment with small amounts of all sorts of yarns and threads to see how the textural finish changes. Choose yarns in various fibers, weights, plies, and novelty plying in the same shade, to see how the weaving changes. Each section will absorb and give off light in a different way, since the yarn surface reacts differently and the one-shade weaving will take on the effect of many. Try other shades for new looks.

Changing the Type of Weave for Texture

When you change the pattern of a weave, you continue to move the weft across the warp in a straight line from right to left or vice versa. There are other kinds of weaves in which the way the weft moves across the warp ends changes. These weaves create new textures in the weaving surface. As the weaves tend to group the warp ends together, they are usually followed and/or outlined by rows of plain weave.

Soumak is a technique derived from Oriental rug making. It's best done with a small shuttle or a needle, as the butterflies are a little harder to handle. To begin each row, you wrap the weft around the selvedge and second warp from the right side and bring it around the right edge to the

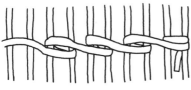
A. First row

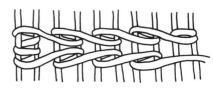
B. Second row

Soumak

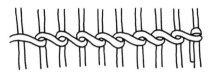 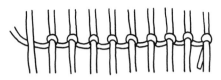

A. One-warp soumak   **B. Reversed one-warp soumak**

Soumak variations

front. Then, bring the weft over to the left for four ends, back down and under two ends, moving back to the right. Take the weft four to the left over the ends, and two to the right under the ends, across the warp.

Soumak can be done on every other row, alternating with the plain weave, beating each row fairly loosely. For a denser, more textural weave, do every row in soumak and beat firmly. If several rows of the stitch are not beaten tightly together, they tend to pull the warp out of line. As you do the weave, don't pull the weft as you move forward four and back two. The ends should remain flat and even and not pull together. You can make small sections, covering only part of the warp, or larger ones. Soumak is woven in one color, or several, as you prefer. The technique is often worked within larger sections of plain weave in different colors, in a method that is sometimes called inlaid, as the soumak areas are set into the plain-weave background. It can also be single warp, or reversed.

Brook's bouquet is the name of a type of weave in which the object is to gather the warp ends together. It is always done in a single row, preceded and followed by several shots of plain weave, which hold the warp in line

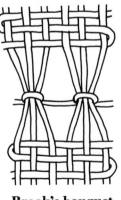

Brook's bouquet

65

for the rest of the weaving to proceed. The weave itself is a wrapping of the warp in which you choose a small number for the groups of warp ends to be wrapped. For example, if you choose to use a multiple of three ends, you start by bringing the weft from underneath, around at the left of the first three ends at the right. Then you take the weft over the three ends to the right and under them again. Tighten a bit so that the three ends group together, with the middle one in the group running in its usual parallel position. Continue the row, bringing the warp under the following groups in the same way, wrapping over from the left around to the back on the right. Make sure that the weft between the wrapped bundles is left with enough ease that the groups aren't drawn toward each other.

Wrapped warp is another wrapping method, which covers the warp completely in a tube or column of weft yarn. You can wrap one or several ends at a time, although it's easiest at first to wrap two or more, as they make a wider core. Bring the weft around the group of ends from the bottom of the area to be wrapped. Move the weft under the ends to the left, up, over and around to the right, under to the left, and up to the right just over the first wrapping. Try to wrap the yarn evenly so that the weft wrappings don't overlap. Continue up the warp ends, making the wrapped column as long or as short as you like.

As the area between columns of wrapped warp is left open—for what would be called the negative space in a design—you use these areas as part of your plan. To vary the effect, take several bundles of weft yarn and

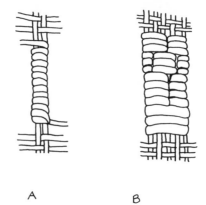

A   B

Wrapped warp techniques: A. Wrapping two warp ends, B. Varied wrapping over five ends for a branching effect

wrap over three or four warp ends at a time. Use the separate wefts to wrap out warp branches, sometimes wrapping around all of the ends in the group, then around one and two at a time. You can change the patterns of wrapping as you wish, creating a series of wrapped branches and closures surrounded by open space. Wrapping is almost always done from the bottom up, since a column wrapped from the top tends to slip downward into a spiral rather than the column, which looks like a neatly stacked pile of tires.

The *Greek knot* is a wrapping technique in which each end is wrapped three times, from the top down. Each wrap is locked in place as you bring the weft over to the next end. To do it, you move the weft over the first end from the right, then under it on the left side to the back, around and up on the right, under at the right to the back, leave a loop at the left, bring the weft under to the right and up around through the loop. Tighten the individually wrapped warp ends, but leave enough room in the weft as you bring it to the top of the next end to continue, so that the warp ends don't pull together. Wrapping as a finishing technique is described in the next chapter.

The Greek knot

Spanish lace is an open weave, usually done over three warp ends at a time. You can vary the number, as long as each area is done in consistent groups. Weave from the right, make five shots of plain weave, forward and back over three ends, move up to the top right of the next three ends and continue.

Spanish lace

Changing Colors

The most basic color variation that you can do is to make horizontal stripes. End off the first color after you finish a complete row. Cut the weft and wrap it to the back of the weaving around the outermost end, to be woven in when the entire weaving has been finished. Start the next color by rewinding the shuttle or taking a new one, as you never wind on top of existing yarn. If you're not using shuttles, thread a needle or make a new butterfly. Start the next shed with the new yarn, just as you would for the beginning of your weaving. The yarns are ended off after each color section.

To make plaids, you plan the warp in more than one color, winding it out in different sets of threads. The warp is visible in all but the tightly beaten weft-faced weaves, so that a plaid forms as you weave a multi-colored warp with crossing weft yarns in different colors. In traditional plaids, the weave is balanced, or worked with an equal number of warp ends and weft shots per inch, in the same sets of colors, in the same order of progression, using one kind of yarn.

To change colors in a weft-faced weave, you need to change only the weft, since the warp isn't visible. Tapestry techniques such as slits, diagonals, interlocks, and such are naturally suited to multihued weavings, as the color areas are ended off as they are completed. Push all tail ends to the back of the weaving. If you carry the yarn from one area to the next without weaving it into the warp, it tends to pull the work together.

Vertical stripes are made in a weft-faced weave, using two shuttles or bundles of yarn. Each is wound in a different color. The first is taken from right to left in the standard first shed. Then, you take the weft around the selvedge end to secure it. Take the other shuttle and weave it through the second shed from left to right and secure the end in the same way. Continue, working each shuttle through one shed in one direction and the next through the next in the other direction. In the standard two-shed weave, firmly beaten, vertical stripes will form, as all of the overs in the odd threads are one shade and all of the unders in the even threads are another.

Ending Off Your Weaving

There are as many ways to end off weavings as there are weavers. The choice is up to you, depending on your own preference and the design of your free-hanging weaving. If you have used interesting weights, they are often left in place as part of the design. Heavy ceramic beads are often chosen as weights for this reason. Whether you have used weights or not, the last shot of weaving is secured in one way or another or the weaving will eventually begin to unravel. The most widely used ending is to add a row of knots, tying off two or more warp ends at a time. The knots are small and functional, or visible as part of the design. For decorative knots and endings, see the chapter on knotting and macrame. As you tie the warp, you can leave the remaining ends hanging below the knots to make fringe, or cut it quite near them. You may want to make small knots and fold back the ends, working them into the back of the weaving for a smooth edge. You can also add further knotting, wrapping, and other knots to the remaining warp instead of trimming it off.

Another method for finishing a free-hanging weaving is to add another dowel, forming a stretched, even wall hanging that's sure to hold its shape. At the end of the weaving, take a dowel of the same weight, length, and texture as the top one—or one that contrasts if you prefer—and weave it into the warp, using the standard shed. Make one knot with every group of ends—each group from two and up—below the dowel to hold it in place. The hanging ends can be further finished with knotting or wrapping, or can be cut close to the dowel. You may find it easier to plan the weaving if you add in the dowel earlier on, to see just where it will be and then weaving with it in place. It will also serve to hold the warp ends more evenly as you weave.

Finishing Your Weavings

For wall hangings and other articles that will be finished by the ending-off techniques, that is all you have to do. If your weavings have a definite purpose, you finish them to fit that function. For example, if you're making a free-style weaving into a pillow or a tote bag, you plan and follow the weaving so that it is the right shape and size to be sewn and assembled with seams. You don't cut the weaving itself as you would for a fabric woven on a loom, which has many ends per inch and is much more tightly beaten in most cases. Since your free-hanging weavings are done with few warp ends per inch, and a less dense weave, you make the article to fit its final shape. You can work in small sections, using a heavy cord instead of a dowel for the top to form curved beginning weavings, or combine various off-loom methods, as some allow shaping to be made, in parts that will be assembled, with great ease.

Planning a Weaving

Free-style weavings are conceived with a sense of design. You create your own patterns and designs with the idea that they will be enjoyed for themselves. Choose several shades and textures of yarn that appeal to you and begin to weave with them. Be adventuresome in your choice of technique and color. See what the weaving suggests to you as it takes shape.

Hanging on twiglike branch, in novelty yarns, finished with one large overhand knot to gather lower warp ends into one tassel form. By Pat Banakus.

If you prefer, weave a small sampler, to see how the yarns relate to each other and to help you plan a larger work. Many weavers start each new design with several samplers in different weaves and hues. When you choose the one that seems to be most exciting for the current project, you'll have the others as good reference points for future works. Weave with contrasts in color and texture, or in basic shapes and forms. For wall hangings, sculptural forms, and other decorative articles you can literally work in many directions, as the finished weaving won't have any actual use to withstand. The lines of your weaving can change in real terms, as the possible blending of techniques makes the warp and weft bend and turn. Or, you can change direction visually, as the colors of the yarns create a path for your eye to follow as you look at the work. When you plan things that will be worn or used, think more of the variations you can achieve using color and texture, rather than the open spaces and looser effects that go so well in weavings which will be hung or otherwise displayed in a stationary manner. As you get to know the methods of off-loom weaving you'll find that they inspire ideas for all sorts of weavings.

Sculptural Forms and Unusual Attachments

Once you are proficient in free-weaving techniques, you can expand the scope of your work, making new forms in three-dimensional weavings. You can use a double warp, with twice as many ends, and weave two layers simultaneously. This is called a *double weave*, which can be done as two separate entities, with two weft yarns, with areas of the top layer worked in slits or other exposed warp or open space to show the weaving beneath. You can also use a continuous weft, which is woven through the warp in two passes, one of which goes around the edge and back through the back layer of ends to form a tubular weave. In both cases, you divide up the warp so that every other end is on a different weaving plane, and weave each set as a single layer. You may find it easier to use two dowels, or top attachments, so that the two sets of warp are distinct. Usually, you weave the bottom layer first, using every other end or those on the lower dowel, and then the top layer, with the remaining ends or those on the upper dowel. Another method is to part the upper warp, put each half to one

Warping a hoop or ring held flat

side, and weave the bottom layer first. Then, you work the top set of ends to suit the design formed by replacing the ends and weaving with the bottom layer in mind. For tubular weavings of this type, you take the weft around the edge, alternating the shots from one layer to the next, with the weft being the connective part.

Metal rings, hoops, tree branches, and all sorts of found objects can be used for the top of a weaving. Their form may even suggest a design. This type of foundation, unusual in itself, can be strung with a warp in the same way you tie one onto a dowel. For the warping, you skip the winding step and suspend the hoop, branch, or other object by tying a strong rope at either end or placing it on a tall shelf. Then you work the warp directly on the article, tying it in place in the areas suggested by the form of the object. Fold a long warp in two, cutting as you place it, and leaving it longer than you might expect, so that you have plenty of room to weave. As you tie on the warp ends, keep your mind open to the pattern created by the object with its hanging warp yarns and use the image you receive to aid in your choice of weft yarns. As you work with new shapes, you'll see how they evoke their own themes for the weaving itself.

Stuffed and padded double weave hanging in deep gold weft on olive warp by Joyce Cross. Wrapped coil in gold curves into and around the main form for added dimension.

Hoops and rings can be suspended by one cord placed on one edge so that they hang flat. You can warp the bottom with ends, from ¼ to ½ of the circumference of the ring. The weaving then begins on a base of curved warp—a reversed arc of attaching threads. You can also suspend a ring horizontally, tying cords at four equidistant points around the ring. Then you can place warp ends around the circle, or on parts, to form a tubular column as you weave it with the weft yarn. These forms take on the qualities of sculpture. You can add new rings into the weaving, below the first one, as a means of weighting the warp, or as part of your design. The finished weaving can be stuffed or padded for true soft sculpture.

If you're using two rings, it's often best to place the top ring as usual and add in the lower one before you begin to weave. Slip the lower ring into the warp, placing the ends over one, under one around the hoop, and tie it in place with pairs of ends in simple knots under the hoop. If needed, as you weave you can lower the hoop, adjusting the warp length. When used as a weight, the hoop or ring can be removed altogether when you are finished.

Another unusual attachment is to find an object which has previously served another purpose. As an extension of the weaving, the object is incorporated into the design. As an example, you can remove the covering fabric of a lampshade, exposing the wire beneath, as detailed in the projects chapter. The warp is placed, using the wire as an armature, giving a weighted type of warp which can be woven easily. Many different objects, even those with dissimilar functions originally, can be used in this way, as long as you can tie on the warp and find open areas through which you can weave. Look around you with the idea of using the things that you see in new ways, creating unique patterns in off-loom weaving.

4

KNOTTING AND MACRAME

Tying intricate knots, on threads held in series or individually, is an ancient form, no doubt derived from the basic two-strand knot. The carefully counted and planned cords of *quipus*, or necklacelike strips with radiating cords knotted at specific intervals along their surfaces, were an Incan means of communication. In that Peruvian society, well-developed centuries before Europeans came to the Americas, each knot in the pattern had significance and could be interpreted.

The more standardized form of knotting that is called *macrame* most likely had its origins in the Near East, as the word is thought to be of Arabic derivation. Throughout the world, macrame was practiced on ships by sailors during the long voyages of the Age of Exploration. The popularity of macrame was at a low ebb in the last century when the Victorian Era rediscovered the art and put it to wide use in knotted fringes, edgings, borders, and other decorations.

Today's off-loom weavers include many knotting and macrame techniques in their working vocabulary, as they are both versatile and attractive. On its own, macrame is most often done using sturdy but flexible cords. Soft yarns and threads, which droop in your hand, work best in areas of dense knotting or tightly repeating rows, since they won't hold their position well in open area knottings. Open knottings are made with the negative space between the cords and knots in mind as the cords become part of the pattern and are carried from one knot to the next. The area left between cords or knots is an essential ingredient in the design. This type of pattern is best supported by medium- to heavy-weight cords and yarns. Just be sure that you don't choose one that is too thick to bend and knot well.

Left: Cape Cod by Polly C. DeVito. Macrame, in clove hitch and square knotting; wool in shades of blue, green, and blue-green; tassel in avocado, brown wool with wooden beads.

Below: Cosmic Bowl: Inner Eye by Renie Breskin Adams. Macrame and crochet, 11″ x 20″, detail.

To try out your knotting skills, make a sampler, as you did for free weaving. Among the best cords to use for this are: woven cotton cording, which usually comes in white or off-white but takes dyes very well and has just the right combination of stiffness and flexibility to knot well; polished and pearl cottons in medium weights, which come in a variety of colors; medium-weight twines that are fairly smooth (the coarse types can be irritating); lightweight rope, which is usually made up of three multiply strands and works well if the ends of the rope are taped so that they don't unravel as you knot; sisal and jute macrame cords, which are made for the purpose and come in many bright shades; and just about any other well-made twine or cord that you like. Slippery ones, such as rattail, are terrific in later works, but can be tricky to use when you are learning the knots. Some types of hard-twisted or standard plied yarns fall into the same category, being used to advantage in many works when you know the knots well but a bit difficult at first.

Bernadyne Antin, macrame purse, in deep teal blue with beads

77

You will also need a board, on which you do the knotting. Choose one that you can stick pins into and can mark with a one-inch square grid, for a handy guide while knotting. Good choices are an 18 x 24-inch sheet of Styrofoam or other plastic foam, a large sheet of cork, one-inch thick, or backed as for a bulletin board, or a soft wood sheet in the same dimensions, such as pine or pressed board. Additional equipment includes: push pins, rustproof and strong (the T-shaped ones are particularly useful); a ruler or tape measure; a pair of sharp, pointed scissors; and a short dowel or heavy cord on which you mount the knotting cords. Other articles, which are helpful but not essential, are: wooden or plastic yarn bobbins to hold the ends of the cords as you knot and keep them under control; friction tape to wrap around the ends of cords which are likely to unravel or unply; white liquid glue for the same purpose, which dries clear, but can't be used if you intend to unply the yarn or cord as a finishing touch when the knotting is complete; ceramic, glass, or wooden beads with large eyes to thread onto the knotting cords for accent and design; C clamps or a board with two strong nails in it to help you wind out the cords.

When you make a basic knotted pattern, such as this sampler, you use the knotting cords folded in half and then mounted or attached to the holding cord or dowel. The knotting cords are wound out beforehand, as for a weaving warp. They are usually made four times the length that you want the finished knotting to be. There are exceptions, such as heavy cords which take up a lot of cord with each knot, densely knotted patterns or a series of intricate knots, which also take up a lot of cord. As an allowance, add a couple of more lengths to be sure that you have enough.

Since the cords are doubled, you make them that way, placing the C clamps or winding rods the distance of one-half the total length of each cord. For example, if you want the finished sampler to be 12 inches long, you make each cord 8 feet long, placing the winding rods 4 feet apart. If you're doing a larger work where the placement of the winding rods that far apart would be a problem, make each cord in 1- or 2-yard lengths, forming it in two or more turns around the rods. For the basic sampler, make eight 8-foot cords, which are folded into sixteen individual knotting cords and mounted on the holding cord or dowel. If you prefer to work over a smaller area, make four 8-foot cords, which will amount to eight knotting cords.

Macrame sampler with seashells (with the holes ready-made by predator mollusks) knotted onto cord ends. By author.

Mounting the Cords

A thin, foot-long dowel or a 14-inch length of strong cord are good foundations for your knotting cords. If you're using a dowel, drill two holes near the ends, thread a cord through the holes and tie it in place around the knotting board so that the dowel is parallel to the top and a few inches below it. When using a cord, make one knot at each end and pin it in the same position as the dowel, sticking one pin through the center of each knot.

Cut the knotting cords off the winding rods. Draw one cord out of the group, holding it by the fold at the middle of the cord. Take the folded middle behind the dowel or cord, bring the loop formed by the center fold, up and over the top. Slip the ends of the cord through the loop and tighten it in place on the holding rod. This is a reverse lark's head knot. A lark's head knot, also used for the top attachment, is made by bringing the fold over the top to the back and then drawing through the ends of the cord.

As you place each cord, make sure that the ends are the same length. If you're using bobbins, wind each end of cord onto one, leaving about 12 inches of cord between the wound bobbin and the knot. Without bobbins, you can wind butterflies out of the ends. Place the end in your palm and wind the rest of the cord in a figure eight, crossing over itself in

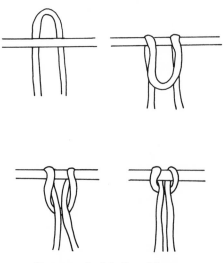

Reverse lark's head knot

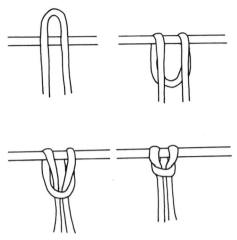

Lark's head knot

the middle of your hand, winding between thumb and pinky. When there are 12 inches left, slip the butterfly off your hand and wrap the center with a small rubber band. As you use up the cord while knotting, just pull lightly on it as it goes into the rubber band and it will unwind without disturbing the rest of the wound cord. When you use bobbins or similar cord holders, unwind as needed.

Add the cords to the holding cord or rod from the center out, placing them right next to each other for the sampler. In later works, you may want to space them differently for open cord patterns and plans. For articles which will be used, or shaped at the top, a cord rather than a dowel is used. It can be the same cord as your knotting cords, or one that is thicker or contrasts in color or texture.

Making the Knots

In macrame, knots are made with groups of cords in sequence. The cords hang in an up-and-down position from the holding cord. Working on a knotting board allows you to see exactly what is happening and will help you place the knots correctly. As you get to know the knots, you can work them just about anywhere, suspending the holding cord from any stationary object, such as a door handle, a drawer knob, a hook of any sort, or the top rod of a chair back. Almost anything will work, as long as you can see, reach, and work with the knotting cords, holding them under a little tension provided by the object you are using, as you loop the holding cord around it and pull as needed.

When you are working with a holding base which will become a part of the finished knotting, such as a found object or other unusual beginning, suspend the object as you would for free weaving to attach the cords and make the knots. If it's a fairly small article, you can tie a cord around it and pin it to your knotting board. When you combine the techniques of off-loom weaving, the dowel rod and found object top attachments are widely used. The up-and-down cords of macrame are comparable to the warp in free-hanging or weighted-warp weaving. The weft in a weaving can also be used as a knotting cord, so that the techniques lend themselves well to combination.

The most widely used knots in macrame are the lark's head, square knot, and clove or double half hitch. These basic knots can be done in so many different ways and sequences that they are often the only knots used in a pattern. You already know the lark's head, both standard and reverse, from the attachment of the knotting cords to the holding cord.

The Square Knot

The macrame square knot differs from the one you may be familiar with in that it is tied with at least four strands. Two of the four are the active knotting cords and two serve as a passive center or core. These passive cords are referred to as *knot bearers* in macrame, because they are not knotted themselves. You can also make a square knot around more than two cords, in designs that call for it, or to finish hanging ends by gathering them in a group. The basic knot is made with four cords.

To make a square knot, start with the center four cords on your sampler's holding cord. As you make the knot with the outer cords, keep the two center cords in their vertical position, flat and even. Hold one outer cord in each hand, the left in your left hand and the right in your right hand.

Take the left cord and curve it a bit as you bring it over the middle two and under the outer right cord. Hold it in place and with your other hand,

82

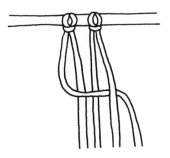

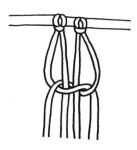

A. Left cord over two, under right

B. Right cord under two, over left

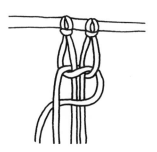

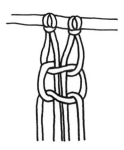

C. Right cord over two, under left

D. Left cord under two, over right

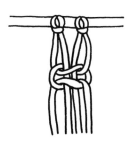

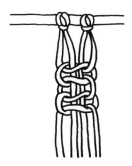

E. Knot tightened

F. Two square knots

take the right cord under the middle two and through the curved loop of the left cord, going over the left cord as you go through the loop. This is the first half of the knot. For the second half, take the cord that is now on the outer left, curve it and bring it under the middle two and over the outer right. Take the outer right cord, bring it over the middle two and through the left curved loop, going under the left cord. As you do each half of the knot, tighten it in place. The two halves together are the square, or reef, knot. Work one with each set of four cords in your sampler, moving out toward the edges from either side of the first knot, alternating sides as you complete each knot. This helps maintain an even and balanced placement of knots. In an article with a balanced pattern, it's usually best to work from the center out in this way, so that each side is always the same as the other side.

A series of square knots, worked over the same four strands, make a chain of knots which is called a *sennit*. A sennit is an up-and-down band of solid knots, which creates a strong vertical design element in any work. In your sampler, make several square knots over the same sets of cords to see how they look. Do at least four complete square knots with each set of four cords.

Sennit of four square knots

The *alternating square knot* is knotted with a different set of cords on alternate rows. For the first, and all odd-numbered rows, make the square knots with the same set of cords that you use to form the sennits on your sampler. In other words, you do the first row using all of the cords, in sets of four. Many macrame projects are planned with knotting cords in mul-

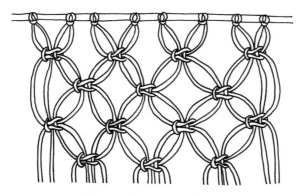

Alternating square knot

tiples of four so that you have an even number to work with.

When the first row of square knots is done, you can work from either side, rather than from the center out, since the pattern of the knots is established by the row. The second row starts two cords in from the right edge, or the left edge, if you find it easier to work from left to right; it makes no difference. Omit the first two cords and make a square knot with the next four cords, two coming from each of two knots on the previous row. The right cords in the new group are the two outer left cords in the first row's first knot, and the left cords are the two outer right cords on the first row's second knot. Move to the next group, taking two strands from each of the nearest two knots in the previous row. In this case, the next group is made up of the two outer left strands of the second knot and the two outer right strands of the third knot on the first row. Continue across the row up to the last two cords, which are left unknotted. For the third row, you knot, using the same four cord sets as the first row, and for the fourth you use the same ones as for the second row. Do the same for all following odd and even rows. If you pull the cords tightly as you knot, you'll get a densely knotted pattern. If you work with them in a looser way, you'll get a more curving, lacy, open effect.

Half square knots are used to make sennits that twist into attractive tight spirals. To make one, you work the first half of a square knot repeatedly over the same four cords. Bring the outer left cord over the middle two and under the right, and the right cord under the middle two and over the left as it goes through the curve at the beginning of the left

85

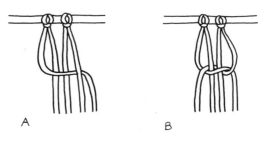

Making a spiral sennit

**A. Left cord over two, under two, B. Right cord under two, over left,
C. Repeat the same sequence, D. A spiral sennit**

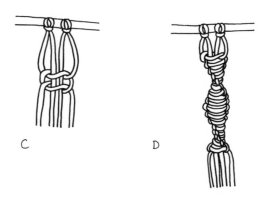

side. Tighten. Repeat the same half knot over and over, without doing the second half of the knot. The finished knots will start to spiral as you make and tighten them. This sennit will spiral to the left as the side ridge formed by the half knots twists to the front. To make a sennit that spirals to the right, in the opposite direction, do the second half of the knot instead of the first. Bring the right outer cord over the middle two and under the left, then the left cord under the middle two and over the right as it goes through the loop. For the sampler, knot at least eight half knots in each sennit to see how the spiral occurs.

Short square knot sennits, of complete knots, are used to create a large, rounded shape called the *square knot button, bobble,* or *popcorn knot.* To do it, make a sennit of six square knots. Then take the two core strands and lift them up to the beginning of the sennit. At the top of the first knot going into the chain bring the cords through the top of the knot, between its cords. The center cord on the right from the bottom of the sennit goes

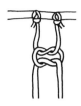

A coreless square or granny knot (above)
A multistrand core within a square knot (right)

in between the first and second cords from the right at the beginning of the sennit, and the left center cord goes in between the third and fourth cords at the top. When the two cords are at the back of the chain, pull on them until the chain loops up toward the top and forms a rounded shape. Then bring the two cords back down to their starting position at the bottom of the sennit and make a standard square knot with the four cords. The same center and outer cords are used. This square knot holds the button in place and allows you to continue knotting with the cords in their original position. For tighter, harder shapes, make a sennit chain of four knots. For a loopy, open form, make a sennit of eight or more, adding a forward- and upward-moving three-dimensional loop to your knotting.

A square knot made using only two cords, omitting the core, is called a *granny knot*. The two halves of the knot are done as usual; you just don't work around a center of two more cords. Often this knot is not pulled tight so that it is open looking.

Square knots made over a core of four, six, or more center strands are often planned as the beginning or end of a project. They make an effective end or finishing touch in a free-style weaving as well. The additional cords or yarns which move in toward the center as the knot is tied around them should be well shaped. Count out the number of core strands that you're using. Take the center two and place them in the usual up-and-down position. Allow those on either side to move in toward the center two on a graceful, curving diagonal so that the strands, or work above them, are not gathered or pulled together too tightly. You then make the square knot around the group with the two outermost strands as usual, while maintaining the position of the group. If you're using this as an ending on a work with lighter weight strands, you can use sets of two on the left and two on the right to make the knot, using each set as if it were a single cord. When

87

the square knot, or possible sennit of square knots is completed, the effect of many strands moving into the knot with ease is somewhat like a sheaf of wheat. As a finish, you can trim the ends below the knot so that they are even, or follow the natural curve that will take place as the outer core strands are drawn up by the position of the knot.

Exposed cord effects are created with square knots by planning the placement of the knots on any portion of the knotting cords that you choose, rather than straight across every row. Use the knotting board's grid as a guide. You can begin to knot some distance away from the holding cord instead of immediately below it. As long as you make a knot with all of the cords eventually, you can leave them unworked for large areas of the design. The exposed straight cords, in the parts that are unknotted, create a change in texture and pattern in the knotting.

The Clove Hitch

The clove or double half hitch is the third basic knot. With the three knots—lark's head, square, and hitch—you'll be able to create literally thousands of patterns.

The clove hitch is a "one strand at a time" looping knot, tied around what is referred to as an anchor or knot-bearing cord. To do it, put a pin into the outer left-hand strand about ½ inch from the previous row of knots. Take the strand and fold it over all of the other cords, so that it forms a right angle at the left edge, held in place by the pin. The cord should run straight across the others. Pin it in place on the other side, about ½ inch away from the last cord on the right. The cord should be pinned so that it is held taut.

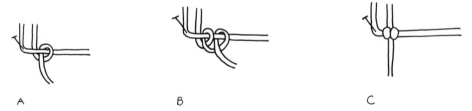

A   B   C

Making a clove or double half hitch knot: A. A half hitch, B. The second half hitch, C. Tightened clove hitch

Take the next cord from the left and bring it up around the anchor cord. Carry it to the back between the beginning of the anchor cord and itself, moving first to the right as it comes over the anchor cord, and then down to the left as it goes around and then down behind the anchor cord. This is a half hitch, the first half of the clove or double half hitch knot. The second half hitch is made with the same knotting cord. Bring it to the right of the just completed half hitch, then up, over, and around the anchor cord to the back. As it goes to the back, bring it through the loop formed by the cord itself as it begins to move around the anchor cord. This loop forms just below the anchor cord as you bring the knotting cord from the first half of the hitch to the second.

Tighten both halves of the clove hitch after the second has been completed. They should be tight enough to be smoothly wrapped around the anchor cord without bending it at all. To continue, you do the same with the second knotting cord from the left, found just to the right of the first one. At the end of the row you add another pin to the anchor cord at the right, about ½ inch down from the first one. Then bend the cord back to the left, crossing over all of the cords again. Pin in place on the left side, ½ inch outside the last cord, keeping the anchor cord taut. Remove the pin directly above, as it's no longer needed. On the second row, you knot from right to left. The knot is basically the same, but the directions are reversed so that it can move to the left across the anchor cord. Bring the cord up and around, then down between itself and the anchor cord at the outer right, then up and around on the left side of itself and through the loop below both hitches at the bottom toward the right.

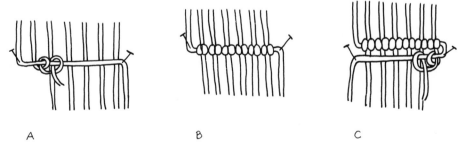

A   B   C

Clove hitching across a row: A. Starting the row, B. Completed row, C. Beginning the second row

Above: Stormy Transposition by Renie B. Adams (40″ wide). Mixed fibers, knotted in clove hitches, rainbow palette of colors. Moving across the bottom from left to right, mixtures of golds and greens, through blues, violets, red, and browns, blending and crossing in the design above.

Left: Renie B. Adams, detail. Area from golds and greens through blues, shows the density and intricacy of the clove hitched knotting and the movement of the cords as they knot. The clove hitching is mainly horizontal along the bottom, intersecting and crossing in diagonals above.

90

Each row of double half hitches forms a solid, wrapped ridge of knots. For an extremely dense knotting, work several rows in this way. If you use up the anchor cord, you can add a new one at the beginning of a row by pinning the end of the new cord outside the knotting cords and bringing it across and pinning to the other side as usual. The loose end can be worked into the backs of the knots when you have completed the knotting.

You can make a diagonal of clove hitches. Pin the anchor cord at the outer edge, bring it across the knotting cords on an angle and pin in place. Then you make the hitches around the cord and they move on angle just as the anchor cord does. You can make rows that move in all directions, curving and on angles, just by placing the anchor cord in the desired line.

A variation in the knotting procedure is to take the anchor cords from alternating sides, rather than using the same one for every row. This method is particularly good when you are knotting a large section, as the cords are used up more evenly.

To make an X shape in double half hitches, you work on the diagonal with two anchor cords. The lines formed by this pattern are quite attractive, as there are triangles of exposed cords between the branches of the X. Take the outer left cord and pin it in place, going across the knotting cords on a 45-degree angle, and pinning again at the outer right. Take the outer right cord and do the same, moving left, so that the two anchor cords cross in the middle over a space between the two center knotting cords. Do a diagonal double hitch around the upper left cord, moving down the cord to the crossing in the center and stop. Do the same along the upper right anchor cord, down along it to the center of the cross, and stop. Unpin the

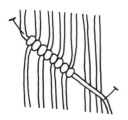

Clove hitching on an angle

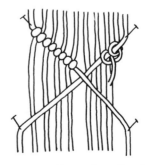

Making an X in clove hitching

anchor cord coming from the left, taking out the pin at the outer right edge. Use the left anchor cord as a knotting cord for one double half hitch only around the right anchor cord. Then repin the cord so that it is in its original position, at the lower right-hand corner of the X. Continue knotting diagonally down, completing the left and then the right lower parts of the X. The only time you knot with the anchor cord is once, in the center, so that the X shape is completely covered with knots.

Diamond shapes are made with the same clove hitch formation as the X shapes. You can either make a series of X shapes, which will naturally form diamond shapes between the bottom of one X and the top of the next, or you can make one diamond by using the two center cords as anchor cords. To do this, you pin each in place about ½ inch down from the previous knots or holding cord, then bring each out to its respective side and pin in place just outside the knotting cords. Then, you knot from the outer right edge up to the center and then knot the other side to the left from the bottom up to the center at the top. Then, take the anchor cords back in toward the center and pin them into their original position, each slanting down toward the middle on the same angle as they moved out. Knot the right side in and the left side in as usual to complete the diamond shape.

As the anchor or carrying cords, as they are also called, form the foundation of the ridges of knots, once you know how to do the basic forms you can make all kinds of shapes, according to the way in which you pin the anchor cord. You can pick up any knotting cord at any position in the group and pin it for use as an anchor cord, opening up many areas for knotting.

The vertical clove or double half hitch creates a solid looking bar or ridge that runs up and down. It is done with the outer cord, and the up-and-down cords are the anchor cords in this case. The outer cord, which does the knotting, is used up very quickly. You can plan for this by making an extra long cord at each end, or add in cords if needed, pinning them in place at the outer edge. When the knotting is all done, the loose ends of added cords are worked into the back of the work and trimmed off.

To knot, start at the left. Pin the outer cord to the knotting board, ½ inch from the previous knots. Hold the next cord to the right taut with

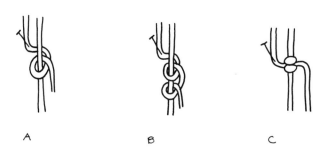

Vertical clove hitch: A. Vertical half hitch, B. Second half hitch, C. Tightened clove hitch, D. A row of vertical clove hitches, E. Starting the second row

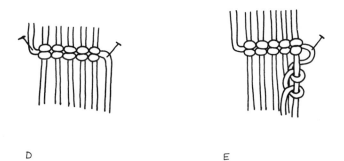

your hand as you bring the left cord under it. Bring the left cord around to the front, up and to the back, then through the loop that began the hitch, around the taut cord and up, back through the loop that forms as you begin the second half hitch. Continue by taking the same knotting cord under the next cord to the right, hold it taut and make two half hitches vertically with the knotting cord. Do the same across the row. To work from right to left, pin the knotting cord at the outer right edge. Hold the next cord to the left taut and bring the knotting cord under it, then up and around, through the loop at the back, to the front and around, then through the second loop and tighten.

Half hitches are just that, the first half of the knot done for the clove or double half hitch knot. The half hitch on its own is done with two cords. You hold one cord taut as you wrap and knot the second one. When you work from the right, you hold the left-hand cord of the pair taut and bring the right one under to the left, to the front. Then take it over and around

93

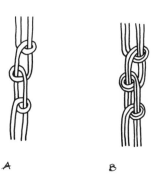

Alternating half hitch chain: A. Two strand, B. Four strand

to the right between the two strands of the cord as they go into the knot from the top. Be sure to hold the carrying cord tight enough so that it doesn't bend or knot at all with the other cord. It remains straight while the knotting cord loops. When you knot from the left, hold the right-hand cord of the pair taut, wrap the left cord under it, moving to the right, up to the front and around and through the loop. A chain of half hitches is made by alternating the left and right hitches as you make the knots along a pair of cords. As you do the knots, make the first one from the left, the second one from the right, the third from the left, and so on. This makes a strong chain. For a thicker chain, work with four cords, holding and using two at one time, just as if they were a single cord.

Overhand Knots

Overhand knots are often used as the finishing knots for macrame and off-loom weavings of all kinds. They are simple, one-strand knots, made by looping the strand up and around itself, then through the loop that forms. Most often, you make overhand knots with sets of threads, such as the cords at the end of a macrame piece or the warp ends of a free-style weaving. The knot itself is good looking, doesn't have to be pulled so tight that it loses its nice texture, and is a secure way to tie off sections of completed working yarns or cords. You can make one overhand knot, or several along a strand, or group the strands and make a row of overhand knots in the strands.

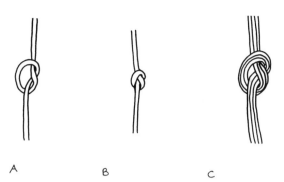

A B C

Overhand knot: A. Making the knot, B. Tightened knot, C. Multistand overhand knot

Wrapping

Wrapping is a technique that has come to be associated with macrame and knotting. It is widely used in many different off-loom works for vertical texture and design and as an attractive finishing technique for groups of strands.

Wrapping is done in several ways, according to the type of yarn or cord you are using and the desired effect. To wrap a group of cords with a cord from the group, hold them all together neatly. Then take the outer right cord and bend it to the left over the group of cords, placing the bend at

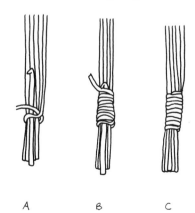

A B C

Wrapping with a cord from the group and a crochet hook: A. Beginning the wrap, B. Catching the end of the hook to draw it through the completed wrap, C. Completed wrap

Using an extra piece of cord instead of a hook

the bottom of the area to be wrapped. If you have a fairly large crochet hook that will catch the diameter cord that you're using, slip it under the crossing right cord, hook up. Slide it up so that the hook is above the designated end of the wrapping's height. If you don't have a crochet hook, cut a length of any strong cord, so that it can be folded in half and still be longer than the total height of the wrapping. Place the folded cord under the crossing cord, loop from the fold at the top of the area to be wrapped. Then bring the right wrapping cord around the left to the back, through the loop formed by its first bend and continue wrapping, around to the left and under to the right. Make sure that the wrapped cord doesn't overlap itself and is neat and well wrapped.

When you have wrapped the group of cords to the height that you want, put the end of the wrapping cord in the hook or through the loop of extra cord at the top of the wrapped area. Ease the hook or cord back through the wrapped section. Go slowly until the end is all the way through the wrapped section. Tighten it if needed by pulling lightly on the wrapping cord, removing the hook or extra cord when the wrapping cord's end has reached the bottom and has been pulled through. Smooth the rest of the wrapping cord back into the group that was wrapped. If the wrapping seems too loose, because you wrapped it with an addition which was removed, tighten it by twisting carefully in the same direction as the wrapping was done. As you turn, hold and pull lightly on the wrapping cord at the spot where it emerges from the bottom of the wrapped area. Don't pull too hard or the wrapped coil will start to pull down into itself.

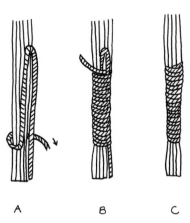

**Wrapping with another cord, Peruvian style: A. Beginning the wrap,
B. Slipping the end through the loop, C. Completed wrap**

Wrapping with a separate piece of cord or yarn is done for color contrast,
or to maintain the number and length of the cords being wrapped, or to
obtain a tighter wrapped coil. When you wrap with one of the cords in the
group, it will naturally become much shorter than the rest. This type of
coil is tighter, as the additional cord used to lock in the end of the coil is
wrapped in place and left there.

The separate cord style of wrapping is often called Peruvian, as it is
derived from the Incan and other Indian weavers of the area. You can use
it to wrap in many colors, or one. Whichever you choose works well with
this method. To do it, you wrap from the bottom up as in the technique
just described.

Use a wrapping cord of about 18 inches. Hold the group of cords or
yarns that are going to be wrapped and place the wrapping cord on top of
them. The end should point to the ends of the group, far enough down on
the group so that it extends below the area to be wrapped. Then, bring
the cord up above the area to be wrapped and fold it so that there is a
loop at the top of the area to be wrapped. Bring the rest of the cord down,
along and next to itself, to the starting point of the wrapping. Wrap from
the bottom up, just as you would with an existing cord. Move the cord
around from the right, over to the left, under the back to the right, and
so on. When you reach the end of the area in the height you want, thread

the end of the cord through the loop formed at the beginning. Pull on the end until all but an inch—or two, for a longer coil—of cord is through the loop. Then pull lightly on the beginning tail end at the bottom of the wrapping and the loop pulls itself and the end of the wrapping cord into the coil for about ¾ of an inch. The upper cord will form a loop that goes into the coil with the lower cord's loop. For longer coils, pull the ends until the locked loops are about halfway through the wrapped coil. Snip off the wrapping end at the top right next to the last coil, pull very lightly on the bottom cord to bring the end in, and cut the bottom end right at the coil. Work the last bit of the bottom into the coil carefully.

Adding Beads and Other Objects

As each section of macrame is knotted with loose strands, it is quite easy to add all sorts of interesting beads, in glass, ceramic, wood, and metal to complement the predominantly natural fibers used in macrame. Just make sure that the eyes or openings in the beads you choose are large enough to accommodate the width of the cord you're using. Then, at any point in the work, you can unwrap the bobbin or butterfly or use the end of the cord when working with shorter pieces that don't need to be wound up. Slip the bead onto the cord, slide it up to the desired spot, and continue the knotting.

All kinds of objects can be knotted into macrame. Shells and other small, hard items can be drilled with holes or knotted into the work by tying knots around them or surrounding them with cords. Bits of driftwood, feathers, small stones, shiny metal washers, and other shapes can all be incorporated into your knotting.

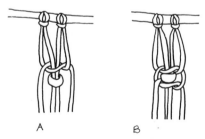

A   B

Adding a bead into a square knot

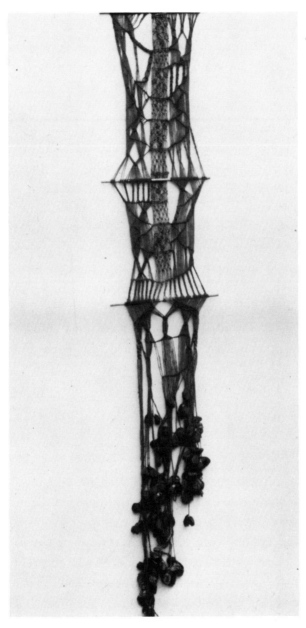

Macrame hanging by Bernadyne Antin. Orange and gold in central densely knotted area. Work in progress with the ends of the cords wrapped into bundles for easier knotting. The wrapped bundles themselves can become part of the design, which incorporates three metal rods.

Finishing Macrame

One of the most enjoyable aspects of macrame is that you are finished as soon as you tie your last knot. The knots naturally tie off the piece, ending it for you. In most articles, the hanging threads or cords are trimmed to the right length and included as part of the design. Groups of ends can also be wrapped, forming tassel-like shapes, or you can leave them hanging loose. For articles in which a fringed or wrapped finish is not wanted, you can work the ends of the cords into the back of the knots after trimming them to about an inch. Use a blunt-tipped yarn needle or a crochet hook in an appropriate size. It's almost impossible to weave them into the backs of the knots without a needle or hook, as they start to come unplied or unraveled.

Another method you can try for plied twine, rope, or yarn is to unply the ends into many soft strands with a nice texture. The greater the number of ply in the strand, the more effective the outcome will be. If you're working with a ply strand that you don't want to unply in the finished article, when the ends have been trimmed, dip each end into a small amount of white liquid glue. Wipe off any excess glue on a piece of paper so that it doesn't make a blob. The glue dries into a glossy, clear finish that isn't visible in small amounts at the bottoms of the cords.

Working in Shapes

When you plan an article with a definite shape, such as a vest, you pin the holding cords into the desired shape for the top sections of the article. You usually work in sections, doing, for example, the fronts and back in three pieces. The holding cord for each can be pinned in any position, as needed. Use a paper pattern to guide the cord placement. For a clothing pattern, cut off the seam allowances, or ignore them, and pin the holding cord along the solid lines at the top of the pattern parts. Then, knotting cords are added as needed to fill in the pattern shape of the holding cord. In curved areas, add cords at the beginning and knot them as you get to them. When the knotting for all sections of the article has been done you can sew side seams with a blunt-tipped needle and strong thread in a matching color.

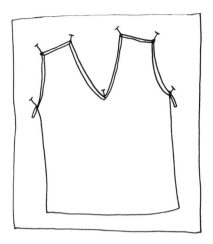

Working in shapes—the placement of the holding cord for a vest

You can also create your own patterns and designs for knotting. Draw out your ideas on paper, using full-sized models. As the knotted cords tend to stretch a little, especially in open knotting, plan the article a bit smaller and shorter than you want it to be. Take the drawn paper shape, pin it to your knotting board, and place the cords as directed by the pattern. Holding cords are put along the top and curved sides, and knotting cords placed along them. Then you can plan your knotting design to work the cords. Extra cords can be added into the knotting, if needed, simply by folding and looping the new cord into an existing cord or knot with a lark's head or less visible half hitch.

Sculptural Knotting and Three-dimensional Forms

You can knot in three dimension, working over a padded form, rather than a flat knotting board. As you can pin and place holding cords at the top, or anywhere you wish, you can then knot around the form with your knotting cords. For tubular forms, use a wire ring or hoop as a holding cord. If you want to be able to flatten the top of the tube when it is knotted, place a holding cord around the ring, holding it in place with small extra knotted threads. Then add the knotting cords to the cord, so that the ring can be removed when the article is done by cutting and taking out the knotted threads.

If you plan to suspend the knotting when it is finished and want it to maintain its shape, knot directly on the ring and leave it in the knotting. To form a small round, place the holding cord in a circle and add in new knotting cords as you work around the inner circle outward. If you continue to add in cords, the shape will be a flat circle. For a curving, spherical shape, place the pinning circle on a pillow or other form in the shape you want to make. Begin the knotting with a small circle, add in new cords as needed, and follow the padded foundation to form a hat, basketlike form, or whatever you plan.

Another idea for knotting is to work on an existing article, such as a cane chair which has lost its caning, and knot in a new seat. As you can find a way to attach holding cords, and then the knotting cords, to just about anything, the versatility and strength of knotting has great appeal.

Chinese Knotting

Oriental ornamental knottings use the same type of cords and knots as macrame, but the Chinese style depends on bold, individual knots tied along one set of cords. The original cords used in China were always made of fine silk, but many heavy cords in cotton and other fibers with a nice texture will work well. To try out the technique, use only one cord, folded into two strands. The aim of the knotting is to form flat, interesting knots, separated from each other along the cord by unknotted spaces, which are part of the pattern. Basic square knots, made without any center cords, are often used in between the larger, more intricate knots.

The Josephine, lover's, and looped double overhand knots are used to make the larger, more complex knots in the pattern. The flat version of the Turk's head knot is tied with a single cord, but two can be worked next to each other in a two-strand work. After making the basic knots several times, you can use four or more strands, holding half in one hand and half in the other. Then they are knotted as if they were single cords. Multiple cords should run flat and parallel to each other throughout each knot, as if you were knotting with flexible ribbons.

The *Josephine knot* is made in several steps. Begin by taking the left cord over the right, making a loop and bringing it back over itself and

102

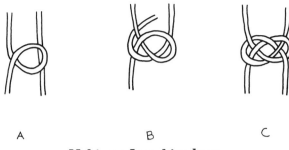

A   B   C

Making a Josephine knot

down. The loop remains on top of the right cord. Lift the right cord, bring it under the left one below the loop, under and through the top of the loop, over itself in the center of the loop, and then under the bottom of the loop. You tighten both cords just enough so that the knot is flat and even.

The *lover's knot* looks difficult, but it's based on two simple overhand knots. Make an overhand knot in the right cord by bringing it up and around in a loop, then through the loop, under the center cords of the loop, over the bottom and down. Leave the knots quite loose. Make the same knot in the opposite direction in the left cord, bringing it through the left-hand side of the right knot as you make the first movement. The knots should look like a linked mirror image. Then reach under the bottom outer loop of each side with both hands, taking the center of the loop on either side of the middle of the knot with the respective hand. Pull slowly outward toward the left and the right, bringing each of the center loops out to the sides, forming a new loop at each side. Check to see that all of the loops are even and nicely shaped.

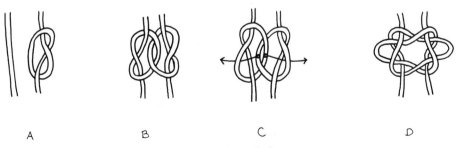

A   B   C   D

Making a lover's knot

103

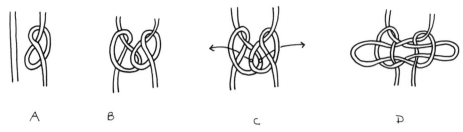

A   B   C   D

Making a looped double overhand knot

The *looped double overhand knot* is made up of two double loosely made overhand loops that are not knotted themselves or linked together in the center at first, so that it is also called the *noninterlocking overhand knot*. To do it, take the right-hand cord, fold it out and up, then behind itself, and down toward the right so that it crosses over the loop formed without going through it. Do the same with the left cord, working toward the left in the opposite direction. Then reach into either knot with either hand, pull the lower left loop through the right-hand knot, and the lower right loop through the left-hand knot. Pull out toward each side, making two new rounded loops. This knot is a variation of the lover's knot and has a similar appearance. Adjust the finished knot so that the cords are even and both sides look the same.

The flat *Turk's head knot* is made with one cord. Knotted loosely, it is a flat knot; pulled tight, it makes a round button shape. Fold the cord out to the right, take it up and then behind itself and down. Make another loop in the same way, just below the first so that the top of the second loop is in the center of the first one. Then bring the cord around toward the left, over itself at the top, under the top right-hand loop, over the top of the second loop just below the first one, then under the bottom of the first loop,

Making a flat Turk's head knot

104

and over the bottom of the second one just below it. Tighten as desired by pulling both ends lightly and slowly at the same time.

Ornamental Top Attachments

You may want to add an ornamental edging to the top attachment's folded cords in some articles, instead of the relatively flat lark's head knots. A small, large, or multiple *picot*, or looped edging, can be made. To form a picot, knot the cords onto the holding cord, using two clove hitches. In between the first and the second, form a loop, heading up above the holding cord. To be sure that the loops are even, in a series, place a pin into the top of each loop as you make it. A multiple loop attachment is made using several cords at a time. You make the first clove hitch with one cord at the left edge. Leave the rest of the cord untied, add two more cords next to the first, moving right. Arrange the arched picots in order, first tying the second clove hitch in the third cord, just to the right of it, then the second half of the second, and the second half of the first, all moving toward the right. Make each picot a little taller than the previous one, so that they

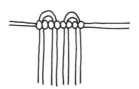

A. Picot with clove hitch top attachment

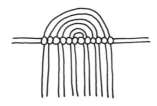

B. Multiple loop picot with clove hitching

arch over each other in three concentric semicircles. A knotted picot is made by adding an overhand knot into the cord so that it falls at the top of a picot, alone or in a group. If you're making a series of knotted picot, place a pin into the knotting board for each one before you start them, and make the overhand knots around the pins. In this way all the knots will be the same.

Combining Knotting with Free-hanging Weaving

The use of parallel hanging cords in knotting and free-hanging weaving makes a combination of the two a natural. Series of rows of clove hitching and wrapping are two of the methods that are most often combined with free weaving. Clove hitches, made with the weft yarn over one sturdy warp end, placed over the others, is particularly effective. As you bring the weft to the back of the anchor cord, wrap it around the other warp ends, one at a time as you come to them. When you are weaving a warp of medium- to heavy-weight yarns, you can make the clove hitching, using the warp ends just as you would use macrame cords.

When the methods are combined, you'll find that you can't predict the warp or cord length as you can in weaving. If you plan to knot a free-hanging weaving, make the warp much longer than you would ordinarily. Place the weaving on a knotting board. Wrap the longer ends into butter-flies, and pin each warp in place above the bundle. This will hold the warp in line, and you can take out a pin as needed to use an end as an anchor cord or for any other procedure. When you know the method well, you can work with the warp free hanging, holding the anchor cord with one hand, the wrapping or hitching cord with the other. You can also add in new ends if needed. They can be tied to the previous row or begun as for a weft. When the weaving is complete, you can weave the tail ends into the back of the work.

As you learn the off-loom techniques, you'll see how well they all combine. The sequences and procedures are so compatible that they inspire a great range of creative directions in shape, form, and pattern.

5

SUPPORTING FORMS IN OFF-LOOM WEAVING

The essence of off-loom weaving is the creation of weavings in the freest possible manner. Occasionally, however, you'll find that certain shapes and structural forms you want to make just can't be woven on free-hanging threads without a supporting device of some sort. The possibilities of creating articles with a specific, preplanned shape are greatly expanded when you consider the use of a foundation on which to build your weaving. There are several alternatives, depending on the finished effect you have in mind.

Coiling, knotting, and crochet are particularly adaptable methods, which are made into the desired shape or form on their own fiber foundation. You can use them to begin a form, as for a sculptural work, or set the outlines for a shape. The base made can be knotted or looped with additional threads, to serve as a warp on which you can weave. You can also complete the weaving using one of the same methods. In this kind of design, the shape made in one technique is planned to complement the weaving to follow and is a part of it. Sketching out various patterns and combinations on paper will give you an idea of which will work well together in an article, even if you make only the barest outlines, filling in the specifics as you weave.

Objects that are incorporated into the design of an off-loom weaving, such as the basic dowels, wood or wire hoops, metal rings, tree branches, and other found objects are another way in which you add structural support. In this type of weaving, the *armature* is an integral part. As the armature is woven, knotted, crocheted, or otherwise worked into, over, around, and within, the weaving and the object become inseparable. To create more

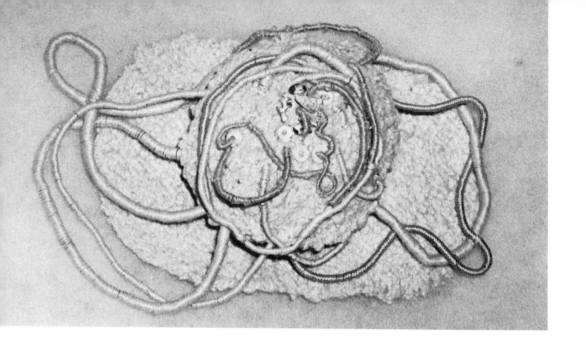

Above: Top view of Precious Pillow by Laureen Vlaisavljevich. Round pillow woven on a cardboard loom sits on its own oval mat. Wrapped coils move in and out of the pillow. Precious shells embellish surface of mixed fibers; 4″ x 10″ x 2″.

Left: Circular form woven on a wrapped metal ring, 24″ in diameter, by Betty Lovejoy. In golds, white, grays, and oranges, finished with multicolored Peruvian wrapping and feathers.

complex or elaborate armatures, use medium-weight wire. It should be strong enough to support the weight of the yarns or cords, but still flexible enough for you to bend it into the shape you want. Then, weave around the wire form, attaching and hanging the yarns or cords in the usual fashion.

In a variation of this technique, dowels and rings are added into both the top and bottom of the work, stretching the warp out taut. When the weaving is finished, they are taken out, having served their purpose in aiding the weaving process. In this sense, they are creating one of the basic functions of a loom, while the threads are still held in a suspended position.

For articles with specific shapes and sizes, you'll find that many other kinds of supporting devices can be used to advantage. These all become looms of a sort, as a loom is any structure on which threads are placed tautly to be woven, but you can plan and weave shapes that are precise. In many cases, you'll start an off-loom work on one of these materials for a good foundation, and then take it off to complete the pattern in free style. In other works, the entire weaving is carried out in place.

Among the articles that you can use are: sheets of strong cardboard, which don't bend out of shape easily, found in corrugated boxes that are cut apart or left in one piece for other effects; heavy artists' drawing board, called Bristol board, which is bought by the sheet; insulation board; Styrofoam and other plastic foams, which often accompany your food purchases in the form of small trays and bowls; cylindrical cardboard boxes, such as the familiar oatmeal and salt boxes used to make tubular forms; soft pine or other woods which can be stuck with pins; your macrame knotting board; cork, in sheets or in bulletin boards; old picture frames; artists' canvas stretcher frames, which come in all sizes and fit together at the notched corners to form a frame. The list is almost endless, as you can thread a warp in so many ways, on so many articles, that you'll find them by looking around your house. Each type of support is used to stretch out the warp and allow you to weave it in a preplanned shape. For articles which are flat but need outline shaping, such as the parts of a garment, use cardboard or other flat sheets of suitable material. To make round or tubular shapes, use cylindrical boxes or wide cardboard tubes. To create a ready-to-hang weaving, add the warp into the back of an attractive frame and weave it. Naturally, within the weaving itself, you can use any weave, knotting pattern, or other method, but the basic support will be there so that the finished shape is more predictable.

You choose the type of support according to the kind of shape you are planning. Each has its own merits. The warping is done directly on the foundation, but the way in which the threads are placed varies somewhat.

Cardboard Templates

Cardboard templates are cut out in the actual shape that you want to weave. You'll need paper and pencils to draw the pattern, a sheet of cardboard, sharp scissors intended for paper cutting (cardboard will dull scissors used to cut yarns and fabrics), rustproof push pins, yarn that's strong enough for the warp, any yarn you like for the weft, and blunt-tipped yarn needles that have large eyes to hold the yarn as you weave. Draw the actual shape of the weaving on paper and cut it out. Trace around it on the cardboard, making the outline ½ inch wider to allow for small V-shaped notches to be cut around the edges. Cut out the larger outline. Snip a small notch into the ½-inch allowance along the edges for the warp, which are usually opposite each other. To weave in the round, make a notched circle. The notches are placed so that each will hold one or two passes of the warp as you place it. In a basically rectangular shape, the notches are placed directly opposite each other along two parallel edges

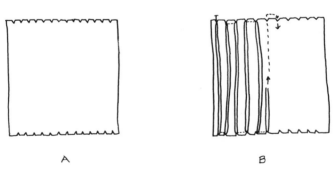

A   B

Making a notched edge cardboard support: A. Notched edges, B. Warping the shape. Secure the first and last ends of the warp to the nearest warp loop, tying in place so that the warp is a closed unit.

Spring Woods by Betty Lovejoy. Woven on a light green warp on a notched Masonite board, in light greens, beige, white, yellows, browns, and gray, with the ends of the warp finished by alternating rows of knotting. The branch was added into the upper warp as it was removed from the board.

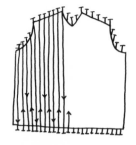

Warping a form with a wider edge. Place the warp two notches on the wider edge for every one notch on the narrower edge.

Pin warping on a cardboard vest shape. Tie each end of the completed warp to the next or preceding warp loop to secure it. The end cannot be left as pinned since it would allow the weft to slip off once the weaving is finished.

of the cardboard. Either set of edges can be used; it depends on the direction in which you want the vertical warp ends to be in the article. For shapes which are irregular, or curved, make an equal number of notches along the opposing edges. On the wider of two edges, you place the notches farther apart, so that they are directly across from the notch on the other side. When the two sides are greatly different in length, you make two notches on the longer edge for each single notch on the shorter one. The warp yarn is threaded onto the cardboard, starting at one end. Pin the tail end at the first notch in the upper corner and bring the yarn down to the opposing notch, go around it and to the front, up to the next notch, around it and down to its opposing notch, and so on. The warp is placed so that the threads are parallel in square and rectangular shapes, including those that curve along one edge only, such as the top shaping on a vest. On round sections, you warp from one side directly across to the other, around the notch to the next one on the right, down across the first warp to the next notch at its left, and so on, following a clockwise path around the circle. The crossed center warps will have the same distinctive curving texture as those found in works warped on hoops and rings.

For other effects, round pieces can also be warped off center by beginning with notches that aren't directly opposite each other. In curved and

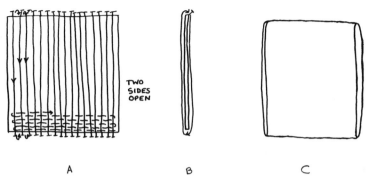

Weaving a tubular shape on cardboard: A. Path of warp and weft, B. Side view of warp path, C. Shape of finished weaving

flaring shapes, the warp ends aren't parallel but converge toward the shorter edge. In pieces that have twice the number of notches along the longer side, so that the ends don't become too far apart to weave well, you take the yarn around each of the single notches two times, once for each of the two opposing notches. After the cardboard is threaded, you can add in new warps, if needed to fill in wide spaces between ends, by putting two push pins into the cardboard, one at either edge, and wrapping another warp around the pins.

A variation of this method is to use both sides of the board at once, making a double warp. To achieve an open end, so that the weaving forms a flattened tube, or is closed on three sides and open on the fourth, as for a bag or ready-to-stuff pillow, you have two possible plans. The first is to place the warp so that the weft will run vertically in the finished article. As you weave you leave one, or both, sides unwoven so that they form long slits. The warp is placed on the board by taking it all the way around it, to the same notch on the other side, over around the next notch, down around the board to the first side, up to the same notch, and is continued in the same manner. The second method is to place pins along the notches at the top. For all of the front wraps of yarn, you go around the notches. For the back wraps, you go around the pins instead. As you weave, you can go all the way around the article, and at the top, where the pins take the place of notches, there will be an opening in the finished piece. In the first method, you can either weave a tube, by weaving the front and then up

113

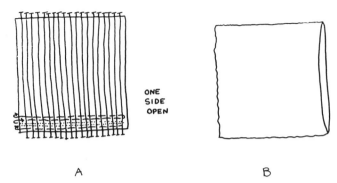

A   B

**Weaving a form with three closed sides and one open one in one piece:
A. Path of warp and weft, B. Shape of finished weaving**

around to the back, and down to the beginning, or a sort of envelope
shape, with three closed sides and one open one, by weaving from the front
around the left side to the back, across the back to the right side. Then
you go back, to the left, around to the front, to the right, and back to the
left. In the finished weaving, the open right side, for articles such as bags,
will be the top. In pillows, it can be either the side or the top; it makes no
difference.

Pin Warping

On large sheets of cork, soft wood, and Styrofoam, you create the shape
you want your weaving to be entirely with push pins. You can lightly draw
the shape on the board with pencil, or use a paper pattern, taped securely
to the board. Around the outline of the shape, at warp edges, place pins,
spacing them as far apart as you want the warp ends to be from each other.
Usually, they are between ¼ and ½ inch, depending on the size of the
weaving. In larger works, they can be farther apart, and in smaller ones,
closer together so that the weave created suits the proportions. Place each
pin into the board at an angle, out away from the center, so that the warp
doesn't pull them out. Place the warp yarn from an upper corner. Make a
slip knot in the end, take out the first pin, put it through the knot and
replace it. Bring the warp down to the opposing pin, go around it and the
next pin, up to the next one, around it and the one next to it, down to the

114

BOTTOM

Pin warping on cork, plastic, or wood to make a shape that is not the same as the outlines of the supporting material.

Warping path for a closed bottom cylindrical form

next set, and so on. Keep the yarn fairly taut, and end off as you do the last pin, with a knot as for the first one.

Boxes and cylinders are warped with pins so that you can make the warp in the same shape as the box. Interesting basketlike weavings can be made along the four sides of a box wrapped with warp, going around pins set into the open edges around the top. In square or rectangular boxes, the warp ends will cross over each other along the bottom. You can weave them into each other, doing one set first on two opposing sides of the box and then weaving the second set, from the other two sides, into the warp as

Stuffed doll Gloria by Betty Lovejoy. Made in orange warp on a cylindrical salt box, with a body of gold, white, yellow, tan, and red. Hair is looped and knotted white, brown and rust mohair added after the doll was stuffed. Arms braided wools in yellow, white, and rust; legs braided wools in rust, gray, and lime green; wrapping at wrists and ankles. Brown bead eyes aren't visible under the hair.

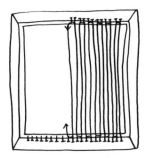

Warping the back of a picture frame, using small brads instead of pins for a permanent attachment

you place it. Then, when you start to weave around the sides, the bottom will be done. For additional strength, merely cross the sets as they are done and further weave them, in any weave between one set of ends, or in knotting, wrapping, coiling, or twining. For cylindrical boxes, such as salt boxes, place pins around the top and make the warp as you would for a circle, forming the center crossing at the bottom of the box.

Frames can be pinned, for a temporary holding as you weave, or you can use small brads and a hammer in frames which will stay in place in the finished weaving. You'll find that judicious placement of pins and small or decorative nails will allow you to weave within just about anything. For example, you can make a sort of stained glass tapestry or open lacy covering in a window by warping the frame of the window itself and weaving in place.

Weaving the Prepared Warp

The weaving on your prepared warp can follow any direction or pattern that you like—tapestry techniques, inlay, knotting, twining, wrapping warps, leno, in short, whichever technique strikes you for the shape of the piece. In articles that have interesting shapes of their own, you can echo them in the design or use a plain weave in different colors or textures.

Blunt-tipped yarn needles are the best way to weave this type of warp, since you need them to get into the small areas between the ends, and the narrow spaces toward the top. Cut lengths of about 18 inches of weft, and thread the needle. If you're using several colors or textures, it's a good idea to use several needles, threading them all when you begin so that they are ready to go when you need them. Using the plain weave, or any other that you choose, weave over one and under one, using the needle to weave from the bottom up, or center out as the case may be. Use a blunt-tined fork or tapestry beater, if you have one, to beat the yarn into place. All of the procedures are the same as those for free-style weaving with the exception that here the threads in the warp are taut, and the weaving is usually done from the bottom up, rather than the top down.

For cylindrical and round works which have an even number of warp ends, be sure to change the over, under pattern in each round so that the tabby weave is created. As you continue to weave around in an even-numbered warp, you change the weave on even-numbered rounds to follow the over, under alternately. For odd-numbered warps, this takes place automatically; you end a series of odd-numbered warps on an under if it began on an under, and vice versa. Continuing, the next round will begin with an over.

In all of these supporting forms, the placement of the warp is such that the individual lifting of warp ends with a needle is preferable to shuttles or thread-lifting devices called *shed sticks* which are used on simple looms, as the needle can work through the warp easily. The pins or notches holding the warp aren't strong enough to take the added tension of a bulky shuttle or the simultaneous lifting of alternate ends created by weaving in a shed stick and turning it on its side to open the shed. You can usually work several ends onto the needle before you bring it through to pass the weft, so that the needles work well and can go quickly.

Finishing the Weaving

At the end of a weaving, there is a narrow opening between the last few shots of weft and the top of the warp. To finish a weaving threaded with notches or pins to the exact shape of the article, weave into the opening as many weft shots as possible. You want to fill in the area completely, so that when the weaving is taken off the board, by lifting it off the notches or taking out the pins, it is complete. If the warp seems a little loose at the

Hanging by Pat Banakus. Knotted onto a dowel, slit weave above and below central design area in plain weave. Slits become strips at the lower edge, with beads knotted into fringe made out of the warp ends.

Batik on handweaving by Margaret B. Windeknecht. Exposed warp leno sections show the combination of dyeing techniques with weaving.

top loops, you can add more weft with the needle, working into the loops. The top or edges can be further finished with wrapping, coiling, or crochet for added strength and design.

When you make a warp that is larger than the article, for example, if you threaded a square form and filled in only the center of the warp, you can take the ends off the notches or pins or cut through them with a scissor at the pins to leave the pins in place for another weaving. The loose ends can be turned to the back of the work, trimmed and woven in, or further finished with knotting, wrapping, or used to create a fringe.

Combining Techniques

Combining techniques in supporting form works is done in several ways. As you have seen, when the weaving is underway you can switch to other methods within the article itself. The finishing techniques are often a blend of methods, as knotting and wrapping are often added when the warp is longer than the article, as described above. You can also plan a weaving for a mélange of methods by making the warp much longer and wider when working in a circle or other unusual shape, allowing for additional techniques to be worked upon the extra warp after the weaving is underway. The ends can be cut, or worked in the loops that naturally form when the weaving is taken off notches or pins without being cut.

Get out your board, pins, and yarns and make small samplers, trying out various weaves, combinations of techniques and patterns that come to you as you weave. The samplers make fascinating studies in themselves and can be mounted as a group for a wall on an attractive sheet of wood, cork, or fabric stretched around a frame and stapled or thumb-tacked to the back. They'll also give you many plans that you'll want to use in other works on a larger scale. Once you start, you'll find it hard to stop, as you enjoy the many variations possible in off-loom weavings of all kinds.

6

FINGERWEAVING AND PLAITING

Fingerweaving and *plaiting* are related forms, thought to have been developed by the Indians of North America. Although fingerweaving is used to refer to several different weaving techniques, the Indian method is one that most resembles a complex braid. The simple three-strand braid is the basis of fingerweaving and plaiting, as they are both braids of many cords.

The term fingerweaving is often applied to free-style weaving in which you work with hand-manipulated sheds and one long outer cord used as a weft. In this sense, you already know the technique. The only change here is that the weft thread is attached to the outer right-hand edge of the top attachment, along with the warp ends. Then, you weave with the weft in the regular way. However, in fingerweaving as practiced by the Cherokee, Osage, and Hopi tribal groups, which are the best known for this weaving style, the warp and weft are combined in one set of threads that are woven together interchangeably. There are two types of braid which can be made. The first starts from the outer edge and is braided across, and the second is worked from the center out.

Both methods are done with a set of threads, premeasured and attached to a short dowel or rod, as for free weaving and knotting. You can use any type of yarn that appeals to you. To start out, a hard-twisted wool, such as the Scandinavian two-ply rya rug yarn, is easy to use and produces a lovely texture. Make the set of threads in the usual way, winding on a set of rods or other supports, making the yarn ends about three times longer than you want the finished strip of fingerweaving to be. The width depends on the number of ends that you make and can be as wide as you wish, once

Mary Shell, Cherokee from North Carolina, demonstrating finger-weaving, 1973.

Assomption by Mary Shell. Wall hanging, fingerweaving, four-ply knitting worsted wool, length 30″, width 18″, 3½″ fringe, 1973, Cherokee Community.

the basic method is well in hand. Usually, the weavings done in this way are strips, up to 5 or 6 inches wide. You can make wider works by combining finished strips, or weaving in sections, as the yarns are held in your hands and can become difficult to handle when there are a large number.

Outer-edge Fingerweaving

For the outer-edge fingerweaving, make an even number of ends, starting with a base of ten, so that they are easy to work with. The actual weaving is quite simple, once the threads are set up on a dowel or other support. Hold the yarns in your left hand and lift the outermost right end with your right hand. Take it over the next end to the left, under the next, over the next, and so on across the threads. The last thread will be an over pass, and you then smooth the end down along the left side so that it rejoins the group. You hold and weave the threads fairly loosely, so that they form a 45-degree angle to the horizontal top attachment. You can also weave them more tightly, by beating them upward as you would on free weaving, with a fork or tapestry beater.

To continue, you lift the outer right-hand thread and follow the same pattern, beginning and ending on an over pass of the thread. You'll notice that as you complete a series of threads that they work back toward the other side as a natural progression, and eventually the same thread is on the right again. When working with the threads angled, as you create a diagonal pattern, you'll also see that the upper left-hand corner is left unwoven, with the ends leading down to the first thread that you wove to the left in their original parallel hanging position. You can create weavings

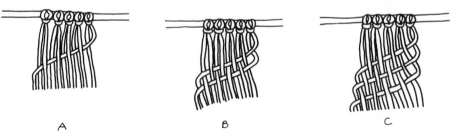

A   B   C

Outer-edge fingerweaving: A. First strand, B. Second strand, C. Third strand

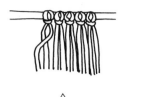

A   B

Filling in the left upper edge before starting

C   D

with these exposed threads as part of your design, or you can fill in the area before you start.

To fill in the area, begin at the left. Take the second thread and bring it over the outer left thread. Take the fourth thread from the left and bring it over the third, under what is now the second and over the outer left thread. Then, lift the sixth thread from the left, take it over the fifth, under the next, moving left, over the next, under the next, and over the outer left. Take the eighth thread from the left and bring it over the seventh, under the next, over, under, over, under, and then over. Now you can begin to work with the outer right-hand thread, which is the tenth from the left-hand edge. You move the right thread in the usual pattern, as the upper left has already been woven. If you find it easier to work from left to right, you can reverse the directions. Weaving the strands from the left outer edge by going under the next thread, over, under, across, and ending on an under pass is the same pattern. In this case, the ends at the upper right will be exposed, but you can weave them beforehand in the same manner as the upper left by following the directions for filling in the upper left, substituting an under for each over and an over for each under, and counting from the right-hand edge.

123

The ends can also be worked with an odd number in a weaving that is already underway by starting from the right with an over and ending on the left with an under pass, after completing the line across the row as usual.

You'll find that as you make the braid, it is actually the same as weaving free style in a basic pattern, as you go over and under each end, just as you would in the tabby shedding pattern. Another style of holding the ends in braiding is to lift all of the threads which are to be passed under with your left thumb and then passing the right-hand strand through them just as you would a weft.

Working from the Center Out

This technique is often referred to as Osage braiding, after the group of Native Americans which perfected it. It is particularly effective when woven in more than one color, as the weaving produces a distinctive V shape. The different shades show the chevron pattern to advantage. You can begin a new piece, starting with ten ends, or five strands doubled and mounted on a dowel, or add the new pattern to your right-sided braid.

To begin the pattern, split the strands down the center, holding them

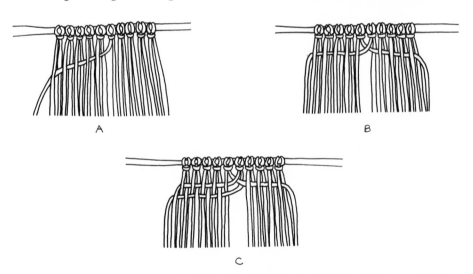

Center out fingerweaving or Osage braiding: A. Right center strand out toward left, B. Left center strand out to right, C. Second right strand out to left

124

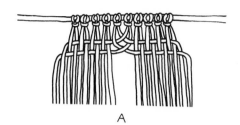 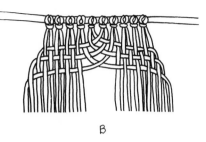

A. Two sets of strands woven, B. Three sets of strands woven

apart so that you can easily reach the two middle strands. Start by bringing the right center strand over the left one, and take it diagonally down to the left by going under the next, over the next, ending on an under pass, and taking the rest of the strand down along the left-hand edge. Then, take the left center strand, and as it has already been crossed over by the right one, take it over the next strand to the right, under the next, over the next, and ending on an over pass. Bring the rest of the strand down into line along the right-hand edge of the strands. Continue working from the center out and diagonally down, always taking the right center strand over the left and following the same pattern. You can also work by crossing the left center strand over the right to start the weaving, as long as you maintain the same pattern throughout any single section.

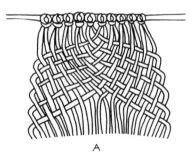 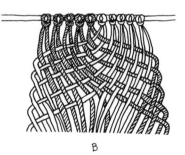

A. Five sets of strands woven, B. Two colors

You can reverse the technique, working from each edge in toward the center, crossing the two strands as they meet. In this pattern, you always bring the right outer strand under the next and then in toward the middle, and the left outer strand in by going over the next strand at the start of the

125

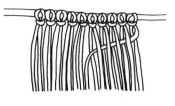
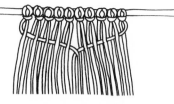

A

B

Outer edges in toward center
A. Right strand in, B. Left strand in

row. You can combine the two, or work in sections, with more ends in various color and weaving groups for different patterned effects.

Braiding

Basic braiding can also be worked in weaving, as it can be done with any number of odd or even threads as long as you follow the same rule. In braiding, the left-hand outer strand is crossed over the next one and left in that position. For an even number of strands, you move to the right outer strand and take it under the next, over the next, and so on. For an odd number of strands, you take the outer right strand over the next strand, and then across. In both cases, you stop when you reach the outermost left strand and begin the next row by crossing it over the one next to it on the right. You can braid with any number of strands as long as you remember to take the outer right strand under when using an even number and over when using an odd number of strands.

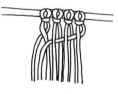

A

B

Basic braiding, even number of strands shown

Pair of tassels, Italian, textile trimmings; braided, knotted, and crocheted, XVII Century. *Courtesy, Metropolitan Museum of Art, Gift of Mrs. J. Pierpont Morgan, 1921.*

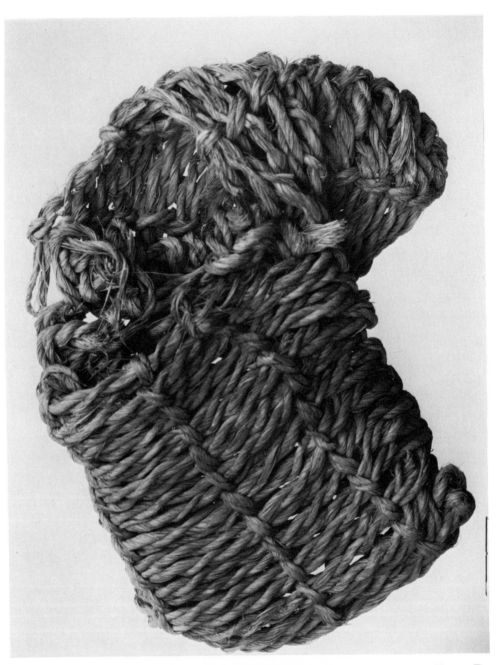

Egyptian donkey bag model, palm fiber rope, twining in coarse fiber, Dynasty XI, Province: Thebes. *Courtesy, Metropolitan Museum of Art, Rogers Fund, 1931.*

7

TWINING, COILING, AND WEAVING IN THE ROUND

Basketry is one of the most ancient craft forms, and perhaps the only one that has never been duplicated by a machine. The techniques were developed to suit the interlacing of flexible reeds, canes, grasses, and split strips of thin wood to fashion durable carryalls. Decorative designs and patterns are added by changes in the weave, materials, or colors. These methods are also well adapted to softer fibers such as those in yarns and ropes and are a welcome addition to off-loom weavings of all sorts.

Baskets are made in three basic ways. *Twining* is the weaving of more supple fibers around stiffer ones, in a manner that can be compared to the warp and weft in free weaving. *Coiling* is a wrapping technique, in which fibers are worked around a thick base and then coiled or formed into rounded shapes and laced together. *Plaiting*, or braiding, is the third method, which usually consists of a standard three-strand braid which is sewn or laced into a basket shape. The twining and coiling methods are of greatest interest to off-loom weavers, as you can use them to add texture and sculptural form within other works or on their own for fascinating shapes and useful articles.

Twining

In basketry, twining is also referred to as weaving, as the upright spokes are used in the same manner as warp ends and the twining fibers are called *weavers*. The weavers are worked around the spokes as you would work with a weft, so that the technique can be used in a fiber weaving.

Use a sturdy warp in place of the spokes or staves in basket making

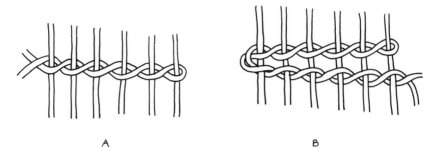

Twining: A. First row, B. Second row

and any medium-weight yarn for the weaver, or weft. Place the warp ends on a dowel or thick cord held taut to learn the method thoroughly before your work on a free-standing rounded form.

The basic twining, also called Salish or Indian twining, is done with a folded weft. Start at the right of the warp and take an 18-inch length of the weaver. Fold it in half and slip the weft around the first warp end. Twist it once, in between the first and second warp ends, take the two ends of the weft around the next warp, with one going to the back and one coming to the front of it. Then twist once and move to the next warp. Continue across the warp in the same way. At the end of the row, bring the half of the weft that is leading from the back of the twist around the warp to the front, and the front half around it to the back, so that they cross along the outer edge of the last warp in the row. Then start the next row just below it, bringing the ends around the same warp. When you are weaving a basketlike shape, you often work from the bottom up, but the method is the same. When you use up the first length of weft, bring both ends to the back and start again in the same spot with a new length of yarn. If you can see clearly at the start that the weft will be used up before the end of a row, it's easiest to end off the old yarn and start the new one on the first warp of the new row rather than waiting for the middle of the row.

Twining gives you a densely covered warp, which usually does not show at all in the finished weaving. When you are using thicker materials, or for an open look, you can space the passes of weft so that the warp can be seen in the finished weaving. In this case, you twist the weft more than once at the end of each row so that it begins the new one higher up, or lower down, depending on the direction of your weaving. Then twine the row as usual, leaving the warp exposed between the row you are weaving and the previous one.

Two-color Twining

A two-color twining can be done in many ways to produce patterns in the finished weaving. For an up-and-down stripe, use two colors of weft and twine them as if you were working with one, folded weft. Since you twist the ends together outside of the last warp in the row, when you begin the next row, the same colors are in the same places, so that the continued twining produces a vertical stripe.

To vary the vertical stripe, make two twists between warp ends at the same spot throughout several rows of weaving. This will give you a check, as the colors will reverse themselves in the weave. The most usual check is balanced, in that you space the double twists evenly throughout a row, and then you continue the pattern for the same number of rows, resulting in checked sections that are the same in relation to each other. For example, make double twists in between every four warp ends, then weave four rows in the same way. For the next four rows, you change the colors at the beginning by twisting twice at the outer edge, then continuing across, making the double twists in the same spots, every four ends, as the previous rows. However, as the colors were reversed at the beginning of the row, the new set of checks will begin to build up and you continue them for four rows.

To create a twill weave effect, using a two-color weft, you just cross the two yarns over each other on the outermost warp so that the next row

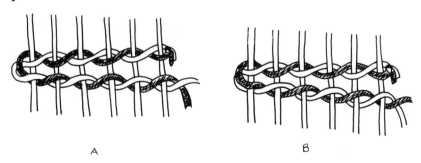

A   B

Two-color twining: A. Forming vertical stripes, B. Twill twining

begins with the opposite color over the shade in the previous row. Continued rows of weaving in this way will start to show the twill-like weave.

For horizontal stripes, you use two colors, but each row is woven with one folded weft. The next is done with the same shade. On the third row, you use the second color and repeat it on the fourth. This will produce a two-weft-wide horizontal stripe. For wider stripes, repeat the rows several times before changing colors.

Changes in the Twining Weaves

Pairing is the use of four strands of weft in a row, which gives a thicker, denser effect. The pairs of weft yarns are used as one, so that you follow the basic twining pattern, but use two around the front of each warp and two around the back. This is sometimes referred to as *double twining*. Another variation of basic twining is to weave with a single weft, just as you would weave in the basic pattern in free-hanging weaving. A triple pair is three in front and three behind, or six wefts for each row.

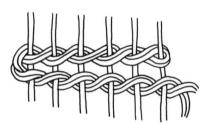

Pairing or two-strand twining

Another interesting technique used with sturdy fibers that maintain their pattern is to make a three-strand braid and weave it as for a standard weave, one over and one under each warp end. In basketry this is called *waling*. It is usually done in between twined rows for a change in texture.

Free-standing Twining

Free-standing twining is used to create basket forms. You can use the same fibers, working them in the round. In basketry, the stiffer spokes or

132

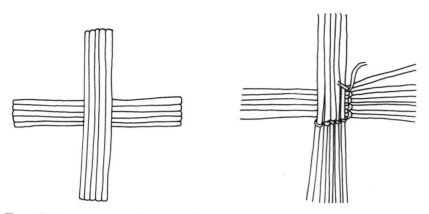

Foundation rope lengths in an X; starting to twine around the spokes

staves are crossed to form the beginning foundation of the weaving. They are often held in place by the weavers, or may be split so that one set is slipped into the other, creating an X shape. The spokes are fanned out so that they can be woven individually. This method can be used to begin a soft weaving by using fairly thick cord or thin rope as the warp. To start out, cut ten lengths, about 18 inches. Place the first five flat on a table or work surface, so that they line up and are parallel to each other. Take the second five and place them over the first to form an X. This will be the bottom of the basket shape, or the outside of the weaving. Take the first length of weft, fold in half, and begin twining around each of the lengths of rope. The first few rows will be tricky, as you want to keep the foundation in shape, while at the same time spreading the ends out so that they

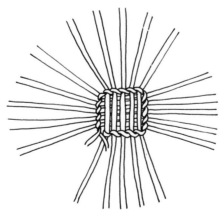

First round of twining completed

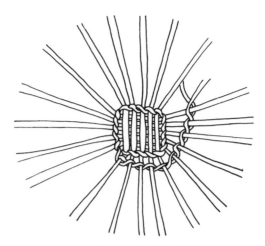

Second round of twining

radiate from the crossed center foundation. Rather than working in separate rows, you continue the twining around in a clockwise circle, merely going one above and over the first row to start the second. When you use up the weaver, slip the ends to the back and start a new piece. The ends can also be held in place along the bottom and the twining woven around them to secure them tightly in place. Continue to weave in a circle until you have a diameter of about 4 inches. You'll notice that the spokes, or warp, seem to be getting too far apart to continue in the same shape. If you want to make a large shape, add in new spokes, folding them in half and weaving them into the twining between two existing spokes. This can be done in several spots around the circle, as long as you place the new spokes evenly, with the same number of existing spokes in between each set of new ones. The new spokes should be trimmed so that they are the same length as the existing ones.

To begin the upward curve, which will form the sides of the shape, work the weaver a bit tighter as you go around the circle. If you have not added spokes, this is quite easy, since the existing ones will be spaced far apart and can be woven together more closely by merely pulling the weaver as you twine. At the point where you want the weaving to curve upward, turn over the basic shape. (The bottom has been facing up until now.) Weave the following rows from the outside, moving up from the bottom. To make

Bending down the spokes to end off the top

a basic tubular shape, just continue to work with the same number of spokes. To vary the shape, causing it to bend inward, work two spokes as one, spacing evenly throughout a row. You can add new spokes, or decrease the number that you have, for different widths and shapes, as you gain control over the technique. For the basic work, make a tubular shape, decreasing the number of spokes toward the top if you want it to curve in or leaving the same number for a columnar shape. Decreasing the number of spokes near the top will give a more rounded, ball-like shape to the basket.

To end off the top, fold the spokes into the basket and weave two rows or so, catching the top of one spoke and the folded end of the next in one twining step. Do this until they are all securely woven in place and the twining goes right up to the folded tops of the spokes.

Basket shapes in twining can also be woven from the top down, so that you begin with the opening of the basket. To do this, you estimate the number of spokes you'll need and make a set of rope lengths that is twice the length and half the number needed. You fold the spokes in half and weave the twining into the spokes right at the fold, which becomes the top of the basket. It is simplest to twine with the spokes placed in their folded

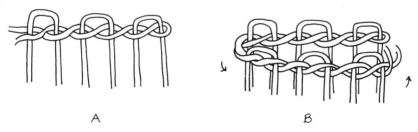

A   B

Twining from the top down: A. First half of the round, B. Bringing the second half of the round over to meet the first and continue twining in a downward direction

135

Fan with a wrapped handle, twining in colored stripes on radiating spokes

Octagonal basket in natural shade twining, straw on straw. Author's collection.

Letter holder in natural cane on shaped cane base

position, with the fold at the top, on a table. You twine as usual, until you have encompassed all of the spokes. Then you carefully lift the beginning end and bring it up to the last twining step and continue in a circle by working the next twine around what was the first spoke. In this manner, you complete the top and start to weave the sides all in one step. As you get to the bottom, you decrease the number of spokes. The very center of the bottom can be woven in until you cannot continue, since the spokes are too close together. Working from the inside of the basket, draw in the ends, crossing them to form the bottom and secure them by tying them with a piece of the weft inside where they will not show. Check to see that they look neat and even on the outside. The bottom will not be visible when the shape is sitting on it, in any case, but should be well formed.

To avoid the problem of finishing the bottom, many baskets are worked from the bottom up, as previously described, or done on a wooden base. In basketry, the stiff spokes are set into the base, which is drilled with holes to accommodate them, in a type of work called *upsett stakes*. For softer fiber forms, you can use the same kind of wooden base with holes around the edges by slipping the rope or other soft fiber spokes into the holes and making an overhand knot on the bottom. You can then weave the sides between the tied-in spokes.

Portuguese basket with single willow weaver on base of upsett stakes

Coiled basket with a lid in natural hue, and twined basket in three colors with a lid and braided strap to open the basket. Author's collection.

Coiling

Coiling is an interesting method, as it is simple to do and can be quite colorful, since you are able to change the colors within the rows with ease. In basketry, the base of coiling is usually groups of pine needles or bundles of grass wrapped with raffia or other flexible materials. The more flexible the inner material is, the better it is to work with, which is why pine needles are popular. For the basics of coiling, you should use a regular rope, not too thick or it won't be flexible enough, and wool or other yarn of medium weight. A blunt-tipped needle, such as one used for rug making, or a curved one, called a *sailmaker's needle*, is quite useful, both to wrap the coils and lace them together as they get long enough.

To begin coiling, use about a yard of rope and several ounces of knitting worsted or other medium-weight yarn. Trim both ends of the rope on an angle, so that the rope tapers to a point. Cut a length of yarn, about 20 inches, and thread the needle. Place the long end of the yarn on the rope so that its end is running along the rope in the opposite direction of the tip of the rope. The end of the yarn should be 1½ inches from the point of the rope. Then, bring the rest of the yarn to the tip and start to wrap the yarn around the rope at the tip, enclosing both the rope and the tail end of the yarn. The coiling method is very much like wrapping a set of warp

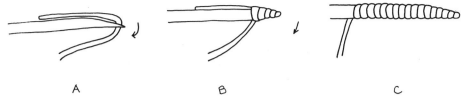

| A | B | C |

Beginning the coil: A. Placing the yarn, B. Starting to wrap, C. Wrapped coil

threads, in that you want the coil of yarn to be smooth and flat without overlapping itself. Wrap the rope from the point back, covering the core completely. As you get to about 1½ inches from the end of the rope, wrap up the tapered end into a circle of covered rope coil. Then, take the needle into the middle of the circle once, to secure the round shape. Hold the circular base in one hand and continue to wrap the rope with the other. There are several styles of attaching the next round of the coil to the previous one. The one you choose depends on the effect you want to create. Basically, you are wrapping the yarn around the rope, bending the newly wrapped area to fit around the base coil and taking one overcast stitch, which goes around the coil in the previous round. You can make these stitches fairly often, after every three or four wraps of the yarn, or less often, for a looser attachment. When you want the coil to be quite sturdy, take the needle and yarn around the previous coil after every two or three wraps of the yarn. For a faster, looser binding, take the yarn around the previous coil after four or more wraps.

Once you have made a flat coiled circle of about 3½ inches in diameter, you can begin to bring up the sides to make a cylindrical basket shape. To form the sides, all you do is lay the new coil directly on top of the previous

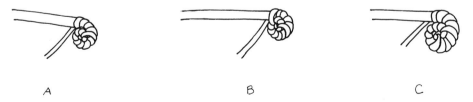

| A | B | C |

Forming the shape: A. First circle, B. Second pass into the center of the circle, C. Continuing to wrap

Coiled foundation, showing path of the overcasting attachment stitches into previous rounds of the coil

Cylindrical coiled basket form

one, rather than placing it around the edge. When you continue to wrap and overcast, placing the next coil directly over the previous one, you get an even tubular form. To make a form with outward curving sides, place the next coil on each round just a bit outside of the one before, so that the sides begin to move outward as well as up. When you reach the end of the rope, start to overcast a bit more often, so that the tapered, wrapped end is smoothly attached to the previous coil. Bring the needle inside the basket, run it along into the backs of a few wraps, and cut the yarn. There's your first coiled basket shape.

To add in new yarn, if you use up the yarn in your needle as you coil, bring the end of the old yarn along the coil in front of the wrapping. Place the new end of the yarn in the same place and begin to wrap where the coil left off. As you wrap, both ends are covered by the wrapping yarn and are held in place.

Coiling in Colors

To coil with more than one color, you'll find it easiest to work with the same number of needles as you have colors of yarn. All of the colors are brought along the base of your coil, as you do the actual wrapping. When you want to coil in the next color, you place the first one along the coil and wrap around it with the new color. As you see how the coiling forms into its three-dimensional shape, you'll also see how to place the different colors in your wrapping yarns to form patterns and designs, such as are seen in the Hopi coiled placques. These are made with natural and dyed yucca plant strips around a base of grasses or thicker parts of the yucca plant. The control of the pattern is dependent on the placement of the coils in their different shades. As you work with the technique, you'll come to see just where you want to place the colors, according to what has happened on the previous round.

Coiling Variations

There are many variations that you can make in the actual coiling technique for changes in the finished appearance of the coils. The *Apache coil*,

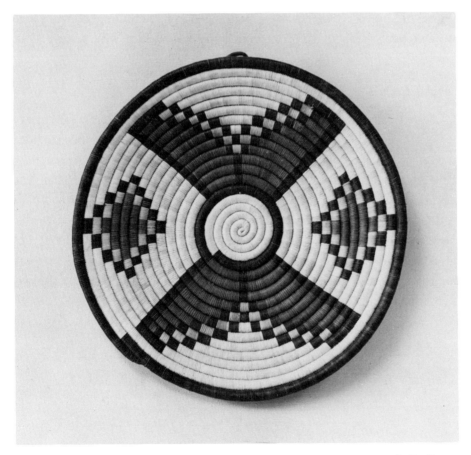

Placque by McBridge Lomayestewa (Hopi Pueblo). Yucca, coiled, diameter 14⅝", 1966.

named after the tribal group which excels in creating intricate baskets and distinctive water bottles, is one in which you bring the wrapping through the previous row's wrapping material, rather than around the entire coil. To do it, you just catch one strand of the wrapping on the previous row each time you make one wrap of the yarn or other wrapping material. A variation of this technique is to bring the yarn through the yarn of the previous coil every few wraps, instead of every time.

When wrapping with a fairly wide material, such as a thick soft yarn which will flatten out on the coil, or the more traditional flat grasses, you can make what is sometimes called the *lazy stitch*. In this type of coil, you go once around the coil, then once around the previous row, all the way around the work. The resulting pattern shows alternating one-coil and two-coil thick wrappings for an interesting flat surface with texture.

Looped Coils

Looped coils can be made to extend out and beyond the regular surface of the coiling. They can bend and form outward loops and other rounded or oval shapes. To make a loop, you simply wrap the core for the length of the desired loop without overcasting it to the previous round. Then you bend the newly wrapped coil out to the desired shape, bringing the end back to the spot where it started to move away from the basic shape. Overcast the loop in place, once or twice, depending on the size of the loop. For larger or heavy-weight material loops, overcast twice to be sure. You can build up new areas of coiling, using the loops as a base, or leave the one layer loop for an open effect.

Looped coil

Curving lid

Combining Techniques

Coiling is an effective way to begin and form sculptural shapes, as it forms a sturdy foundation for the weaving to follow. If you are planning a twined basket you may find it easier to make the flat bottom section in coiling and attach the spokes for twining by wrapping folded, double lengths into the last round of the coil. In this way, you have a good flat base and your warplike spokes are ready to be twined. There are also many works in which you'll find that coiled sections add strength and dimension, particularly in forming soft sculptures.

Coiled circles and ovals can be made to fit many works which you want to have a definite top and bottom, with other techniques worked between the sections of coiling. For covered baskets, coiled lids are both useful and easy to make, since you follow the basic shape. To make a lid you can plan a slightly arched shape. Place each coil just a bit up from the outer edge of the previous one so that the lid curves gently upward. You can check the size of the lid on the opening of the basket itself, ending off the coil when it fits over the top securely. For a cylindrical basket, or one that ends in a tubular top, you can make a flat coil lid, one coil's width wider than the opening of the basket and add a few rows of tubular coiling. The short lip that forms will fit snugly on the basket. A buttonlike top is added to either lid shape by making a beginning coil about 1½ inches wide. Then you

Basket shapes in coiling

143

Basket with Fitted Lid by Jan Knutson. Coiling technique worked in wool fiber crochet over sisal rope foundation. Coils are linked to each other with crochet stitches rather than overcasting.

coil the next row directly over the last row in the small coil and continue the rest of the lid as usual.

Changing the Shape

As you begin a coil with a tight rounded inner coil, the following shape is naturally round, as you follow the basic shape to continue coiling. The sides are varied, by curving out, or in, or moving straight up as you coil, but the bottom and top remain circular. To change the round bottom you can use one of several variations. The easiest to do is to make an oval coil to start out by merely folding the wrapped beginning end over to the following coil for about 1½ inches. As you continue the coiling, the base will become oval.

A square coil base is made by wrapping a longer beginning end than usual and folding it sharply back toward itself. Then you continue coiling

Oval and square coil foundations

up to the beginning end, make another sharp bend so that the next row will be placed alongside the second one just completed. Repeat once more, so that the fourth row follows the third and continue in the same way until a square is formed. To make a rectangle, extend the length of the first row and add just enough additional rows to form the desired shape. Once the base is made, you work around its edges as you would for a round coil, going into the bends with the overcasting as you pass them. The basket will follow the shape of the coil, giving you a square or rectangular form with softly curving corners.

To modify the base shape even further, you can make irregularly shaped bases by adding in new areas with looping of the coil. As you can continue to build on the additional loops of coiling you can make all kinds of different shapes and patterns. You'll discover that coiling is such an effective way to make sturdy forms that it is invaluable in many applications.

Traditional Basketry

Baskets of traditional form are made with different materials and basically the same techniques as soft fiber works. Reed, cane, rattan, and wicker, which all come from the same plant, a tropical palm grown in the Far East, are popular materials because they are flexible and strong. *Reed* is the core of the plant, made in round, flat, or caning, and round on one side and flat on the other. *Cane* is usually made from the smooth outer part of the stem, and is often used to make the seats in bentwood or hardwood chairs. The different widths, from about ⅛ to ½ an inch, are found in one-pound, loosely wound groups. When the diameter of the round or the width of the flat type increases, the material is usually called *wicker* or *rattan*. The increased thickness makes wicker and rattan suitable for things which will

145

get a lot of use, such as furniture, huge baskets, and trunks, all of which are made following the same principles as simple baskets. The most widely available color is the natural tan, but you may come across darker brown or black.

Raffia is made out of strips of leaves from another palm tree. It is flat and thin, available in several widths and many colors. The pliant strips are well suited for use as the outer wrapping material in coiling techniques. You can also use many different kinds of wide, flat grasses, such as marsh or sea grass. They can be picked and allowed to dry in a shaded area. For the core in coiling, groups of pine needles, added as needed while you are making a coil, or bundles of dry sea grass, rushes, and just about any other flexible fiber can be used. Sisal and jute, loosely spun or unspun, are popular choices.

Split strips of different types of wood are used most often for the spokes in woven baskets. Willow is grown for basketry and comes in varying widths so that it can be used for both the spokes and the weaver in two thicknesses. Other woods such as hickory, birch, ash, linden, and oak are made into wider strips called *splints*. These are stiff in the completed basket, for strength and durability, and are most often used as spokes. Split bamboo is found in various thicknesses, but it can be difficult to work with at first.

All of these plant fibers are soaked in water for at least five hours for spoke materials. Reed and other stiffer materials are also soaked when used as weavers. The raffia and flat grasses for coiling don't usually need to be wet, but if you find that they aren't pliant enough to work with, water is the answer. Use a pail or pot large enough to immerse completely.

To make baskets, you'll also need a work surface covered with a sheet of plastic or other waterproof fabric, a really sharp knife and scissors, and thin, pointed pliers to help bend up the spokes forming the sides. When you are weaving a tightly woven pattern, you'll find that a knitting needle or similar object is helpful for opening up areas as you work.

For twined baskets, the basic pattern is to create a base of crossed spokes with an odd number and to weave with a single length of weaver. The weaving is done just as for any under one, over one pattern, all the way around the spokes. On the next row, you go over the unders and under the overs of the previous row. In this type of weaving, pairing is the use of two

An assortment of wicker and cane baskets, showing single weavers, braided top edges, and foundations of different numbers of crossed spokes.

weavers in a regular twining pattern. Double pairing is the use of four weavers following the same pattern. Triple pairing is done with either three or six weavers.

One of the most important aspects in making a basket is to start out with a good, flat bottom. There are several different ways to begin the basket, which are chosen according to the shape and type of basket that you are going to make. The spokes form both the bottom and side foundations of your weaving so that they must be well done for the best results. The style of weave that you do on the spokes can be chosen for its visual pattern and texture. The actual shape or outline will be determined for the most part by the placement of the spokes.

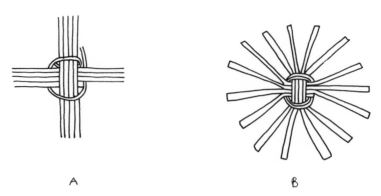

A. Placement of foundation spokes and weaver to secure them, B. Two wraps of weaver to secure the spokes and the spokes bent into a circle

One of the most basic beginnings, for a basket made with a fairly thin spoke material, is to make a crossing of two sets of spokes. The sets are of equal number, usually four and four for a small, learning basket, but one spoke is cut shorter than the rest to give the odd number needed for the basic weave. Place four next to each other on your work surface, so that they line up and they are running horizontally. Place the second set on top of them vertically to form a cross. The shorter spoke is placed in the middle of this group, and should be cut after you see how the placement works. It should be just long enough to cover the horizontal group and extend for about ¾ of an inch and the same length as the other spokes at the top of the group. Take a piece of the weaver and put it under the vertical spokes just above the cross. Bring it up and around, over the top of the same group and to the horizontal group next to the beginning end of the weaver. Bend the weaver to shape as needed, while you weave it. Then, take it under the horizontal group, over the next vertical, under the next horizontal, and repeat once. As you complete a round or one complete turn of the weaver around the spokes, push it into place, so that it interweaves with the spokes. On the next round, take the pliers, cover its two metal sides with scrap fabric to prevent their marking the surface of the spokes, and start to bend the spokes out from their position, so that they form a multipointed star shape. The outermost spoke in each group is bent at the sharpest angle, as they are the farthest from each other. Each spoke should

148

be an equal distance from the next. To help align them and get the basket underway, take the next round of the weaver, moving clockwise, and go under one and over one all the way around. Tighten it after each half round for the first few to maintain the right distance between the spokes and make a firm foundation for the basket. On the next round, you follow the same pattern and continue up to the beginning of the sides.

Up to this point, you have been working with the bottom of the basket facing up. Now, turn it over so that you can work the sides from what will be the outside of the basket when it is finished. Take the pliers and bend the side spokes up into place. Be sure that they are still damp so that they bend instead of breaking. If you bend them on a right angle, the sides of the basket will be straight and cylindrical. When you use less of an angle, they will flare out. The degree of bend is up to you. At first, the knack of getting the bend in the same spot on each spoke may seem elusive, but it will come to you.

Now take the next round of the weaver so that it follows the shape of the spokes as bent. You continue weaving from the bottom up to fill in the spokes for the sides of the basket. You can vary the weave as you like, trying out different twining and plain-weave patterns to see how they work. To end off and finish the top of the basket, the spokes are dampened if necessary and can be worked into the sides in several ways. The first is to bend each spoke so that its tip runs along the top of the next spoke, which is in turn bent over to meet the next, and so forth. The weaver is then twined around each spoke and end spoke as if they were one. As you get up near the bends, it may help to use a knitting needle or other article to work the weaver into the openings. You want to weave as close to the bends

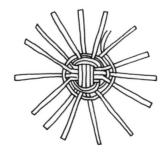

First round of the actual weaver with the second round begun

149

as possible for a strong finish. Another way to do this gives an open, loopy rim. You need slightly longer spoke ends, and you bend them at a wider angle, meeting the second spoke moving toward the right. Then you lift the one that was skipped and bring it to the third spoke, and so on. The weaving is stopped somewhat below the loops, as they are part of the design. You can also work this with every third spoke, for a less open-looped effect. As you finish the basket, you may need to cut the spokes to suit the ending technique. If you do, cut them with a sharp knife, always cutting away from yourself, carefully, making an angle as you cut. The tapered tips will be easier to cover and also may be worked directly into finished rounds of twining, if it is not too tight. The spokes can also be left a bit longer than usual and braided, using each spoke in turn in the braid so that it moves around the rim of the basket. As a spoke is used for one part of the braid, the end is pushed to the inside of the basket, or into the twining below, whichever works out well in the type of weaving you are doing. When working with spokes that are round but thick, you will probably find the simplest finish to be best. They can be begun more easily if you make a slit in the vertical spokes and slip the horizontal ones into the slits. This does take practice, though, since the spokes sometimes continue to slit on their own as you place the others inside.

Baskets made with wide splints for the spokes are often constructed so that the weaving doesn't begin until the sides are bent up into place. The spokes are all cut the same length, soaked, and set out in a radiating circle. As the width of the overlapping points in the circle of splints fully covers

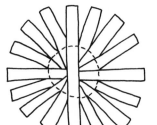

Wide splints in formation for the bottom and sides

150

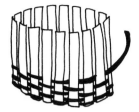

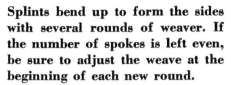

Splints bend up to form the sides with several rounds of weaver. If the number of spokes is left even, be sure to adjust the weave at the beginning of each new round.

Lacing another wide splint around the top to finish the edges of a basket

the bottom of the basket, you begin to weave with a thinner weaver at the point where the spokes start to separate enough to be woven. Bend the spokes upward and use a standard twining weave. The top rim of this type of basket is usually finished by taking an additional strip of the spoke and bending it to shape around the outside edge of the basket. Then, the weaver is used to lace the rim in place, overcasting around the top to secure it. The outer rim is placed and woven in this way, as you can't bend the spokes back into the weaving and they are cut to the same length as the height of the basket.

Square or rectangular baskets are usually made with the same material in both spoke and weaver, as they are interchangeable on the bottom, or beginning, of the basket. You make each strip the length of the total of two sides and the bottom of the basket. For a rectangle, one set of strips is made longer than the other. You start the basket by placing all of the strips for the width of the bottom next to each other, parallel and vertical, on a table. Then, take the first strip for the crossing weavers, and weave it into the vertical strips, as you would for any plain weave. Position the strips as you weave them into the vertical ones so that the tops and bottoms of the vertical strips are left unwoven for the height of the sides, and the horizontal weaving strips are unwoven along the sides for the same distance. When the bottom is finished, these extending strips are bent up to form the spokes for the sides of the basket. You can weave them in the same pattern or a different one. The top can be worked in any of the usual

151

Working the bottom of a square basket with wide splints, leaving the sides in place unwoven

finishes. For variation, you can use another material for the sides, or work in more than one shade, if more are available. A further variation is to weave the bottom in a basketweave, or two over two, two under two.

Wide splints are used to make entire baskets in square or rectangular shape in the same way. The top is finished with an additional splint, formed to shape, and placed on the woven top edges. To secure the outer rim, you can use tiny brads, driving them through the rim into the spokes in an even pattern so that they don't look out of place. You can then bend down the ends into the basket, if needed. Another finishing method, more in keeping with the basket style, is to use an overcasting lace of reed or other thin material and wrap it around the rim and the weaver beneath, overcasting all the way around the basket. You can overcast with wide spaces or close together for a wrapped look.

Wooden bottoms are made from ¼- to ½-inch wood, cut to size, and drilled around the edge with the same number of holes as you want to make spokes, or staves, in the basket. In this way, you can begin with a strong, flat bottom of just about any size or shape. Use good wood glue to secure the spokes in a step called *upsetting*. The spokes in this type of work are also called *stakes*. Just be sure that the drill bit is the same size as the width of the spokes so that they fit snugly.

Other basket shapes are woven from the top down on a splint bent into shape for the rim. A set of flexible spokes is set on the rim by wrapping

Squared end fireplace match holder, woven in white and purple with flat weavers, 18″ in height

Split bamboo chair from the Philippines with looping and wrapping in flat raffia. Square split bamboo basket.

each end around it several times, then bringing it to the spot directly opposite and wrapping it in place there. The spokes are allowed to curve more toward the center, so that a shallow basket is made. The weaver moves from side to side, around the rim at each edge, in any weaving pattern you choose. This style works best in a rim of rectangular shape, woven to form a basket with the up-and-down spokes acting like the warp in weaving.

Coiling with basketry materials is done in the same way as previously described for rope and yarn. The base, or core, is started with a tapering group of grasses, pine needles, or other material. The rest of the coiling proceeds as usual, with raffia or a wide grass as the wrapping. When working with pine needles, you gather them yourself—you can't buy them—and soak them until the little bottom covering comes off. Then wipe off any of the pine resin at the tips and allow the needles to dry. They don't need to be wet when you use them, since their length and grouping is so flexible. As you use up a bundle while coiling you can slip in several new needles, in place of the old. They interlock as you continue to coil around them. Pine needle coiling is sometimes done with an open wrap, so that the distinctive texture shows through.

Weaving in the Round

The basic shapes and forms of basketry add a new direction to your off-loom weavings, as you begin to think of weaving in rounds, rather than rows back and forth over a flat surface. The round weaving done to create tubular and sculptural forms in free-style weaving on a ring base has given you an idea of working in the round. For a circular weaving, you begin with a base of crossed warp ends, like the crossed spokes on the bottom of a basket. Since warping materials are usually more flexible than those in basketry, you can cross them in any style you choose, in radiating spokes or crossed horizontal and vertical patterns. You can continue, using any weaving technique you want upon the warp spokes.

To strengthen the weaving you can use a wire hoop or ring as an armature. Then, you wrap the spokes of warp from one side of the circle to the other, crossing in the middle. Take each end around the ring once, across

Mandala or Magic Circle by Betty Lovejoy. Weaving in the round on a spoke foundation of crossing warp ends in shades of brown, beige, and rust. Woven in plain, soumak, reversed soumak, twill, slit, and other weaves, finished with a fringe, wooden beads, and pheasant feathers.

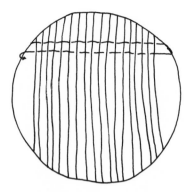

Vertical and horizontal warp and weft on a round shape

the center, around the other side once, and back across the ring. Move each just a bit over, to form an interesting center shape as they cross over each other in sequence. This textural pattern is exposed in the finished weaving as you weave into the spokes themselves just beyond the crossing. Lots of different yarns and weaves can be combined to add further design to the weaving. Using a round extension of the weaving like a hoop allows you to work with much thinner warp yarns. In free-standing flat or round weavings, you need to use a thicker warp to hold the shape as you weave.

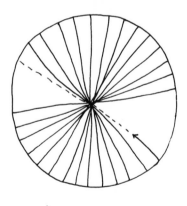

A

Warping a ring for the center crossing spoke pattern: A. Path of the warp spokes, B. Detail of ring edge being warped

156

B

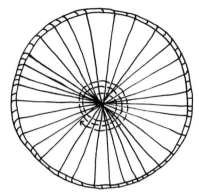 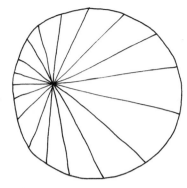

Path of the weft yarn on warped ring   Off-center warping of the ring

The exposed ring can be a part of your pattern, or you can wrap it with yarn as for coiling after, or before, you place the warp spokes. Other variations on this theme are to use two or more rings, placed inside of each other concentrically, opening up more weaving surfaces as the warp moves between the sets of rings. The warp is placed in two directions, up from the inner ring to the outer one, and in toward the center from the inner one. The warp will hold the rings in place once it has been completely threaded on a flat work surface. You can then lift the rings, holding them in any comfortable working position to weave.

A small ring can be placed in the exact center, leaving an opening in the weaving as the warp is threaded from the outer ring to the inner one and back. You can also place it off center for an entirely new form. The warp can be varied, strung at angles or with exposed areas, without any additional ring for other effects.

The creative potential of basket-inspired shapes and methods adds a lot to your off-loom weaving repertory as you see how they are used alone and concurrently with other techniques.

8

KNOTTED AND KNOTLESS NETTING AND LOOPING

Netting, or open-work weaving, can be created with knotting for a securely held and formed net, or in a twisted-thread, knotless netting technique that is also known as *sprang*. *Bobbin lace* is a further variation of knotless netting, in which you create the characteristic twists while holding the threads on small bobbins. *Looping* is another method that is related to netting, as is it generally worked in an open, lacy network. Technically, it is somewhat closer in form to knitting, which forms tighter loops in series, but the overall effect of looping generally places it within the realm of netting as an off-loom method.

These techniques have come down to us through the ages from all areas of the world. Netting done by people for fishing is found everywhere and is one of the most obvious uses. The art of netting—knotted, knotless, and looped—has been practiced by inland people as well, to make useful bags, carryalls, comfortable hammocks, and many other articles. The methods of bobbin lace making, which sound far removed in name and seem to be in reality when worked in the complex patterns of the European Renaissance, are a form of netting since the basic structure of even the most intricate lace work is simply twisted threads.

Knotted Netting

Knotted netting is just that—an open-work net, with diamond-shaped negative spaces between the threads and knots which create the pattern.

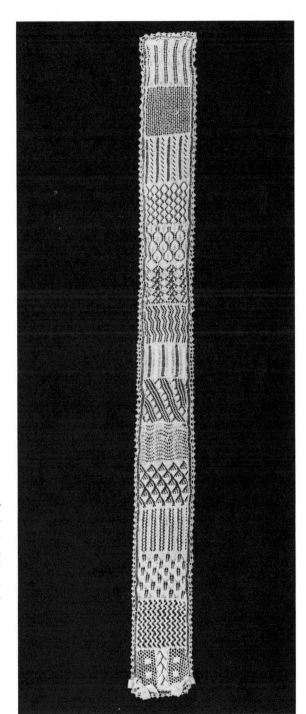

Lace network sampler, cotton. Germany, XIX Century. Length 4′ 5⅛″, width 5⅛″. *Courtesy, Metropolitan Museum of Art, From the Collection of Mrs. Lathrop Colgate Harper, Bequest, 1957.*

A

A. Netting needle, B. Gauge

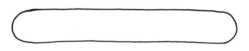

B

You can make knotted netting with many different types of thread, cord, or twine, changing the size of the netted spaces to go with the thickness of the material. When you use a fine thread you make the net with small loops and knots. Correspondingly larger open areas are made to go with heavier or thicker cords and twines.

Netting is done with a netting needle, which is more like a shuttle than a needle and holds the thread as you use it to form the net. A gauge is used to insure evenly sized loops. It is optional; many work without one, using a thumb to loop around. You'll probably find it easier to begin using a gauge. The needle and gauge are usually made out of wood and are available from craft supply and marine stores. You can also make them out of strips of wood, cut to shape and sanded smooth. You'll also need the twine or thread and a couple of feet of cord to act as a top attachment or anchor

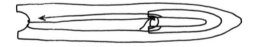

A

A. Beginning to wind thread onto the needle, B. Wound needle

B

cord. Seine twine or any light- to medium-weight polished cord or thread can be used for the net and any sturdy cord or rope for the top.

To net, tie the ends of the anchor cord into a knot and hook it onto the type of object that allows you to reach it easily. The cord is the base on which you begin the first row of actual netting. Wind the thread onto the spine in the opening of the netting needle. Tie the end of the thread to the spine. Then wind down around the notched bottom of the needle and then up to and around the spine from the other side. As you bring the thread around the spine, bring it back down along that side to the bottom and then up to the spine again from the first side. Be sure to go up and back from side to side, not around the needle as with a shuttle. Wind on thread until you are within ½ inch of the tip of the spine.

Take the end of the thread leading from the needle, cut it from the ball of thread, and tie the end to the anchor cord. Hold the gauge in your left hand. Take the needle with your right. Bring it down to the gauge and hold the thread on the gauge, in front of it, with your left thumb. Between the knot on the anchor cord and the gauge, leave a length of cord that is twice the width of the gauge. Then bring the needle up, behind the gauge, and put it through the anchor cord from back to front as in figure A of illustration for first netted loop. Bring the needle and thread down to the gauge as in B. (The needle is not shown in each figure for clarity, but it is there as you knot.) Hold the thread next to the first end with your thumb. Bring the thread out toward the right, forming a loop held by your thumb as shown in C. Then bring the needle from the right, behind two threads and over the third and fourth, moving left, which you are holding in place on the gauge with your thumb as in D. Pull the needle and thread out toward the left and you've formed the basic netting knot as in E. Adjust its position and tighten in place, halfway between the top of the loop on the cord and the bottom of the loop, and remove the gauge as shown in F.

For the second knot, place the thread leading from the knot over the gauge and hold it in place with your thumb. Then bring it up and through the anchor cord, after going behind the gauge, as in figure A of illustration for making second loop. Make a new loop on the gauge and continue the knot as you did the first one, as shown in B. The completed second knot is shown in C. You repeat the same steps across the anchor cord until the

161

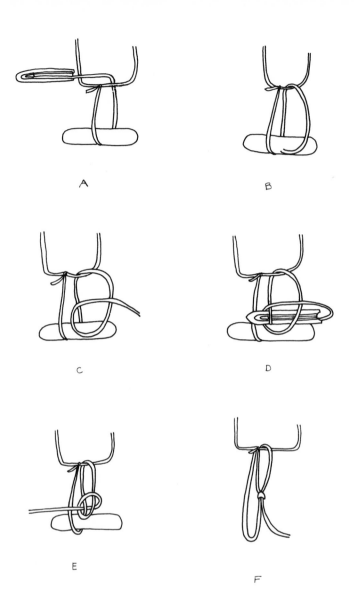

Making the first netted loop

number of knotted loops is the width you want the netting to be. The loops will tend to hang together, so that you should spread them out on the anchor cord periodically. Untie the anchor cord and stretch it out, attaching it to any good foundation. For the second and all subsequent rows, you work the knots with the loops of the previous rows. As the knotting should always be done from left to right, turn the entire work around each time.

A B

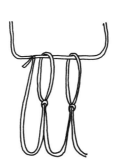

C

Making the second loop

The thread, which is now leading from the last loop of the previous row, is now on the left.

To work the second row of knots, hold the thread on the front of the gauge and bring it down behind the gauge and then up through the loop above, from back to front. Hold the thread in place next to the first thread on the gauge. Make a new knot, moving the needle from right to left, under and behind the two threads of the upper loop and over in front of the two you are holding on the gauge as in A of illustration for making second row. Tighten the knot on the bottom center of the upper loop as in B. Continue across the row, using the loops above to form new knots and loops. As you continue to work through the same number of loops each time you make a row, the net forms uniformly in a rectangular shape. To make the net narrower, slip the gauge into two loops at a time as you make the knot.

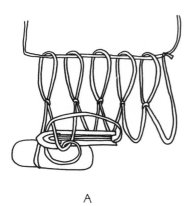 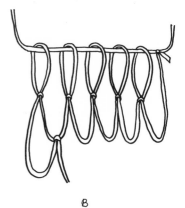

A B

Beginning the first loop in the second row of netting. The work is turned after every row so that the loops are always knotted from left to right.

To increase, or widen the net, make two new loops and knots into one loop above. To form a triangular net, make one base loop, then work two below it. Increase on every row for a wide triangle or every other row for a narrower one. You can also decrease from the triangular shape to form a diamond of netting. Since the knots lock into place, you can end off the netting as you wish, cutting the thread beyond the last series of knots. The top of the finished netting, and the bottom, can be threaded onto a dowel instead of the cord, as for a hammock, or you can use the anchor cord, or remove it entirely, to suit your plan.

Knotless Netting

There are many variations of knotless netting. The technique using several threads at a time, often referred to as *sprang*, is one of twisted threads used to form a network. The basic twists are also used in bobbin lace, which is sometimes easier to control, as the work is done on a supporting pillow and often pinned into place as you work. The second general type is called *looping*. It is done with one continuous strand and a needle. The loops are formed in rows, working back and forth. In twisted-thread methods, many threads are set out and worked across a row, using the threads in pairs.

To start out with the twisted thread technique, use bobbins and a support.

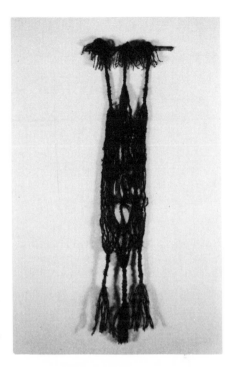

Right: Hanging on a small branch by Pat Banakus. Knotted and knotless netting, wrapped warp, and tassel-like finish.

Below: Hammock in knotless netting of 22 rope cords slipped through wooden bars with holes drilled in them. Tied with additional cords to form the hammock itself in single twists on alternating rows. The strength of this construction allows for years of use.

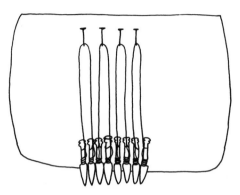 

Bobbins and supporting pillow for knotless netting or bobbin lace

How to wind the thread onto the bobbin

Since the threads are wound onto bobbins they are easy to work, and the support, called a pillow or cushion, helps to regulate the shape as you pin down the edges.

The bobbins are small, about 4 or 5 inches in length, and you can make them out of lengths of notched wooden dowel instead of buying the ready-made sort. The supporting pillow can be any fairly firm surface that you can put pins into to help maintain the desired edges. Once you get used to the technique, you will be able to work with free-hanging threads, even combining the technique with others, and omitting the supporting pillow. For the first trial piece, you will find it best to work with a small number of bobbins, such as eight, and a support. If you have a knotting board, as for macrame, you can use it for the support. A fairly thin thread, such as pearl, or perle, cotton, with its distinctive sheen, is a good material to work with at first.

The basis of the method is two movements—the twist and the cross, which are made with pairs of bobbins. The first step is to wind the bobbins so that you are ready to start. For the basic pattern, four bobbins are needed, so that using eight will give you an amount of flexibility in working. The netting resulting from a small number of bobbins will resemble a braid more than a net, as it will naturally be fairly narrow, but you will be able to see how the twists and crosses are made. To wind the bobbins, you use

 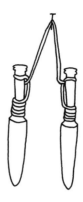

Using a short notched dowel for a bobbin   Two bobbins and the top pin to hold the thread in place

two of them for each length of thread, winding up the ends and pinning the center to the top of your work surface. Start out with threads about a yard long, so that each, when folded, is 18 inches in length.

The bobbins are notched about ½ inch from the top, and held with the notch at the top to wind the threads. Fold each thread in half and pin the folded center to the work surface. Start to wind about 3 inches down from the notch and wrap the thread around the bobbin, wrapping around the beginning end to secure it in place. Continue to wind on the thread until about 4½ inches are left between the pin and the notch. Secure the thread around the notched top of the bobbin with a half hitch. Then wind the rest of the bobbins in the same way. As you work, you'll use up the thread. Undo the half hitch, unwind another couple of inches and replace the hitch, so that the bobbins can hang down without unwinding.

Start to work with the four bobbins at the right. For the first basic movement, the twist, you merely hold two bobbins in each hand and twist them once around each other, so that the right bobbin moves into the place of the one that was previously on the left. Do this with each of the two bobbins in each hand. Then do the same with the other set of four bobbins at the left. For the second twist, go back to the bobbins at the right. Leave the outer ones of the four at each side in place and take the middle two. Make a twist in the same way, turning so that the right moves over the left, using only the center two bobbins. Go to the other four bobbins and do

167

A B C

A. Right over left, twist, B. Left over right, cross. These steps repeated and pulled together tightly make a braid, loosely, a network. C. The double twist.

the same. Take the center two, between the groups, and make a second twist with them to balance the group. The outer threads on the far right and far left are unworked in this step. For the next row, repeat the first one. Do a series of lines or rows to see how it works.

The cross is a further step, which interlaces the areas of the work. To do it, you take the right-hand bobbin of each two-bobbin pair and bring it over to the right, crossing the right-hand bobbin of one pair over the left-hand bobbin of the next pair, moving toward the right. This step repositions the bobbins, allowing further variations in the basic netting. As you go, you will find it handy to pin down the outer edges of the strip of netting that you are forming so that the outer threads, which are often unworked as the twists and crossovers continue, are held in place and the sides remain straight up and down. The basics of the technique are only these: the many patterns which you create are done using the two movements—twist and cross. You can pull the threads tightly, for a really braided effect, or leave them loose, for a more netlike effect. In sprang, the main movement is the twist, most often done over many threads across a line. A double twist is also employed, but you just turn the bobbins an extra time in order to make it.

As you work with the bobbins, making different combinations of twists, crosses, and double twists, you'll see that many patterns and shapes can be created. By pulling the bobbins out toward the left or right as you work, you can make shaped outlines in the same technique. To create changing shapes within your netting, make some areas tighter, others looser, allow

Hot Fudge Sundae by Renie Breskin Adams. Cotton, crochet, macrame, and knotless netting, 2″ tall. Coin shows the scale of this work.

A   B

C

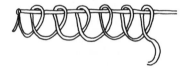

D

Looping in the left to right basic pattern. Use your thumb as a base to form the loops and control their size and shape.

the threads and patterns to bend and turn, forming new shapes and directions in your netting.

The looping method of knotless netting is worked on a base of cord, such as the top attachment in free weaving and macrame. Stretch out a length of cord on a knotting board or other work surface and use the same thread as for your bobbin lace sampler. A blunt-tipped needle is helpful here, since you pass the thread through the loops as you make them and a needle makes this much easier to do. If you want to work in a thicker material, do so, as all sorts of threads and twines are well used in this method of knotless netting.

To start out, make the basic set of loops across your anchor cord. Tie the end of the thread you are using to the cord and thread the other end through a needle. Take the needle down and then up around the cord, passing it through the loop just created as you bring it through to the

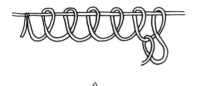

A

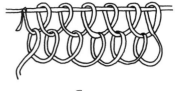

B

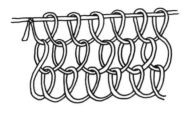

C

Second row of looping, right to left. Third row as first.

bottom again. Use your thumb as a guide to hold the desired length of each loop as you make it. Pull the loops evenly, making sure that each is even and equal in size. Move from left to right, making a number of loops. Once you know the technique, you can experiment with all sorts of changes in loop size and shape, but for now, concentrate on making them all as even as you can. For the second row, you move from right to left. Make the same loops through the bottoms of the loops in the previous row. You can add or subtract the number of loops quite easily, by making two loops in one to add, or skipping one altogether to subtract.

An interesting variation on the looping techniques is to make the loops of a following row around the crossing strands of two loops in the previous row, rather than working into the curving loop strand itself. This produces a more uniform, knitlike appearance.

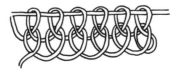

Looping through the crossed bottoms of the previous loops

Looping can be done in any work, as you add the loops to the bottom of a section of worked yarn. The section above may be knotted, woven, or whatever; it's up to you. By changing the way in which you make the loops, pulling them tightly, adding several into each area above, forming irregular shapes, you can make all kinds of shapes and designs in looping.

9

CROCHET AS AN OFF-LOOM TECHNIQUE

When you think of crocheting, the most likely aspect that comes to mind is the use of the method to fashion garments and other useful articles that are meant to be worn. Yet, crocheting has been expanded as a creative technique that is invaluable in off-loom weaving. The beauty of crocheting in this regard is that it is one of the most flexible forms, being worked with a single strand that locks itself in place as you finish a section. You can add crochet to an off-loom work that is combined with other techniques, or use it on its own to make shapes and forms with ease and simplicity of materials.

Indoor Hammock by Jan Knutson. Mixed techniques of crochet, wrapping, and rya knots, 40″ x 90″.

Foundation of Indoor Hammock. Crochet in wool, single crochet stitch, chain stitch added in lengthwise rows for reinforcement.

Red Fungiform by Kathleen McFarlane. Crochet in sisal string.

For standard crocheted articles, the size of the hook and the type of yarn being used are closely associated, as you must relate them to each other in order to make an article that matches the one in a pattern that you are following. In off-loom crochet, conventions are cast aside and you can work with hooks of all sizes, even eliminating the hook altogether and forming the stitches with your fingers, using all kinds of yarns, threads, ropes, and other materials. You can crochet in the round, working in a circle as you might for a basket-inspired shape, or form free-style designs. The versatility of the method allows you to apply it in many ways.

The basic stitches are the same as those used in crocheting for garments and other articles; it is the freedom with which you can apply them that changes here. In standard crochet, you always start with a chain stitch base, but you'll discover that you can crochet along the edges, or into the bottoms, of all kinds of off-loom weavings with fascinating results.

To learn the stitches of crochet, if you are not already familiar with them, you'll probably find it best to start out with a size G or H crochet hook, available just about everywhere in aluminum or plastic, and a small skein of knitting-weight worsted yarn. These are the basic tools of crochet of all kinds, and they will be well suited to show you how to do the stitches. To begin, make a sampler, incorporating the stitches into the edges of the previous ones to see how the different stitches look and change in texture and appearance.

The starting foundation of crochet is a chain, made with the chain stitch. Take the yarn and make a slip knot in the end, about 3 inches in from the tip. To form a slip knot, make a circle in the yarn, crossing it over itself at the top of the circle. Slip the hook into the circle, catch the overlapping

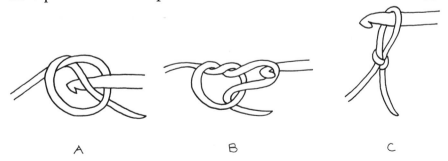

A   B   C

Making a slip knot

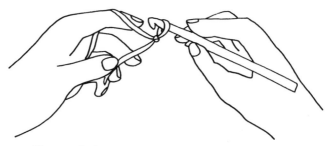

How to hold a crochet hook and yarn

strand, and pull it through the circle to form a loop. Tighten the loop on the hook so that it is loose enough to move easily but tight enough to maintain its position. Hold the hook in your right hand, or left if you are left-handed, as you would hold a pencil, with the hooked end where the point of the pencil would be. Place the yarn leading from the slip knot over the index finger of your other hand, then under the second and third fingers and over the pinky to the skein to help control the tension of the yarn as you make the stitches. Then, hold the short end leading from the knot

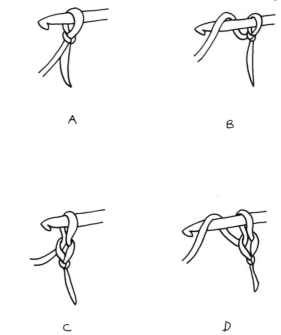

Making a chain, the foundation of crochet stitches

between your thumb and second finger of the same hand.

To make a chain, wrap the yarn around the hook so that it goes behind it and then up and around, and under the hook. Never merely catch the yarn without wrapping, as the tension will be incorrect. You can move the hook or the yarn to do the wrapping, whichever feels the most comfortable. Draw the wrapped yarn through the slip knot to form a loop on the hook. That's the first chain stitch. Following chain stitches are made in the same way, wrapping the yarn under then over and around the hook, and drawing through a new loop. Make a chain of about twenty stitches. The stitches are made on the chain foundation. As you count the chain, the loop on the hook is not included in the number, and as you complete a stitch, there is always one loop left on the hook. In instructions, ch means chain stitch.

The single crochet stitch, abbreviated as sc, is made by putting the hook into the second chain stitch from the hook. Wrap the yarn around the hook, draw through a loop so that there are two loops on the hook, wrap the yarn and draw it through both loops. As you work into a chain, you'll see that each stitch is made up of three strands. When you put the hook into the chain, be sure that two of the strands are on top and one is beneath and that the chain doesn't twist as you crochet.

To continue the single crochet stitch, go into the next chain stitch moving left, wrap the yarn, draw through a loop, wrap the yarn, draw through both loops. Work a stitch into each chain stitch across, being sure to count the slip knot as a stitch at the end of the row.

To turn the work and reach the next row, you make a turning chain.

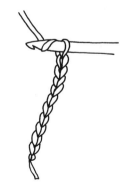

Crochet chain

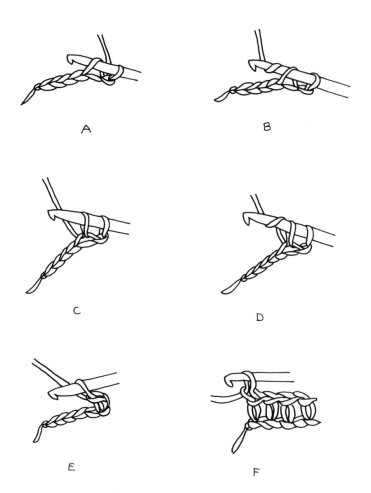

A   B

C   D

E   F

Single crochet stitch. Turning chain made at the end of the row (F).

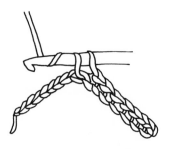

Single crochet stitches

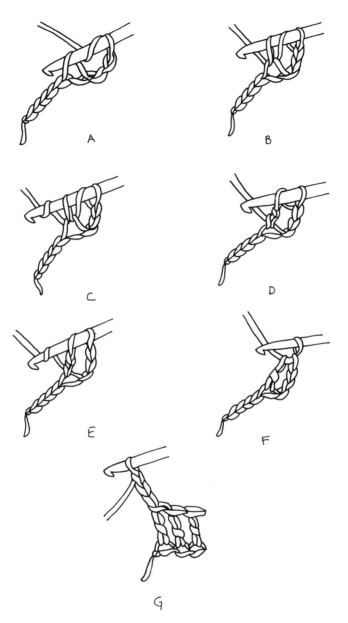

Double crochet stitch. Turning chain at the end of the row (G).

This is done at the end of one row or the beginning of the next after you have literally turned the crocheting around in your hands. For single crochet, the turning chain is one chain stitch. It is considered the first stitch

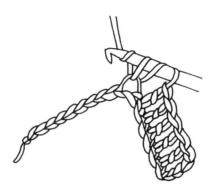

Double crochet stitches

in the next row, so that you go into the second stitch, placing the hook into both V-shaped strands of the top of the stitch in the previous row. The single crochet stitch is then continued across the row, just as you did for the first one.

Double crochet, or dc, is a taller stitch, made by wrapping the yarn once around the hook before you go into the stitches of the previous row. You can work it on top of the rows of single crochet stitches or begin with a new chain. When working on previous stitches, make a turning chain that is three chain stitches. On a new chain, put the hook into the fourth chain from the hook. Then, wrap the yarn and draw through a loop, so that there are three loops on the hook. Wrap the yarn, draw through two of the loops, wrap once more and draw through both remaining loops. Continue across the row in the same way, adding three chain stitches after the last stitch for the turning chain.

Triple crochet (tr) is an even taller stitch that goes very quickly, because it covers a lot of room with each stitch. To work on a previous row of stitches, make a turning chain that is four chain stitches in length and go into the second stitch in the row. Working on a chain foundation, go into the fifth chain from the hook. Wrap the yarn around the hook two times, go into the stitch below, wrap the yarn, draw it through only the stitch on the hook, giving you four loops, wrap the yarn, draw it through two loops, giving you three loops on the hook, wrap the yarn, draw it through two loops, giving two loops on the hook, wrap the yarn and draw it through the last two loops. Although this stitch sounds complicated, it's really quite

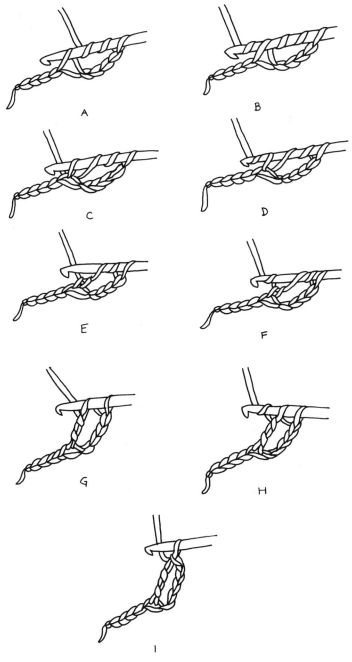

Triple crochet stitch

181

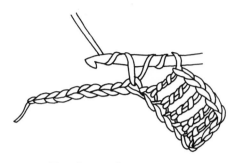

Triple crochet stitches

easy, as are all of the crochet stitches.

The slip stitch, or sl st, is the shortest stitch in crochet. It is usually used to join sections, to make cords on a chain base, and to work in the round. To make a slip stitch, insert the hook into the first stitch from the chain, wrap the yarn and draw it through both the stitch and the loop on the hook in one motion. When joining sections, you put the hook through the edge stitches of both parts, draw through the stitches and the loop on the hook at once. When you work the slip stitch in the round, you use it to join a chain into a circle, giving you a round foundation of chain stitches upon which you can build a flat circle or column of stitches.

To crochet in the round, make a chain of the required length and join the last stitch on the chain to the first one with a slip stitch. If you want to make a flat piece in the round, make a chain of from four to six stitches in length. Then work the first row of stitches, called a round here, into the opening in the chain circle, not into the stitches themselves. For the first round, you make approximately twelve stitches. At the end of the round. In flat crochet, you use increases to make the piece wider, adding

A   B   C

Making a slip stitch

182

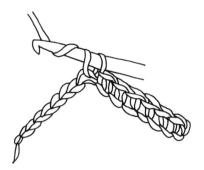

Slip stitches

chain, the length of the usual turning chain for the stitch that you are doing. Then, you go into the next stitch from the chain, without turning the work over in your hands. To make the crocheting flat, increase the number of stitches, usually multiplying by two, or making twenty-four stitches on the second round.

Increasing is done by making two stitches into every one of the previous round. In flat crochet, you use increases to make the piece wider, adding as many stitches as are needed in a row, spacing them evenly through the row, rather than placing them all in the same area which will make the crocheting pucker up. In round crochet, you double the number, adding two in every one so that the circle stays flat. As you continue for several rounds, and if you want the work to start to curve into a basketlike shape, you make less increases on every row. To make the work columnar, you stop increasing altogether, building up the sides of the column with the same number of stitches on every round.

Decreasing is done when you want the piece to start to curve inward

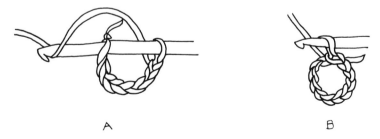

A   B

Joining a chain into a circular foundation with a slip stitch

183

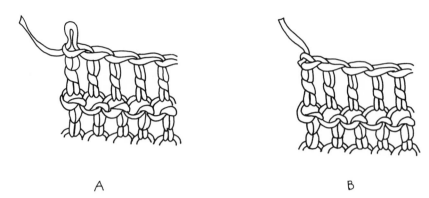

A   B

Ending off a crochet section, shown with the double crochet stitch. The same technique is used in all crochet.

again. To decrease, you skip a stitch anywhere in a round. If you skip every other stitch, the work will bend sharply inward, returning the number of stitches to that of the last round of increases. You can also skip fewer stitches, so that the curve is more gradual. In flat crochet, you decrease to narrow the piece, usually by skipping the last stitch in the row, which would ordinarily be worked into the turning chain from the previous row. To sharply narrow a section, you make several decreases, spacing them through the row so that they are evenly distributed, or by stopping before the row is done and turning.

To end off any piece of crocheting, you merely cut the yarn and draw it through the single loop remaining on your hook. Pull to tighten and the crocheting is securely ended.

Adding new yarn when you run out in a larger piece, or changing the color of the stitches, is done by cutting the old yarn and placing the end

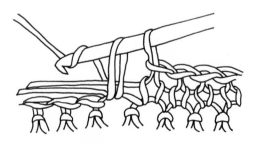

Adding in new yarn

along the tops of the stitches in the previous row or round. Then, you add the new yarn, placing its end in the same way along the tops of the stitches and work the subsequent stitches around both pieces of yarn, locking them in place.

Shapes and Variations

As you work with crochet as an off-loom medium, you'll find that it is extremely flexible. You can make all sorts of shapes by increasing and decreasing as needed. If you want to make a tubular shape, open at the end, you start out with a long chain, join it with a slip stitch, and then crochet as for working in the round. Crocheting in this manner allows you to make different shapes as you increase and decrease. If you want to create a sculptural form, you can work tubular and other shapes in the round and then stuff them when they have been completed, using loose batting or pillow stuffing of any kind.

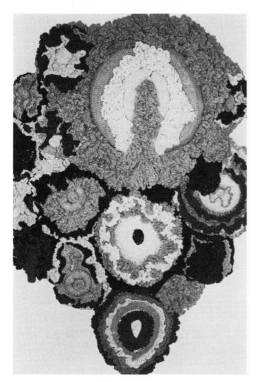

Left: Circumvention by Jan Knutson (3′ x 6′ x 10″)

Detail, below, crochet stitches of all types

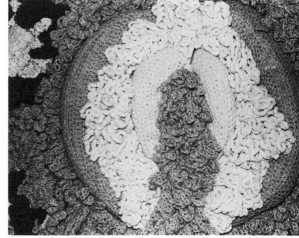

185

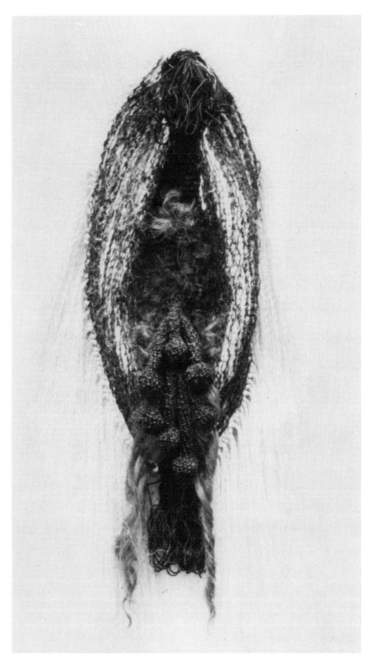

Triffoid by Kathleen McFarlane. Sisal, weaving, and crochet. White warp with deep grays and rust, unplied fibers; crochet in lower center is deep gray.

Basket by Jan Knutson. Wool fiber crochet and wrapping with feathers over sisal, 12″ diameter.

Other variations can be made by working on an armature or found object. You can make a chain around the openings of the object by slipping the hook through the opening, or by working the stitches around the wire of a hoop, for one example. You can work back and forth, using chains and other stitches to fill an area. You'll also find that a crochet base allows you to work in other techniques, adding in new threads and securing them in place with crochet stitches. The new threads can become warp or weft for all sorts of weavings and knottings.

Other variations can be made by working crochet onto the existing loops or weft passes of another technique, or making the crochet stitches themselves in different pattern variations. You can leave open spaces in your crocheting by merely chaining across the space, then stitching again in the new spot, wherever you like. By making the stitches loosely, you'll get an open lacy look, and by varying the actual stitches themselves within one row or round, unusual textures will ensue. For combined works in heavier yarns or threads, you may even abandon your hook, using your fingers to draw through the loops, crocheting in large, open stitches. The creative variations are limitless once you know how to do the basic stitches.

As in all off-loom weaving, you should let your imagination take over as you work, following the forms suggested by the piece itself. For more structured designs, in which you know exactly what you want to happen, you can make a sketch or paper pattern, full size. This will allow you to plan out just where the work should be increased or decreased, or where you are going to add in a new element, perhaps in another off-loom technique. Small or lightweight articles are easily worked into a piece as you loop around them with the yarn and hook. Just about anything is possible, as you draw inspiration from the techniques of off-loom weaving.

10

HOW TO CREATE ORIGINAL PROJECTS

Now that you know the basics, you'll enjoy making all kinds of articles, in both decorative and functional applications of the techniques of off-loom weaving. Because all weavings are, and should be truly personal statements, general plans are presented which give you an overall view of how practical patterns are developed and followed. In some articles, two or more methods are combined, depicting the use of a blend of techniques. As you think out and then follow through to complete your own weaving projects, you'll acquire a working knowledge of actual design procedures. As you delve into the pleasures and possibilities of these related means of expression, you'll want to form unique works, drawing inspiration from the literally hundreds of sources that surround you every day. Even if you feel somewhat unsure of just what you want to do first, you'll discover that you can create your own designs in off-loom weaving without problems if you stick to basic forms in early designs. Start with any shape or medium that you like, make a set of base cords or a warp to suit, and work it with appropriate yarns in appealing shades. As you weave or knot the threads, you'll see that the very structure suggests design ideas. Each new combination of fibers, strands, and methods will give you new thoughts on patterns and forms. It's a good way to develop your creative potential as you weave.

You may enjoy keeping a design notebook, in which you can jot down any concepts that come to you. It's also quite helpful to make a record of each weaving, including the type of yarn, amount used, techniques employed, and any other pertinent information. With all of these facts at your fingertips you'll find it much easier to plan future projects. For a truly complete listing, add snippets of the actual yarns and sketches of the design used. Other items which you can add to your design notebook are photographs, pictures from magazines and catalogues, and any other pictorial references and sources of design possibilities that you see. Soon you'll have so many ideas that are just waiting to be put to use that it will be hard to decide which to do next.

For all off-loom weaving projects, be sure to have all the essential equipment on hand before you begin. You'll need: two pairs of scissors, one sharp, pointed pair to cut yarns and cords and one larger pair for cutting paper and cardboard; sheets of drawing paper to plan design outlines and patterns; pencils; colored markers, pencils, or crayons to test out color schemes on paper; a ruler and a tape measure; blunt-tipped, large-eyed yarn needles, called tapestry or rug needles; sewing needles and threads; a knotting board, preferably marked with a one-inch square grid for easy reference; rustproof push pins; sheets of cardboard or rigid plastic foam; a tapestry beater or fork; white liquid glue; and a set of rods or clamps on which to wind out measured cords or warps. Although you won't need all of these things for each project, they are good to have ready in one place as you weave.

The project ideas presented are intended to give you an indication of how the concepts were achieved, showing you how design and weaving procedures are followed in off-loom weaving. The steps in the process are explained in order to give you a solid understanding of how plans are made and articles are completed. As this is such a personal craft, the plans are open to variation and interpretation. They aren't rigid patterns, as you would have for a crocheted garment, which must be duplicated exactly for the article to come out right. Rather, you can use this section as a point of departure to learn how to relate your ideas and express your individuality. In all weavings, the major purpose is the fundamental charm of the weaving itself, not the precise reproduction of any specific article. As each weaving is unique, the emphasis is on this freedom of expression. Once you see the results of your first project, you'll be pleased and surprised. As you weave, following basic structures and adapting them to your work, you'll find that your own technique and style will establish themselves. As you acquire a firsthand knowledge of these methods, and how to make things using them, you'll understand why they are gaining the popularity they richly deserve.

The Light Tube designed and woven by Betty Lovejoy. Shades of brown, rust, tan, olive, green, beige, and gray, in soumak, reversed soumak, twill, and plain weaves.

The Light Tube

You can transform a plain lampshade into a woven light tube. The textured weaves and different yarn textures and colors form fascinating patterns when the lamp is lit. The one shown is made on the wire base of a shade that was stripped of its original covering. You can create a light tube in colors that suit the room, using an old shade or buying an inexpensive one. Make sure that it has two rings, connected by vertical bars. You can tell how it's made by looking inside the existing shade. There are usually four side wires, but some shades are made out of just two metal rings held together by a stiff paper lining. When buying a shade, if you can't find one with side bars, it's simpler to buy two metal rings of the appropriate size from a craft supply store and use them to make a hanging lamp. Shades with side supports are stripped of their covering and warped. Then they can be woven in any comfortable position since the warped shade becomes a unit that is portable. For a hanging lamp made with two metal rings, you suspend them for weaving in the exact relationship to each other as they will have in the finished lamp.

This light tube has the standard flaring shape of many lampshades. You can also work on cylindrical forms, following their shape, or drawing in the sides as you weave for a graceful inward curve. A hanging lamp will be cylindrical if the rings are both the same size, and flaring if the bottom ring is larger than the top. The dimensions of the lamp shown are: top diameter, 6 inches, bottom diameter, 9 inches, side bars, 7 inches in height. The warp is cable twist mercerized cotton. For a lamp of up to 10 inches in height, you'll need one 120-yard skein. You can also use any medium-weight cotton or linen warp-strength yarn, or a hard-twist wool, such as rya yarn. Once the shade is warped, the bars are wrapped with wool, in a medium weight. This yarn should be one of the yarns within the work, and you'll need about 4 ounces. The weft is several different kinds of wool, cotton, and novelty yarns in small amounts. Because many types of yarn aren't available in amounts of less than 2 ounces, you can buy a good assortment, such as six different colors and/or types of yarn. You'll have yarn left over, but you'll find that there's always a use for extra yarn. Also, the extra yarn will allow you to do any type of weave that appeals to you in the lampshade, secure in the knowledge that there is enough. The colors are up to you; they should go well with the room in which you plan to place the lamp, but there is no need for them to be identical. The lampshade shown is made up of many yarns, in browns, tan, rust, shades of olive-green, beiges, and grays. You can choose fewer colors, or use small amounts of yarn on hand that complement the predominant hues in the chosen scheme. If you're making a larger shade, of over 10 inches in height, you can figure out how much yarn you'll need by using the rough estimate of 1 ounce per inch of weft. As there are several shades of each color, you can always buy more yarn if needed. The dye lots will not be a problem in this case.

To make a shade, strip off the covering, exposing the wire frame. Place the warp on the frame by beginning with one knot, attaching the end of the warp yarn to the top ring. Then, wind the warp onto the frame, up and down between the rings, wrapping once around the ring at the end of each pass, so that the warp is positioned well. The warp should be taut, but not extremely so, as it is taken up or tightened a bit by the weaving process. In the one shown, there are a total of sixty-two warp ends, or thirteen per quarter as defined by the side bars. When the warp is complete, wrap the entire wire frame with one of the yarns, covering the side bars as well as the warped top and bottom rings.

For a hanging shade, suspend the top ring by four equidistant cords. Decide what height you want the shade to be and wind out warp ends four times that length. If you were using an 8-inch ring, for example, you would make thirty-four warp ends, as they are doubled in use. Cut through one end of the wound warp and attach each warp to the suspended ring with a lark's head knot. As you place each doubled warp on the ring, put it right next to the previous one, so that they are well spaced. Each knot gives you two hanging warp ends. In the example just given, you will have sixty-eight. If your ring isn't covered by the original number, or for a larger shade, make more ends. If there are too many to fit well, use less. Place the bottom ring into the warp, where you want it to be in the finished shade. Loop the bottom of each pair of ends to the ring with a half hitch knot. Make sure that the two rings are level and parallel to each other and the floor. The warp ends should be taut throughout the weaving. If the warp gets too tight, it can be adjusted by loosening the half hitches, but this is unlikely. You can wrap the warped rings with one of the yarns in the weft. If you do it before the weaving starts, you can't adjust the warp, as it must be trimmed and then wrapped on the bottom ring. You

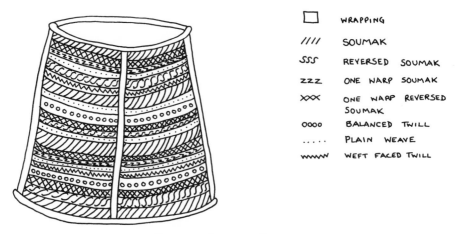

☐	WRAPPING
////	SOUMAK
ʃʃʃ	REVERSED SOUMAK
zzz	ONE WARP SOUMAK
xxx	ONE WARP REVERSED SOUMAK
oooo	BALANCED TWILL
. . . . .	PLAIN WEAVE
wwww	WEFT FACED TWILL

Suggested weave diagram

may prefer to wrap only the top ring and do the second one when the weaving is almost complete. If you wait until the shade is completely woven, it will be harder to wrap.

To weave, use a blunt-tipped needle. You can follow the suggested weave diagram or use any sequence of weaves that appeals to you. Change colors as often as you like. Weave from the top down, from the outside of the shade. If you're using a barred side foundation, make sure that the weaving goes under each wrapped bar. For a different look, you can omit the wrapping and weave over the bars. Just be sure that the weaving goes consistently under or over throughout the work. If it feels more comfortable, you can hold the frame upside down and weave in an upward direction. For suspended rings, weave downward for best results. The weft should be kept fairly loose, so that the sides don't draw in. For variation, you can tighten the weft near the center, and then loosen toward the bottom again for a graceful inward curve.

For larger shades, repeat the weave pattern as needed. For a new effect, add in open-work leno, slit, or exposed warp sections, placing them above and below the spot where the bulb will be so that the bulb doesn't show. If you prefer, you can line the shade with translucent white paper, made especially for the purpose, and place open-weave areas anywhere you wish.

As soon as you complete the last round on the wrapped wire frame, your shade is finished. For a suspended shade, as you near the bottom

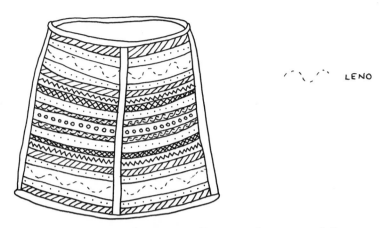

LENO

Alternate weave diagram with areas of open work leno

ring, retie the warp ends with double half hitches if it was not wrapped at the beginning. Trim the ends close to the knots and wrap with a weft yarn to complete the ring. Then, continue to weave right up to the finished ring. In the light tube shown, additional threads were added with a wooden bead at each end. If you plan to add beads, cut lengths of thread that are twice as long as you want and knot each one onto the rings at the bottom. Slip on a bead and make an overhand knot to keep it in place, with one on each end of the added threads.

To create further variations of this shade to suit various rooms, choose different warp yarns. Heavy linen natural-tone rug warp, cotton navy cord, or sisal twine will give a more rustic effect, as the weft will be more widely spaced due to the width of the warp threads. The weft can be of any sort, or combination, that you choose to complement the texture and weight of the warp. You can also change the weaves, add in other knotting techniques, or make any tapestry-weave pattern that you like. For a figurative pattern, use the same type of yarn throughout the weft, changing colors to create the design.

Hanging Plant Holders

As living plants of all sorts continue to find great welcome, the search goes on for interesting ways to place them in different settings. One of the

195

Hanging Plant Holder, in natural tan sisal twine with purple and clear glass crow beads. By author.

best is the simple knotted plant sling. As this classic form, shown in an Egyptian work that is centuries old (page 12), has come to be almost synonymous with today's plants, you'll enjoy making several.

The basic sling is one of the easiest projects in knotting. It provides attractive, useful results, and can be knotted up in an hour or so, so that it's a nice project to do. There are so many possible variations and additions that you'll enjoy this concept. With the basic plan, you can make hundreds of different ones, just by changing the length, spacing, and density of the knotted areas. The steps in making the one shown are described in detail to show you just how easy these hangers are to make.

This plant hanger is made out of natural-hued tan sisal twine, in medium weight, found in almost any hardware or variety store. One ball will be enough for at least two slings. The large-eyed glass crow beads are available through craft supply stores, but you can choose any type of bead that appeals to you. Just be sure that the holes are large enough to allow the beads to be threaded onto two strands of twine. You can also leave off the beads entirely, for another effect.

Wind out eight 16-foot-long cords. Fold them in half and suspend them from a hook for knotting so that you have sixteen knotting cords, each 8 feet long. If you know exactly where you want the plant to hang, attach a sturdy hook into the ceiling and use it to check on the length and positioning of the knotted areas. If you are placing the hook for the plant, always screw it into a beam, as many ceilings can't support the weight of a plant. As you knot, use another hook that is in a more convenient position, or tie a cord through the tops of the folded cords and loop it on a doorknob or chair back.

Take two cords on each side of the fold. Make sure that they are the same two on either side for best results. Begin to knot a spiral sennit about 2 inches down from the fold, using the two cords as one on each side to form the half square knots. In the example shown, the spiral is 6½ inches long. Then, leave the cords unworked for 10 inches and separate them into four groups of four cords each. Use each group in turn to make four spiral sennits. Use the first sennit as a guide to make the other three in exactly the same position on the cords. The sennits in the sling shown are 10 inches long. Then, separate the cords again, into four groups of

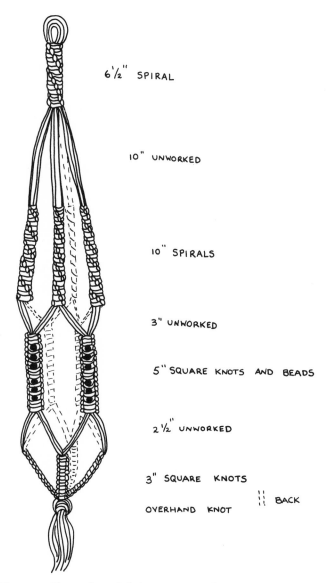

6½" SPIRAL

10" UNWORKED

10" SPIRALS

3" UNWORKED

5" SQUARE KNOTS AND BEADS

2½" UNWORKED

3" SQUARE KNOTS

OVERHAND KNOT   ¦¦ BACK

Knotting diagram. Lengths of the sennits and open areas can be changed as desired.

four, each comprised of two cords from the right of a sennit above and two cords from the left of the adjoining sennit to the left above. As this particular hanger was made for a fairly narrow diameter pot, the next set of sennits begins 3 inches down. For a larger pot, or to fit the standard

198

plastic hanging pot of 9 inches in diameter, make the new sennits at least 9 inches away from those above. The next sennits are square knot sennits. Make each in turn, using the four groups of cords. For the beading shown, make three square knots, slip a bead onto the two core cords, make one square knot, add one bead, make one square knot, add one bead, make three square knots, add one bead, make one square knot, add one bead, make one knot, add one bead, make three square knots. Make all four in the same manner. Then, there is an unworked length of 2½ inches. Separate the cords into the original groups of four, taking two cords each from the sennits above. Make four standard square knot sennits, each 3 inches long. Gather all of the ends together and make one large overhand knot right at the end of the set of sennits. Tighten in place. In the hanger shown, purple beads are used within the sennits and then purple and clear are added to each hanging strand of the cords leading from the overhand knot. Add the beads where you will, trimming the ends after each bead is tied in place with an overhand knot. Here, each end has one bead and they are trimmed to be deliberately uneven. Find an appropriate plant and it's ready to go.

You can make many variations of the basic pattern by following the same structure and changing the parts that make it up. The sennits can be longer or shorter, spiral or square knotted. You can add beads into the spiral sennits, add them more closely, leave them out altogether, or use different types in complementary shapes and sizes. Use different knotting patterns to make the top knotting denser, or to cover the pot more completely. The hanging tassel can be cut short for a pom-pom effect, trimmed so that all of the ends are the same length, or worked back into the overhand knot for no tassel at all. Once the cords have been wound out and started, you will be able to make your own plans for a new look within the same framework. And so it is for all articles, as you naturally develop the sense of design which off-loom weaving offers.

Star Placque

One of the most fascinating aspects of off-loom weaving is the appearance of similar design motifs in works from widely distant sources. The three coiled works shown provide a fine example of this interesting occur-

Papago basket by Margaret Saraficia. Yucca, coiled, diameter 17⅜″, 1964.

Chinese coiled basket with a lid. Star motif worked in added fiber on basic coil of the lid. Author's collection.

Placque from Upper Volta, Africa, diameter 15″. Author's collection.

rence. The first coiled placque is a Native American Papago Indian basket. The second is a Chinese coiled basket with the star motif worked into the coiled top strands with an overlay of natural-hued strands on the basic coil. The third work is a placque from Upper Volta with the star design worked in the coiling itself, as in the first work. As you can see, there is a remarkable similarity of motif, while each work is unique.

You can create your own star placque in either basketry materials, such

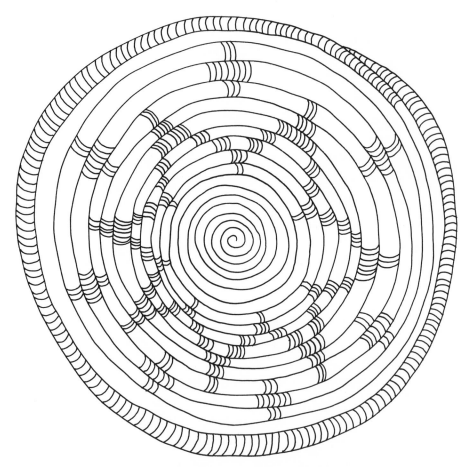

Suggested star coiling pattern

as were used in the examples shown, or in wool yarns on a rope foundation. The use of coiling materials in two or three different colors, in specific sequence to form the design, is an exciting challenge. Once you have made a coiled work in this manner you'll know just where to place the coiling materials to form patterns in the round. If you're using basketry materials, buy three shades of flat coiling, such as raffia, and a soft, flexible core, such as natural fiber rope or bundles of grasses. The same design is equally effective in earth tone yarns on rope, if you prefer a softer finish.

To begin your placque, make a standard coiled circle for a round shape.

In the articles shown, the center is coiled in only the basket top, while the Indian work has a woven base, and the African one of basic coiling over-wrapped with one of the colors in the design when the inner coil is one inch wide. In all cases, the following rounds are made in coiling with the wrapping fiber being worked into the outer edge of the previous coil, rather than the usual overcasting after every three or four wraps. To form the coil, make the center foundation and then coil by taking the raffia or other fiber, or yarn, once around the coil and once into the outermost edge of the previous coil. This gives you a sturdy attachment with a smooth finished look. Continue in one shade for about eight rounds. Near the end of the eighth round, wrap in the beginning ends of the second and third colors so that they are ready to use when you need them.

Then, follow the diagram for suggested placement of the different shades to form the star pattern. Coiling with three colors isn't hard, once you get the knack of wrapping the colors which are not in use into the coil along with the foundation. The diagram shown presents one version of a star pattern that you can use but feel free to vary the design as you like. The finished placque can be as large or small as you wish. As the first star outline establishes itself in the coiling, you can add another one, outline the motif with bands of color, in short, follow the ideas which come to you as you weave. The locked-in-place nature of this particular style of coiling allows you to stop and think through the pattern as you go. When you are satisfied with the size of the placque—the Indian one is 17⅜″ in diameter, the African one is 15″—you can end off the coiling. For an added finishing touch, the outermost coil can be overwrapped, as in the first work, with a single strand of the deeper shade of coiling material. Or it can be coiled with another stitch, as in the latter, which has a final round of coiling in alternating colors, which is worked into and over the previous round on every other wrap, so that you wrap once and overcast once to create a sawtooth effect. Other variations you may like to try include wrapping with the coil slightly up on the previous round for a more bowl-like effect, or coiling with the standard technique to form a spiked look where colors meet within the same basic motif. The possibilities are limit-less, as you work with different materials, shades, and designs in coiling.

Designed and crocheted by Vince Adesso untitled pattern crochet hanging, all in single crochet stitch, 3′ x 2′. Five shades of gray, white, and tan yarns form the design.

Crochet As an Art Form

The versatility of crochet stitches lends itself well to the creation of art works in softly textured fibers. The two works shown are presented to give you an idea of the scope of this technique. As you begin to think about the type of work you want to make, be it a wall hanging with a basically two-dimensional design and geometric shape in rectangular or square outlines, or a sculptural form in three dimensions, get several sheets of paper and draw your concepts. Even the most fundamental of sketches will help you plan a design, so you needn't feel that your drawing is the final pattern. Rather than trying to make a complete design on paper, make several small sketches on one sheet. Then, choose the ones which are more appealing and elaborate on them on separate sheets. You can then start the crochet itself and allow the textures and patterns suggested by the yarns as you work with them to influence the design.

The hanging shown is an untitled study in five shades of gray, from pale through charcoal, with white and tan. The entire work is done in single crochet, with changes in color providing the design. The design itself is assymetrical, or what is called informal balance, as the forms within do not repeat themselves exactly anywhere in the composition. They are created by carrying the shades of yarn as they are used. Pattern crochet offers a tremendous latitude in design concepts, as you can bring the colors to any section as you work. In many cases, you'll find it best to end off the yarn when you complete a section, rather than carrying it to the next area. When yarns are carried, they should only cover a fairly short distance without being worked, or they will tend to pull the crocheting out of shape.

As you plan your work, color in the drawn sketches to develop the color scheme. Choose several shades of the same type of yarn. In pattern crochet, the changes in shade provide the design. If you change the type of yarn as well, you'll find that the different weights or textures work up quite differently and you won't have a nice squared outline. Before you begin, you should also plan the kind of top attachment you want to use. In the work shown, three bands of crochet are looped over a Lucite rod in a form that complements the design. The top can also be finished with a solid border, then folded over and around to form a hem through which

Rock Sculpture designed and crocheted by Jan Knutson, in fibers of wool, linen, and cotton using many different crochet stitches.

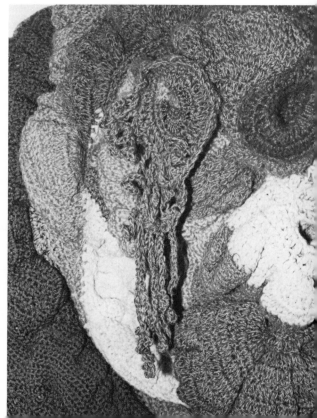

Detail of Rock Sculpture, showing the use of increases and decreases with added chains

you can slip a dowel or other rod, or you can crochet directly around a rod at the top for another look. If you feel at all unsure about the direction your design and finishing are taking, make a small version, crocheting with the same yarns and hook to see how well they work. The interesting thing about crochet is that the results are visually pleasing, in even the most basic of design forms. You'll enjoy making the small versions so much that you'll soon be ready to crochet your own wall-sized hanging.

Sculptural crochet has the added dimension of form. In the Rock Sculpture shown, the fibers of wool, linen, and cotton are combined with many crochet stitches to create the convoluted, rocklike shape. The hills and valleys formed by using a blend of yarns and stitches are further defined by use of increases and decreases with added chains for further surface texture, as shown in the detail.

Here again, preliminary sketches are very helpful in planning your own design. Another possibility is to begin a piece in yarns that you like and see where it leads. Some of the most inventive works are created in a free-form manner. To add definition and shape to your sculptural work, add in a good stuffing material such as polyester fiberfill. You can stuff a piece when it is partially complete to see how it affects the design, and continue to work around the filling, or wait until the crocheting is finished. In the latter case, you leave an opening that is large enough to stuff easily and then crochet it closed.

Whichever form of crochet you choose, you're sure to enjoy the crocheting itself and the finished results. Crochet stitches, which lock themselves in place as you do them, are so easy to do that you can concentrate on the design and shape.

Designs in Twining

This wall hanging was made in Africa in patterned twining. The vertical threads are held in place on a frame or loom to keep them taut and even while the weft is twined into them. In the two patterns shown, the vertical threads are roughly spun natural tan wool twined with dark brown natural wool, off-white cotton, and dyed red wool. Their bold, simple outlines are quite attractive and are easily adapted to many works. You can create

Wall Hanging, Africa, twining in dark brown, white, and red on natural tan wool warp. Author's collection.

the same type of design for a wall hanging, tote bag, pillow, or any other work with a two-dimensional design surface. You might even use them for a crocheted piece, such as the hanging described above.

There are several ways in which you can proceed. If you want to try the twining techniques, you can follow the drawn diagrams which reproduce the house and bird motifs shown. Another possibility is to work in tapestry weaves on a supporting form, adapting the designs themselves in diagonal, interlocking, and slit weaves. The designs seem to work best in natural tones, vegetable, or other natural dyes on wool yarns.

Diagram of the bird design

Diagram of the house design

209

Whichever plan you choose to follow, you'll find it best to work the yarns on a foundation, such as a piece of Masonite or cardboard. You can also use an old picture frame or a set of artist's wooden canvas stretchers. Thread on the vertical or warp yarn. In the patterns shown, each is 10 inches wide by 9 inches tall. The selvedges, or side threads, define the width, and the vertical threads are used in one long section, weaving the pattern blocks one at a time on the long warp. In the finished work, the blocks can be cut at any point as the twining is fairly secure and a small space is left between one block and the next. To make your own patterns, you can use one long warp or make one precisely the right size on a board with pins or notched edges, so that the weaving is complete as you do the last row. The warp ends are spaced here at four per inch, as the twining threads are in the medium to heavy weight range and you need the room between vertical threads to work the twining. A standard twining pattern is followed using one thread folded in half so that you have two ends, and the design comes out the same on both front and back in the finished work.

To follow the designs in either twining or tapestry techniques, you'll find it very helpful if you make a scale, or same size, copy on a sheet of drawing paper. Then, slip the paper under the vertical warp threads. You can then work the sections easily as the design is right there. The same is true for any variations you plan or for any figurative weave where accuracy in pattern is important. In tapestry weaving this type of pattern is called a cartoon. The design placement is important as you weave the sections in order, from the smallest details to start, through the surrounding design parts, then the background, and lastly the enclosing border. Without a guide to follow, this sequence is somewhat harder to master. Another method you can try is similar to that used by Navajo rug weavers, in which you weave up from the bottom, using each thread in turn, so that you create the design one row at a time. As you do your first figurative works, this working plan is also easiest to do with a copy of the pattern in place behind the warp ends.

Weaving in the Round on a Ring or Hoop

The process of weaving in the round on a wire ring or a hoop to create decorative wall hangings is ably demonstrated by the Mandalas shown.

Mandala designed and woven by Betty Lovejoy. Beiges, grays, natural tans, white and pale gold. Natural beige warp spokes, wooden beads on added pale gold and tan fringe, with pheasant feathers.

Mandala designed and woven by Betty Lovejoy. In brilliant blues, deep blues, and bright greens. Deep blue warp spokes, fringe added in deep and bright green with deep and bright green wooden beads with peacock feathers.

They are part of a striking series of color studies in weave and texture, all based on the same type of foundation and weave structure. Another example is shown on page 108.

To make your own weaving in the round, buy a metal ring or hoop at least 12 inches in diameter. Use a good strong thread to make the warp spokes, such as a number 3 pearl cotton. Two 2-ounce tubes will be more than enough; if you space the spokes farther apart, one will do it. The weft can be any combination of wool, cotton, and novelty yarns in contrasting, neutral, or natural shades. For new effects, handspun yarn in various textures can be bought, if you don't spin yourself. The texture of the yarns and the occasional open warp spokes are part of the design, so that you should aim for a group of yarns that have a central theme which relates them to each other. In the works shown, the colors are closely related in hue and shade within each weaving. The light colors are beiges, grays, natural tans, white, and pale gold on a warp of natural hue. Added threads form a fringe in gold and natural tan, with wooden beads that echo the color scheme, and pheasant feathers worked in near the fringe attachment are brown and beige. The dark shades are a mixture of brilliant blues, deep blues, and olive greens on a dark blue warp, with added fringe in bright and deep green, accented by bright and deep green wooden beads and peacock feathers.

To begin the weaving, wrap the hoop with one of the weft yarns. Then, warp the hoop with the warp yarn, spacing the spokes carefully and overlapping them in the exact center of the hoop. To weave, use a blunt-tipped yarn needle. Start at the center and work out. The first several rounds should be plain weave in a fairly lightweight yarn or thread, as the warp spokes are closest together at the center. Then, you can add the different yarns in plain weave, slit weave, soumak, reversed soumak, and twill weave, as the yarns suggest and your design indicates. For a work such as this one, the very textures and patterns created by the yarns as you use them are a design in themselves, so that you can feel free to follow any plan that suits you. Once the warp is in place, the weaving is very portable and fun to do just about anywhere. As you complete the last round, the weaving is also complete, as the wrapped ring needs no further finish. If you want, you can add fringe or any other ornamentation that you like. To hang up the weaving, use thin, transparent fishing line and place it on a wall. It will also look attractive in a window, but remember that the yarns will tend to lighten in the sun if you place it in a sunny window.

Rings of all sizes and types can be used to make designs in the round. You can try different warping patterns, adding more open areas, and any other variations that you think of. The potential in weaving in the round is so great that you'll have a good time seeing the results as you weave and gain further insight into the technique.

Netting and Weaving in Tubular Forms

The complex tubular weaving shown is a fine combination of twisted-thread knotless netting and free-style weaving on four wire rings. The work is comprised of three sections, defined by the metal rings. From the top down, the rings are first 7 inches in diameter, followed by a section of knotless netting, then a 9-inch ring, followed by a middle section of free-style weaving, another 9-inch ring, a second section of knotless netting, completed with a 7-inch ring. The basic yarn is a cotton thread in a natural light-beige tone used for all of the netting and to form the warp for the woven section. Small amounts of wool yarn are woven, leaving large exposed warp sections in deep and light burgundy and orange. The weaving is accented with short beaded lengths of the basic thread, holding beads made out of natural wood and nuts. This work was made in India and can be used as a sculptural hanging, or even as a light tube with a low wattage bulb which won't harm the threads.

To plan your own tubular weaving, you should decide how many rings you want to use, perhaps drawing out your ideas on paper to see how they look. As the rings are placed parallel to each other, they define spaces between, which you fill with netting or free-style weaving as you prefer. If you use three rings, you'll have two areas to be worked, with four rings, as shown, there are three, with five rings there would be four, and so forth. If you are making your first work in this design you may find it best to work with fewer rings, until you get this technique completely under control.

In the work shown, there are 72 doubled threads, for a total of 144

Tubular hanging in knotless netting and free-style weaving in natural beige cord with woven wool areas in deep and light burgundy, and orange. Author's collection.

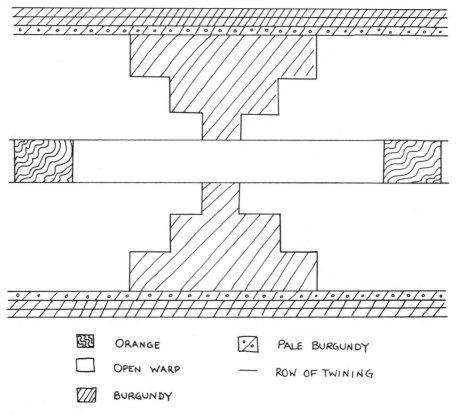

	ORANGE		PALE BURGUNDY
	OPEN WARP	—	ROW OF TWINING
	BURGUNDY		

Diagram of a suggested weave pattern. All in plain weave on double warp ends.

Pattern for twists for the netting:

Row 1: Single twists

Row 2: Same, with alternate pairs

Through Row 13: Repeat

Row 14: Same, placing two pairs together after each twist to braid

Row 15: Crossover of center two threads in each set

Row 16: Outer pairs twist to complete braid steps

Row 17 through 20: Repeat standard network steps

Row 21: After row is complete, split into groups of three pairs

Row 22: One crossover between each group, rest single twists to make braid at crossovers

Row 23: Cross last two in each group, move toward the first pair in the next group to the right

Row 24: Twist across, leave pair that moved over space separate twist it alone to make braid

Row 25: Single twist, work one as the first of three in the next group, as the last pair in each is now in the following group

Row 26: Repeat braid and subsequent open space making steps seventeen times in all; or sixteen after the first time for a total of seventeen rows

Row 42 through 49: Twists for open network

Row 50 through 53: Repeat the first set of spaces as in rows 14, 15, and 16

Row 54 through 57: Single twists up to ring

Warp and do free weaving

Repeat netting below next ring

End off at last ring by looping around it and working ends back up into the netting, cut off

working threads. Unless you are already familiar with the netting process, you'll find it best to work the first section on a padded form or pillow rolled into a cylinder for the first several sets of twists in the netting. To begin the netting, and lay the foundation for the rest of the weaving, wind out the required number of threads on a set of rods. Each thread should be at least 4 yards long if you plan to make a weaving of similar height. Hanging up, this work is 18 inches long, but the netting and weaving take up a lot of yarn. The threads are used doubled, as for netting, so that you should wind up the loose ends on bobbins, short lengths of dowel, or other holding devices after they have been cut off the rods. For a beginning work, there are too many threads in this design, as you need to have a good working knowledge of the process, so that you can halve the number and space them more widely around the top ring. This will give you a more open effect that is simpler to accomplish but doesn't lose its impact.

If you want to create the same type of open-work netting, for the first section, suspend the top ring. Place the threads, wrapped onto bobbins, on the ring, putting each over it at the center fold of the thread. Each thread then forms two working threads as it hangs off the ring. Place the ring so that you can add in a soft support, such as a pillow rolled to size, which will help hold the threads on the ring and add form to the netting as you do it. The pattern for twists is given, but you can follow any one that you wish, even staying with the basic single twists throughout. In the work shown, the netting is tightened toward the center of the area to form a graceful inward curve. It is then worked more loosely toward the next ring.

In this case, the second ring is placed into the netting 7 inches down from the first. The threads are taken once around the ring and then are unwound, off the bobbins, for 5 inches, and then taken once around the next ring and secured with a loose knot. This adds in both of the central rings and creates a warp out of the previously netted strands.

To begin the woven section, thread a blunt-tipped needle with one of the warp yarns. Work a plain weave all the way around just below the second ring in the work, taking the warp over two and under two threads for at least three rounds. This plain weave section secures the threads for weaving and spaces out the warp ends. In the example shown, the warp is used throughout with two threads as one. A double parallel set of threads is twined into the center of the exposed warp to hold it in place. The sections of plain weave are added in slit fashion wherever you please. At the bottom of the woven section just above the third ring, another complete round of plain weave is done, also for strength and spacing. If you are using half the number of threads, work the weave in the same way, using only one end and you will have the same visual results. When the woven section is complete, you untie the loose knots below the third ring and begin netting again. The same pattern is followed from the top down to the last ring. Add in the last ring and loop the ends of the threads around it when the netting is finished. Trim the ends and work them back around the ring so that they aren't seen. If you like, you can add on bead trim in any spots on the rings that you choose.

As you work with tubular forms, you'll find that they do present somewhat of a problem in an open work such as this one, until you gain dexterity in handling the numerous ends, which you will with a bit of practice. However, the results are so enchanting that it's well worth the effort. If you use a padded form to do the netting, work in a more cylindrical fashion, as the curve inward will not occur when the form is in place. For the weaving, it isn't needed, although you can add small weights to the third ring as you weave to maintain a good tension on the warp. The lower section of netting will be easier to do, as you will already be quite familiar with the technique from the first section.

This type of design is readily adapted to all sorts of weavings. You can use the basic form to create tubular weavings that are completely woven, completely netted, or a combination of knotting, weaving, and netting. Once the basic threads have been started on the first ring, they will give you ideas for patterns you'll want to follow. Just let your imagination be your guide and you'll be sure to achieve the results you want.

Black Sheep Weaving and Craft Supply
315 SW Third Street
Corvallis, Oregon 97330

Dick Blick Co.
Box 1267
Galesburg, Illinois 61401

**Knitting and Weaving Yarns
Briggs and Little Woolen Mills Ltd.**
Harvey Station
New Brunswick, CANADA EOH 1HO

Contessa Yarns
P. O. Box 37
Lebanon, Connecticut 06249

Coulter Studios, Inc.
118 East 59th Street
New York, New York 10022

CUM Textile Industries Ltd.
5-7 Roemersgade
1362 Copenhagen K
Denmark
    Sells only through authorized dealers in the United States. Will send local listing if requested.

Frederick J. Fawcett, Inc.
129 South Street
Boston, Massachusetts 02111
    Linen yarns and threads

Filature Lemieux Inc.
St-Ephrem, Beauce,
Quebec, CANADA GOM 1RO

Greentree Ranch Wools
163 N. Carter Lake Road
Loveland, Colorado 80537

J. L. Hammett Company
10 Hammett Place
Braintree, Massachusetts 02184

The Handweaver
1643 San Pablo Avenue
Berkeley, California 94702

The Handweaver
460 First Street East
Sonoma, California 95476

Walter Kircher
Alte Kasselerstrasse 24
Marburg-Lahn, 3550 GERMANY

Belding Lily Company
HW Dept.
Shelby, North Carolina 28150

Magnolia Weaving
2635-29th Avenue West
Seattle, Washington 98199

New England Earth Crafts, Inc.
149 Putnam Avenue
Cambridge, Massachusetts 02139

Schacht Spindle Company
P. O. Box 2157
Boulder, Colorado 80306

School Products Co.
1201 Broadway
New York, New York 10001

Texere Yarns
9 Peckover Street
Bradford
West Yorkshire BD1 5BD ENGLAND
    Wholesale only

Village Weaving Center
434 Sixth Avenue, 5th floor
New York, New York 10011

Village Wools
3719 4th N.W.
Albuquerque, New Mexico 87107

The Weaver's Shop
Wilton Royal Carpet Factory
Wilton near Salisbury
Wiltshire SP2 OAY
ENGLAND

The Weaver's Shop
39 Courtland Street
Rockford, Michigan 49341

Index

Dark Ancestor

The Literature of the Black Man in the Caribbean

O. R. Dathorne

Louisiana State University Press
Baton Rouge and London

Designer: Albert Crochet
Typeface: VIP Trump Medieval
Typesetter: LSU Press
Printer and binder: Thomson-Shore, Inc.

LIBRARY OF CONGRESS CATALOGING IN PUBLICATION DATA

Dathorne, O   R   1934–
  Dark ancestor.

  Bibliography: p.
  Includes index.
  1. Caribbean literature—Black authors—History and
criticism. 2. American literature—Afro-American
authors—History and criticism. I. Title.
PN849.C3D37   809'.896   80–22581
ISBN 0–8071–0759–X

For Hilde Dathorne
For Jahn, Lydia, the Herskovitses,
and other believers

Contents

Acknowledgments

I must thank a great many people for help, assistance, and encouragement. I was never fortunate enough to attract grant monies for this project, and thus I appreciate all the more the generosity of The Ohio State University. Through Florida International University I had the opportunity to come down to Miami and continue this work in 1974 and 1975, and at the University of Miami, thanks particularly to Dr. William Babula, I was able to complete it in an agreeable atmosphere. There were individuals at all stages who seemed to believe that there was more than sea and sunlight to this, and I thank them for their faith.

For help with specific sections, I must first of all express my gratitude to Ricardo Pau-Llosa for assistance with the Spanish sections and to Ernesto Pichardo, my first *santero*, who stayed around long enough to become a friend. Liz Bell and Adele King assisted with the French and Haitian Creole, and Gerald Curtis and Rose Watson with sections on Portuguese. Robin Dobru's visit reactivated my interest in Sranan-Tongo and Dutch. Lydia Cabrera and the late Janheinz Jahn talked with me, always. Eleanor Sapp worked initially on the typing, and Marlene Leroy was very patient, painstaking, and helpful. Ana Bradley and Marianne Messina were rigorous with the proofing. My family endured the readings over dinner. To all I owe my gratitude and thanks.

In the late stages of the manuscript, several work-study students at the University of Miami were helpful. In particular, I wish to thank

Lewis Archer, Patrice Bowie, Rosalyn Jones, and Saadia Ortiz for the help with the bibliography—an arduous undertaking. I would also like to thank Walter Rhett, one of the most dynamic graduate assistants with whom I have ever worked. To all I owe a debt of gratitude. The bad judgments remain mine.

Dark Ancestor

Introduction

The southern rim of the United States, eastern Mexico, and the Caribbean regions of Central America, Brazil, Venezuela, and the Guyanas demarcate the borders of that area of the Black man's New World terrain that is significant in this discussion. The inner zone of this area, especially the Caribbean Islands, provides the focus of this study, although I will consider Canada, the United States, and Central and South America when relevant.

In large measure, to allude to the Caribbean, or indeed to the New World, is to confirm the presence of the Black man in its evolution. The Indian presence, when it was not virtually extinguished, was rendered culturally neutral; but the black presence afforded these areas an air of new cultural autonomy and bestowed a pattern different from that of the old worlds of Europe and Africa.

Within the Caribbean the Black man has manifested his culture in a number of diverse ways. Some generalizations obviously apply, but there is much divergence within these common manifestations. More precisely, the New World Black who lives in the United States is culturally, economically, and socially different from his New World counterparts in Nicaragua and Panama. Eugene D. Genovese, in *The World the Slaveholders Made* (1971), gives an early warning for those embarking on a study of this nature.

> Historians usually treat all slave classes as if they also exhibited monolithic similarity, but few of these historians would adhere to the only principle justifying such a procedure—that blacks are blacks. At one extreme, in the Old South, the blacks were largely creoles [American-born], at least during the mature period of the slave regime. At the other ex-

1

treme, in Saint-Domingue on the eve of its great revolution, the blacks were overwhelmingly newly imported Africans. Between these two we find various combinations at different times in Cuba, Brazil, Jamaica, and other slave countries. Among the African-born we find quite different peoples, with markedly different political, social, and cultural backgrounds. The mere fact that Bahia, Brazil, witnessed large-scale Moslem-led revolts during the early part of the nineteenth century ought to be enough to put us on our guard.[1]

Hence, there are also important differences between the Jamaican and Virgin Islander, the Cuban and the Haitian, the Trinidadian and the Barbadian, the Guyanese and the Brazilian. The diverse nature of the culture contact with the New World metropolis and, perhaps more importantly, the initial indigenous ethnic culture to which specific African groups belonged account for this.

Although in the area we are examining there are clear indications of Spanish, Portuguese, French, Dutch, and English influences— even if one ignored latter-day influences from Canada and America —certain filialistic resemblances between the inhabitants of some of these areas and parts of Africa are very apparent. In turn, this establishes their relationship with one another. The religious association of Blacks in the Oriente Province in Cuba with those of the Yoruba in Nigeria shows their comparative similarity with Blacks in the Bahia Province of Brazil. Yoruba culture is the mutual denominator, not the Iberian cultural enclave in which both of these small groups are encompassed. Historians seemingly have overemphasized this latter aspect.

The slave trade clearly illustrates the manner by which peoples from various parts of Africa entered a cultural ghetto; equally significant is the evolving pattern. While easily admitting that the New World Black is a product of West and Central Africa, one also has to conclude that there are important cultural varieties that can only be accounted for by symbiotic and acculturative factors.

At the inception, a researcher has to inquire about the nature of the common features, inherited or locally manufactured, that Blacks in these areas share. One argument might well show that four centuries of differing culture contacts (albeit within the European New

1. Eugene D. Genovese, *The World the Slaveholders Made* (New York, 1971), 4.

World framework) account for variations that would seemingly have little bearing on the original parent culture of Africa. Differences might also be seen as arising out of involvement within hybrid African New World societies that were not merely content with European New World patterns. Hence David Brion Davis' comment can be disputed. He says:

> No doubt there is much truth in even the idyllic picture of the Brazilian "Big House," where slaves and freemen pray and loaf together, and where masters shrug their shoulders at account books and prefer to frolic with slave girls in shaded hammocks. But we should not forget that West Indian and North American planters were fond of idealizing their own "Big Houses" as patriarchal manors, of portraying their Negroes as carefree and indolent, and of proudly displaying humane slave laws which they knew to be unenforceable. . . . There is little reason to doubt that slavery in Latin America, compared with that of North America, was less subject to the pressures of competitive capitalism and was closer to a system of patriarchal rights and semifeudalistic services.[2]

He concludes that "it may be that differences between slavery in Latin America and the United States were no greater *than regional or temporal differences within countries themselves*. And such a conclusion would lead us to suspect that Negro bondage was a single phenomenon, or *Gestalt*, whose variations were less significant than underlying patterns of unity" (italics added).[3]

One ready answer to this argument is that this ignores the slave's *Weltanschauung* completely. It is a view from the master's world. *Slave*, a new word that had many connotations, referred to a member of an African group who spoke an African language and had been initiated into an African society. In addition, the New World Black, despite European affiliation, does think and act, however superficially, in a manner that would denote a rejection of European mores. Certainly because of curious parallels, there are common manifestations that have to be accounted for. But they overlap the artificial perimeters of Old World European allegiances and seem to reflect the Old World character of African man instead.

2. David Brion Davis, "A Comparison of British America and Latin America," in Eugene D. Genovese and Laura Foner (eds.), *Slavery in the New World: A Reader in Comparative History* (New Jersey, 1969), 73.
   3. *Ibid.*

What is perhaps equally important is that Afro-New World man has altered and transformed himself, not only in terms of his immediate environment, but also with regard to the new African and European cultures immediate with him. Hence, a hypothetical Black man who is a product of English-speaking Guyana is, because of his cultural and historical heritage, conscious of Spanish, Dutch, and French intrusions into his adaptation of an English culture. This is in addition to his absorption of a variety of African cultural norms. He is, therefore, much more fully aware than his White counterpart of the meaningfulness of the varied culture experience in the New World.

In addition to "being" several European men, this hypothetical man is not only a product of a single regional African ethnic group, but a combination of several. The politics of slavery had brought this about, yoking Africans together in an unusual bond. Before the New World Black had become aware of the varieties of European culture, he knew of the way by which his own specific indigenous culture flourished for him independently and in relation to the cultures of other Blacks around him. This was the training school of the Middle Passage. Before, there was Africa, but no African existed— only a person within a group. In the slave holds he sought a compromise that would later have ramifications in the enforced adaptation of the slave shacks. He absorbed the various Black and White cultures around him and made them part of his being. If the argument is made that Afro-New World man is New World man, then White becomes an appendage to the cultural fortifications the Black man erects.

This is why there is so much confusion in the view from outside the culture of the Black man in the New World, why, for instance, Eric Williams in *British Historians and the West Indies* (1964) can praise Adam Smith for a "broad international outlook," and yet rebuke him for succumbing to "the tradition of sentimentality." He can also criticize Thomas Clarkson for his "humanitarianism and breadth of vision [which] were seen at their best in his attitude to the question of Negro inferiority." Williams deems it absurd that "not a voice was heard, not a funeral note against this betrayal of the humanitarian cause" when Thomas Carlyle clearly advocated a per-

manent state of servitude for Blacks in his *Occasional Discourse upon the Nigger Question* (1849). Williams is equally incensed with Anthony Trollope, who was "convinced that emancipation bred idleness."[4] Surely it becomes pointless to rebuke the best minds of that generation for failing to understand that "slave" had no cultural meaning for the person enslaved. Subject had become object—unknown to subject.

A study of Caribbean literature can only expect to chart currents through which Black writers have chosen to move, and emphasize their similarities and differences. When discussing the New World, one comes up against the intriguing point that not only is the New World a Black invention, but the writer at the same time is engaged in threading a synthesis into literature. Because of the texture and variety of this synthesis, Afro-New World man is in many ways unique, and his literature reflects this.

The first aspect of this uniqueness emerges in the group affinity of the Black man, and there are many sides to this point. Slavery broke down the smaller groups and initiated, almost by default, the advent of Afro-New World man. This new man was in the process of becoming an individual, for slavery (and this cannot be emphasized enough) meant the separation of person from group. Both Ottobah Cugoano and Olaudah Equiano (or Gustavus Vassa) emphasize precisely this aspect in their personal accounts of capture written in the eighteenth century. Cugoano comments: "Next morning there came three other men, *whose language differed from the others*, and spoke to some of those who watched us all night, but he that pretended to be our friend with the great man, and some others, were gone away. . . . We went with them again about half a day's journey, and came to a great multitude of people, *having different music playing*."[5] The isolation is confirmed through the initiation of the Middle Passage. Although still in Africa, the slave has wandered far, and his admission of otherness is the start of the transmigration of body.

It is, of course, no accident that Equiano's account is not very dif-

4. Eric Williams, *British Historians and the West Indies* (New York, 1964), 20, 23, 81, 91.
5. Ottobah Cugoano, *Thoughts and Sentiments on the Evil and Wicked Traffic of the Slavery and Commerce of the Human Species, Humbly Submitted to the Inhabitants of Great Britian* (New York, 1969 [1787]), 9.

ferent at this point. The foreignness that he and his sister experience is translated into cruelty—another important lesson that the subject had to learn when beginning the archetypal journey of generations which would result in his change to object:

> The next morning we left the house, and continued travelling all the day. For a long time we had kept to the woods, but at last we came into a road which I believed I knew. I now had some hopes of being delivered; for we had advanced but a little way before I discovered some people at a distance, on which I began to cry out for their assistance; but my cries had no effect than to make them tie me faster and stop my mouth, and then they put me into a large sack . . . and in this manner we proceeded till we were out of the sight of these people.[6]

Being removed from the security of the group meant, as both Cugoano and Equiano point out, that they were not physically with their ethnic groups when they were kidnapped; this aloneness was later to become a way of life and a theme for literature.

Despite the separation on the sociocultural levels, there were obvious survivals of African cults in the form of secret societies, which proved useful bastions against slavery. In Brazil, the Hausas and Yorubas maintained their own indigenous societies as ethnic, cultural expressions of their groups; in Cuba and Haiti, Yoruba and Ibo group affinity was preserved through religious ritual.

Neo-African revivals take the form of lodges, friendly burial societies, and churches. During the nineteenth century, brotherhood cults were founded exclusively for buying freedom. Consequently, group associations meant the preservation of some of the group ideology. In many instances they met a practical need; throughout the Black New World, basic banking procedures (in Guyana, called "the box," and in Jamaica, "susu") began as ways of helping freed Blacks toward achieving a measure of economic stability. Communalistic efforts in the sharing of work and construction of houses and village roads were also part of the group affinity imported by Afro-New World men.

Group activity ensured not only the preservation of the basic and the combined cultures but also their enrichment. This process of ac-

6. Olaudah Equiano, *The Interesting Narrative of the Life of Olaudah Equiano, or Gustavus Vassa, the African* (London, 1969 [1789–92]), I, 61.

cretion was significant because it allowed for the addition of new culture groups to the larger one, resulting in historical and psychological changes that occurred as Europe waged its wars.

Kinship matters were important within the smaller, extended family system of the New World, and the mother still plays a very important role. Without delving into a sociological debate, one can assert that a Black mother was not molded by slavery and postslavery demands. Although it has become commonplace for social anthropologists to assert that the masculine sort of Black mother stereotype in the New World is the direct consequence of slavery, it is definitely not so. According to the arguments of such anthropologists, the Black male had never been assigned a responsible role to play in his society, and therefore the Black woman had been conditioned to the acceptance of the dual responsibility of mothering and fathering.

Further investigation reveals that in the original African context, role playing is indeed essential. The woman—childbearer and wife—is also provider; in West Africa she is a farmer and market seller. For the Black woman to continue to assume these roles, therefore, is a natural extension of her traditional place in African society and not a distortion of this position. When Afro-New World writers describe the mother stereotype, extended in some instances to the glorification of the Black woman, they are relating a historical and sociological fact. The *dozens* (oral verses praising the mother figure through apparent condemnation of her) in the United States negatively assert her positive status, as do mother rhymes in the Caribbean.

Role fulfillment was also significantly emphasized for the father and other kin, both in the African and New World context. The father in Africa was not only expected to be a farmer but to take on the economic responsibilities of the extended family. This included the obligation of rearing a dead brother's family, for example, and was part of the family system disrupted by slavery. Children have traditionally owed allegiance and obedience to their parents. Black writers frequently utilize mother, father, and children, not as individual characters, but as stereotypes for the transmuting of African culture.

Within the New World, the ethnic group becomes a race. The process is a slow one. First, the smaller group becomes "African" for the

first time, and later, when there is a blending of the subject (how the Black man perceived himself) and the object (how he is perceived by Whites), "negroization" takes place. This is both positive and negative; on one hand, a larger group comes about; on the other, this larger group is almost invented by the dominant White group in the New World. The "Negro" thus becomes a figment of the imagination.

The slave captain, a kind of prehistoric immigration officer who assigned nationality at whim, is greatly responsible for the artificiality of cultural boundaries for the Black man in the New World. No longer was he an Ashanti, an Ewe, or a Yoruba. In his own mind he became an Afro-New World Black man; to others he was a "Negro." Those Blacks who were "negroized" would not assert themselves. Instead, they played out the stereotypes assigned them, as demonstrated in the literature. The "negroizers" (the White inhabitants of the New World) saw, not the Ashanti, the Ewe, the Yoruba, but the antipathy of what they themselves were. Thus a myth becomes a misinterpretation of history and later a fact. This is compounded by the desire of the Black person to free himself. First, from the "darkie" syndrome he asserts he is a Negro; later on that word takes on a servile quality, and in the 1960s the Black person emerges. Demythifying is almost complete.

Male and female relationships also constituted an important element of the new way in which the New World Black man was perceived. Traditional roles could not be enacted within the confines of slavery; instead, other parts had to be assumed. The woman became the mere producer of children, and the man was reduced to being the stud. Slavery and postslavery economics continued to interfere with traditional and authentic roles. Writers, therefore, have had to define and redefine these relationships within the social framework.

Contact within the New World was very physical. Sexual contacts were often interracial, and the Mulatto (mule) was the sterile product of this meeting. He is interesting in literature because he confines within himself the explosive potentialities of two totally different worlds. One side to this—in reality the perverted end product of the collision of the old worlds—is the emergence of the "cultural Mulatto" as a theme in New World Black literature. Winthrop

Jordan makes a point that adds to the confusion, albeit from the master's standpoint:

> All European colonists in the Americas faced the problem of racially mixed offspring. In the Portuguese and Spanish colonies there rapidly developed a social hierarchy structured according to degrees of intermixture of Negro and European blood, replete with a complicated battery of terminology to facilitate definition. In contrast the English colonists in Maryland, Virginia, and the Carolinas created no such system of ranking. Although cultural differences among the colonizing nations may have done something to effect this divergence, it is significant that the English reaction to racially mixed offspring was not everywhere the same, that men bearing the same cultural baggage reacted differently when dealing with racially different conditions in the New World.[7]

Part of the task of the New World Black was therefore the transformation of his cultural environment into a Mulatto society. African words were intermingled and introduced into the new languages of Europe. His New World tongues differed from the metropolitan parent tongue. The consequences this would have for European languages have been documented, yet it has not been pointed out that the Yoruba of the New World is not the same as the standard, modern Yoruba in Nigeria. Cuban Spanish, Guyanese French, and Jamaican English differ radically from one another and their European equivalents. The language of Afro-New World men infused these tongues with a different rhythm. Léon Damas tells his readers of an early encounter with a concerned mother who reminds him that it is necessary to speak "le français de France" (the French of France).[8] This conflict with language is to continue within the writing of New World Blacks. At one extreme Robin Dobru adapts Surinamese as a literary language and Louise Bennett utilizes Jamaican Creole as her sole medium, and at the other extreme early writers like the Cuban Plácido and the American Phyllis Wheatley use European cultural attitudes in their language.

Similar structures exist in the religious pantheon. Spain bequeathed to the New World the concept of Cristo Negro as seen in Guatemala

7. Winthrop Jordan, *White Over Black: American Attitudes Toward the Negro, 1550–1812* (Chapel Hill, 1968), 167.
8. Léon Gontran Damas, "Hoquet," in *Pigments* (Paris, 1962 [1937]), 35.

and El Salvador. In addition, Roman Catholicism, indeed New World Christianity, was substantially altered by Blacks. The call and response routine, possession, and attitudes towards the Christian god as person rather than as removed deity are all manifest in orthodox African religions and later in Afro-New World faiths. The literature of Afro-New World man confirms that the Christian religion of the Black was very different from the White.

The developing Black institutions, with their incorporation of White ones and the intrusion of standard white values (including those of immigrants continuing to come from Europe), are important. Writers demonstrate this as an important area of tension, though they cannot take sides (even the middle is uncomfortable). At times the New World Society subscribes to neither African nor European values, for it is neither. The nature of what has been remains significant, and thus writers respond to what was oral. Therefore, prose, poetry, and drama become meaningless as separate genres, and the New World Black writer usually unites them in a given work of art.

The purpose of the art adheres significantly to African intention. It is *for* a people and (with few exceptions) speaks *to* a people. The writer is group spokesman. It is a moot point whether the group addressed is middle class and White; what seems more important is that the role of the writer is one in which he sees himself as a spokesman for the "negroized."

But the process that invented Negro, *évolué*, and *assimilado* had to terminate. Writers began to question the thrust and purpose of their westernization. They were themselves products of this type of education. But the so-called Harlem Renaissance; Négritude in France, Haiti and Senegal; and Negrista in Cuba (all movements of the 1920s and 1930s) ask important questions of the intent of European culture, and of the Black man's significance in the making of the New World. The legitimacy for this investigation is authorized by Europe—a true, yet ironical point.

In looking at the literature of the Black man in the New World, one realizes that even if answers are not readily forthcoming, the very role of writer is being questioned. One comes up with stunning factors with regard to the nature of acculturation. Therefore, Graham Greene in Haiti or Havana, and Saul Bellow in his imaginative en-

counters in *Henderson, the Rain King* become like Black men—like, in the United States, writers such as Imamu Amiri Baraka (LeRoi Jones), Don L. Lee (Haki Madubuti), Nikki Giovanni, and Sonia Sanchez; in Cuba, Nicolás Guillén; in Haiti, Jacques Roumain; in the Guyanas, Martin Carter and Léon Damas; in Jamaica, Andrew Salkey, and in Barbados, Austin Clark. Parallels of experience can be drawn, and their significance is part of a common quest for "Afro-Americanitude" within the complex framework of New World culture using Africa and Africans as the touchstone. Caribbean literature adequately shows the arduous penetration of minds into this fertile but bewildering wilderness.

1 Africa as Source

A distinction has to be made at the very outset between Africa as it literally extends itself into the New World, and Africa as the myth and realization there. It is possible to view the entire New World as a cultural province of Africa, and this assertion becomes even more evident when clear reasons can be advocated for it. In the first place, contrary to what is usually believed, Africans were in the New World probably before, and certainly with, the advent of the Spaniards. José Antonio Saco comments thus:

> De un pasaje de Pedro Mátir de Anghiera a Anglería, pudiera inferirse que en aquél continente existieron negros antes que los hubiesen introducido los españoles y aún quizás que Colón lo hubiese descubierto. Asegura aquel autor, que cuando Núñez de Balboa hizo su famosa expedición en 1513 para descubrir el Mar del Sur, ya encontró negros. Dice así: "Allí encontraron negros esclavos en una región distante de Quarequa dos días de camino, los cuales solo engendran negros feroces y muy crueles. Júzgase que por robar pasaron en otro tiempo de la Etiopía, y que habiendo naufragado, se fijaron en aquellos montes. Odios, intestinos existen entre los quarequanos y estos negros, y alternativamente se esclavizan ó matan."
> Ningún historiador de América ha dado al pasaje de Pedro Mátir la importancia que merece. Tres cosas deben notarse en él: la., si existió tal pueblo de negros; 2a., si Núñez de Balboa encontró algunos de ellos esclavizados cuando en 1513 fué a descubrir el Mar del Sur; 3a., cuál era su procedencia.

From a passage by Pedro Mátir de Anghiera, or Anglería, we can infer that blacks already existed on that continent [Central America] before the ones who were introduced by the Spaniards and perhaps even before Columbus discovered America. The author assures us that when Núñez de Balboa made his famous expedition in 1513 to discover the South Sea,

he already found blacks there. He says as follows: "There they found black slaves in a distant region two days' journey from Quarequa. This region only produces ferocious and cruel blacks. It can be concluded that because they were thieves, they had come at some other time from Ethiopia, and because their ship had sunk they settled in this wilderness. Great internal hatred existed between the Quarequanos [Indians] and those blacks and they alternately enslaved and killed each other."

No historian of the Americas has given this passage of Pedro Mátir the importance it deserves. Three things should be noted in it: first, whether such black people existed; second, whether Núñez de Balboa found some of these enslaved when in 1513 he went to discover the South Sea; and third, where they had come from.[1]

Saco proceeds to cite, apart from *De Orbe Nove* (1587), the works of López Gomara, Juan Ochoa de Saldo, Juan Rotero, and Bartolomé de las Casas. Referring here to towns in Darien, the northern section of the Isthmus of Panama, Saco confesses that the presence of Blacks is a mystery for him. But he attempts to explain it with disastrous consequences.

Las Casas supports an early Black presence, as Saco recognizes. When describing an expedition by Vasco Núñez, Las Cas to King Quarequa who resisted the Spaniards. The "Indians" were obliterated, and "the Black king and lord was killed with his important subjects." Furthermore, Saco shows that Gonzalo Fernández de Ovideo also supports this, claiming that a Spanish explorer journeyed near the area and was told that "certain people who were black lived there." Herrera, another explorer of the time, also mentions this, stating that "Blacks lived there who had managed to save themselves from the ship."[2] From this Saco rightly concludes that despite a conspiracy of silence on the part of some historians, Black people did exist and might have come from Africa. But Saco does not feel that "savage Blacks" were capable of making such a journey, either from East or West Africa. He posits, therefore, that they came from Polynesia.

Of course, it is more than likely that Spaniards thought the Indians were Blacks. It is also equally likely that Black people did make

1. José Antonio Saco, *Historia de la esclavitud de la raza Africana en el nuevo mundo y en especial en los países Americano-Hispanos* (Havana, 1938), I, 118n2.
2. *Ibid.*, 118–19, 119–20, 121–22.

the journey from Africa and that they indeed shared the New World with indigenous inhabitants (the so-called Indians) before they were discovered by Columbus. Whatever the tentative conclusion, the base for Africa as the source of culture in the New World must surely begin with this historical interrogative.

Long before the introduction of the slave trade, Africans came as explorers. John Hope Franklin argues:

> Even if Pedro Alfonso Niño of the crew of Columbus was not a Negro as has been claimed, there were many Negroes who accompanied other European explorers to the New World. . . . Thirty Negroes, including Nuflo de Olano, were with Balboa when he discovered the Pacific Ocean. Cortés carried Negroes with him into Mexico and one of them planted and harvested the first wheat crop in the New World. Two Negroes accompanied Velas in 1520. When Alvarado went to Quito, he carried two hundred Negroes with him. They were with Pizarro on his Peruvian expedition and carried him to the Cathedral after he was murdered.[3]

In addition, Blacks were with the Spanish and Portuguese explorers as they moved into North America. Estevanico, or Little Stephen, was instrumental in pioneering entry into New Mexico and Arizona. Blacks helped the French open up Canada and the Mississippi valley, as Franklin points out. He adds that "it is not without ironical significance that Negroes were thus extensively engaged in the task of opening the New World for European exploitation."[4]

Therefore, the New World became a physical extension of Africa and hence, a cultural and literary one. Where early settlers and explorers left off, slaves were to continue. Maureen Warner, in an excellent article on Africans in nineteenth-century Trinidad, shows just how cultural mores were preserved after emancipation in this British colony in 1834. "The slaves deserted the plantations after apprenticeship and set up in villages which often skirted the plantations. There they reverted to patterns of life to which they were traditionally accustomed. For most African societies, particularly the ones from which many of the slaves came, life centered around agriculture. Their association with the land was further cemented by the agricultural emphasis of New World plantation existence. . . . Their link with the

3. John Hope Franklin, *From Slavery to Freedom* (3rd ed.; New York, 1969), 46, 46–47, 47.
4. *Ibid.*, 47.

land had never been broken, nor for those enterprising West African and Congolese women, their love of trade and bargaining." Kru (from Liberia), Coromanti and Ashanti (from Ghana), Yoruba, Ibo, Fula, and Hausa (from Nigeria), various groups from the Congo (including Nsundi, Mbama, Luba and Wanda)—all lived side by side in nineteenth-century Trinidad. Warner continues that, "home—the site of the buried navel string—is of such pivotal importance to the African psyche that African cultures have generally found ritual methods of returning to its psychic centre the spirit of the man who dies far from home."[5] This ritual is a very important way of preserving the culture of the group, and an examination of the group's literature confirms that the New World had become an extension of Africa.

A few other examples should suffice to show the variation of African groups within the New World. Philip Curtin accounts for sixteen groups from West Africa, eight from Central Africa, and three from Southeastern Africa, all located in Mexico and imported towards the end of the seventeenth century. Between 1771 and 1780, nineteen different groups from West and Central Africa were in Haiti and the Dominican Republic. On a single sugar estate in Surinam in 1690, there were twelve different groups. Frequently, the groups included individuals who were called Senegambia, Ginea, Congo-Angola, or Mozambique, which would indicate even greater variations. "The United States," Curtin states, "was only a marginal recipient of slaves from Africa. The real center of the trade was tropical America, with almost 90 percent going to the Atlantic fringe from Brazil through the Guianas to the Caribbean coast and islands." This is the very area of our concern. Because "more Africans than Europeans arrived in the Americas between, say, 1492 and 1770," and did not total "less than 8,000,000 or more than 10,500,000" by Curtin's conservative assessment, it is therefore possible to assert quite definitely that, independent of early Black inhabitants or explorers, the New World was demographically African a century and a half ago.[6]

These facts have large ramifications for this study, because they

5. Maureen Warner, "Africans in Nineteenth-Century Trinidad," in *African Studies Association of the West Indies Bulletin*, No. 5, n.d., pp. 30, 48.

6. Philip D. Curtin, *The Atlantic Slave Trade: A Census* (Madison, 1969), Table 32, p. 113; Table 56, p. 193; Table 53, p. 189; pp. 89, 87.

indicate the possibility of retaining the culture, though in a different form. Because of the relatively small number of Whites, there were at that time few alternative cultural modes. True enough, the White was master, but the slaves ate, worked, and slept together. Necessity formulated a *modus vivendi* that would accommodate differing ethnic patterns and relate itself to the White world.

II

African culture, therefore, managed to preserve itself by its sheer volume. Synthesis took place, first, within the cultures that were more closely related to each other and, later, through the process by which Blacks tended to define themselves in terms of their similarities with one another and their differences from overseer and slave master.

Despite being numerically superior, the Black man was "qualitatively inferior," and thus European White cultures constantly sought to make inroads. Resistance took the form of suicide, uprisings, and revolt, of which Haiti is the supreme example. But the separatism that escaped slaves practiced was equally important to ensure culture protraction. In Brazil, Africans escaped from enslavement and established *quilombos* along the lines of the village system they knew, and so they created, in Palmares, perhaps the best example of a separatist state.[7] In Jamaica, the Maroons set up their own settlements in hill country; in Bequia (a small island near Saint Vincent) Africans from a shipwrecked slaver intermarried, feuded with the Caribs, and had a separate state well into the latter part of the eighteenth century.[8] In Surinam, the Djuka provide another interesting example of cultural autonomy. Escaped slaves, they established their own towns and laws in the hinterland. Melville and Frances Herskovits found a great deal of interrelationship between the language and culture of those whom they termed "Town Negroes" and those whom they termed "Bush Negroes" (the Djuka). For instance, they gave a phonetic transcript of how Ba Tiger enslaved Ba Toad.

There were Ba Tiger and Ba Rabbit. Then Ba Toad was sitting on the road. Then Ba Tiger was passing. Then Ba Toad asked him, said, if he

7. Nina Rodrigues, *Os Africanos no Brasil* (São Paulo, 1932), 111–43, and Arthur Ramos, *The Negro in Brazil* (Washington, D.C., 1939), 42–57.
8. William Young, *A History of the Black Caribs in St. Vincent* (London, 1975),

wouldn't loan him a little money? He said to him, said, he would pay him back when he grew up. Tiger said to him, said, "Yes." Then Ba Rabbit said to Tiger now, said, Ba Toad isn't going to pay him, because Ba Toad won't be able to earn money. He won't grow up any more. Little as he is, so he will remain. His mother and his father are like that. Then when Ba Tiger met Ba Toad he took him away with him, because he was his slave. He took him because he was a slave for the debt.[9]

Ba Rabbit obviously belongs to the separatist Djuka element. The moral of his lesson was meant to help propagate values and ensure the longevity of the "fugitives." Their journey to freedom had taken them up the Marowijne River, past the Arminavellan Falls and into safe villages. Surinam had been Dutch since 1667, and for over a century the Dutch had unsuccessfully attempted to recapture the Africans. Finally, they gave up and signed a peace treaty in 1761. The Africans numbered 25,000; their lot had at least been better than that of the Blacks in Palmares and Saint Vincent, who were constantly in conflict with the Europeans. In Florida they were to seek shelter with fleeing Indians and set up villages in the Everglades. The sorry tale repeated itself throughout this area.

In West Africa, secret societies were an important means of passing on the culture. In the New World, when separatism was not possible, secret societies flourished. For instance, in Bahia Province in Brazil, the *candomblé* was a "highly complex organization of ritual and belief."[10] Basically it was centered around the perpetuation of Yoruba and Ewe beliefs that were fused together.[11] Various *seitas* (shrines) were located in several places, dedicated to different *orishas* (Yoruba gods), each of whom had his specific day, food, colors, dress, and praise songs. As in Yoruba land, he could manifest himself to a person and take possession. The *seita* was in charge of a *pae de santo* or *mae de santo* (father or mother of the *orishas*), which is close to the Yoruba *babalawo* (diviner), or "father of mysteries."[12]

123, 125. Also see Elsa Goveia, *A Study of the Historiography of the British West Indies to the End of the Nineteenth Century* (Mexico City, 1956), 37.

9. Melville J. Herskovits and Frances S. Herskovits, *Suriname Folklore* (New York, 1936), 158–59.

10. Donald Dickson, *Negroes in Brazil* (Chicago, 1942), 275.

11. Rodrigues, *Os Africanos no Brasil*, 320.

12. For a scholarly study of the Yoruba pantheon, consult E. Bolaji Idowu, *Olódumaré: God in Yoruba Belief* (London, 1962).

African religious and cultural expression took root in Cuba in the Ñañiguismo secret society. Lemuel Johnson comments: "There was a force, a *ñanga*, which infused and animated all visible phenomena. There is thus a *ñanga* of trees, of rocks and the like. This all pervading force could be harnessed for good or for evil. There are charms, *embo* or *mayumba*, which determine how to use and direct that force."[13] Janheinz Jahn, in *Muntu*, makes the connection with the repository of African religion.

> In Cuba, as in Yoruba-land, Bon Dieu is called Olorun. But since the absolute transcends all human understanding, no temples are built to Olorun either in Yoruba-land or in Cuba, and no sacrifices made to him. On the other hand, the life force of the creator is thought to be present in all creatures and in all things, especially in the *orisha*, who in Yoruba-land were originally human beings, important ancestors from whom the Yoruba people are descended. Their extensive spiritual and physical progeny demonstrates that they are forces, life forces, which share, just as you and I do, the primal life force.[14]

Here again, the parallels are present. One need only observe a Yoruba shrine or festival in Nigeria, and several ceremonies in the New World become meaningful. In English-speaking Guyana the food that was left for the "fair maid" was really an offering to Yemayá, embodiment of the sea. Yemayá, associated in Cuba with the Virgen de Regla, represents one of the more interesting aspects of Afro-Cuban culture, in which it underwent the stages previously described. This included the blending of African cultures into *Lucumí*, their acculturation, and finally their acceptance, not only by the Roman Catholic church, but by White Cubans in whose *botánicas* in Miami Christian saints and African gods stand together. Their worship, termed *santería*, is yet another factor in African colonizing of the New World, and along with Haitian voodoo constitutes the most important.

On the religious and popular levels, Africa continues to live in Cuba. As we have seen, religion is present in *santería* and *brujería* (or *mayombé*). Black nurses helped transfer their culture to the White

13. Lemuel Johnson, *The Devil, the Gargoyle and the Buffoon* (Port Washington, 1969), 140.
14. Janheinz Jahn, *Muntu: An Outline of Neo-African Culture* (New York, 1961), 63, 70–78.

world. Children were told of their African past while adults learned of remedies and herbs. The reverence accorded to the wilderness, or *monte*, and to the *orishas* who inhabited the moss tree and the royal palm tree was imitated by Whites and incorporated into their own beliefs. The gods explained the world of nature and affirmed its presence. Through ritual, the Yoruba language preserved the integrity of the religion. The drums remained, for they heralded the gods. When possession then occurred, man became god. Stones that contained the spirits of the ancestors and the gods were preserved. As a result there was no death, because the life force continued to exist in stones.

To be fully initiated as a *santero*, or priest, a novice must first have a series of necklaces woven for him. Each necklace, with appropriate numbers of beads for the specific *orishas*, is worn. Seven necklaces are used, and Obatala, Oshún, Yemayá, and Shango are the essential *orishas* represented. For initiation of priests, white is worn and the head is covered. So one must bear in mind the religious nature of all this, as well as the voodoo, when considering the chants and folklore. Of course, with *santería*, unlike *brujería*, a child is baptized before going through the African ceremonies. No contradiction is seen in the belief in African and European gods. Association is made through common symbols, functions, or accompanying legends.

The *santero* is an ordinary priest; the *babalawo* is the spokesman for the oracle. Neither was foreign to the Roman Catholic church, since exorcism was as much a part of Catholicism as of *santería* or *brujería*. The correlation is surely in the acceptance of mystery and magic and the attempt on the part of people to understand themselves and others. Offerings to saints and gods, belief in an afterlife, and ceremonies to mark birth and death are part of Catholicism and African religions.

Early churchmen effected a compromise between the two religions. They felt, both in Cuba and Brazil, that this was one way in which they could bring the two worlds together. What perhaps they could not foresee was, first, that this would help preserve the African religion and the African way of life and, second, that as a result, Roman Catholicism would be seriously altered for all in these countries.[15]

15. These facts were expressed in lectures by Father Augustin Roman at St. Bren-

Fernando Ortiz, author of *Los negros brujos* (1906), and Lydia Cabrera, author of *El Monte* (1954), are the two authorities on Afro-Cuban cultural survivals in the New World. These two writers suffer from some obvious prejudices. Ortiz, though well informed, is a product of his time and is not averse to viewing the Afro-Cubans as "savages" and their religion as "heathen." Cabrera has entered much more sympathetically into the Black gods or *orishas* who inhabit the jungle and hilly places of Cuba—the *monte*.

In addition to Spanish, Blacks in Cuba speak some seven different African languages, including Yoruba and several languages within the Bantu group. Why Yoruba (or Lucumí, as it is called in Cuba) predominates is not an easy question to answer. Curtin does not show any substantial number of Yorubas from Nigeria between 1817 and 1843.[16] However, Yorubas probably did exceed numerically any other group in Cuba; so that when the primary synthesis took place between, say, Africans from Congo and those from Nigeria, there was a preponderance of Yoruba words, beliefs, attitudes, customs, and religion. Cabrera refers to this context as *sincretismo congo-lucumí*.[17]

Not many Cubans, let alone Caribbean people, realized the cultural implications of the secondary synthesism, especially as it extended into, and related itself with, the White world. Cuban Spanish has borrowed not only words from African languages but its music, such as the *son*, the rhumba, and *guaguancó* (with its spontaneity, background drums, and singing). It is with religion—*brujería* (which is authentically African) and *santería* (in which the synthesis with Europe takes place)—that one sees the greatest expression of Black Cuban thought.

Religion survived and perpetuated African culture because it effected a compromise. Blacks changed the names of gods or, rather, alternated the names with those of Christian saints. They altered the sexes of their African gods, distorted their functions, and fused their mythology as deliberate devices for survival. This is why one becomes impatient with Fernando Ortiz, despite his excellent pio-

---

dan's School, Miami, Florida, on September 26, 1974, and Father Sosa at Florida International University on October 21, 1974.
16. Curtin, *Atlantic Slave Trade*, 247.
17. Lydia Cabrera, *El Monte* (Miami, 1971), 134.

neering work. He sees international distortion as poor pronunciation, and cites Saint Hubert and Saint Albert as cases of obvious confusion of roles. His love-hate relationship with *brujería* causes him to attack the religion throughout his book and to support police raids that were made on the *brujeros*. At one stage he argues that since Blacks could not comprehend the doctrine of purgatory and hell, they "confused Satan with the souls in purgatory and could not make their vulgar concepts of these subjects of dogma more subtle and thus in forming their iconographical equivalents make great mistakes."[18] Hence, at the base of his book *Los negros brujos* is the absurd theme of Catholicism as manufacturer of a New World African religion.

Certainly there was confusion, as Cabrera demonstrates, but the survivals demonstrate to an amazing degree, much cohesiveness. For instance, in orthodox Yoruba belief, Olorun or Olódùmaré is the high god. He was removed and apart, "not represented by an idol of any kind." In fact, because the high god had no *practical* function to perform, he disappeared, as Rodrigues confirms in referring to Blacks in Bahia, Brazil. He is not found in Cuba either. Both Rodrigues and Ortiz agree on a number of points, for example, that Obatala, Shango, and Ifa are among the primary gods; that there are numerous secondary gods; and that the wearing of amulets and other ornaments constitutes a specific part of the worship of the gods. A hierarchy of priests existed. Ortiz disagrees with Rodrigues by stating that priests took advantage of the common people's ignorance and seduced women by blackmail. This, according to him, was sanctioned by African custom, in which "women are slaves."

Rodrigues does not see the Portuguese in the way that Ortiz views the Spanish, as being more humane to slaves than the Dutch and English were. This will be discussed in a subsequent chapter, for despite the recent contentions of the latter-day slave authorities, I contend that the denial of freedom cannot have degrees. One is either free or not free; slavery was bad in all aspects. It does little for those who would advocate Spanish clemency to recall that Spain did not fervently clamor for abolition.

Although Ortiz authoritatively describes the religious practices of

18. Fernándo Ortiz, *Los negros brujos* (Miami, 1963 [1906]), 29.

Black Cubans, he adopts a moralistic attitude. "The intellectual re-
tardation which made many Whites descend to the point of having
faith in the *embós* and made them maintain within their own [non-
African] cults emblems which would mark them as fetishes—made
them become believers in idols. This dragged them down to their belief in the divinatory powers of these African magicians."[19] Lydia
Cabrera, though not as naïve as Ortiz, seems very puzzled about the
validity of the Black cultural impact. "In Cuba *santería* was always
widespread although it was usually a well-kept secret. Now it is out
in the open, especially in Miami. I've known many people, some of
them belonging to Cuba's most respectable families who believed
and practiced *santería*. It was simply incredible; some of them had
lived in Europe for decades and still kept their sacred rocks and amulets. Such was the enormous influence of the Blacks in Cuba on
White society and culture."[20] Of course it ought not to be surprising, for if we go along with the argument that the presence of Blacks
was a process of cultural colonization, then obviously, Whites would
be affected by their presence.

The Whites absorbed the culture for a number of reasons. Black
was a powerful force, despite the debilitating nature of the Black experience in the New World. The indifference of Spaniards (and Europeans in general) to their own religion, and their materialistic quest
for gold and sugar profits, left them exposed to new cultural attachments. Life in the Caribbean for most Europeans had, in the early
stages, a temporary nature; the slave was there for life. Ortiz points
out that the occult was obviously not unknown to Spaniards, and
books of this nature were widely read in the New World. Furthermore, as Black adaptations of Christianity ably demonstrated, the
origin of man, mortality, and the significance and meaning of gods,
all had parallel places in African and European thought. In addition, since church and state were equated, it is not unlikely that,
especially with the Spanish-American wars, many Caribbean territories no longer felt any linkage with the Christian church. True
enough, the physical church was there, but the oral tradition of the
Africans was too strong to resist. So, as Ortiz states, "The slaves continued to practice their beliefs in the sugar mills with the consent of

19. *Ibid.*, 171.
20. Lydia Cabrera, interviewed by author, in Miami, Florida, November 12, 1974.

their masters. They were allowed to have altars with St. Barbara, the Virgen de Regla, etc. . . . St. Barbara was not St. Barbara for Blacks but the orisha Shango, and the Virgen de Regla was Yemayá."[21] Masters exerted a *physical* control, but the slaves retained a *spiritual* dominance. Preservation of the group—the necessity for the perpetuation of a familiar religion—was their most insistent reason and existed throughout the New World.

Rodrigues shows that, in Brazil, Obatala, the creator of God, was associated with Christ and Saint Anna, the mother of the Virgin Mary; Ortiz shows that, in Cuba, Obatala was the Virgin de las Mercedes and Jesus Christ. The logic of the equation need not concern us, although it is there. Instead, what is important is that Obatala was preserved. In both Cuba and Brazil, Shango, god of lightning and thunder, was Saint Barbara, saint of storms; in Bahia, the god's wives are Oyá (the Niger), Oshún, and Oba. Obvious sexual confusion might seem to occur here, but it was intentional distortion. For Africans to preserve their heritage, Shango had to have an androgynous association. It was easy to do this with Obatala, who in strict Yoruba theology had such an origin. But with Shango no such authority existed in the Yoruba canon. Other attributes were given him in Afro-Cuban theology. "The most popular of the *orishas* is Shango. 'Alafi-Alafi, king of Oyo and king of kings.' Shango or St. Barbara is inseparable from the most beautiful and evocative tree in Cuba. 'Where you find the palm tree, there you find Shango, breaking the branches and planting as if he were in the tower of his *ilé olódun* [castle].'"[22] Shango is not an image of Saint Barbara; Saint Barbara is Shango, and far from being syncretic this is a blatant assertion of African belief. Indeed, the Christian saint pays homage to the primary African deity.

Ifa, the great oracle of the Yorubas, is personified in the New World as "the one who reveals the occults." Probably because of the secret nature of the oracular manifestations, there is no European equivalent. Ortiz comments that "Nina Rodrigues [in Brazil] does not cite a Catholic saint which is similar to Ifa nor have I been able to find one."[23] Naturally this is so; the Blacks of the New World needed secret ties to bind them together.

21. Ortiz, *Los negros brujos*, 153.
22. Cabrera, *El Monte*, 129.
23. Ortiz, *Los negros brujos*, 34.

Yemayá is important. She is worshiped in Brazil as Our Lady of Candeias and in Cuba as the Virgen de Regla. Jahn rightly argues that in Yoruba land Yemayá is the sea itself, and disagrees with Arthur Ramos that she is goddess of rivers and springs.[24] Osho-oshi is god of the hunters, armed with a bow and arrow; the worshipers have power over snakes. In Bahia, Osho-oshi is naturally equated with Saint George, for slaves had seen representations of Saint George fighting a dragon on horseback. The correlation between a dragon and a snake was not difficult to make.

Ogun, Shango's brother and god of war and fighting, is the *orisha* of iron. Saint Peter kept the keys (equated with iron) of heaven and so it follows, in Cuba and Haiti, that Ogun is Saint Peter. In Brazil, he is Saint Anthony. Oshún, one of Shango's wives, is the Virgen de la Caridad del Cobre in Cuba. Here again there is an obvious association, since as patroness of sailors, the Virgen guided them safely, much as the Yoruba Oshún as goddess of a river. In Cuba, Ortiz writes, Oshún and Shango meet in dance "and surrender themselves to a fervent dance of love in an unconcealed and incomparable imitation of carnal lust."[25] With this Jahn correctly disagrees. "In the Yoruba tradition in Africa, however, Oshun and Shango never meet. The Shango-Oshun dance would be impossible in the country where the cult originated, since the embodiment of the orisha takes place one at a time in strict serial order."[26]

Other examples are Orunmila, who is Saint Francis of Assisi in Cuba, and Olorun, who is John the Baptist. Babaluaye is the god of infectious diseases; his obvious Christian counterpart is Saint Lazarus. Cabrera describes Osein as "diviner and lord of the jungle areas and the *monte* as well as the vegetation." He is associated with the earth and has a large head, one foot, one eye, and one large deaf ear and another small and extremely sensitive ear. He leaps as he walks, and he seems to correspond to the Wan Foot Jumbie whom Creoles of Sierra Leone took back with them to Africa from the New World. Here an interesting process has taken place. The god traveled to the

24. Jahn, *Muntu*, 67–68.
25. Fernándo Ortiz, *Los bailes y el teatro de los negros en el folklore de Cuba* (Havana, 1951), 260.
26. Jahn, *Muntu*, 67–68.

New World, underwent alteration, and then returned to Africa where he changed again. The Wan Foot Jumbie is therefore a New World creation, reexported to Africa. According to Cabrera, Osein's symbol is a rod or arrow with a round disc or ball with six feathers, three vultures, and three owls.[27] Such details apply to the separate symbols of identification for each god.

Eshu, perhaps the supreme cultural link in the Black world, is the trickster god in Yoruba belief. He was very necessary in the New World, where "slave cunning" formed an everyday part of the existence of Africans. His lay equivalents are legion: Anancy in Jamaica and other parts of the Caribbean; High John de Conquer, Stagolee, Shine, and the Signifying Monkey in Afro-American folklore.[28] But it must be reiterated that in Yoruba land Eshu is a god, and like other *orishas* he has to be placated. He is responsible for strange quirks of misfortune, but his clownish quality is conspicuous in the New World, as Jahn comments.

> The dancer who is possessed or "mounted" by Eshu wears a red and black jacket, a red and black cap as tall as a chief's, and knee breeches in the same colours decorated on the knee band and belt with shells, pearls and bells. His dance is grotesque. He makes faces, plays with a top or with marbles, steals the hats of the onlookers, takes the cigarettes out of their mouths, waggles his buttocks and hips.... At the same time he hops and turns on one leg, improvises capriciously, and surprises and delights the spectators by his acrobatics and his virtuosity.[29]

This probably amused the slave master, and thus Eshu remained altered and transformed, perhaps even in aspects of Papa Legba in Haiti.

However, New World Blacks saw to it that Eshu had his parallel in Christian theology—the devil. Ortiz rightly disagrees, stating that "Nina Rodrigues makes an accidental identity between Eshu and Ogun"; but he wrongly argues that whereas Ogun is benevolent, Eshu is malevolent.[30] Certainly, his Christian namesake is Satan in

---

27. Cabrera, *El Monte*, 70, 134.
28. For a good discussion of some Afro-American folk heroes see Roger Abrahams, *Deep Down in the Jungle* (Chicago, 1970), Arna Bontemps and Langston Hughes, *The Book of Negro Folklore* (New York, 1958), and Zora Neale Hurston, *Mules and Men* (Philadelphia, 1938).
29. Jahn, *Muntu*, 64.
30. Ortiz, *Los negros brujos*, 35.

Brazil and he represents the souls in purgatory in Cuba, not the devil, as Jahn states. But this does not make him malevolent, and he is worshiped secretly in both Bahia and Cuba. The New World Blacks carried on an important African tradition that has confused these researchers; for in Yoruba land "to identify Eshu with evil is to misunderstand the basic principles of Yoruba philosophy" as well as to confuse the principles of New World Black theology.[31] For neither good nor evil is personified in Eshu but instead are recognized as forces operating in the world; the worshiper therefore placates.

III

A voodoo ceremony in Haiti recognizes the need to operate within a world in which good and evil intermingle. Voodoo influenced *brujería* and *santería*, although Ortiz contends that "these [roots] are only superficial and only in the Eastern province [Oriente] owing to the immigration of numerous planters and Haitian Blacks." At the time of the Haitian revolution, White planters left with their slaves for Cuba, Jamaica, and Louisiana. Yet voodoo survived in a distorted form, and Ortiz adds that "sacrifice is made to them [the voodoo gods or *loas*] out of necessity for being in good relationship with them."[32] This does not accurately describe voodoo, which is a form of African worship as complex as *brujería* and *santería*.

A process of multiple syncretism occurs with voodoo in Cuba. It is properly Haitian and is basically Dahomean, although Yoruba, Ibo, Congo, and other ethnic groups contributed to it.[33] It is "the rites, beliefs and practices of the Vodoun cult built around the similar religious systems of the Dahomeans and the Nagos [Yorubas]."[34] Jean Price-Mars gave voodoo respectability. As he points out in *Ainsi parla l'oncle* (1929), voodoo had a distinct theology; there were gods, or *loas*, priests, worshipers, temples, altars, and a ritual preserved by the oral tradition.[35] It has already been mentioned that this oral tra-

31. Ulli Beier, *Sacred Wood Carvings from One Small Yoruba Town* (Lagos, 1957), 9.
32. Ortiz, *Los negros brujos*, 47–48.
33. Harold Courlander, *The Drum and the Hoe: Life and Lore of the Haitian People* (Berkeley, 1960), 317.
34. *Ibid.*, 8.
35. Jean Price-Mars, *Ainsi parla l'oncle: essais d'ethnographie* (New York, 1954), 32–37.

dition was the supreme cultural counterbalance to the book learning of Europeans. In Haiti's case there were not only always large numbers of Blacks, but the terrain was difficult and Europeans never had more than a toehold in the island; thus the lengths to which Afro-Cubans had to resort for preservation were unnecessary. Of course, Spain had slave laws dating from 1680 that encouraged Blacks to escape from Dutch and English territories and seek refuge in New Spain, where they would be saved by the Spanish church and state. Likewise, France's Code Noir attempted to repress African religious practices, but it was even less rigidly administered in Haiti, Guadeloupe, and Martinique than in Spanish areas.

Primary synthesism occurred out of necessity, but the secondary synthesism—the association with Europe—was not so necessary. A few cases can be cited: Papa Legba, comparable in some measure to Eshu because he is a lame old man, corresponds with Saint Christopher; Damballa, who lives in swamps and springs, is a combination of Moses and Saint Peter; Erzulie Doba, a sea goddess, is the Virgin Mary; and Ayida Wedo is Saint Patrick. There the correspondences end, despite the numerous *loas*. All that occurred in voodoo was a remodeling of an African form into a new Black religion that suited the Caribbean.

Hence we have the comparisons with *brujería*. Cabrera spoke of how, in Cuba, "the Black man spiritually penetrates the jungle which is the heart of the *monte*. No doubt the direct contact which he establishes with supernatural forces there, in its own dominions, surrounds him. Whatever space of the *monte* is there one can perceive an invisible and sometimes a visible force or spirit. He considers this very sacred. 'The Monte is sacred.' Because in it resides the divinity."[36] It should come as no surprise, then, to discover that the Black men of Haiti also peopled their landscape with African gods. "In addition to having homes in Africa or below the water, most *loa* have special residing places in Haiti, such as stones, caves, waterfalls or springs. One may come across a boulder or a bamboo grove sacred to a certain *loa*, and food offerings are likely to be seen there. Many *loas* are identified with some specific variety of tree

36. Cabrera, *El Monte*, 1.

and will 'inhabit' all such trees throughout the country."[37] So Papa Legba, the interpreter of the gods, and he who must be invoked first in a voodoo ceremony, dwells at the crossroads. Damballa, a Dahomean import, lives in watery places; his symbols are the snake and the rainbow. Agwé Woyo is ruler of the seas; Erzulie Doba and Simbi Dleau, whose symbol is the snake, are near fresh water. The synthetic process included the Ibo; Takwa, for instance, is a manifestation that speaks unknown tongues, and Congo Savane, a man-eater, fierce and strong, pounds people to death in his mortar.[38]

Certain concepts are mutually held by voodoo and *brujería* worshipers. Certain *loas*, though conceived as one, manifest themselves in seven moods. The Arara cult in Cuba shares this. "Dambala remains one of the chief gods of the Dahomey cult in Cuba," Courlander tells us; and he adds that "he survived into the last century in New Orleans." Papa Legba "is remembered elsewhere in the New World, notably in Dutch Guiana [Surinam], Brazil and Cuba. Until recently he was known among the Negroes of Louisiana by the name of Papa Lebat."[39] Ogun Feraille is of course a part of Ogun himself, and we have already noted his active presence in Cuba.

So an ingenious process is observed here. Africa exports a religion; it is recollected in a dismembered form and put together by New World Blacks in their response to the needs of intermingled African ethnic groups. Then the primary synthetic form of the religion is exported to another Caribbean island, where it comes into contact with another African religion that has developed independently under different pressures and evolved into a secondary synthetic form. Thus a semicolonizing process extends itself.

My recent observation of a voodoo ceremony showed how the African cultures had absorbed what they wanted of the European with little apparent strain. Candles were used for the worship of Damballa on Tuesday, the day reserved for him. Drumming by male performers at the end of a circle set the mood. Some female novices about to be initiated, and other women, danced counterclockwise;

37. Courlander, *The Drum and the Hoe*, 21.
38. *Ibid.*, 317–31.
39. *Ibid.*, 27, 318, 321.

the novices wore red and white, and the initiates wore Damballa's color, white, with their heads covered.

As with an African ceremony, dancing, chanting, and drumming formed part of the routine. Intricate steps were executed as the dancers circled. Then came a sudden interjection from Europe—a kneeling motion and a sign of the cross (of course, Papa Legba's symbol is a cross, representing the divine and the mortal). The incantation from the *houngan* (priest) and a *hounsi* (spirit wife) came; the drums became silent. The ceremony now resembled the liturgy of a Christian mass. Amid the singing of Creole voices, the name María was clearly heard. She has her African counterpart in Erzulie Doba, the beautiful sea goddess.

The pattern of dancing now changed. No longer together, women danced singly, turning in one direction and holding the hem of their dresses. The emphasis in the dance shifted to the men. A male initiate appeared with a sword (was this symbolic of the sword that had pierced the heart, symbol of Erzulie Doba?). Then the *houngan* with his gourd of beads rang a bell. Two women were in the center—one with a red flag, the other with a light blue one. It seemed as if some crisis were about to happen; then the dancing started again. Suddenly and inexplicably, a woman fell in violent convulsions to the mud floor. A fire had been lit in the center, and her bare feet came in contact with it. The *houngan* above her seemed to control her every movement, leading her, with eyes staring into distant nothingness, to the center of the circle. There the god mounted her and she became the vehicle of the *loa*. Through her the god could act and speak.

The *houngan* had a potion that he used; he spat around the circle. Another woman became possessed; leaves were brushed on her body. She rolled herself on the ground, a basket of fire on her head. Then the dancing started again, but more solemn and subdued this time, as the sacrificial goat was brought into the circle with candles on its horns. There was chanting and singing and then the sacrifice, blood dripping into a bowl.

Flags had been draped over the women who had been possessed. They lay almost in a state of coma until they were moved out of the

circle and beyond the designs that had been scrupulously made for Damballa on the mud floor. The intricate designs had been almost completely erased by the steps of the exultant dancers.

The ending was triumphant. One had a feeling of having participated in joy. The drums quickened their pulse and at one end of the circle the priestess waved her flag triumphantly. There was no more singing, only the heavy, intensive sound of the drum. At this point, if one looked at the entire *hounfor*, designed by the *houngan*, one could observe a central pole supporting a straw roof through which the *loa* had come. There was a small building nearby containing the serpent and rainbow paintings of Damballa, iron crosses, dishes, and bowls. The uninitiated were not allowed to inspect the altar.

I had seen, but I had not understood, for I was an outsider. Voodoo permeates all of intimate Haitian life—initiation, birth, death, illness, and even crops. Bon Dieu is supreme, but the African *loas* must first be supplicated.

Just as I had not understood all that had taken place, there were many Westernized Haitians who had failed to come to terms with their culture. Jean Price-Mars recognized the necessity to teach them about their own past. He had studied medicine and anthropology in Paris. He knew of the work of Black Americans and the Harlem Renaissance, and he saw the beginnings of the négritude movement of the Senegalese Léopold Sédar Senghor, the Guianese Léon Damas, and the Martinican Aimé Césaire.[40] Their work complemented each other's. These authors all had in common one belief—Africa was the source. As a scholar Price-Mars "invites Haitian thinkers and writers to free themselves from the prejudice which binds and constrains them to a servile imitation of the French and to make use of the materials within their reach."[41] This was necessary, for few Haitians, though voodoo was secretly practiced, wished to be reminded of the past which surrounded them. When he pointed out that Haitians had "un complexe psychologique qui donne à la com-

40. In *La relève*, Jean Price-Mars published three articles; in the first he commented on the impact of the Harlem Renaissance on music (July, 1932). His second article focused on James Weldon Johnson and W. E. B. Du Bois (August, 1932), and his third discussed the work of Jessie Fauset, Du Bois, Claude McKay, Johnson, Langston Hughes and Countee Cullen (September, 1932).

41. Naomi Garret, *The Renaissance of Haitian Poetry* (Paris, 1963), 63.

munauté haitienne sa physionomie spécifique," Westernized Haitians were naturally surprised that an *évolué* should opt so clearly and categorically for the culture of the bush.[42]

This indeed is what began to happen with Ortiz, as his later works demonstrate; by the time Price-Mars followed, the so-called Harlem Renaissance, which was to influence large corners of the Black world, was in full swing. The significance of Black literary output as a result of these ethnographical studies may not be disputed, and interest developed in Black folklore and in the imitation of Black rhythms. One considers it imperative to mention that André Gide's *Voyage au Congo*, Eugene O'Neill's *Emperor Jones*, Stravinsky's experimentations with ragtime music, and Picasso's blatant copying of African sculpture had much to do with the validity of Afro-New World artists seeking legitimacy in this pursuit. Minds like those of W. E. B. Du Bois, Alain Locke, and James Weldon Johnson charted the perimeters.

The result was the increase of interest in Afro-New World folklore. The colonized had altered the cultural vision of the colonizer. The extent to which they did this is apparent in the difference between the literature of the Old World metropole and the New World provinces. Folklore must be our main area of concern in order to see the manner in which the Afro-New World person comes to terms with his challenging experiences.

42. Price-Mars, Preface, *Ainsi parla l'oncle*, i–ii.

2 Oral Literature and the Reality of Africa

Afro-New World men conceived of their abodes in the New World as extensions of Africa. For them Africa was real and a part of where they lived and belonged now. This is most evident in Cuba and Brazil, where one not only finds actual statements of forgotten African tongues but also restatements within the format of African lore.

The Cuban *guagauncó* exists on the popular level, although it contains religious references. This is the most African of all Cuban musical genres and consists mainly of background drums and a singer who sways as he performs. The *guaguancó* exhibits an early stage of the synthesis, termed *primary transculturation*, or the blend of African ethnic cultures relatively untouched by European contact. On the other hand, the *son* is in the state of *secondary transculturation*, in which European and African sounds come together. It is characterized by repetitive rhythms incorporated with North American jazz.

Celeste Mendoza is well known in Cuba for her rendition of the *guaguancó*.[1] In one of her songs, the singer, a streetwalker, relates her infidelity to her husband. There is a solo and chorus effect in which the chorus asks the name of the singer. In another, the singer describes her jealous husband who would not let her go to the carnival. These themes, taken from everyday life, have much in common with North American blues. The bongo is used, and the rhythmic variations have names like *columbia* and *yambu*. Guaguancós, originally from Oriente Province, are now usually played in the back-

1. Celeste Mendoza, *Celeste Mendoza*, Rumba Record Recording; Roberto Maza, Panart Records, LP 2055.

yards in Cuba—the *solares*—basic, Black urban units with five or six rooms leading out to a central patio. Usually, an authentic *guaguancó* is improvised and has themes about love. Thematically, it differs from the religious music of the *bembé*, during which converts gather to worship and feast in honor of a specific saint. At the *bembé* sacred *bata* drums would be used, while the *guaguancó* makes use of different drums and different rhythms and music.

If one examined the spoken ritual of *santería*, *brujería*, voodoo, the *queh-queh* (or wedding songs from Guyana), the Shango shouts in Trinidad, and the songs of Pocomania and Myal in Jamaica, he would readily observe that these constitute an important body of African oral literature, especially as it extends itself into the New World.[2] This occurs in Samuel Feijóo's *Cuentos populares cubanos*, in which one witnesses change and transformation from the original body of African folklore, as many of these stories are based on relationships between the races. They satirize rural and urban modes of behavior and values. For instance, "El hijo blanco de Francisco," shows Francisco's predicament when he discovers his son is White. To Francisco's concerned question, Francisca replies, "No sea bobo, Flancisco, ¿tú no a bito cómo gallina prieta pone huevo blanco?" (Don't be a fool, Flancisco, you no see how a dark chicken lays white eggs?)[3]

Black-White relationships are also a part of the story about Jigué, a Black midget who inhabits rivers and lakes. The jigué, who has small feet, large ears and hands, and a large belly, will drown a person and take him to his cave. There are two boys in the story—one is the Black son of a slave woman and the other the White son of one of the plantation masters. The Black boy wears the used old clothes of the White boy and thinks he can become White if he bathes in a certain well. Jigué appears and drowns him.[4]

Even if the basic theme of the story were not the Black boy's crisis of identity in the New World, one would know that this was not an

2. For a general treatment see James Haskins, *Witchcraft, Mysticism and Magic in the New World*, (New York, 1974). Also Henry H. Bell, *Obeah: Witchcraft in the West Indies*, (Westport, 1970 [1889]).

3. Samuel Feijóo, *Cuentos populares cubanos* (Havana, 1962), II, 69.

4. See Ramón Guirao (ed.), *Cuentos y leyendas negras de Cuba* (Havana, 1943), 124, 79–80.

authentic African account, but one invented to meet the cultural necessities of Afro-New World man. In addition, contrary to the tradition of African oral literature, there are descriptions of landscapes with birds singing and the sugarcane blowing in the wind. The main reason for Jigué's intervention is to remind the Black audience of its place in the world and the necessity to understand the claims, not of a small ethnic group, but of the larger group of Afro-New World man.

II

It is possible to isolate some of the ritual and to regard it in a strict literary framework. One must, however, always be conscious of function. The creator god, Obatala, decides to test Orula to see how fit he is to rule the world. The test, typical of African folklore, is to cook the best meal ever, then the worst. When asked to explain, Orula gives these reasons:

> Con la lengua se concede "aché", se ponderan las cosas, se proclama la virtud, se exaltan las obras y maneras, y con ella se llega, también, a encumbrar a los hombres. . . .
> Entonces te dije que era la mejor, pero ahora te digo que es la peor, porque con ella se vende y se pierde a un pueblo, se calumnia a las personas, se destruye su buena reputación y se cometen las más repudiables vilezas.[5]

> With the tongue, "aché" [inner being] is accepted, things are taken into consideration, virtue is proclaimed, works and forms are exalted, and with it, men are also elevated.
> At that time I said to you that it was the better, but now I tell you it is the worse, because with it, people are sold and lost, human beings are slandered, their good reputation is ruined, and the most censurable infamies are committed.

The substance instead of the form of the account matters here. The presentation in the European language can either be in prose or poetry, but important African ideas are being carried on, here aided by the use of the Afro-Cuban word *aché*. For instance, Mama Inéz is the African earth mother in Cuba; she is the mother of the household and of the slave family. Later, poems by Nicolás Guillén, Ramón

5. *Ibid.*, 17–18.

Guirao, José Tallet, Emilio Ballagas, and Marcelino Arozarena, among others, utilize this figure. The folkloric antecedents appear as a recurring motif, as in one work collected by Guirao, which contains the chorus "Ay, Mama Iné" throughout.[6] The musical chain-gang quality is in keeping with the social tone: a group of Black men tells Mama Iné that the estate supervisor does not want to pay them for their labor in cutting and processing the sugarcane. This kind of oral verse takes us back in style to the *guaguancó* with its heavy reliance on repetition and rhythm.

Throughout the Black world one finds this type of form. Frequently, as in the United States, the song can be used to convey a social message clear only to the immediate audience.

> Afro-American oral verse dates back to slave days when the plaintive (and symbolically loaded) poetry of spirituals was sung in front of white folks, and the lyrics of seculars and work songs were more commonly sung among friends. Today many of the same devices—repetition, verbal irony, private symbolism, etc.—may be found in the work of the finest black American writers. Just as spirituals, seculars, and work songs were to develop from sacred music and clandestine clarion calls, through the beautiful transition to blues, so did their forms permeate the products of important American writers such as Charles Chesnutt, Langston Hughes, Ralph Ellison, and Gwendolyn Brooks.[7]

The researcher, therefore, must understand the significance of Afro-New World oral literature in order to appreciate the work of later writers. In the United States, although the state of secondary transculturation has existed from the beginning, careful examination reveals the relationship between the Afro-American heroes and their Old World counterparts in Africa.

Some accounts in Cuba are still preserved intact in the original African languages. Guirao gives one that was translated from Ganga into Spanish. It begins with a chant, termed *curuguango*, which can stand on its own as a musical piece. The chant calls the attention of the audience to what is going to happen:

6. Ramón Guirao, *Orbita de la poesía afrocubana 1928–37* (Havana, 1938), 10. There is a good selection in this anthology of oral verse. Also see José Lezama Lima, *Antología de la poesía cubana* (Havana, 1965), III, 171–87.

7. Gerald Haslam, "American Oral Literature: Our Forgotten Heritage," *English Journal* (September, 1971), 718.

>
> Curu-guango guango Curu-guango guan-go Coru-
> guá Para-mí Aguanó—Curu—[8]

To say that this means "Pay attention for I am going to describe something extraordinary" does not tell us of the deep rhythmic tone, of
the onomatopoeic sound, of the hypnotic effect the repetition gives,
and of the international break at the end that gives one a feeling of
anticipation.

The story is about a woman, Maurú, but time is taken to acquaint
a foreign reader with African customs like polygamy, upbringing of
children, and the significance of agriculture. In Ganga, the story contains no such explanations, and their inclusion indicates changes in
custom, not in language.

Ecue-Ibonó is Maurú's husband. On one occasion, he tells her not
to fish for a certain type of fish, *siquillán gama*; but when he goes
away, she encourages the other wives to catch this fish. When they do
catch the fish, it sings from the net and escapes. Its song is: "Siquillán-
gamanga manga manga Sigui llanga / Kurr-Yon Siqui."[9] Knowing
the name of the fish, the reader easily understands the refrain. But
what of *kurr* and *yon*? *Kurr* is the sound of the fish rubbing against
the net and *yon* is the sound of its fall into the water. The women
serve the fish to their husbands. The head and gills are stored away,
but as soon as Ecue-Ibanó tries to eat the fish, the head begins to sing:

>
> I am the man of the river
> which you said they
> should not catch.[10]

Every time the women ate the fish, they had to dance for three days
and nights.

As is customary with the narration of an African folktale, the lis-
teners join with the singing and dancing. The "un-Africanness" of the
story continues as the husband eats with a spoon while the women
prepare rice "en aquellos grandes pilones africanos" (in one of those

8. Guirao (ed.), *Cuentos y leyendas*, 33.
9. *Ibid.* See Fernando Ortiz in *La africanía de la música folclorica de Cuba* (Havana, 1965), 119. He supports the view that Afro-Cuban oral literature relies on tonal
languages, song, rhythm, poetry dance and pantomime.
10. Guirao (ed.), *Cuentos y leyendas*, 36.

large African mortars).[11] The foreign listener is again being given an explanation.

Eventually, Maurú's misdeed is discovered; the fish is returned to the river, where it sings again. The husband makes his wives leave the house. They had not merely gone against his dictates, but had offended the natural order of life. This was no ordinary fish, for it resembled a snake and sang like a human being. The snake is, of course, sacred.

Other good examples exist of how the African languages were used. The carnival, in both Cuba and Brazil, was an excellent opportunity for New World Blacks to revive their beliefs and customs and also to "play mass," as the Trinidadians refer to their own carnival. José Lezama Lima has used African language in an account of an excellent ritualistic confrontation between the snake (Damballa's symbol and Maurú's downfall) and a young Black girl. The snake, who is the Devil in a straw outfit and bright colors, has power to inflict curses on individuals or to take them away.

(Negrita)

—¡Mamita, mamita!
Yen, yen, yen.
¡Culebra me pica!
Yen, yen, yen.
¡Culebra me come!
Yen, yen, yen.
¡Me pica, me traga!
Yen, yen, yen.

(Diablito)

—¡Mentira, mi negra!
Yen, yen, yen.
Son juego e mi tierra.
Yen, yen, yen.

(Negrita)

—¡Le mira lo sojo,
parese candela! . . .

11. *Ibid.*, 37.

¡Le mira lo diente,
parese filere! . . .

(Diablito)

—¡Culebra se muere!
¡Sángala muleque!
¡Culebra se muere!
¡Sángala muleque!
¡La culebra murió!
¡Calabasó-só-só!
¡Yo mimito mató!
¡Calabasó-só-só!

(Negrita)

—¡Mamita, mamita!
Yen, yen, yen.
Culebra no pica
Yen, yen, yen.
Ni saca lengüita.
Yen, yen, yen.
Diablito mató.
¡Calabasó-só-só!

(Diablito)

—¡Ni traga ni pica!
¡Sángala muleque!
¡La culebra murió!
¡Sángala muleque!
¡Yo mimito mató!
¡Calabasó-só-só![12]

(Black girl)

Mother, mother!
yen yen yen
The snake bites me!
Yen, yen, yen.
The snake eats me!
Yen, yen, yen.
He bites me, he swallows me!
Yen, yen, yen.

12. Lima, *Antología*, III, 177–79.

(Devil)

That's a lie, my black girl!
Yen, yen, yen
They are just games of my earth
Yen, yen, yen.

(Black girl)

I see his eyes
they look like fire!
I see his teeth
they look like needles!

(Devil)

The snake is dead!
Sángala muleque!
The snake is dead
Sángala muleque!
The snake has died
Calabasó-só-só
I myself killed it!
Calabasó-só-só

(Black girl)

Mother, Mother!
Yen, yen, yen.
The snake does not bite
Yen, yen, yen
Nor sticks out its tongue
Yen, yen, yen
The devil killed it.
Calabasó-só-só!

(Devil)

No! He does not swallow or bite
Sángala muleque!
The snake has died!
Sángala muleque
I myself killed it!
Calabasó-só-só

Even after translation, the piece conveys its rhythmic effect. The
interpolation of African words with black Cuban Spanish heightens

the confrontation between the young girl and the Devil. Nina Rodrigues states, with reference to Brazil, that "we in Bahia call Nagós (Yorubas) all Negroes from the Slave Coast who speak the Yoruba language." She feels that the preservation of Yoruba retarded the acculturative process, although Donald Pierson contends that "the ritual of the more important fetish-cult centers was, and still is, carried on in this language."[13] In other words, the ritual language is the same in Brazil and in Cuba, and the language imparted significance to the ritual.

African language, like culture, in the New World is never isolated. It is true that secret societies in both Cuba and Brazil did preserve elements of linguistic and cultural autonomy.[14] But such societies were small, even though their influence was widespread. What actually occurred was that the African words spilled over into the mixture of New World tongues. Gilberto Freyre is in agreement with respect to Brazil.

> What Brazilian, at least from the North, feels any strangeness about such words as: caçamba, canga, dengo, cafuné, lubambo, mulambo, caçula, quitute, mandinga, muleque, camondongo, muganga, quibêbe, quengo, batuque, banzo, mucambo, banguê, bozo, mocotó, bunda, zumbí, vatapá, carurú, banzé, mucama, quindim, catinga, mugunzá, malungo, birimbau, tanga, cachimbo, candomblé? Who prefers to say "mal cheiro" instead of "catinga"; or "garoto" instead of "muleque" or "moleque"; or "trapo" in stead of "mulambo"? These are terms which correspond better than Portuguese words to our experiences, our palates, our understanding and our emotions.[15]

And Pierson gives versions of some surviving songs to *orishas*, for example, "Egbêji moro ô ri, okorin-kam / orolu mori ô ri, okorin-kam," which seems to me like a song of praise for the birth of twins.[16] These are Yoruba words and *egbêji* means "twins." The cultural context of the functional use of art shows the language in action.

13. Rodrigues, *Os Africanos no Brasil*, 157; Donald Pierson, *Negroes in Brazil* (Chicago, 1939), 72.
14. Lydia Cabrera, *La sociedad secreta Abakuá* (Miami, 1970).
15. Gilberto Freyre, *The Masters and the Slaves* (New York, 1946), 101–102.
16. Pierson, *Negroes in Brazil*, 291.

III

Afro-New World man had imported his awe and respect for land, and an ancient ecology became part of the new order. Little matter that the land was not legally his; he did not see it in this perspective. His relationship with land had an almost magical significance, and it fortified his religion and expressed itself in totality in his oral literature.

Reverence for landscape is constantly emphasized in Cabrera's stories in *El Monte*. In one account she cites the legend of a poor man who hears two ceiba trees talking and as a result obtains a remedy to cure a sick girl. Likewise, Erubbá is barren, but through her offerings to an iroko tree, she obtains a child.[17] The landscape for African and Afro-New World men is alive; its trees speak and dance.

Leaves of the ceiba tree are used in *brujería* rites, adding still another dimension to the belief in landscape. Hence the account of the Black man who cut down a ceiba tree is important.[18] He is a stern person and threatens a goat because it eats grass. The goat gives him a horn and he tries to exchange it for a fish. The ocean at first refuses but finally agrees. A blacksmith agrees to give him fire to cook the fish, but he almost burns off his arm. Another smith provides him with a hammer, which he exchanges for an ax. He expects to become rich with this ax and stupidly "stabs" a ceiba, with the result that the tree falls and crushes him to death.

This is the familiar "stepladder" story form from Africa, but here the progression is toward a climax, without a reverse process. The New World story thus follows an African pattern with differences. It is emphasized that the chief character is Black, which in the African legend would be taken for granted. In addition, the main character is not a mere stereotype. Stupidly oblivious to the claims of the living landscape, he is an example of New World individuality. Another difference from the African pattern is that material things do not always link the sequences. For instance, when the Black man cuts down the ceiba tree, he gives nothing to the first blacksmith in exchange for the fire to cook the fish. When the fish is burnt, he has

17. Cabrera, *El Monte*, 155, 156.
18. Guirao (ed.), *Cuentos y leyendas*, 95–97.

nothing to give to the second blacksmith. He can only claim that
the fire which the second blacksmith put out was needed by him.

Since the slave was in daily contact with his overseer, supervisor,
and plantation manager, all Afro-New World oral literature could
not be purely African. For our purpose though, it is important to note
that several existing links securely associated the Black man of the
New World with his African counterpart.[19] In "El Mono, La Monita
y El Garbancito," the female monkey complains to the king, queen,
mouse, cat, stick, fire, water, and ox, and receives negative results
until she goes to the ant. As she moves from one to another, the action of any one agent will precipitate a chain reaction on the part of
the next until the ultimate satisfaction—here the acquisition of the
bean—is achieved. The ant agrees and conditions are reversed. The
request to the ant reveals the pattern of the tale.

> Hormiga, pícale el culo al buey, para que el buey se beba el agua, el agua
> apague la candela, la candela queme el palo, el palo le dé al gato, el gato se
> coma al ratón, el ratón le coma los vestidos a la Reina, para que la Reina
> se pelee con el Rey, para que el Rey prenda al monito, para que el monito
> abra su palmita y me dé mi garbancito.[20]

> Ant, bite the ox's ass, so that the ox will drink the water, so that the
> water will put out the fire, so that the fire will burn the stick, so that the
> stick will beat the cat, so that the cat will eat the mouse, so that the mouse
> will eat the queen's dresses, so that the queen will fight with the king
> and the king will arrest the monkey, so that the monkey will open his lit-
> tle palm and give me my bean.

This point is reinforced in this New World African story by the *refusal* of the various agents to permit the action of the forerunner. In
an African tale, order is restored by the positive force of one action
upon the other; here the ant's *yes* affirms the world order and contrasts with the *nos*, as the subsidiary agents pleaded against the
consequences of action. By a type of default the original order is restored.

Ortiz shows that Yoruba, Dahomey, "Carabalí," and "Conga" elements went into the musical lore of Black Cuba. But he assumes
that what survived of Africa in the New World were merely "musi-

---

19. See José Franco, *Folklore criollo y afro-cubana* (Havana, 1959), 84–88.
20. Guirao (ed.), *Cuentos y leyendas,* 89–92.

cal chants" that meant nothing. Without the Spanish element, Ortiz contends, there could be no Black oral literature.[21] Enough has been shown of the way in which Africa culturally extended itself into the New World to demonstrate that Ortiz does not make a valid observation.

When allusion is made to extensions of Africa, one immediately realizes that part of the process of primary transculturation involved the assigning of a place for the *oyinbo* (the White man). African oral literature had few references to him, but naturally, because it was a form of functional art, it could hardly ignore the presence of reality. Therefore, the literature of the Black man in the New World evolved from efforts to define his place as a slave in the new society.

Two types of characters found in Afro-American oral literature take the slave's part and portray his role. Roger Abrahams lists them as trickster and badman.[22] One such character, the Signifying Monkey, fools Lion and has him fight Elephant. Lion loses the battle and the Monkey laughs. In Jamaica, Anancy is a trickster figure. Andrew Salkey recaptures his character well in a retold story in which Anancy decides that he can live just as well in Kingston as in London or America.

> Anancy wife say to Anancy one day, when sun hot in them yard in Balcarres, that is time, now, that Anancy start bettering himself, like how Zacky and Man Boy and Cephas and Macky did go way and fix up themself in 'Merica and Englan', some year aback. But Anancy look straight down 'pon the sun shining out of a condense milk tin and know to himself that he not going pick 'pon either 'Merica or Englan'. When story pop, he got him eye fix 'pon the Sain' Andrew people same place where he living in the Islan'. He like short travel and short catch. As he name Anancy, he got to do things f'him own way. Him wife don' like this sort of contrary business he usual go on with at all.
>
> She say: "Wha' wrong wit' 'Merica an' Englan', Anancy?"
>
> He say: "Them don' have the right sort o' weat'er an' right mind."
>
> She say: "Non o' we go way f'the weat'er an' the mood o' the people who live over foreign. We usual way f' the money we can work. Not so?"
>
> All he say to that speechifying is: "Money right yah so, special down by Sain' Andrew top."[23]

21. Ortiz, *La africanía de la música folclorica de Cuba*, 107–108, 118.
22. Abrahams, *Deep Down in the Jungle*, 62.
23. Andrew Salkey, *Anancy's Score* (London, 1973), 157.

Anancy's real job is to look after the sexual needs of his employer. He is such an excellent employee that she has to find another gardener.

The trickster in African lore was a god—an embodiment of Eshu. But with his passage to the New World, he merely became the spoiler of the White masters' schemes. Anancy and the Signifying Monkey both have little strength and must battle with their wits. Obviously this is how Afro-New World man saw himself. Imprisoned as he was, within the confines of slave shack, "slave cunning" was the only device open to him.

Often this trickery is expressed in clear and unequivocal terms; the trickster, here directly called "nigger," is sometimes completely fooled.

> God let down two bundles 'bout five miles down de road. So de white man and the nigger raced to see who would git there first. Well, de nigger out-ran de white man and grabbed the biggest bundle. He was so skeered de white man would git it away from him he fell on top of de bundle and hollered back: "Oh, Ah got here first and dis biggest bundle is mine." De white man says: "All right, Ah'll take yo' leavings," and picked up de li'l tee-ninchy bundle layin' in de road. When de nigger opened up his bundle he found a pick and shovel and a hoe and a plow and chop-axe and then de white man opened up his bundle and found a writtin'-pen and ink. So ever since then de nigger been out in de hot sun, usin' his tools and de white man been sittin' up figgerin', ought's a ought, figger's a figger; all for de white man, none for de nigger.[24]

The laughter in the New World is often cynical. Directed at self, it frequently alludes to the intrusive presence of Whites who would seek to dominate all. As one "Aunty" said, the creatures were living quite happily until the coming of the White man; then they left, for "Mr. White man come for to stay."[25] The gravest vilification is made here; the European is a usurper of the natural order.

The other type typically present in many of the New World folktales, the badman, is represented in America by Stagolee, "a mean man, a purveyor of violence."[26] The master is brutal, but in many instances he wills the intervention of the slave. In one instance, he

24. Hurston, *Mules and Men*, 102.

25. Mari L. Owen, *Voodoo Tales as Told Among the Negroes of the South West* (New York, 1893), 139.

26. Abrahams, *Deep Down in the Jungle*, 75.

promises to release the slave but fails to keep the promise; in another, he does this again. The third time around the slave says, "Si tú queré que yo te salve . . . fímalo bajo agua" (If you want me to save you, sign for my liberty under water).[27]

Stagolee is not a slave. He fights for the sheer love of it, out of an enormous race hatred that is alien to any other part of the New World. He kills the sheriff, makes love between daring acts, and stages a shoot-out with the deputy. According to Julius Lester, in *Black Folktales*, even Death has difficulty in getting him to die, until finally God has to send a thunderbolt.[28] When Stagolee goes to heaven, he finds conditions most unsatisfactory. He opts for hell instead, where air conditioning has been installed and good music is played. Finally, in another version, he makes love to the devil and his wife and takes over hell.

In Cuba the badman is a rebellious slave. He is openly defiant and brings an end to his condition. First there is the ruse against him, and in this case the master Don Ramón decides to punish the rebellious Francisco.

> El negro Francisco era algo rebelde, por lo que, constantemente desobedecía a su amo Don Ramón.
>
> Don Ramón, cansado de regañar a Francisco, ideó la forma de castigarlo, para ello escribió una carta, la que dió al negro, para que la entregara al Mayoral de la finca.
>
> Francisco, obedeciendo al amo, llevó la carta al Mayoral. Este al leerla, azotó al negro, pues la carta le recomendaba dicho castigo.
>
> Un día, al realizar un viaje Don Ramón, en unión de Francisco, tenía que cruzar un río y, al intentarlo, se cayó del caballo, siendo arrastrado por la corriente.
>
> Don Ramón le gritaba a Francisco para que lo salvara. Pero el negro le contestó: "Cribí, cribí ahora pa mayoral." Y el río se llevó a Don Ramón.

> The black man Francisco was a bit rebellious and as a result of this always disobeyed his master Don Ramón. Don Ramón was tired of reprimanding Francisco and thought up an idea of punishing him for good. He wrote a letter that he gave the black man to give to the supervisor of the farm.
>
> Francisco obeyed his master and took the letter to the supervisor. The

---

27. Feijóo, *Cuentos populares*, 72.
28. Julius Lester, *Black Folktales* (New York: Grove Press, 1969), 113–35.

supervisor, having read the letter, took out a whip and began to whip the black man, because the letter recommended such a punishment.

One day Don Ramón, on a trip together with Francisco had to cross a river and, as he was attempting it, fell off his horse; he was dragged by the current downriver.

Don Ramón yelled out to Francisco to save him but the black man yelled out, "Go ahead now, write your letters to the supervisor." And the river dragged Don Ramón off.[29]

In the United States the end of the master occurs in a similar manner. On the *Titanic*, Shine exhibits more patience; thrice he warns the captain that the ship is sinking, but to no avail. Finally, he jumps from the ship, and neither the lure of money nor the promise of the captain's daughter can urge him back. He swims ashore and the *Titanic* sinks. Shine (formerly a derogatory word for a Black man), unlike Stagolee, seeks accommodation. To see, in his threefold attempt to speak with the captain, the continuously ignored and rejected attempts on the part of Afro-Americans to adjust to the Anglo-Saxon world is not extending the meaning of folklore too far. Finally, out of the rejection comes the hate born of hate; the Black Liberation Army and the Black Panthers are latter-day testaments to this.

IV

As in Africa, combinations of song and dance survived in folktales. For instance in the *siguillángama* in Cuba there is narrative, singing, and dancing.[30] The call-and-response routine is also present, as it is throughout the Afro-New World, and in Cuba those present act as chorus to the narrator. Thus the speaker is the primary narrator and the audience becomes the secondary narrator because of its artistic participation in the creative process.

Within the framework of this art, the audience is part, not only of the performance, but of the creation itself. In West Africa, when the storyteller relates a legend or tale, his audience is brought nearer to the account in a variety of ways. Local references are made, certain common jokes are shared, and from the center of the circle, the supreme vantage point, the narrator physically moves backwards and forwards to bring his audience into the meaningfulness of his narration. The chants and questions help as much as the songs, hand-

29. *Ibid.*
30. Guirao (ed.), *Cuentos y leyendas*, 125–126.

clapping, and gesticulating. In the New World this important tradition of audience action and participation was carried on; this is evident at funerals.

The African dirge is naturally part of the repertory of Afro-New World man's oral heritage.

> Cundingui,
> cundingui,
> dín, dín, dín!
>
> Bamo llorá
> muetto pobre.
> Mañana toca mí,
> pasao toca tí
>
> Cundingui,
> cundingui,
> dín, dín, dín!
>
> Cundingui,
> cundingui,
> dín, dín, dín!
>
> We are going to cry
> poor dead man.
> Tomorrow it's your turn;
> day after it will be mine.
>
> Cundingui,
> cundingui,
> dín, dín, dín![31]

The central portion could well be a solo piece from the leader, whereas the two refrains obviously survived from a half-forgotten African tongue and would be intoned by the secondary audience. They remain definitely as part of the mythical assertion of the African presence. These *jitanjáfora*, or African-sounding words, were used by new poets of the 1930s to acknowledge the importance of their African world.

Songs, whether associated with folktales, praises, weddings, carnivals, or storytelling, emphasize the musical element. Testifying to this is the proliferation of a variety of drums and also the *sansa*, or *likembe*, which is made of steel springs and played with the thumbs. In Cuba and Haiti it is termed a *marimbula* and in Brazil it is known

31. Guirao, *Orbita*, 13.

as the *marimba*. It was used in early Trinidadian calypso bands and in masquerade bands in Guyana.

In folktales, the songs, while providing moments of dramatic suspension, enjoin the audience to take part. In the Haitian tale in which Tortoise tries to outsmart Uncle Pierre Jean, who has caught him, Tortoise sings:

> Colico Pierre Jean Oh!
> Colico Pierre Jean Oh!
> Si'm capab' m'pito volé, enhé
> C'est regrettant ca, m'pa gaiyain zel.[32]
>
> Colico Pierre Jean, oh!
> Colico Pierre Jean, oh!
> If I could I would fly, *enhé*!
> What a tragedy, I have no wings.

This type of rhythm was to have a strong influence on White musical genres, as we have seen in Cuba. In New Orleans, Black music "affected all other forms of music in the city," and in Brazil, the Black man "has adopted all the traditional festivals ... lending to them his own colorful interpretations, the rhythm of his songs and his dances, the *samba*, the *maracatú*, the *batuque*."[33] It is the history of New World adaptation to Africa.

In Brazil, "the samba, which is in effect the soul of Carnival, has a ritualistic origin that goes back to a day when tribal ceremonies were still fresh in the mind of the Negro slave."[34]

> The dance was a deep-rooted institution among the Negro peoples from which the slaves for the Brazilian trade were drawn; religious, funeral, hunting, war and love dances. The Sudanese and Bantus both carried to Brazil the tradition of their religious and war dances. The *quizomba*, for example, the wedding dance of Angola, influenced to a very marked degree the sambas and *batuques*, typical Brazilian Negro dances. Many of the forms of religious dances were incorporated into the *macumbas* and *candomblés*. There are no Negro religious ceremonies without the accompaniment of dances by the faithful. Some of the characteristic dances

32. Courlander, *The Drum and the Hoe*, 179.
33. John W. Blassingame, *Black New Orleans* (Chicago, 1973), 140; Courtenay Malcolm Batchelor, *Stories and Storytellers of Brazil*, (Havana, 1933), I, 176. Also consult Mário de Andrade, *Compêndio de história de música* (São Paulo, 1933), and Renato Almeida, *Historía de música brasileira* (Rio de Janeiro, 1942).
34. Batchelor, *Stories and Storytellers of Brazil*, I, 31.

of the *candomblés* lost their strictly religious meaning and became popular as the *batucajés* with steps or variations called by local Brazilian names: *alujá, jeguede* and *jaré*.[35]

Plays are also prominent at festivals. Portuguese *autos* (or medieval miracle plays) were adapted and converted into African forms. One form, the congo, dramatized the African kings and queens, and one was performed as early as 1706 in Iguarassú in Pernambuco, Brazil. The plot involves the death and resurrection of Prince Mameto amid scenes of rejoicing. Another type of play, a *quilombo*, commemorates the events of the separatists in Palmares. In Bahia, Rodrigues has noted *ternos*, or *ranchos*—pastoral plays in which shepherds or shepherdesses accompanied by musicians go from house to house singing. In neighboring Guyana, this type of event also occurred at Christmas, but the masqueraders who wore gaudy costumes frequently were seen as forms of punishment. They carried whips and would flog children for any alleged wrongdoing.

Alceu Maynard Araújo traces in Brazil the geographical location and history of what he terms *congada*.[36] His account, with musical notation, shows the Christian and European elements as well as the African rhythms. The king is addressed in very formal manner and the play is made up of a multiplicity of characters, some named by their occupations (ambassador, general, secretary), some by African names like Séfe and Zambásio, and others by Portuguese names. The holy nature of the play is never lost sight of, nor is the music, dance, or the Africanness of the Black king. This extract in Black Portuguese shows this.

> (*Rei*)
> Prinspe e secretaro
> devie de está escuitando
> lá no campo do bataia
> sinal de guerra estão dando
> e o tempo já é chegado
> e o dia vai se acabá
> forma toda nossa gente
> pra danca principiá

35. Ramos, *The Negro in Brazil*, 107.
36. Alceu Maynard Araújo, *Folclore nacional* (São Paulo, 1964), 216–86.

(*Secretário*)
Saberás meu reis de Congo
e que sem demora já vai:
deserta o céu e a terra
e a estrêla do seu lugá,
êle prêmio vai nos dá
nós da Lua nãofalamo
é porque ela que nos cria,
lá no céu na eterna glória
e a estrêla será nossa guia.
toca-me, toca-me essa marimba
que são instrumentos de afagos
que eu hoje quero mostrá
esses meus dançá trocado.[37]

(*King*)
The prince and the secretary
should be listened to
in the discourse of the fight.
They give the sign of war
and time is now passing
and soon would be the end of day.
Everyone get ready
For the principal dance.

(*Secretary*)
You should know, my king of the Congo,
Who stays too long should go.
Sky and earth are empty,
a star is in its place.
St. Benedict is in heaven
and he will give us a gift.
We don't speak of the moon
because she raised us.
Eternal glory is in heaven
and the star will guide us.
Touch me, touch me, this marimba,
instrument used for ceremonial dance
For today I want to show all
how I can change my dance.

With these forms of road theater, Africa had exported one of its most important genres. The festivals that occurred in Yoruba towns had

---

37. *Ibid.*, 286.

come to the New World and been modified, yet they retained their essential African quality. A somewhat prejudiced account by an early traveler survives in English.

> A score of men, after promenading through the settlement, came to the *Casa Grande*. They were dressed, as they fondly imagined, after the style of Agua-Rodada House, descended from the great Manikongo and hereditary lords of Congo land. But the toilettes though gorgeous with colored silks and satins, were purely fanciful, and some wore the Kanitar or plumed head-gear, and the Arasira or waist fringe, and carried the Tacape or tomahawk belonging to the red man. All were armed with sword and shield, except the king, who, in sign and dignity, carried his sceptre, a stout and useful stick. The masked old man, with white beard, trembling underjaw, *chevrotante* voice, and testy manner, was clearly represented by a young black from Sabará. On his right sat the captain of war, the Premier; on his left the young Prince, his son and heir. Of course the buffoon of the Dahomean court was there, and the fun consisted of kicking and cuffing him as if he were one of our clowns. . . . The "play" was a representation of . . . a slave hunt; the march, accompanied with much running about and clashing of swords, which all handled like butcher's knives; the surprise, dragging in prisoners, directions to put to death recreant ministers and warriors, poisoning and administering antidotes. . . . His Majesty freely used his staff, threshing everybody right regally. The speeches were delivered in a singsong tone; the language was Hamitico-Lusan, and there was an attempt at cadence and rhyme. Slaughtering the foreman and drinking his blood were the favorite topics, varied by arch allusions to the Superintendent and his guests.[38]

Allowing for the jaundiced interpretations, one still can observe the use of masquerade, dress, parade, characters, singing, music, and a plot sequence. The year was 1869. In 1899, Rodrigues knew of Os Pandegos da Africa (The Clowns of Africa), one of the four active carnival clubs, and saw their float representing King Labossi in an enormous seashell, surrounded by his ministers. Nearby the Zambesi River was represented. Two other floats followed. She adds that they represented "a colossal *candomblé* traversing the streets of the city."[39] Our previous account of the dialogue between the king and his secretary shows the enactment of this in words: under pretense of preparing for "war," arrangements are made for dance. The high

38. Richard Francis Burton, *Explorations of the Highlands of Brazil* (New York, 1869), I, 282.
39. Rodrigues, *Os Africanos no Brasil*, 271.

point of the drama is in the dance, in the acrobat-like execution of bodily precision; even the Church (Saint Benedict) will bless this.

A great deal of the African culture was preserved in the mountainous regions of the Guyanas. The Europeans stayed on the coast, usually in the capitals. Various types of music and dance were retained for specific occasions such as wakes and weddings, since African art was functional. The pattern discussed before is evident here.

> Jonah, you nah see none body pass yah
> No, me fran
> Oh, two ah me dumplin gone
> Nah tell me so
> Me pretty little dumplin gone
> Nah tell me so
> Two ah me dumplin gone
> Nah tell me so
> Nice Nice dumplin gone
> Nah tell me so
> Only little dumplin gone
> Nah tell me so
> Me own sweet dumplin gone
> Nah tell me so
> Me sweet sweet dumplin gone
> Nah tell me so.[40]

The call and response alternates throughout this *queh-queh*. The tale is an amusing one, such as would be used to liven up wedding guests. The refrain "Nah tell me so" (Don't say that!) is very effective because it has a point in the development of the song and at the same time encourages the lead singer to repeat his statement. The reference here might not be immediately obvious; *queh-queh* songs usually have sexual undercurrents in them. The "dumplin" could be a reference to the bride's breasts or to the bride herself, and the lament might well come from a former lover.

At Christmas in Guyana, primary transculturation took place. African masqueraders came out with Mother Sally, tall and erect, on stilts. Comfa drummers would perform short, quick, elaborate steps.

---

40. Recorded by John George of Parika, Guyana, on *Our Kind of Folk*, a record produced by Peter Kempadoo in 1972 for the National Folk Development Unit of Jarai. Accompanying booklet not paginated.

This was the point at which music, song, and dance were fused into a supreme combination of poetry.

At times, the acculturative process would seek to make whiteness from blackness. Xavier Eyma, a Brazilian, set "O Jornal do Recife" (1861) in Louisiana. He is concerned with the theme of the "tragic Mulatto," and hence he is interested in Francina, who is part Black. But the description of her on the auction block is not the description of a Black woman.

> Sob seus traços de uma delicada finura, parecia haverem-se extinguido, mais que do costume, pelo cruzamento das raças, todos os traços de origem africana; o seu nariz era aquilino, os seus labios estreitos, suas faces pareciam antes queimadas do sol que ennegrecidas pela natureza, e as maçãs do seu rosto, salientes como as de todas as mulheres do novo mundo de qualquer origem, enrubesciam -se por instantes te um sangue rosado.

> Under her delicately fine features, the traces of her African origin seemed to have disappeared more than expected by the mixing of the two races; her nose was delicately shaped, her lips were thin, her skin looked sunburned rather than dark by nature, and her cheeks protruded like those of any women of the New World and blushed at times from her pink blood.[41]

Neither synthesism nor transculturation can explain this. This is Africa removed. "Limpiar la raza" the Spanish said, and the African "Congo," caught up in the realities of societies that emphasized color gradations, passed through stages of mixed blood (tinta, moko, guayabudo, javado) in his struggle toward the final achievement—becoming a White person. At all costs *salto atras* (leaping back) had to be avoided; the African's path was one of whitewashing himself into a new society.

Fortunately the cultural remains in functional oral art preserved the significance of staying Black. Throughout the New World, when Blacks were not physically isolated, as they were in their *quilombos*, they were to some extent culturally autonomous; this is the real comparison that the Brazilian writer saw when he set his novel in Louisiana. Blassingame informs us: "There were several other distinctly African features of the slave's culture. In Louisiana many African religious rites were fused into one—voodoo, the worship of

---

41. Xavier Eyma, "O Jornal do Recife" in *Jornal Semanal*, III (January 19, 1861), 17.

Damballa or the snake god. The king and queen of the voodoo sect in New Orleans were 'Dr. John' and Marie Laveau who exacted blind obedience from their followers. Claiming a knowledge of the future and the ability to heal the body and to read the mind, Dr. John and Laveau exercised great control over the Blacks."[42] These are cultural alleys into which the mad "progress" towards White civilization became diverted. The culture was preserved even in the master's quarters, because "generation after generation repeated these tales in the *senzala* (slave quarters) and in the kitchen of the Big House" in Brazil; and the Black women, as children's nurses, also carried these stories into the Casa Grande.[43] As in the United States, Cuba, and the entire Caribbean, "circumstances in Brazil were such as to favor the taking over by Whites of certain African elements."[44] In other words, Africa was civilizing the New World.

Where there was a small White population, the preservation of African culture was not in serious jeopardy. Surinam is an excellent example of how the Djuka, mainly Ashanti and Ewe, who escaped into the hinterland of the country, preserved the mental territory of Africa. Carving was used to relay intimate messages, especially between lovers. Women would reply by carving on calabashes, "I'd prefer to see your heels rather than your toes," indicating a firm negative. Similarly the way in which a woman braided her hair or tied her headkerchief would convey messages. The manner in which a woman wore her clothes had proverbial implications, and hence meaning. The statement, "You thought I was eating butter and cheese on my plate but you don't know you took a snake off my neck," referred to a woman who had taken away another woman's husband and who ended up by being beaten by him.[45]

The *refránes* collected by Cabrera in Cuba in original Lucumí (Yoruba) show the preservation of the wit and acute observation of the Black ancestors.[46] Much of the suffering and oppression of Afro-

---

42. Blassingame, *Black New Orleans*, 5.
43. Batchelor, *Stories and Storytellers of Brazil*, 21; Freyre, *The Masters and the Slaves*, 34.
44. Pierson, *Negroes in Brazil*, 102.
45. I am indebted to Robin Ravelas for some of the information contained here on Surinam.
46. Lydia Cabrera, *Refránes de Negros viejos* (2nd ed.; Miami, 1970).

New World man also is there; consequently, proverbs constitute an important part of the African heritage. Cabrera distinguishes between Lucumí proverbs and Abakúa ones. Some proverbs, like All the chickens go along with what the mean rooster says and Happiness has a very thin existence, seem to stress the unhappy conditions of slave life. As with the Djuka proverbs, they use immediate experiences in the New World to make significant statements. Sometimes the sayings in Surinam, among the Saramacca, are sexually suggestive and wily: "Seki no gogo a go seki na baka" (The more the woman moves her buttocks, the more the man's back will move). The Herskovitses naïvely explain, "This is a woman's proverb, and carries the significance that one person must help another."[47] Obviously, the reference is to a woman who is a good lover and who is able to excite her partner. In both instances, it should be noted that these sets of proverbs continue to extend the cultural territory of Africa, since they indeed exist in African tongues as well as in languages spoken by New World Blacks.

V

The reality of the African presence in the literature of the Black man of the New World is indicated by the presence of two qualities. The first is that the literature—wedding song, dirge, legend, tale, proverb, or riddle—is in an African language, in a combination of African languages, or in a local version of the metropolitan language.[48] The second is that in seeking to preserve the African reality through the similarity of form, oral literature in the New World clearly shows elements identical to those in Africa—call and refrain, use of the trickster and badman figures, relationship of the art with a specific occasion.

Narrative in the New World, as in Africa, contains verse interjections, drama, dance, mime, and music. Themes might be different;

47. Herskovits and Herskovits, *Suriname Folklore*, 479. Proverbs in Srantongo, or Taki-Taki, as Herskovits calls it, belong more rightly to the invention of Blacks in the New World.

48. In addition to her *Refránes*, Lydia Cabrera has put together a useful vocabulary of Lucumí in *Anago, vocabulario Lucumí* (2nd ed.; Miami, 1970). She shows that transculturation has had no effect on Lucumí; indeed most of the people she interviewed spoke little or no Spanish.

the New World hero might have to assert the combined values of the Black world instead of specific African ethnic values, but he is still, like the artist, a group spokesman. The interaction in which the artist plays primary audience to a secondary audience embodies the nature of Old World African art. The primary articulator in the New World may frequently serve as a reference point for African values—the sanctity of land or the importance of the earthiness of the gods. He might also explain African customs to his Black New World compatriots, who might be unacquainted with some of them. This is an important New World addition to the functions of the Black oral artist.

Whites are present, directly and indirectly, in New World accounts. The authenticity of African folklore is still present, for the White person has merely taken on the attributes of a contributor to cosmic disorder. The hero seeks to restore an even pattern, and one may argue that, through the process of primary and secondary transculturation, his new relationship vis-à-vis Whites has defined new qualities for him. For example, though Anancy survives, he is not credited with any relationship with gods, as exists in Africa; he is a foil to Whites and becomes a trickster who seeks to outwit them.

Santero songs make apparent the pattern of secondary transculturation. The same singer can request protection from a guardian angel and in Lucumí invoke Papá Candelo. A belief in God, in the song "Del Más Allá," does not prevent the singer from acknowledging the presence of bewitching spirit. "El Embrujáo" tells of protection with herbs and prayers. In "Santísimo Justo-Juez," the singer requests protection from people who would harm her; in another, roses are brought to the Virgin so that "each day she will make my destiny better." These are, in every way, the requests of African songs —first the invocation and later the solicitation for favor. The singer is conscious, not of a dualism, but of the real acceptance of two worlds; "Jésus Predicó" relates the significance of Christ's death, while "La Madama Juana" relates the African concept of the presence of the dead.

> When I was in my earthly life
> I did good deeds when I could.
> Pray a Pater Noster for me

And I'll come and help you.
My spirit goes to the world
Helping all those who need help.
I am the black mother of humanity.[49]

Celia Cruz, Bola de Nieve, and Eusebia Cosme—all Afro-Cubans —continued to keep alive throughout the New World the spoken and sung nature of this transcultural art that combined African sounds and European instruments. Celia Cruz's songs, backed by the Sonora Matancera Band, kept alive the life of Africa in Cuban Spanish. "El Congo" is about a Congo (a very black person) who wants to dance. "Afro-Mambo" shows the blend of authentic African and European styles into the novel New World style. Because her approach is a popular one, she has to be mentioned in an assessment of the transculturative process. Her band provides the rhythm section which includes bass, a thing unheard of in Africa, but her powerful voice frequently uses African-style chants and at times seems to overpower the band.[50]

Bola de Nieve (Snowball) used a piano. His real name was Ignacio Villa and, despite the derogatory connotation of the name he took, it is interesting that like the African artist, he sought refuge in anonymity. His importance must surely lie in his contribution to the idiom of the music. In the lullaby "Lacho," he addresses a Black boy, Lacho, in Black Cuban Spanish, and he describes the boy's mother, a maid, and his father, who is a *babalawo*.

Pregones, or street chants, inspired his song "El Ducero." Here again he makes use of the Black Cuban idiom. One profound piece speaks of a *brujero* who kills scorpions. The ritual and rhythm in his songs came from Africa.[51] Like Celia Cruz he popularized the culture of his people, though he also sang in French and Portuguese, and his voice was paramount, with piano and bongos in the background. The voice frequently led the piano—at times singing, speaking, cajoling—much as the African oral narrator would have done.

At first, the *son* was peculiar to Afro-Cubans in Oriente. But again

49. Sung in Spanish on *Santeros Cantados*, Antillano LP 25.
50. Celia Cruz, *Album aniversario de la sonora Matancera*, Solo Records, New York, SS-3.
51. Bola de Nieve, Record Kubaney Mt-320.

the blend takes place; this time it was popularized by a White man, Antonío Marió Romero, who intermingled the Oriente sounds with the colonial dance. Paulina Alvarez, a Mulatto, then used her own style to sing some of the fifteen hundred *sones* he composed.

Both Eusebia Cosme and Luis Carbonell were reciters. Cosme continued to recite in the 1950s and 1960s, when the type of poetry she used was considered passé. Indeed, the very Cubans who had ignored her now applaud her. Luis Carbonell was a composer in words, an entertainer, a singer, and a humorist. He too helped keep African art alive in the New World. Not only did he recite the poetry of others, but he composed verse that described the experience of Blacks in Cuba. His style lies in the effective use of parody; he mocks the pretensions of the middle-class Mulattoes like himself. In "Yo quiero ser comparsera" (I Want to be a Comparsa Dancer), a mother chastises her daughter for wanting to be a *comparsa* dancer, until she herself is caught up in its rhythms. He involves the color-caste system in "Me priva la sociedad" (I Love Society), in which a very Black girl wishes to read in the society columns of all the parties she is denied because of her status. "Mademoiselle Merci" also knocks the pretensions of the Cubans who went abroad and returned speaking French; even a girl who was a *santera* and danced the *bembé* now professes to be one such person—as the personal servant of the rich Cuban. And "Celos Negros" (Black Jealousies) makes fun of a Mulatto girl who dances "fox," drinks highballs, and speaks like an American. The humor lies in the use of Black Cuban Spanish and in the exposure of cultural hypocrisy.[52]

This is a very good example of the positive and negative effects of transculturation. Those who pretend to be European are considered foolish and silly, and what is fashioned out of Africa becomes desirable. Some genuine "Rezos de Santos" (Prayers of the Saints) include typical African praise songs to Elegua, Shango (or Saint Barbara), Iroko (a tree in Africa but a saint in the New World), and Obatala, or the Virgen de las Mercedes. Among these there are some odd equations; Saint Raphael is associated with Osein, Shango is called "the youngest of the orishas," Saint John is seen to be the same as Ogun,

---

52. Luis Carbonell, *Estampas*, Record Kubaney MT-161. Vol. II.

and Saint Lazarus is described as "also known as Dahomey."[53] It is interesting that these equations are made, although they do not necessarily tally with previous research. One cannot doubt the authenticity of these *oro*, as they are sung in Arara and Lucumí. What is interesting to note at this stage is the manner in which the transculturative process becomes an active ingredient of oral literature.

Cruz, Bola de Nieve, Cosme, Carbonell, and other popularizers of Afro-Cuban oral literature must be included in any discussion of the presence of the Black man in New World literature, since they clearly show the nature of the alteration of the African form. In large measure the later poets and writers of the Negrista, Négritude, and the Harlem Renaissance movements, which will be discussed later on, were never able to compete with these reciters and performers. They were known only to a small circle of intellectual elites, whereas the *son*, the *guaguancó*, Cosme, Carbonell, and Bola de Nieve, as well as *santero* hymns, gained a larger audience. Perhaps it is not so ironical that Cosme's visit to Puerto Rico was to inspire Luís Palés Matos to compose *Pueblo negro* in 1925, when he had as yet not written anything with a Black theme.[54]

The point must be repeated that although one hears the "African" narrator, and though his output is oral and not written, it cannot be dubbed African for a number of reasons: some of the performers were Whites or Mulattoes; the Blacks were three or four generations removed from Africa; and the language was an adaptation of a European one. The art was thus a compromise between European written art and African oral art; the result was surely the symbol of the New World. Instances abound in our area of concern. It cannot be overemphasized that this is what gives autonomy to regions that seem so disparate.

> A national culture is not a folklore, nor an abstract populism that believes it can discover the people's true nature. It is not made up of the inert dregs of gratuitous actions, that is to say actions which are less and less attached to the ever-present reality of the people. A national culture is the body of efforts made by a people in the sphere of thought to describe,

---

53. *Rezo de Santo*, Maype record, 180, Continental Recordings, Miami, Florida.
54. Cesareo Rosa-Nieves, *La poesía en Puerto Rico* (San Juan, 1969), 243.

justify, and praise the action through which that people has created itself and keeps itself in existence.[55]

This must surely be in the justification of what we have been considering. It is this apartness from the Old World of Europe and Africa that converts New World man from a hybrid to a synthetic man.

55. Franz Fanon, *The Wretched of the Earth* (New York, 1963), 188.

3 Africa Affirmed in Afro-American Literature

So far I have stressed oral sources, because the Spanish, Portuguese, Dutch, and English writers in the New World have been influenced by African cultures. The realistic extension of Africa into the New World is exemplified in religious belief and secular proverbs and riddles—all orally expressed. Exceptions are writings such as Namba Roy's *Black Albino*, John Hearne's *Land of the Living*, Wilson Harris' *The Secret Ladder*, and Herbert G. de Lisser's *White Witch of Rosehall*.

To indulge intentionally in selection of specific works is to invite controversy. How, indeed, does one detect the "Africanness" of a work by a New World writer? My concern, however, is more with the utilization of real African experience in our literature than with attempting to establish a private terrain of "African literature" by New World writers. I merely wish to distinguish between Africa perceived as a real extension into the territories of the New World, and Africa visualized as a prophetic and mythical encounter in a never-never land.

I

Harold Cruse's *Crisis of the Negro Intellectual* (1967) deals extensively with the background of the Harlem Renaissance. Perhaps what he fails to stress is most important. This is that Carl Van Vechten's parties, Ethel Waters' songs, Josephine Baker, Duke Ellington, and Louis Armstrong were more important in the final analysis than were the poets and novelists.

Cruse points out the split between the West Indian and Afro-

American Black, but there was also the conflict of individuals. *Infants of the Spring* (1932) reveals that surely Wallace Thurman could not have cared greatly for anyone. He was a bitter, disillusioned man. Zora Neale Hurston and Jessie Fauset died in relative obscurity, poor and uncared for by their fellow Black Americans. The assertion of individuality within the total Black conflict, however, does not negate the argument that the Harlem Renaissance was a powerful social, intellectual, and unifying force.

Indeed, what was taking place might be seen as a reinforcement of unity. Although Eric Walrond and Claude McKay might be seen as usurpers, more European in their outlook than American, they obviously did share, as Afro-Americans, one thing in common. Ghettoism and colonialism were natural enemies to both, and they combined their efforts to rid themselves of it. Understandably, Langston Hughes and McKay flirted with the Communist party because it seemed to be a remedy for shared ills.

Politically, therefore, the decade from about the end of World War I shows the heavy reliance of Black on White. White liberal artists sought out Europe as their cultural mecca; Pound, Eliot, and Hemingway were in this way no different from their Black counterparts who also sought out Europe. The interesting point is that the Black writers talked Black and espoused Black ideas, but wrote White. Why? Because they had no role models and because leftist White writers and those who sought a romantic rebirth in the "savagery" of the Negro were intellectual bypasses as well as approval stamps to the Black man's understanding of himself.

Underlying, and opposed to, all this is Marcus Garvey: he is "uneducated," "un-Westernized," and has a large mass of followers. His United Negro Improvement Association (UNIA) is largely independent of White support, unlike Du Bois' Niagara Movement (later the NAACP), A. Philip Randolph's Brotherhood of Sleeping Car Porters, or the Urban League. Garvey is, in a way, what they all seek to be but do not dare; and so, other Blacks revile and attack him. He can be seen as a single rallying point for the spokesmen of the Harlem Renaissance. For Garvey believed in a *physical* journey back to Africa. He made preparations for this and conceived of the Black Star Line for the return of Blacks to Africa. His failure was not one of ide-

ology, for he was fiercely committed; he was, however, opposed by the powerful voices of the Black intelligentsia—the talented tenth.

Du Bois recognized that "the rise of a talented tenth within the Negro race, whether or not it succeeds in escaping to the higher cultural classes of the white race, is a threat to the development of the whole Negro group and hurts their chances for salvation."[1] On the other hand, Du Bois conceded, "It may be said that the rise of classes within the Negro group is precisely a method by which the level of culture is going to be raised." Yet he clearly states that "Negroes, particularly the better class Negroes, are brought up like other Americans."

Garvey was both in and out of the American social context. He was Black but not Negro and helped raise the level of the culture. But he remained, in the eyes of his colleagues, an unintellectual person of a lower order. Pan-Africanism could have been, but never was, the banner around which the dissidents could have formed. Du Bois' eventual option for Ghanaian citizenship is ironically significant. The African center was, only in the final analysis, the link and the positive force, if it could be taken out of the rhetoric of Garveyism. Hence, Margaret Butcher in *The Negro in American Culture* (1969), makes use of material from Alain Locke's papers to come to a similar conclusion. African traits exist in the New World in varying degrees, and folk material in the United States is the true link between the Afro-American and his peer in the New World. It can be said that "Uncle Remus and the spirituals are enough to establish the high quality of the unadulterated product."[2] Africa survives but New World man does not recognize it.

II

Hence the literature and culture of Afro-Americans must begin with references to the past in Africa. Not only have Africanisms and Black movements stressed the link with Africa, but the African presence was never destroyed. At times, under the pressure of slavery or economic integration it went underground, but it would emerge at peri-

1. W. E. B. Du Bois, *Dusk of Dawn* (New York, 1968), 189, 191.
2. Margaret Just Butcher, *The Negro in American Culture* (New York, 1956), 32–33.

ods when the need for national ethnic assertiveness was greatest.

In very practical terms the association with Africa manifests itself in three important ways: first, as a means of racial solidarity; second, in the form of cultural survival; and third, as religious nationalism. These combined in varying degrees at given periods of history in stressing alternatives to White ethnocentrism and the survival of minority culture.

Eighteenth-century aspects of this association with Africa tended to be both racial and religious. The Free African Society of Philadelphia and the Free African Society of Newport afforded some measure of communality, for at their base was the provision of a decent burial for their members. In 1789, the Free African Society of Newport, not surprisingly, corresponded with the Free African Society of Philadelphia regarding the possibility of a return to Africa. One therefore sees in the life of the Afro-Americans a cultural dichotomy—the need for survival in the new lands and the practical need to seek an urgent return. This is, and has remained, a dominant feature of the lives of Afro-Americans as shown in their art—a feature inherent in all Black art.

Cultural nationalism not only proclaims a separatist doctrine, apart from the transplanted host culture, but it also asserts a superiority. In this context one finds the recent use of African names, the wearing of African clothes, and the learning and speaking of African languages. This is a far cry from Ralph Ellison's *Invisible Man* (1952), in which Ras de Exhorter/Destroyer (modeled on Marcus Garvey) is rejected by the protagonist. James Baldwin, the novelist and essayist, was to add that, for him, the differences between the African and the Afro-American were because "the terms of our life were so different, we almost needed a dictionary to talk." Despite mass identification today, the debate continues.

The most obvious form of religious nationalism would be the Nation of Islam, or the so-called Black Muslims of the 1960s. Their most stringent departure from other forms of Islam was the recognition of a Black man as the messenger of Allah. Another form of religious nationalism is to be found in the association of some Blacks with Judaism. There is no conflict between Jew and Muslim in the Nation of Islam; the unifying factor is God, and God is a Black man.

The Black Muslims' antecedents are the African Methodist Episcopal Church and the Abyssinian Baptist Church.

Racial solidarity, cultural nationalism, and religious nationalism mark three conditions in the movement away from consumer of culture to interpreter, from being Negro to being Black. Naturally, attempts at economic reformation have accompanied this growth in awareness, and the formation of producer and consumer cooperatives, albeit on a limited scale, owe much to the recognition of communalism in the African past.

It may be argued that the Black capitalist (a myth and almost a contradiction) is essentially a product of the bourgeoisie. Similarly, the reformist school of thinking seeks out the ballot box and backs Black candidates. The latter may be contrasted with the Black Panther Party, which urged the overthrow of the "pig." Black people in the United States may disagree on the means, but the only practical goal is nationhood, a clear understanding of the unifying forces of history.

Of course, the real debate between Black Americans has always been whether to integrate or to segregate. Apart from the 1789 proposal of the two societies, there were other expressions of emigrationist ideas and, hence, segregationist sentiments. In 1815, a shipowner from New Bradford, Paul Cuffe, took thirty-eight "free Negroes" to Sierra Leone. In 1818, immigrants from Liberia reported that Africa was their country and their home. This was, of course, never true for the new settlers to Liberia. They always maintained a distance from the "natives." Also, John B. Russwurm was to write in the March 17, 1829, issue of *Freedom's Journal* an editorial entitled "Our Rightful Place is in Africa," after which he went to Liberia.

On the other side of the debate were the Black leaders who in the 1830s were calling for conventions at which Blacks could speak on the issue of whether to integrate or separate. Many militant Whites who were antislavery were also anticolonization in that colonization seemed to be a heartless way of removing a "problem." David Walker spoke out at that time. For Walker and others like him, their Black color carried with it the utmost pride and significance, but the ills first had to be remedied in America. Likewise, the all-Black American Moral Reform Society was against the concept of separatism

and encouraged Whites to participate. But Samuel E. Cornish, opposing their trading of anguish, held that there were no "oppressed" Americans, but, instead, "colored" Americans.

By then, in the middle of the nineteenth century, the argument for segregation had been reinforced by discrimination in the courts, disenfranchisement, segregation in public accommodation, and exclusion from schools. Segregation was no longer an act of will, and whether it had ever been, the majority culture was now imposing it. With the apparent failure of the antislavery campaign, the convention movement was revived, and revolt and emigration were advocated. In a speech in 1843, the Reverend Henry Highland Garnet urged violence, and although Frederick Douglass eloquently argued that this was wrong, the tone of the time was such that Garnet, Alexander Crummell, and Martin R. Delaney (a Harvard-educated physician) all advocated departure from the United States. Crummell himself was to leave for Liberia, "this spot dedicated to nationality," very much in line with Paul Cuffe's petition to the president of the United States in 1814, in which he described himself as "a descendent of Africa."

Out of these has come the modern association with Africa. And it is therefore always a cause for surprise when people speak of the absence of African traditions among Afro-Americans, for it is the persistence of this African need for belonging that led to the formation of various Afro-American allegiances in the latter part of the nineteenth century, like the Afro-American Council formed in 1898 (formerly the Afro-American League). This group ensured a sympathetic reception for Marcus Garvey's UNIA in 1917.

The debate was certainly not one-sided; the influential Booker T. Washington had discarded Africa. Afro-Americans were to live under America's gubernatorial jurisdiction. Du Bois, despite *Crisis*, the integrationist journal he edited, and his peripheral interest in Pan-Africanism, remained a mere exhorter of his "talented tenth"; he depended more on the reservoir of African consciousness that had survived despite the efforts of White slave masters or culture makers, and that was to branch out in various directions. Therefore, whether one associates the twentieth century with Garveyism, Pan-Africanism, Black Power, or the cultural equivalent that the poet LeRoi

Jones (now Imamu Amiri Baraka) places on Black myth and symbol, the ideology is the same—a striving for a sense of history, for the essence of the identity of a people.

Around the oral survivals some of this identity is apparent and links the racial, cultural, and religious aspects of blackness in America. One need not isolate the Gullah dialect, spoken off the coast of South Carolina and rich in Africanisms, nor speak about their attitude toward the "dead who are not dead" to see profound resemblances to Africa that the Black oral literature of America has handed down. African legend survives, as does the African tale. The distinction is a little arbitrary, though important; legend dealt with the local, whereas the tale stressed more universal elements in human behavior.

Within the Afro-American oral context are the "toasts," or adult narratives, of Shine on the *Titanic*. Shine, the ship's stoker, on three occasions comes up on deck to warn the captain that the ship is sinking, but to no avail. Finally, he decides to swim. As he is about to save himself, he refuses to turn back to aid the captain, despite the promise of a monetary award and the captain's daughter offering him her body. Shine's reply in one version is straight to the point. "There's pussy on the sea and pussy on the land, / But the pussy on the land is the one for me."[3] Shine, a symbolic folk hero, is the Black man who first attempts to come to terms with the White man's drowning world. When he does decide he has had enough, there is nothing in the White world that can tempt him back. Therefore, his three visits on deck to the captain chart a history of attempted integration, and when this fails, there is voluntary separatism as Shine abandons ship. The entire debate is contained in this action.

As with an African tale, there is definite polarity here, but unlike an African tale, Shine has supertypical qualities—patience, ability to swim, sexual virility. Also, he is equated with the narrator by the occasional use of the first person as the tale is told. The close identification any Black audience would have with such a tale helps establish a terrain of close communication, much as in an African tale or legend.

3. Abrahams, *Deep Down in the Jungle*, 126–27.

If the toast about Shine on the *Titanic* is a combination of legend and tale, the figures of Stagolee, "the baddest nigger that ever lived" and High John the Conqueror, the slave who outsmarted his master, are folk heroes within a strictly African legendary tradition.[4] In Africa the hero of the account would be tribal, and his feats would have a certain ancestral significance in that they would help to demonstrate to the novices before initiation the excellence of the tribal past. In America this tribal hero becomes an ethnic hero. Stagolee is a good gambler, an excellent marksman, a man renowned for sexual prowess. He is gambling with Billy Lyons and shoots him. Billy Lyons' sister tries to trick him, but she is seduced just before the sheriff's arrival. The name Billy Lyons (bull and lion) probably dates this account to an earlier epoch in the African past. But within the context of this account, Stagolee is required to show his superiority over the White sheriff and to outwit him.

High John is a slave whose cunning is more in keeping with Hare, Tortoise, and Anancy, the three great African counter-heroes who oppose the accepted values of the world and triumph in their revolt. High John, in one account, fools his master into drowning himself in the river. But his importance, like Stagolee's, is that they both defy the canons of the White man's world; they are not even afraid of the Devil himself, and in various accounts they arrive in hell and take over, after seducing the Devil's wife and daughter. On a simplistic level one might say that these tales belong to the trickster genre within the African context. More important, they demonstrate the ability of the Black imagination to surmount the obstacles of the immediate environment and to re-create familiar patterns of African narrative.

With the loss of African languages, few proverbs have survived. Indeed, were the riddle solely dependent on twists of language, it would also have perished. However, in Africa the riddle is by nature a statement of paradox or an attempt at reconstructing similarity from apparent dissimilarity, and it survives in the Afro-American dozens recited by adolescent boys and sometimes by girls. The mother image

4. Julius Lester, *Black Folktales* (New York, 1969), 113. For a good survey of Afro-American toasts, see William Labor *et al.*, in Alan Dundes (ed.), *Mother Wit from the Laughing Barrel* (Englewood Cliffs, 1973), 324–47.

is sacred in the culture of Africa. In a Hare tale, for instance, during a time of famine, Hare agrees to sell his mother for food. But he encourages the other animals to do it first, and when his turn comes, he hides his mother and thus preserves the originator of the life-force. Some of this sacredness is implicit in the attack against the mother which one reciter of the dozens levels against another. Obviously, the mother figure must be held in high esteem; otherwise no offense could be taken by references to her sexual promiscuity. A linguistic cultural manifestation of this legacy is seen in the Afro-American derogatory invective "mother fucker," the most abusive expression in Afro-American English.

The African trickster tales are seen at their best in the survivals of the stories of the Signifying Monkey. In many accounts, Monkey fools Lion into fighting Elephant; he laughs at Lion when he is caught for his "signifying" (trickery) and falls out of his tree into Lion's claws. In still other versions, he escapes again, and in some Lion kills and buries him, leaving an epitaph in the jungle.

In the Afro-American stories of the Signifying Monkey, the setting is the jungle and the animals are African, but the way of dress, indeed the emphasis, belong to postslavery Afro-American preoccupations. In one account Lion and Baboon have a boxing match, in keeping with the experiences after slavery in America.

The need to interpret the world anew has given rise to the preacher tales, which include jokes directed against the Black preacher—his supposed lust for women, his alleged love of money. These tales are comfortably close to African masquerade verse, in which the oral artist is permitted satiric excursions against outsiders—sometimes European—within the society or perverters of the social order such as thieves and prostitutes.

When the group activity could in some way be incorporated into the trappings of the new religion, one finds a definite survival, such as the dirges, which preserve African beliefs of the survival of the dead. In "Lay This Body Down," as in African burial songs, the dead and the living are subtly interwined when the singers chant, "And my soul and my soul will meet that day / When I lay this body down."[5]

5. As quoted by W. E. B. Du Bois in *The Souls of Black Folk* (New York, 1970), 205.

Of course, the Christian sentiments here give this example a survival factor, but beyond this is the refrain and chant, the community-oriented art of Africa, and of course the repetitive refrain such as is found in this Akan dirge from Ghana:

> Kwakye's child,
> I am anxious and troubled,
> Kwakye's child,
> I am anxious and troubled.[6]

Another similarity worth pointing out is that what is spoken and what is sung usually occur in the same piece, and the distinctions that Western critics make between poetry and prose do not exist in the oral literature of Afro-Americans and of Africans.

Not surprisingly, in Black America today, even written literature, especially poetry and drama, is seeking the restoration of pact with audience, an element that had been missing in certain aspects of Afro-American literature because of its compromise with European norms. And the new literature is also seeking verification, a compulsion projected by need. In other words, just as in Africa, where wedding songs, dirges, and birth songs belong to specific occasions, the artist in contemporary America seeks the authority of societal promptings. The new alliance with audience and the necessity for a spokesman have helped reestablish the old and formidable link with the mother land.

III

In a society that has always contained a great deal of interaction among races, one must tread warily when isolating the literature of any one group. This is why the so-called Uncle Remus stories, with all their New World trimmings, are probably more European than African. Too, a consideration of what is sung must only include genuine song and exclude the so-called Negro spirituals. Through the latter, the agony of a race became a commercial prospect, and what were at first the genuine utterances of pride, defiance, and fortitude became the sickly sentimental warbles of Stephen Foster's compositions.

6. As quoted by O. R. Dathorne in *African Poetry* (London, 1969), 21.

When the Afro-Americans had to reinterpret their new world and sing about it, music became a type of therapy. The songs were spirituals, for they did not accept the lot of the slave happily or look forward to rewards in the sky. The type of protest songs associated with Leadbelly, Josh White, and Paul Robeson fit more into the category of true slave songs.

Malcolm X once said that the difference between the household and the field slave was that the former was ever solicitous of his master's well-being, whereas the latter frequently wished he were dead. One humble song states, "Hurrah for good old massa / He give me the pass to go to the city," and concludes, "Hurrah, I'm going to the city."[7]

Because the singing slave was frequently called upon by his master to entertain friends, the references had to have a double meaning. They might be referring to God, but the god was not removed from them and was very much present in the traditional African manner. Their references to the children of Israel were allusions to themselves, and their songs could often give directions for escape—another instance in which Africans conscripted art for the practical service of existence.

Heaven is, therefore, of this world and through many of the slave songs runs the ardent desire for freedom in this world, although the imagery might be couched in the mysticism of the next world. Many references are to God as a symbol of worldly companionship. Also, the slave songs that describe the lot of the singer and bewail the weariness of his plight show not only passionate anger but also contempt for the master and for the entire system.[8]

Slave songs were also used for didactic purposes, as a substitute for forgotten children's tales. They warn of the consequences of evil and tell of the attributes of goodness. Although these are seemingly Christian virtues, in reality the viewpoints are those of the Black singers and artists, dissatisfied with their lot and warning of the ills that attend Blacks who refused to act out the part of folly. Briefly then, slave songs harmlessly warbled to Master and his friends in the

7. As quoted by Eileen Southern, *The Music of Black Americans* (New York, 1971), 155.
   8. *Ibid.*, 128–31.

big house, are the very epitome of slave cunning—teaching survival and protection.

No slave performance would include the entire repertory of the singers, because, as in Africa, art is related to life. Songs that despairingly tell of separation from brothers, sisters, or a mother would remain very much the property of the slave, since the institution of slavery demanded that such separations should occur. At this point, one might compare this type of slave song with the familiar African dirge of the mother bemoaning the loss of her child. In America, the social conditions were certainly different and produced an artist able to transform archetypes and relate them to an Afro-American experience.

In the lyrics for "The Preacher and the Slave," irony combines with scathing references to preachers and to Christianity, in mock reference to slave humility and acceptance of his lot.

> Long-haired preachers come out every night,
> Try to tell you what's wrong and what's right;
> But when asked about something to eat,
> They will answer in voices sweet:
>
>> You will eat bye and bye,
>> In that glorious land above the sky (way up high)
>> Work and pray, live on hay,
>> You get pie in the sky when you die (and that's a lie)
>
> And the Salvation Army they play
> And they holler and they clap and they pray,
> Till they get all your money on the drum,
> Then they tell you when you're on the bum.
>
> If you fight hard for children and wife,
> Try to make something good of this life,
> You're a sinner and bad man they tell.
> When you die you will sure go to hell.
>
> Workingmen of all countries unite,
> Side by side for our freedom we'll fight;
> And when the riches of the world we have gained,
> To the grafters we'll sing this refrain:
>
>> You will eat bye and bye,
>> When you've learned
>> how to cook and how to dry:

Chop some wood, it'll do you good,
And you'll eat in the sweet bye and bye
(and that's no lie).[9]

This would seem to be very much in the tradition of "Joshua Fit the Battle of Jericho" and "Go Down Moses," except that the biblical allusions here are used to exhort the slaves to violence. Both Moses and Joshua speak Black English (for instance, Joshua says "Cause the battle am in my hands"), and the use of chorus with the underlying format of the African praise poem clearly shows the origin and how the old forms were adapted to differing conditions.

Similarly, work songs were adapted to the context of the slaves, who would sing as they worked the land, loaded the steamboats, and built the roads and railways. The topic of the song would reflect the occupation and the occasion, much as in Africa, where a woman pounding her food, or men rowing canoes or hunting buffalo would sing in different ways. The adaptation could mean that the singer was really revealing something about the nature of his world. Therefore, the lines below not only describe a hunt for food and preparations for cooking and eating, but also reveal that the slave was never properly fed and was frequently hungry.

I's gwine now a-huntin' to ketch a big fat coon.
Gwineter bring him home, an' bake him, an' eat
  him wid a spoon.
Gwineter baste him up wid gravy, and add some
  onions too.
I'se gwineter shet the Niggers out, an' stuff
  myself clean through.[10]

This has only surface similarity with the African tales that relate a search for food during a time of famine. An important difference is that in the African tales there is evidence of satisfaction—food is always found—whereas in the lines above, what one finds instead is a wish that hunger could be satisfied. At no point does the singer state that the hunger is actually satisfied—a sorry indictment on his plight.

9. "The Preacher and the Slave" by Joe Hill, recorded by Joe Glazer on *Songs of the Wobblies*, Labor Arts Record.

10. As quoted by Jules Chametzky and Sidney Kaplan, *Black and White in American Culture* (Amherst, 1969), 177.

Slave songs, frequently acted out for the master, had a preconceived notion. The slave, knowing that the master had a preconception of slave life, provided a facsimile far removed from his own real life. Master and guests wished to see happy carefree Blacks, antics, and ridiculous dancing. The slaves, therefore, acted the part of the clown for the master and intentionally gave him back the picture he had himself created. One could be sure that lines about "ol' massa an' ol' missus" ("Jus figin an' a-plannin' / How to work a nigger harder" or "She lived so long, dat er head got ball / And she give out'n de notion a dyin' at all") never reached the ears of the master.[11] But the mockery in them is close to the masquerade verse of Africa, which ridicules outsiders.

Unlike the African sung art, therefore, slave songs tended to have two unrelated functions. One was in keeping with the African tradition; it responded to the urges of the life of the slave and was symbiotic with it. The other was purely ornamental, meant for the consumption of the slave owner and his guests. These dual concepts of the role of the artist have continued to be inherent in all Afro-American art.

The slave artist and his counterpart in Africa both responded to community urges and were spokesmen who did not invent from vicarious experience but responded to, and spoke on behalf of, a group experience. But the artist in traditional Africa was a free man who did not need to refer to his desire for freedom. Secure within tribal mores, he could exalt the attributes of chief or warrior. But the Afro-American, as somebody else's property, could only be an amateur performer, whereas in Africa certain groups were afforded the luxury of having professional artists. The art of the Afro-American had as its audience two distinctly differing types—the group (homogenous, Black, all slaves), and the family and friends of the master. This accounts not only for a twofold interpretation of the nature of art but also for two different types of art. One satisfied the stereotypes desired by the master; the other mirrored the more specific realities of the performers' life-styles.

This duality of approach accounts in large measure for Black and

11. *Ibid.*; Butcher, *The Negro in American Culture*, 103–104.

"nigger" aspects of the Afro-American tradition. The Black tradition was more genuine, rooted quite firmly in Africa and utilizing a voice only when the formal occasion demanded—birth, wedding, death, work, prayer. The "nigger" tradition (or invention) was made up for the specific pleasure of an alien ear. At some point the two traditions converged, but when one infers that slaves were laughing despite their hardships, this is really not completely accurate. They were clowning for the benefit of their masters.

> Way down yon'er 'un de Alerbamer way
> De Niggers goes to wo'k at de peep o' day.
> De bed's too short, and the high posts rear'
> De Niggers needs a ladder fer to climb up dere.[12]

Unlike the derogatory references to the master and his wife, alluded to before, this was obviously intended for the Whites as well as the slaves. Ostensibly all the laughter seems directed at Blacks, but cleverly the slave artist manages to slip in references to the size and height of the bed and to the working conditions of the slaves. Of course no immediate offense could be taken, for the scene was "way down yon'er."

The slave songs reflect the history of transition; different mores appear in them. Luckily, most slaves who were transported would have undergone the rigors of "tribal" initiation; therefore, when they began to act a different part—a role alien from the traditional one of "tribal" Africa—this was both an act of will and of necessity.

One may speak of original emotional rhythms and tones that permit Black song, but without the "nigger" element. The Black song tradition was adapted to new circumstances and gave way to the Afro-American blues, the origin of all New World music. The blues, like jazz and like their precursors (the slave songs), were peasant utterances, but the peasant needs were different ones. In Africa, the land was one with the Blacks; in America, not belonging to the land meant that the songs often had to express *deraciné* concepts.

Lack of land and, paradoxically, the closeness of the slaves to soil

12. Butcher, *The Negro in American Culture*, 102–103. Frances Anne Kemble, *Journal of a Residence on a Georgia Plantation in 1838–1839* (New York, 1961) has excellent information from another standpoint. She spent four months on the plantation and made thirteen separate entries on slave songs.

account for the large number of references to forests, rivers, mountains, and cotton fields. Even songs that lie within the purely Black domain have these allusions and hence the preoccupation of the slaves with the absence of land is readily understood. The White man owned the new lands, but the land within the immediate tribal past belonged to the high god and the group; therefore, what emerges in song is estrangement from God. Despite the many references to the White God within the "nigger tradition," Black slaves instinctively knew that there could be no God without a kin relationship to landscape: God was only a servant. This is readily seen if two references are compared: first, the supposed words of Nat Turner, who led a slave revolt in Southampton County, Virginia, in 1831.

> Being at play with other children, when three or four years old, I was telling them something, which my mother, overhearing, said it happened before I was born. I stuck to my story, however, and related some things which went in her opinion, to confirm it. Others being called on, we were greatly astonished, knowing that these things had happened, and caused them to say, in my hearing, I surely would be a prophet, as the Lord has shown me things that had happened before my birth. And my mother and grandmother strengthened me in this my first impression, saying, in my presence, which they had always thought from certain marks on my head and breast.[13]

The irony seems hardly worth emphasizing; the very White God that had held him captive was to free him, much as the same God of the masters was to free the slaves in the more widely known Afro-American songs and much as the same God was fighting on the side of the slaves for emancipation. The psychological effect that this had, both for slave and master, is readily apparent. The message of freedom could be put out in cryptic lines that ironically echoed the vocabulary and syntax of a hymn.

> Where the great big river meets the little river,
> Follow the drinkin' gourd:
> For the sailor boy's a-waiting' to carry you to freedom
> If you follow the drinkin' gourd
>
> CHORUS: Follow, follow, follow,
> follow the drinkin' gourd!

13. Herbert Aptheker, *Nat Turner's Slave Rebellion* (New York, 1966), 133.

Follow the drinkin' gourd!
For the old man is a waitin' for to carry out to freedom,
If you follow these drinkin' gourd.[14]

As William Lloyd Garrison, who launched the *Liberator* in 1831 for immediate emancipation, was to say, "The whole scope of the English language is inadequate to describe the horrors and impieties of slavery."[15] The slaves not only had to invent new references in their song but had to yoke the English language to alien patterns. The end result, like the African folk art they utilized, was immediate and extremely practical. New World God and land were forced into a pattern of practical alliance.

IV

One aspect of the triangular flow of culture is seen in the play of Afro-American children. The term *triangular* suggests the flow pattern of the slave trade. Men and ideas moved from Europe to Africa to the New World but there was a vast crosscurrent whereby Black ideas flowed to Europe from Africa and across to the New World. In turn, the New World exports ideas previously imported from Africa and Europe. Historical conglomerations like the "mark of Cain," the "noble savage," Inkle and Yarico, Négritude with its New World equivalent in Negrismo and Negrista, and the attention East and South African intellectuals pay to Black American thinkers like Du Bois and Langston Hughes—all are pointers toward the assimilation of Black culture throughout the world. The games of Afro-American children assert the literary borders of Black culture of the triangle.[16]

When Black children play, they are carrying on important oral traditions of their people. In Africa, riddling had been considered as play, but it was also an important factor in the process of heritage and inheritance. Riddling among African children not only helped them to understand and appreciate the age of the language (since many riddles were couched in archaic forms), but also helped in a psychological way. Children were presented with disturbing views

14. "Follow the Drinkin' Gourd," recorded by the Weavers on Decca DL 5285.
15. Quoted in Martin B. Duberman, *The Anti-Slavery Vanguard* (Princeton, 1965), 136, from New York *Anti-Slavery Standard*, June 2, 1860.
16. The examples of play songs that follow are taken from my own recorded collections.

of the world; the solution to the riddle was that they were forced to reassemble chaotic patterns into more orderly ones. This reconstruction was learned, for the answers to riddles had to be memorized. There was logic to the reassembly of fragments; instinct, not formal learning, was necessary.

Similarly, in the New World the games of Black children help keep alive the instinct of the race. For instance, the instinct of self-preservation, the reenactment of the dislocation of tribe, the broken memories of lost African dirges, adjustment in the New World, slave revolt—indeed the entire history of Black peoples in the United States —manifests itself in play. One may be fairly sure of an intact tradition, since Black children played with Black children during slavery and afterwards. Because of segregation in school, house, and church —a segregation that was both cultural and economic—Black children managed to pass down to the contemporary period important reenactments of the ritual and instinct of their people. Play is therefore preservation. Where similarities occur between Black and White children in play, the ritual is understood by each in a different cultural context. Even if some of the games have been European in origin, Black children have reinterpreted them to suit their own special situation.

An example, the game Red Rover, will illustrate both the ritualistic and instinctive concepts of Black play. The children arrange themselves in two lines and one child attempts to move over from one line to break up the other. If the child succeeds, he chooses someone who returns to his line with him. The chant is simple: "Red Rover, Red Rover / Send someone over." This is the ritual of the game, but the instinctive aspect of the game is one of slave cunning. Actually, the two lines of children represent the European master and African slave. The child that is brought over from one line to the other has a definite function to perform—that of preventing the line in which he is standing from winning. Analogies could easily be made with the house slave captured from the field. The game would seek to teach the field slave that if and when he should become a house slave, his function would be to destroy the house and thereby reaffirm his kinship with his apparent enemies.

Games demonstrate quite clearly that in the homes of Blacks in

America confinement (in slave shacks of the past or urban ghettos of today) is an important factor. Not surprising, therefore, is the popularity of many hand-clapping games and jump-rope games, in which African memories seem present (note, for instance, the reference to the Congo in one that follows). But what is perhaps of more importance is that these references combine into an Afro-Euro fragment. For instance, a jump-rope game has the song:

> Old Mary Mack Mack Mack
> All dressed in black black black
> With 24 buttons buttons buttons
> Up and down her back back back

The fragment of ethnic consciousness—the instinctive element— is in *ack*, which carries, through its repetition, references to black. This is carried over to the second verse, in which *back* is mentioned three times, culminating in the reference to the "Fourth of July, lie, lie." Again the reference seems obvious—mourning. The fourth of July ought to have represented freedom for Blacks but never did.

On the other hand, in Funny Little Dutch Girl, a hand-clapping game, the myth of the ancestor is intentionally destroyed and put together in the mock stereotype of the White. Therefore, the Black girls here become White and their assumption of whiteness is liberty enough to voice not only the prejudices of the Whites but also latent prejudices of Blacks.

> My boyfriend's name is Sambo
> He comes from the Belgian Congo
> With a pickle on his toe
> Singing sea I e I o.

Sambo is ludicrous, and here again the instinctive element asserts itself; a Black child would not see herself reflected in Sambo and therefore not in the Dutch girl's attitude toward Sambo. Consequently, the Dutch girl is "funny"; in this way the instinct of cult is preserved.

Black children teach Black children to play, unlike most of their White counterparts, for whom play is often supervised by an adult. Mercifully, little of this has been exploited by culture "superintendents," and therefore it has remained the property of the folk. Be-

cause of this, the only reason for conceptualization and perservation of the play of Black children is that it represents the articulate consciousness of Black people.

One may assume that the ritualistic aspects of the games—standing in line, clapping hands, moving around in a circle—were adapted from the White supraculture, although the ceremonies at funerals of Blacks could have provided a model. Even in the very adaptation there had to be choice, since no game could survive, whatever its instinctive implications, if the ritual could not be performed in close quarters and did not imaginatively demonstrate kinship.

Take for instance the game of Spud. Someone who shouts "spud" throws a ball, and the other children attempt to avoid the ball by swaying from side to side. In Statue Maker, in which one child spins another around and then lets go, the child who is spun around halts, forming himself into a statue. In both these instances, space is restricted and the rigidity of the African mask is dramatized. Obviously, slaves could not pass on the importance of the mask in African rite, because in Africa the person wearing the mask *became* the god. In the New World context, the mask was necessary for its wearer to become something else too, to hide his true feelings; hence, a child becomes a statue. Eventually instinct and ritual merged into a meaningful whole—survival techniques.

In the White man's world in which the slaves found themselves and in which Blacks later moved from rural to urban areas, progress was the ability to absorb an iron discipline. Children in the city have modernized an older game that expresses the concept. In the game played in the cities—Red Light—space is no problem. The leader, who is the red light, stands some distance away, turns his back to the other children and shouts, "one, two, three red light." The other children try to touch him, but the child who is the red light can turn back at any moment and send anyone he detects moving towards him back to the starting point. The game ends when one child finally touches the red light.

Since the idea is to "beat" the red light, the game brings out the instinct of deception that was needed in the New World if Blacks were to survive. Perhaps the game from which this evolved was the one involving a "captain" and children. The captain tells the children

that they could move ahead, but if the child selected does not ask for permission, he is sent back to the starting point. The magic words are "May I?" and if the child fails to say the words he does not move up. As with the red light game, the White man's rules—red lights, saying "May I"—are ridiculous, but the Black man complies to achieve what he wants. The instinct here is the Black instinct of survival; the ritual is the White ritual of custom.

Children's games among Blacks, therefore, ridicule the absence of quality in social and economic progression, based on mastering the rules of the White man's game. What is being enacted in the two games cited above is the ability of the Black man to distort the social rules for his own advancement. Nowhere is this more apparent than in a game called Rock School, which ridicules the educational system of Whites but at the same time enjoins Blacks to participate. Children arrange themselves as if they are in a classroom with the teacher in front. They are sitting on stairs, some distance away from the teacher, who is at the top. They have to guess in which hand the teacher has a rock and if they guess correctly, they move up one step; if not, they remain on the same step. The concept of progress is thus dramatically demonstrated—enlightened guesswork ensures success in the White world.

Old Mary Mack and Funny Little Dutch Girl on the one hand, and Spud, Red Light, and Rock School on the other, show the interaction of Africa and Europe in the New World. Combinations of cultural elements take place between two contrasting rituals and instincts. This does not suggest that the Afro-American play tradition in any way was an untarnished one, but that it is one that often went contrary to the African beliefs. This is another way of saying that an examination reveals that the African oral tradition may be termed *pure* as opposed to the Afro-American, which contains *applied* characteristics.

For instance, in Africa a dirge was a dirge, sung with appropriate solemnity. No dirges existed that were solely the property of children. But within the Afro-American context, dirges exist among children and are mixed with humor. "Aunt Dinah Is Dead" has comedy, references to the Black migration from country to town, and allusions to children, to dance, and to the disadvantages of a lack of

Western education. Within the African context, the death of Aunt Dinah would have been reiterated, her noble qualities would have united the living chanters of the dirge and the dead woman. In the Afro-American context, one child acts the part of Aunt Dinah and mimes the manner in which she dies. The others sing and take cues from Aunt Dinah as they go along. The dialogue is usually performed in this manner:

LEADER: Aunt Dinah's dead.
OTHERS: Aunt Dinah's dead.
How'd she die?
LEADER: Oh she died like this.
OTHERS: O—Oh she died like this.
(This is repeated as often as the child who is playing Aunt Dinah continues to mime the way she died.)
OTHERS: Well she's living in the country,
Gonna move to town.
She's got forty-five children,
She's gonna shake it on down.
Gonna shake, shake, shake it on down,
Gonna shake, shake, shake it on down.

Obviously, the proper tone of awe is absent here, and the lines in which the children shake their waists are reminiscent of another game called Little Sally Walker, in which Sally is told to "wipe your weeping eyes" and in which dancing follows soon after.

Now shake it to the East,
Shake it to the West,
Shake it to the very one
that you love the best.

On the other hand, "Green Gravels" shows the necessary awe in the presence of death. Here, as in the Akan tradition of Ghana, the participators are in a circle and, with linked hands, they sway from left to right, singing:

Green gravels, green gravels,
How green the grass grows. . . .
Mr. [or Miss]——
Your——is dead,
And they wrote you a letter
To turn back your head.

Here the identification is made between living and dead, as within the African tradition. There is an absence of any jocularity, the tone is low, and the movements of the children are subdued. Every child is given the opportunity to play the part of the living relative, and he mimes the words of the song by turning his back on the circle to indicate that he has joined the person who wrote the letter. Each child becomes, therefore, solemnly aware of the fortuitous occurrence of death and the interrelationship between the African ancestors, who are always present, and the living, who only happen to be visible.

This account is intentionally restricted to games that Black children play between the ages of five and eight. I felt that there would be less likelihood of cultural interference, and hence the ritual of the game would in large measure express instinct. It must be emphasized that the games of Black children are useful to anyone interested in the cultural past of Black Americans, since these games would have been considered harmless by slave master and the landowner. And these few examples show the history of a people—their homeland, attempts at adjustment in the New World, survival techniques, and the New World blend of the flexibility of Africa and the rigid nature of Europe.

V

In isolating David Walker, Henry Highland Garnet, Martin R. Delany, and Frederick Douglass for consideration, one is dealing with people who were extremely different in personality but unified by a single idea. Though born Black, they were not subject to the degradation and suffering of their fellow Blacks. The irony of their peculiar situation was as obvious then as it is now, for by averting their eyes they could have afforded themselves some tolerable amount of basic freedom, if not dignity. But they chose to identify themselves with the Black slave and to fight for his emancipation.

David Walker is best known for his *Walker's Appeal . . . to the Colored Citizens of the World* (1830), one of the first expressions of Black assertiveness.[17] Basically, the fiery account, consisting of a

17. David Walker, *Walker's Appeal in Four Articles with a Preamble to the Coloured Citizens of the World but in Particular and Very Expressly for Those of the United States*, 1830. For a good introduction see Herbert Aptheker, *One Continuous Cry* (New York, 1965), from which page references herein are taken.

preamble and four parts, claims that the White "God of armies" will side with the Blacks in their need to revolt. If the Whites do not give in, the Blacks will topple them with the help of this Christian God. God, for Walker, is not to be found in the meek and pious mouthings of the "nigger" minstrel tradition of the slave song. Indeed, Walker goes on to state that Blacks who side with Whites and help to perpetuate the state of ignorance and slavery should also suffer. Education, Walker argues, would free the Black man in that he would no longer be prepared to subject his family and himself to the adversities of slavery.

Walker's firm statement is the verbalizing of years of discontent. Slaves had always been plotting and seeking ways out of their predicament—escape, suicide, revolution. In 1822, Denmark Vesey led an abortive uprising, and nine years after (or two years after Walker came out with his activist statement), Nat Turner's rebellion took place. During this, the best known of the slave revolts, approximately sixty Whites and a hundred Blacks died. Nat Turner himself managed to remain in hiding for over two months before he was captured and hanged. Walker's *Appeal* had contributed in no small way to the rightness of Turner's cause. By 1830, Walker's little booklet, into its third edition, was known in the slave South.

Walker himself had expected no less. He had said that he had assumed he would be labeled "an ignorant, impudent and restless disturber of the public peace" and "a mover of insubordination" (p. 64). Indeed, his odd disappearance from Boston in 1830, when he was only about forty-five, was most likely an indication that he had been murdered. Although he was born of a so-called free mother in the South, he himself must have felt so acutely the pressures of living in a racially maladjusted society that he left for the North when he was in his thirties. But his links with the South helped to make his *Appeal* circulate.

Yet the *Appeal* demonstrates certain attitudes worth pointing out. Although the overall message, poignantly stated time and time again, is that the slaves should seize their freedom, there are certain giveaway parts. For instance, Walker quite obviously sees a distinction in kind between the so-called free Blacks and what he terms "their more ignorant brethren." That is why he wants "colored people to

acquire learning in this country." In turn, this attitude makes him take a firm stance against colonizing. He writes: "The greatest riches in all America have arisen from our blood and tears:—and will they drive us from our property and homes, which we have earned with our blood? They must look sharp or this very thing will bring swift destruction upon them" (p. 131). A firm integrationist, he sees the attempts at founding colonies overseas and shipping Blacks as a devious way of getting over the consequences of Black freedom.

Like Henry Garnet, who in 1843 was to deliver a similar attack, he is suspicious of his fellow Blacks. He can find no accurate comparison between them and the children of Israel and Moses, for he finds that they are "courting favor with, and telling news and lies to, our *natural enemies*"—the same people who would seek to perpetuate slavery continue to exist. For him, God is a rebel, and he advises his fellow blacks that if they revolt "the God of justice and armies will surely go before you" (p. 75). There is something distinctly ironical in the invocation of the very God who was to temper the revolutionary fervor of the slaves. Walker borrows the equipment of the White slave masters and then turns it against them.

Caution is one of the main themes in the *Appeal*. "Never make an attempt to gain our freedom or *natural* right, from under our cruel oppressors and murderers, until you see your way clear." But caution does not mean, for Walker, indefinite procrastination. "It is not to be understood here, that I mean for us to wait until God shall take us by the hair of our heads and drag us out of abject wretchedness and slavery, nor do I mean to convey the idea for us to wait until our enemies shall make preparations, take it away from them and put everything before us to death, in order to gain our freedom which God has given us" (p. 74n). Therefore, Walker continues, "If you commence, make sure work" (pp. 73–74).

Slavery is then, not only a sin; it emasculates the character of Black men. Walker uses the analogy of the Black family broken up by slavery to argue that a man who does not actively resist such harm is not even deserving of pity. At one stage Walker explodes with the words, "Treat us then like men," and he advocates that, in return, the past should be forgotten. In other words (and this fits in with his anticolonization argument), once White faced up to the wickedness and

evil of slavery, and once slaves were free to live normal lives, education (that is, Westernization) would be a means towards integration; and "we yet, under God, will become a united and happy people" (p. 137).

He obviously was quite serious in seeing integration as the reward the Black would give the White for emancipation. In his argument, Walker makes a distinction between "the American" (meaning Whites) and Blacks, usually alluded to in the first person plural. When he speaks of integration and freedom, the first person plural is *not* restricted to Blacks; Walker is talking about Black and White Americans.

In any cold-hearted, present-day examination of Walker, one may be accused quite rightly of ignoring the real issue in what was an emotional piece of writing, intended for a specific people at a specific time. However, it would be tantamount to laxity if some of the discrepancies were not pointed out, because they are indicative of a much larger gap in American life—the polarity, now so painfully apparent, between Black and White, and the lack of definite identity, which has plagued Black life and culture in America. Walker is extremely contemporary in this way, and one detects between the lines an impassioned groping for some solution.

Hence, we see the painful paradoxes of self-recognition; Walker advocates America as a Black homeland and yet describes himself as one of the "wretched sons of Africa." He advocates violence, but what little is known of his own life indicates that his *Appeal* was more a war of the pen. He categorically states that only Black men deserving the status of slave should cooperate with the White overlord, and yet cries out "Treat us then like men." In these lapses, or perhaps indications of his position as middle man, Walker was very much someone of his own time and, indeed, ours.

Henry Highland Garnet, a minister of a Presbyterian church in Troy, New York, spoke out even more forcibly in 1843; yet he left the same culture chasm unfilled. Garnet's contribution, a speech delivered at a convention,[18] begins with an admission that, so far,

---

18. Henry Highland Garnet, "An Address to the Slaves of the United States of America," delivered at the National Negro Convention, Buffalo, New York, August 15–19, 1843, in Richard Barksdale and Keneth Kinnamon (eds.), *Black Writers of*

the conventions had only concerned themselves with the free Blacks. Coldly and precisely logical, in contrast to David Walker, he advocates violence to bring about the overthrow of the White slave master. He examines the institutions of America and Africa, debunking the former and advocating the latter, since, he argued, the very myths of the former had been responsible for the prolongation of slavery.

Still there is the unintentional giveaway, as with Walker. For instance, despite the precise and calculating nature of the argument, he alludes to the nonslave world as "civilized" and regards the slave masters as "enlightened." Although at one stage he speaks of "our ancestors from the coast of Africa," at another he alludes to the descendant of those ancestors as "the untutored African who roams the wilds of the Congo." And what Garnet seems to be saying is not so much that slavery in itself was bad, but that slavery applied to *évolué* Blacks in America was bad, since in fact they were like Whites. The distortion forces him at one stage of the argument to admit as much. "If a band of heathen men should attempt to enslave a race of Christians, and to place their children under the influence of some false religion, surely Heaven would frown upon the men who would not resist such aggression, even to death" (p. 177). And yet, not much further on, Garnet states that "liberty is a spirit sent out from God, and like its great Author, is no respector of persons." And even in stronger terms later on, in a complete association with Africa, Garnet writes of the "undying glory that hangs round the ancient name of Africa," adding, "forget not that you are native born American citizens" (p. 178). The dilemma of the pendulum is once more apparent.

Despite these lapses, the argument is a closely reasoned one. First, Garnet identifies the free Blacks with the slaves and deplores the fact that little had been done to help. He carries the stage of association one step further with a cunning pun that sums up the relationship: "We therefore write to you as being bound with you." Then, like Walker, he invokes the African past, not so much in terms of direct references, but by stressing the extended family links of the

---

America (New York, 1972), from which page references herein are taken. Also see some personal comment by Garnet's friend and admirer, Alexander Crummell, in *Africa and America* (Miami, 1969), 301–305.

Black diaspora. This logically leads Garnet to a further stage in the exposition, for he then writes to the Black slaves, "as such we most affectionately address you," that is, as members of the same Black family (p. 176).

Garnet's imagery is relevant and poignant. Slavery has fixed a "deep gulf" between Black people, which "shuts out" any friendly help, but God provides a "glimmering ray of hope," which "shines out like a lone star in a cloudy sky." Garnet keeps up this powerful language for a paragraph that led to the logical conclusion of thought and image—the point at which life and art synthesize—when he said that the "oppressor's power is fading." Darkness, strong light, fading light, sum up the predicament and hope of the slaves, as well as the ultimate destruction of the slave master.

Garnet's imagery can at times be irritating to the twentieth-century reader. He can, however, write as enthusiastically about Africa as any Black writer of the early twentieth century, as shown in his description of Joseph Cinque, who led a mutiny and freed the slaves at sea. "He was a native African, and by the help of God he emancipated a whole ship-load of his fellow men on the high seas. And now he sings of liberty on the sunny hills of Africa and beneath his native palm trees, where he hears the lion roar and feels himself as free as that king of the forest" (p. 179). But his use of *dark* is annoying. In one place he alludes to the "dark catalogue of his nation's sins" and in another to slavery with its "dark wings of death," although one may concede that he is punning (p. 176).

The tone of his delivery is at times morbid as he relates the horrors of the slave system, at times ironical in describing the hypocrisy of Whites, and at other times fierce as he switches from complaint to exhortation: "You can plead your own cause and do the work of emancipation better than any others" or "Tell them in language which they cannot but understand, of the exceeding sinfulness of slavery" (p. 178).

His logic develops in sequence like a narrative. First, he lists the grievances of certain Blacks who had been enslaved. Next, he plays on the inconsistency of a people who had come to America seeking freedom "and who themselves could enslave others." Then he charts the manner in which slavery was set up to breed a caste of lesser

men, and within this he attacks cherished White American institutions. The War of Independence and the Declaration of Independence
(ironically described as a "glorious document") come in for full-scale
attack. He argues that basically there was a betrayal of God, since
the perpetrators of the evils of slavery were fully aware of the principles of liberty. Therefore, slavery was an intentional attempt by
Whites to emasculate Blacks. This will be mentioned again and again
in Afro-American literature and gives added poignancy to David
Walker's plea, "Treat us like men." And Garnet means as much when
he says later on, "They buy and sell you as though you were brute
beasts" and even more pertinently, *"Rather die freemen, than live
to be slaves"* (pp. 178–79).

He debunks the myth of the so-called heroes of the American Revolution. "From the first moment that you breathed the air of heaven,
you have been accustomed to nothing else but hardships. The heroes
of the American Revolution were never put upon harder fare than
a peck of corn and a few herrings per week. You have not become
enervated by the luxuries of life" (p. 178). The suggestion is that the
slaves were even more ready for the proclamation of their own freedom, since their own courage had been hammered out on the anvil
of their bitter experience. Garnet switches from the formal opening,
"Bretheren and Fellow Citizens," to "Fellow men." The tough texture of oratory has prepared the way for the latter salutation, for he
addresses his audience as men, and he exhorts them to fight as men.
But the implicit question, "Where are the slave heroes?" remained
unanswered until almost the end of Garnet's search.

There are asides that bolster Garnet's argument, such as his reference to "the increase of happiness and prosperity in the British West
Indies" since emancipation—a line that was bound to appeal to the
White farmers interested in profit. This, of course, introduces an interesting aspect of audience appeal that was less present in Walker
and entirely absent in the oral matter, but which comes to be of increasing concern among Black writers and speakers. This is the frequently unacknowledged presence of the third ear. It makes for a
whole new style of writing. The writer/speaker not only addresses
Black people, with the idea that his only concern is the elevation of
Blacks, but assumes that the Whites are also heeding his words.

The argument closes with a factual survey of men who had risked their lives to protect freedom—Moses, Toussaint L'Ouverture, and Washington, as well as "Patriotic" Nat Turner. Basically, they all fought for the elevation of the human spirit, Garnet seems to argue, and so the issue is no mere vulgarian's matching of Black with White; rather, it is the confrontation between captor and captive.

Having made the main points of his argument, Garnet repeats his call to rebellion, with the fact thrown in (which he also repeats) that four million Blacks exist. He chides and mocks the "patient people" who surrender their daughters and wives to their overlords. In conclusion, he merely urges them to resist in the language of the immediate "tribal" past. He says, "Your dead fathers speak to you from their graves," which suggests that the African presences of their ancestral past also urge resistance. The tone is high-pitched towards the end, as he says, "Brethren adieu!" He has returned to the apparent formality of his opening salutation, but not to its docility. The African family ties, the dead presences of Africa, and the true African heroes who stood up for liberty are the actualities of Black life. Garnet seeks to replace the myth of the White hero with the substantial one of the Black.

Walker and Garnet had spoken out. But there were only two major slave revolts, so what were other Blacks doing? The question is a fair one. The answer is not difficult, since one must recognize that Walker and Garnet were not just two men who decided to speak up. Walker had an excellent printing and distribution network behind him; Garnet's speech was given at a national Negro convention, and its resolution was almost adopted. In other words, behind both men was a most effective machinery for propaganda. But neither of them was a revolutionary in the sense that he sought a violent overthrow and would himself have participated. Their importance lies in the fact that they acted as disseminators of thought, of the collective will of large segments of their people. Without them it could not have been possible for Douglass and Delany to have functioned. They set important patterns for others to follow; Douglass and Delany certainly did. Walker and Garnet had plowed terrain that had hitherto been thought of as infertile. The harvest was, and is still, not yet gathered. But the seed had been planted.

National awareness was, therefore, what Martin R. Delany stressed in his book, *The Condition, Elevation, Emigration and Destiny of the Colored People of the United States Politically Considered* (1852).[19] At the time of publication Delany was assistant editor and cofounder with Douglass of the *North Star*, but according to him, the appendix of his book was written when he was only twenty-four. Apart from the commendable practicality of Delany's plan, what surprises the reader who has studied Walker and Garnet is that he should have thought of emigration as the only sensible plan for Blacks in America. He did not, however, stick to this and felt that since "one part of the American people are quite unacquainted with the other, one of the great objects of the author is to make each acquainted" (p. 10).

Within this specific context, Delany's terminology is interesting; Blacks are not singled out as a separate people but as a part of the American people. Delany has moved away from supporting the colonization plan to a "far more glorious one," *i.e.*, of educating Whites and Blacks to understand the nature of their proximity. Therefore, like Garnet, Delany has to disclaim certain myths of White Americans about themselves and about Blacks. This really is the purpose and body of his book.

By the time of the publication of the appendix, Delany had only half-hearted feelings. But the appendix is important, since it provided very practical ideas on the return to the motherland. Delany, who was writing this at a time when it was almost anathema to think in this way, is to be praised for having had the foresight to anticipate the development of the thought of the people. The appendix reveals, or rather predates, the point at which Blacks would question the legitimacy of White Anglo-Saxon middle-class values.

From the first of his account, the cultural dichotomy is present: "We are a nation within a nation," having merged "in the habits and customs of our oppressors" (p. 209). At the same time, he alludes with relish to the "pristine purity" of Blacks prior to their having been "despoiled of [their] purity" (p. 209). This of course, harks back

19. Martin Delany, *The Condition, Elevation, Emigration and Destiny of the Colored People of the United States Politically Considered* (New York, 1968 [1852]), from which page references herein are taken.

to the idea of the noble savage, the Black living at peace with nature and uncorrupted by the advent of the White.

Delany's solution is not in any way a democratic one. There is a certain Socratic/Du Bois aloofness about the "true representation of the intelligence and wisdom of the colored freemen," who are to assemble and make specific confidential recommendations, "to project any scheme they may think proper for the general good of the whole people." The figures Delany gives are interesting: "six hundred thousand free and three-and-a-half millions bond." So his statistics are used differently from Garnet's, who had reminded his audience that they were large enough in numbers to overthrow the Whites. Delany is merely concerned with selecting the best of the best, with convening a council and a board of commissioners "to go on an expedition to the Eastern Coast of Africa" and other places (pp. 209–11).

But, like Garnet, he is aware of his other audience, and he mentions specifically England and France. His idea is that these two countries would help finance the first expedition and the resettlement, since they could hope for "the opening of an immense trade." One is reminded of Garnet's little aside regarding the improvement in the economy of the West Indies since emancipation. The two countries would help Black Americans without a doubt, Delany believes, since they were willing to help "a little nation—mere nominal nation of five thousand *civilized* Liberians" (italics are mine). Delany's resettlement solution reflects his quandary, which, indeed, is the problem of Black people in the New World—paying allegiance to alien gods while timidly clutching the shadows of their own.

His better-known colleague, Frederick Douglass, a slave born around 1817, wrote, "My father is a white man" and, in that short, terse sentence, laid bare the entire situation. Walker, Garnet, Delany and Douglass suffered from the ills of their age—mainly a lack of cultural, ethnic direction. True, Delany had suspected the other half of the argument and stated it, but built into the utterances of all these spokesmen was this directionlessness. This is not a sorry reflection on them but on their times, since being so close to the slave age, they found it (ironically) extremely difficult to think in terms of a

slave culture. In this examination there is evidence that these writers felt the group instinct of their African ancestors.

Therefore, although Douglass writes, in *Narrative of the Life of Frederick Douglass, an American Slave* (1845), specifically to condemn slavery, he alludes to family life and its importance. In this connection, he writes about separation from his mother. "For what this separation had done, I do not know unless it be to hinder the development of the child's affection towards its mother" (p. 24). He mentions this in decrying the practice of the slave masters in the part of Maryland where he was brought up. The fact that his mother died, unknown to him, when he was only seven shows the great importance he set on this relationship, for his priority could not have been derived from personal experience (those near him had no mothers either) but from an awareness of the strong matriarchal society of his ancestors.

The Afro-American scene is, however, Douglass' main concern. He tells of the horrors of miscegenation within the slave society, of Mulatto children being constantly whipped to satisfy the wife of the slave master, who stood by watching "one white son tie up his brother, of but a few shades darker complexion than himself" (p. 26).

Like African art, Douglass' ideas are linked to the people's need to survive. Therefore, he does not spare detail as he tells that the slaves received "as their month allowance of food, eight pounds of pork, or its equivalent in fish, and one bushel of corn meal. Their yearly clothing consisted of two coarse linen shirts, one pair of linen trousers for the winter, one pair of stockings, and one pair of shoes, the whole of which could not have cost more than seven dollars" (pp. 32–33). Douglass' authority came from his own life; he had been a slave and had only managed to free himself after he had escaped for a second time. His statement is not, therefore, an empathetic one of atrocities but a mundane recital of the horrors he had personally known.

He provides an answer to a question previously posed. Why did Blacks not revolt more frequently? They faced the threat of imminent death if they were caught, but more important and more subtle was the "psychological" jurisdiction under which they lived. Their owners would ensure that they became so inebriated during the few

holidays they had, that they would rejoice when it was time to commence work. An intentional effort was made to ensure that they
were not educated because, as one of Douglass' masters said, "Learning would *spoil* the best nigger in the world" (p. 58).

Above all this is Douglass' own story, and it does not suffer half
as much from heavy-handedness in style and biblical rhetoric as,
say, Ottobah Cugoano's 1787 account. The purposes of both are
basically the same—to recount a story and at the same time expose
the evils of the slave trafficking and slave labor. Douglass makes the
reader feel that this is very much his story, that he is not going to be
led away by alien notions of whom he ought to be. His colleague
Delany had complained that "politicians, religionists, colonization-
ists and abolitionists have each and all, at different times, presumed
to think for, to *dictate* to and *know* better what suited colored people, than they knew for themselves" (p. 4). And although Douglass
joined William Lloyd Garrison, the famous abolitionist, he spoke
his language, but did not echo his thoughts.

Not surprisingly, his account describes how he began to subscribe
to Garrison's paper, the *Liberator*, and how, while attending an anti-
slavery convention at Nantucket, on August 11, 1841, William C.
Coffin encouraged him to speak.[20] His story is really about an intelligent Black man who used his talent for oratory. The speech at Nantucket was the starting point, but there had been a lifetime of preparation, beginning with his learning to read. As Douglass comments,
"My stress, in teaching me the alphabet had given me the *inch*, and
no precaution could prevent me from taking the *ell*." He had come
to realize what Walker and Garnet had hinted—the treachery within
his own people. He cites an incident in which, despite the close brotherhood among fugitives in the North, an informer threatened one of
them. A meeting was summoned and this was the result: "Friends,
we have got him here, and I would recommend that you young men
just take him outside the door, and kill him." The nation was coming closer together in having to face common tribulations. After
Douglass' own anxieties of having to face a White audience at Nantucket, he could affirm that "from that time until now, I have been

20. Frederick Douglass, *Narrative of the Life of Frederick Douglass, an American Slave* (Cambridge, 1960 [1845]), from which page references herein are taken.

engaged in pleading the cause of my brethren" (pp. 151–53). He did this long after the abolition of slavery, establishing himself as an authentic voice for Blacks.

His resolute intellectual independence was confirmed by his break with Garrison. He came to believe that the ballot, not the dissolution of the Union, was necessary to end slavery. It was then that he started his paper, *North Star*, which lasted from 1847 until 1860. He followed a middle-of-the-road line in policy and suggested that the Black press play down race and emphasize patriotism. Given the nature of his time and the period of retrogressive measures that were to follow soon, one can see caution and good sense in what he attempted.

Because the end of slavery was the beginning of self-dependence, the cultural dichotomy assumed political overtones: In which direction should the Black man go? toward Africa and the consciousness of kin in the Black diaspora? or towards absorption within the White majority culture? Douglass did not answer the question, though he developed countless possibilities for response, for alternative bases of living. Not until the post-Booker T. Washington era, when the young Du Bois attacked the concept of compromise with a statement of the urgent presence of Africa, was the dormant, but never extinct, debate to explode. Its literary splendor was the so-called Harlem Renaissance, and *Cane* is its perfect illumination.

VI

Jean Toomer's *Cane* (1923) is not a novel; it is a combination of Black folk story, surrealistic sketch, and elaborate pun.[21] Its grand design is that of a spiral with its center on Negroness, or the cultural dichotomy between Africa and Europe. The novel demonstrates through use of skilled, precise examinations, the manner in which Negroness adversely affects Black life. Its central symbol, one of despair, is well delineated in the illustrations of arcs, which are used to demarcate sections in the volume. These are circles that are never completed; home is never found. Each stereotype in the novel seeks completeness in another, and there is the never-ending quest for touch

21. Jean Toomer, *Cane* (New York, 1975 [1923]), from which page references herein are taken.

and understanding. The pattern in each sketch is, therefore, the pairing of dramatic opposites. Their failure to touch is related back to the focal point of the spiral—the Negroness—which fails to be effective.

Seemingly, it is women who, as childbearers, ought to release blackness and give it form and substance. But their character-conglomerates show how they are trapped in a Negro environment that is not of their own making. Each woman, therefore, in the rural pieces, as contrasted with men in the urban pieces, locks off the life flow. Karintha kills her child, and Becky is living testimony to the destruction of the faith of men in each other; Whites and Blacks can only agree to hate her. Carma, despite her strong associations with her African past ("She does not sing: her boy is a song. She is in the forest dancing"), makes her husband revert to the position of slave, and she herself takes on the role of whore (p. 131). Fern does not seek men and has distanced herself from any real world where men could touch her. And when the half-White Esther attempts to confront the reality of King Barlo's world, not the preacher fantasy he talks about, her experience is so traumatic that she becomes frigid.

It is, of course, of particular importance that women are used in these first pieces. The point Toomer wishes to make is doubly made, and the tragic inspection is intensified. These women represent arrested shapes, the aggregate patterns of a mutilated inheritance. Their wombs can bear no lasting fruit. Irony emphasizes the inability to work back to a glorious past. There are no connecting links: "Becky had one Negro son. Who gave it to her?" (p. 5); a mule wagon cannot become a "Georgia chariot" (p. 10). And Esther's acceptance of the savage nobility of King Barlo also speaks to this absence of history; King Barlo is a creature that is a White man's re-creation of power and virility, nobility and awe.

The lack of inheritance is poignantly represented in "Blood Burning Moon," for here the study is focused again on Negroness but is given a different slant. Louisa is representative not merely of the collective qualities of women but also of the land, Louisiana. Strong men dispute the right to possess that land—Stone, whose name suggests hardness and durability, and Burwell, whose name indicates bursting out and growing well. Neither wins, for they do not have

the natural right of possession. Tom Burwell has carried Louisa "into the fields, day after day, after that, an I sho can plow when you is there" (p. 30); but he seeks to usurp an imposed order. Within it he is victim (the peasant) and Bob Stone is the victor (the landlord), as Burwell sees it. His folkloristic attributes of the bad nigger cannot suffice here, for the victor is not a White man who is sole possessor. Bob Stone reminisces that "his family had lost ground," which is no unintentional pun (p. 31). The point here is that they are both "landless," or, in a larger sense, men without a culture. Louisa, as a poet and singer, is forever beyond the reach of knives and the lynch rope, always close to the moon, seeking to go beyond the despairing depths of a diluted inheritance.

An important part of the technique of *Cane* is to show a closeness to this ever-elusive past in Africa. Two character-conglomerations who bring this out are Carma and Father John. But Africa is not close by; it is to do with "Jujumen, gree gree, witchdoctors," (p. 10) a goat path, "two princesses in Africa going through the early-morning ablutions of their pagan prayers" (p. 35). The attempts at evoking a past only introduce a frightful distance—the two arcs again—for these attempts whether flattering or insulting, illustrate the crude inability to know. Knowledge is far outside the spiral, beyond the entrapment of Negroness and the enticement of whiteness.

The narrator does not assume this. He has adapted the style of the African folktale. Besides using stereotypes, he blends the tale, drama, song, music, and dance. The "I" narrator (not to be confused with Toomer) lends the qualities of directness and immediacy to the telling. Use is made of Black English, direct address to the hearer, and onomatopoetic lines to conjure up situation. Like the African tales, the stories are fixed, so that the teller and the listener can anticipate the ending—here, the incomplete arc, the constant triumph of failure.

There is, therefore, no great distinction between the pieces set in Georgia and those set in the city, for the characters still do not touch. What distinction there is, must surely lie in the fact that the Georgia pieces are more primordial in their rendering of passion, more "primitively" articulate in this groping attempt at fulfillment. Perhaps the underlying distinction is that the first part is really about cane, grow-

ing in wild abundance but destined for the sugar factories. The second is about Cain; his murder, described in the first part, means a destruction of his past and of his present. Hence Cain has wandered:

> Money burns the pocket, pocket hurts,
> bootleggers in silken shirts,
> Ballooned, Zooming Cadillacs,
> Whizzing, whizzing down the street-car tracks. (p. 39)

Within such an environment, even the instinctive impulses of the rural environment are no longer present. Instead, there is only the mechanical order that removes man further from the state of his real being—his blackness.

Within these artificial confines, therefore, a "Nigger God" cannot exist, for "He would duck his head in shame and call for the Judgement Day." Rhobert (Robert plus robot), like everyone else except the blind and deaf Father John, is far removed from the ability to connect. His situation becomes even more paradoxical and severe, for his material encumbrances seem to be the very instruments of release; but of course, they are not. Therefore, the house is "like a monstrous diver's helmet," because Rhobert rejects the reality of the outside world for oxygen from a tube. After his archetypal crime, he, the natural cane, has become the mechanical monster, Cain. His paradoxical being is expressed thus: "The dead house is stuffed. The stuffing is alive" (p. 40).

"Avey" is not merely a nostalgic piece about a remembered love. Her name, suggestive of an aviary, leaves much to be desired in her. The "I" narrator speaks of her "sloppy laziness," which is exemplified, in one of Toomer's best passages, as she falls asleep while the "I" narrator seeks "the truth that people bury in their hearts" (p. 46). This is an exploration of blackness beyond Negroness. The "I" narrator is a college student far removed from the earthiness of the earlier collectives of Toomer's rural sketches and from Avey's reality. He has romanticized her out of all existence, and perhaps this is why she finds it difficult to relate to him on the level of fantasy; for she is a real person within the confines of her Negroness. The sketch then becomes another microscopic look at Negroness; here the gap between illusion and fact obscures and blunts Black reality. In a way,

this obfuscation characterizes many of Toomer's contemporaries who romanticize the Black woman to the extreme of nonexistence.

The extent to which there is a backsliding from Black reality in the Negro world of *Cane* manifests itself in the fantasy and dream sequences, which are more pronounced in the urban sketches. This unreality is another instance of the curved arcs that never grow toward each other into a circle. Life here and in Georgia is never rounded and never completes itself. Indeed, the terrain is not dissimilar ("And when the wind from the South, soil in my homeland falls like a fertile shower upon the lean streets of the city . . ." [p. 46]). But on the soil of homeland in the South, total being was not possible. Therefore, how much less possible was it in the city, where the White mind dominated the Negro heart?

Negro movement is ritualized, losing the spasmodic urge of the country. "Theater" and "Box Seat" dramatize this predicament of contemporary, urban Negro man. In the former sketch, neither John nor Dorris is able to face up to the physical consequences of a grave passion; they dream out their fantasies. In "Box Seat," Dan and Muriel are unable to relate because Muriel cannot see the real Black world, cannot accept a rose from the hands of a dwarf or understand the crippling power of the institutions she cherishes and which in turn make her into a thing. If in the rural sketches the environment had distorted people so that they failed to relate, here the distortion is assumed and the inability to relate comes about because of things. A member of the audience at the Lincoln theater, is like "a bolt that shoots into a slot and is locked there." Mrs. Pribby is a "thing" that stands between Dan and Muriel, and "there is a sharp click as she fits into her chair." Earlier on, Muriel "skirts Dan as if to keep the glass between them," a house oppresses Rhobert, and a frantic search for Western materialism stands between the "I" narrator and Avey. The separation seems ultimate in the city.

In the rural pieces, the character-conglomerate Becky, living in an old log cabin near the railroad and the main road, shows the inescapable nature of a peculiar condition. Ostracized by both worlds, she lacks the resources to seek a way out, because she does not desire physical escape, and any spiritual releases lead her to self-hatred. In the urban piece, Bona (suggestive of goodness) seeks out the Black

in Paul. But he too is trapped by a refusal to face his Black self; it only leads him back with the sun to "a pinematted hillock in Georgia" (to his Negroness), and he finds nothing there, for he cannot understand the young Black woman's song of fertility. Eventually he has to return to what he knows ("Paul follows the sun into himself in Chicago"), and he finds himself at Bona's window looking through a dark pane. By the time he is near to completing his own circle ("white faces are petals of roses . . . dark faces are petals of dusk"), he has lost Bona. He has tried to relate back to the scenes in Georgia dusk and has begun the exploration that Dan performed in the theater when he saw the large Black woman "whose strong roots sink down and spread under the river" but nevertheless "disappear in blood-lines that waver south" (p. 62).

Therefore, the South is only the beginning. "Georgia Dusk" had hinted as much.

> . . . the men, with vestiges of pomp.
> Race memories of king and caravan
> High-priests, an ostrich and a ju-ju man
> Go singing through the footpaths of the swamp. (p. 13)

The journey in reverse across the Middle Passage is possible; concubines with "virgin lips," "dusky cane-lipped throngs," can have "dreams of Christ" (p. 13). Hence the possibility of an elevation above the fruitless matings on Georgia soil and the pointless encounters in the city can come about, and, thereafter, a full knowledge of blackness. The last sketch, "Kabnis," demonstrates this.

Kabnis (suggesting slave cabins) in his white, black, and yellow room is the epitome of miscegenation. External descriptions emphasize his plight—the Black mother singing to a White baby and his killing of a hen ("egg-laying bitch") as a symbol of his destruction of fertility. Between Kabnis and his world is himself—an ironic situation. He prays, "Dear Jesus, do not chain me to myself and set these hills and valleys, heaving with folksongs so close to me that I cannot reach them." For "Ralph Kabnis is a dream" (pp. 83, 81). How can one dissolve the self and not destroy?

This is the ultimate riddle that Kabnis has to face, in the last sketch of *Cane*. Compulsion has forced him to return to the South, but he

neither understands nor, at first, cares to understand. All of *Cane* comes together in "Kabnis." There are the character-conglomerates who have been alluded to before: the sensuous woman (Stella); the life-providing Black woman (Carrie-Kate), here only a girl; the well-integrated darkie completely aloof from the failure or even the necessity to connect (Hanby); the man of the earth, a welder, a forger (Halsey); the jive nigger, frequently a feature of the preacher jokes (Layman); and Father John, a former slave who can neither see nor hear and who seldom speaks, ironically, the reservoir of the cultural values of the race.

Not unnaturally, Kabnis at first rejects Father John, as he does his alter ego, Lewis. His reasons are really the same; both have come to terms with their slavery and their environment, each in his own way. Father John has rejected the fundamental deception of Whites; Lewis accepts this rejection and the manner in which it sets Negro against Black. Lewis represents good soil; Kabnis' encounter with Lewis and the moment of his inability to touch, to come to terms with himself in Lewis is well related. "Kabnis, a promise of a soil-soaked beauty; uprooted, thinning out. Suspended a few feet above the soil whose touch would resurrect him. Arm's length removed from him whose will to help . . ." (p. 96). The passage evokes the parable of the sower and his seed, and the crucifixion and resurrection of Christ, except that there is no link. The arcs are still displaced, never touching.

Kabnis' problem is a refusal to face up to his slave past; naturally when he meets Lewis, Lewis "seems to be issuing sharply from a vivid dream." Recall that Ralph Kabnis "is a dream" and cannot assert himself either with White aspirations, which Hanby represents, or through the Black physical ability, which Halsey represents. Nor can Kabnis recognize himself in Layman's tale about the ruse of the cornered Black, who pretended to pray and escape in the cunning manner of a folktale hero, by jumping into a stream. Failing to communicate with the only community there is, the Black church, Kabnis again fails himself. This is not the failure to recognize orthodox Christian doctrine, but to recognize Negro togetherness. Thus the singing from the church and the testifying are sore points for Kabnis. He had said earlier, "A bastard son has got a right to curse his maker

. . . God." Likewise he curses the communal life of the church, which stems from the tribal enclaves of Africa.

Kabnis is the ultimate in Toomer's defeated character-conglomerates. He sums up the total possibilities of negative attributes—lack of community, god, self-identification, belief in worth, and sexual vision and power of procreation, which causes the rejection by Carrie-Kate. Carrie-Kate could have united in him the conflicting opposites, since he is a part of every other stereotype in the Black world of the book. He is an artist like Layman, a manual worker like Halsey, a half-Negro like Hanby, and he has a Black potential for self-understanding, like Carrie-Kate and Father John. But, unlike the unnamed Black woman, he cannot unite "cane—and cotton-fields, pine forests, cypress swamps, sawmills and factories" within him, for he understands neither song nor dusk (p. 103). Song is associated throughout the book with the ability to correspond closely to deep participation in living, and dusk with the assertion of vitality. For him, there can only be his rejection of the singing from the nearby church and a "false dusk."

When Lewis explains Father John to Kabnis, he is really continuing Kabnis' own monologue. For Lewis, Father John is possibly "a tongue-tied shadow of an old religion" or "symbol in flesh and spirit of the past." It is this that Kabnis must seek, as Lewis tells him. First, there is heated rejection ("he ain't my past"), but after Lewis reminds Kabnis of his denial of heritage and environment, Lewis disappears. One suspects that Kabnis has expelled him to the Black world without, and now he has to come to terms with the monstrous part of his immediate self, Father John. In a long monologue to Father John, recognition and identification come slowly. "Do y think youre out of slavery? Huh? Youre where they used t throw th worked-out, no-count slaves . . . th sons-a . . . Why I can already see you toppled off that stool and stretched out on th floor *beside me*" (pp. 113–14). Though he rejects the association at this stage, the young girl Carrie-Kate bringing food to the old man helps Kabnis come closer to an understanding of what the old man wishes to say. Even before Father John can articulate "O th sin th white folks 'mitted when they made the Bible lie," Kabnis has already seen through the trick that history

has played him; he has said to the young girl, "The whole world is a conspiracy t sin, especially in America, an against me. I'm the victim of their sin." Too easily had Kabnis accepted the role assigned him by White history—the role of Cain. There is hope; one does not know if it is with Kabnis, but certainly the circle seems to be com-' plete for at least two people: "Light streaks through the iron-barred cellar window. Within its soft circle, the figures of Carrie and Father John" (pp. 115–16).

Seemingly, then, the failure, the incomplete circle, lies in the inability to relate to the outer area of that spiral, the unquestioned acceptance of the far past. The near past is present in *Cane*, especially in the rural sketches, in which interspersions of song and dance lend vitality to the physical nature of Negro life. But the women in the first part of *Cane* do not make the connection with the far past because they have been rendered as objects. Their environment has brutalized them, so that either they cannot feel at all, or when they do, fecundity is arrested. A child is killed by its mother, Karintha; Becky's sons grow up in hatred; Carma brutalizes herself and her man; Fern recoils from the woman in her; and Esther isolates herself from her only source of release, King Barlo.

In the urban pieces, the character-conglomerates underscore this inability to relate to the life source of strength, to a Negroness that is even more distant. Avey is the romanticized portrait of a Westernized college student; in "Theater," as Dorris dances, John dreams, and when she looks at his face, "she finds it a dead thing in the shadow which is his dream." Muriel, in "Box Seat," places herself where Whites usually sit in the theater in Black Harlem, counterpointing her refusal to face Dan. And neither Paul, in "Bona and Paul," nor Kabnis can move outwards from Negroness to blackness.

The roots are there: Layman's tales to Kabnis; the portly Black woman who sits next to Dan; the remembrance of the goat path in Africa; Stella and Cora, two whores who become African princesses as they comb their hair. But these are only fleeting, momentary possibilities. No one except Father John *is*. And he is deaf, blind, and nearly always mute. If the city man can be stripped of his environment, then an outward way may still be found to the experience of

Africa, which lingers in the songs and dance, in the ritual and closeness to the soil. But first, the human parts must complete themselves; man must learn to live with man, to break through obstacles of understanding, and to retrace the goat's path outward to the Black African kingdoms of princesses and peasants.

4 Responses to Africa

The New World Black man brought some cultural dress. Although he was deprived of a great deal of it, the necessity for it remained, and because it was functional, sheer practicality prolonged its wear. It adorned itself in a new consciousness of place and time, and while it may have lacked style in terms of Old World Africa, it demonstrated a new uniform of necessity. How does one Caribbean writer (White) respond to this practical change of gear? And how do a host of English and White Americans react? The answers are important for our study.

In *Ayapá* (1971) Lydia Cabrera has elevated African myth and legend into a written form. She attempts in these stories to recapture the meaning of the Turtle. She says in her preface:

> El esclavo, al igual que la impedida, inofensiva Jicotea, que no puede medirse con los fuertes, tenía que recurrir a alguna triquiñuela para sacar una ventaja, burlar el rigor de un contramayoral—odioso porque era otro negro—, despitar o embaucar al amo de piel blanca. Podía comparar su condición a la de Jicotea y gozarse con sus fechorías, aplaudir sus trastadas, sus traiciónes y mentiras ingeniosas. La más desposeída y débil de las criaturas, las más conciente de su pequeñez y de su impotencia, era capaz de leones, elefantes, todos temidos, admirados, acatados; grandes figurónes "privilegiados", come se dice ahora, del mundo animal, hinchados de la misma vanidad que los nuestros—capitalistas o jerarcas totalitarios-sucumben cándidamente a sus ardides.[1]

The slave, in the same way as the handicapped harmless Turtle, who cannot struggle against the stronger, had to take recourse at times in trickery to obtain some advantage to laugh at the rigor of his supervisors

1. Lydia Cabrera, *Ayapá* (Miami, 1971), 11.

—it was hateful to him because this supervisor was also Black—to fool the master of the White skin. He could compare his condition to that of the Turtle and enjoy its mischievous acts. He could applaud his misbehavior, his treason and his ingenious lies. The weakest and most dispossessed of creatures, the most conscious of her smallness and her impotence, was capable of taking on lions, elephants, all feared, admired, and revered. As is said today, these were great privileged creatures of the animal world, inflated with the same vanity as ours. Capitalists or totalitarian dictators candidly succumbed to her cunning.

Jicotea (Turtle) is returned to his rightful place by the narrator. He speaks in Lucumí and through the *babalawo* shares the presence of the divine. He knows how to act when Orunmila comes and does not dare to scratch. Jicotea witnesses the sacredness of the *babalawo's* functions as the drum begins to speak in one story of the life of the dead.

Thus an important alteration takes place, and African culture, in becoming Afro-New World culture, is no less practical. What is changed is the manner in which the Turtle, Stagolee, Shine, or the Signifying Monkey happen to be perceived. They become not merely protagonists, but antagonists; they are still culture heroes, but now they *attack* the new cultures that would rob them of their potency. This becomes important in our comprehension of New World cultural stances, which must serve as a racial foil, counter prejudice, and assert dominance when the latter seems least evident. Black art must, therefore, reproduce representative and relevant aspects of Old World African culture and also introduce a New World interpretation.

I

Alejo Carpentier's *Ecué-Yamba-ó* (1933) does just this.[2] Menegildo Cué is a young Black boy and the protagonist of *Ecué-Yamba-ó*. He has to help his parents, who are sugar plantation workers, to work, because the harvest is forthcoming. Problems are complicated, for the Americans are buying the sugar estate factories with the result that owners either sell or go into rivalry. Usebio refuses to sell out,

2. Alejo Carpentier, *Ecué-Yamba-ó* (Montevideo, Uruguay, 1973), from which page references herein are taken.

but he is soon in difficulty and has to sell his cane at half-price.

The boy grows up in this atmosphere of uncertainty. Soon he meets Longina and asks a local *brujero* to help him win her. Menegildo does not know she is married, and one night, on returning from town, he is soundly beaten by her husband, Napolión, a huge Haitian. In an investigation during his imprisonment, Menegildo cannot explain why Napolión was cut up and left bleeding at the side of the road.

While in prison, he hears from his cousin Antonio, of the *ñañigo* secret society. When he is released owing to a lack of evidence, Napolión vanishes and Menegildo gains Longina. Soon he manages to become a member of the *ñañigo* society. Carpentier describes the details of the ritual—the initiation, the confrontation with Eshu, and the offering to the gods. Finally the oath is taken and a liturgy is sung.

In the meantime Menegildo's private life seems to improve, for his wife is expecting a baby. But at a party, suddenly and without warning, they are attacked. Menegildo dies and Longina, after enduring some abuse from her mother-in-law, has his child. He too is called Menegildo.

Janheinz Jahn refers to this story as "the only novel of Afro-Cubanism."[3] Pedro M. Barreda-Tomás called the novel "el primer ejemplo importante de novela negra en la República," because in it Carpentier has made extensive use of his own knowledge of Afro-Cuban culture.[4] Menegildo is representative of the suffering and endurance of New World Black man; his prison sentence, his thwarted love affair, his search for his African roots, and his violent death typify him as a combination of men. He seems, on one level, to be the history of Afro-New World man.

Menegildo's world is one that has a wide compass. It includes Americans, Jamaicans, Haitians, and a Polish shopkeeper. And he has his prejudices. "He felt very strange among so many blacks of other customs and other languages. The Jamaicans were very proud

3. Janheinz Jahn, *Neo-African Literature: History of Black Writing* (New York, 1969), 222.

4. Pedro M. Barreda-Tomás, "Alejo Carpentier: Dos visiones del Negro, dos conceptos de la novela," *Hispania*, (March, 1972), 34.

and they were animals! The Haitians were animals and savages" (p. 45). With a fellow Cuban he feels empathy: "Ese, por los menos, hablaba como los cristianos!" (That one at least spoke like a Christian!) He laughs at a large Jamaican woman intoning a Christian hymn and accompanied by two Salvation Army men.

Near the beginning of the novel Menegildo encounters a mixture of vulgarity and indigenous lore. English words, in some parts devoted to the Americans, are tucked in among the Spanish sentences, emphasizing the discordance. Even the line "varios cantadores guajiros improvisaban décimas" introduces a crude element, as a group of Polish Jews sings songs while chanting about their wares. Here, however, the antiimperialist note is also struck, as Menegildo reflects: "But who thought about tomorrow anymore? It was so very well known that in the long run only the Yankees, masters of the estate, managed to benefit themselves from the meager profits of these ruinous harvests!" (p. 48).

Throughout the novel Carpentier is blatant in his attacks on the capitalistic system. Later, he himself was to criticize *Ecué-Yamba-ó* as being too blatant and too obvious. But it is interesting that the chief character is Black and stereotyped, like the Jamaican and the American. Seemingly trapped within the values of his society, Menegildo is used in this way to attack other stereotypes. He enshrines Cuban antiimperialist values and, having been rejected, becomes an outsider, witnessing to the atrocities around him.

Menegildo is also a witness to the decay of morality in Cuban life. We are prepared for this from the first solemn greeting his Black friend, Antonio, gives in *ñañigo*. Later, the talk is lost in baseball and, apparently, petty politics. A giveaway line for a Cuban audience, however, is "una bañadera cuya agua 'salpicaba' plateado" (a bathtub that splashed silver-plated water), which reveals corruption in vivid imagery. In Cuba, when politicians threw away money, the saying was that "the shark may go into the water but he splashes"; thus, for the politician to keep swimming, he allowed others to share in his misdeeds. They in turn would help to keep him swimming. Thus, Antonio says, matters grow worse and each year the cane is sold for less. Through Antonio, Menegildo hears about electoral

frauds and the punishments meted out to the opposition. Menegildo, the spokesman, represents the author himself, who is imprisoned for opposing the government.

> Menegildo recordaba las fiestas políticas celebradas en el pueblo. Las guirnaldas de Papel, tendidas de casa en casa. Las pencas de guano adornando los portales. Cohetes voladores, y disparos al aire. Una tribuna destinada a la oratoria, y una *charanga* de cornetín, contrabajo, güiro y timbal, para glosar discursos con aire de décima, en que el panegírico del candidato era trazado con elocuencia tronitruante por medio de parrafadas chillónas que organizaban exhibiciónes de guayaberas heroícas, cargas al machete y pabellónes tremolados en gloriosos palmares . . . El apoteósis de las promesas estilizaba el campo de Cuba. Los jacos engordaban, los pobres comían, los bueyes tendrían alas, y nadie repararía en el color de los negros; sería el imperio del angelísmo y la concordia. (p. 49)

> Menegildo recalled the political fiestas celebrated in the town. The paper decorations strung up from house to house. Palm leaves adorning the porches. Firecrackers and gunshots in the air. A tribunal destined for oratory and a *charanga* of a coronet, a counterbase, a *güiro* and bongo, to polish the speeches with the air of *décima* in which the eulogies of the candidate were traced with a thundering eloquence through the rows of screams that organized exhibitions of heroic Cuban shirts, charges with machete in hand and pavilions decked with glorious palms. . . . The apotheosis of promises stylized in the fields of Cuba. The nags became fatter, the poor ate, the oxen would have wings, and no one would criticize the color of the Black man: It would be the empire of angelism and concord.

The bitterness here is unmistakable. As the politicians speak of Maceo and Martí, of Columbus and the sword of Damocles, and as the university-educated sway the masses in one direction or another, Menegildo, like Carpentier, feels that Cuba is up for sale to the highest bidder: "Había que saber ordeñar la vaca lechera del régimen demagógico!?" (Did one have to know how to milk the cow of the demagogical regime?). The graft of the politicians bred further greed on the part of the so-called electorate. The entire demonstration is a *conga* in which Afro-Cuban references to music and dance mock the make-believe revolution that is to take place. The real potential for the revolution is in the Black self and soul of Menegildo, but his entire purpose has been perverted. Even the song "Aé, aé, aé, la cham-

belona," which once launched a revolution, is now a cry of mockery. Menegildo, the Black, has become entrapped in his own history, like the people of his country.

Carpentier manages to convey to the patient reader how this is done. The basic food of the Cuban peasant is presented in the same droll, ironic way: "sardinas pescadas en Terranova, albaricoques encerrados en latas con nombre de novela romántica, carne de res salada al ritmo de ban duneón porteño el bacalao de la Madre Patria y un arroz de no sabía donde" (sardines caught in Terranova, apricots packed in tin cans with the name of a romantic novel, beef salted to the rhythm of an accordion from the port, and salted fish of the mother country, and rice from who knows where [p. 85]). It is all imported; the beef is from Argentina (the country of the accordion), the salted fish from what is ironically referred to as "la Madre Patria" (Spain), and the rice is most likely from the United States. Carpentier, in identifying with Menegildo, reflects on what has become of his country—the New World.

The "dance of the millions" occurred during World War I, when sugar was needed for gunpowder. It was a temporary economic boom owing to high sugar prices. After the war, with the introduction of beet sugar, Cuban sugar was no longer in high demand. This resulted in the great economic collapse of 1918. At that time, large American conglomerates bought up the sugar estates for small sums, with the result that American control lasted tnroughout Machado's dictatorship. A slow process throughout World War II saw the growth of a middle class that was able to regain control over Cuban businesses. By 1940, the picture was a little better. But Menegildo belongs to the 1920s. He is anti-American because most of Cuba is owned by American interests such as the United Fruit Company. It is possible to see the American, not as an imperialist, but as the savior of the Cuban economy; but Menegildo does not. He is a product of sugar plantations that he cannot own. He sees big business only in American hands, and his reaction is a logical one.

Menegildo is important, for only through his kind is preservation of the authentic Cuba ensured. "Sólo los negros, Menegildo, Longina, Salomé y su prole conservaban celosamente un carácter y una tradición antillana. El *bongó*, antídoto de Wall-Street! El Espiritu Santo,

venerado por los Cué no admitía salchichas yanquis dentro de sus panecillos votivos! . . . Nada de *hot-dogs* con los santos de Mayeyal!" (Only the Blacks, Menegildo, Longina, Salomé, and their kind conserved Caribbean character and tradition zealously. The bongo was the antidote of Wall Street! The Holy Spirit, venerated by the Cué,, did not allow American sausages in its bread rolls offered as vows! . . . No hot dogs for the saints of Mayayal! [p. 86]). The denials that will affirm Menegildo as a *ñañigo* are there. They confirm him more strongly in his own Black faith and belief in his country. They also turn him toward a revolutionary path. He has become "el macho," armed with a knife. He is a furious man, and the revenge he exacts against Longina's husband is a direct result of the pressures he feels. He has to pay for being an outsider; he has dared to defy the colonial society, and when he is arrested by the "guardia rural," it is not for his political leanings. Napolión, Longina's Haitian husband, has apparently been killed.

This is a disappointing way for a hero to go. Carpentier, accused of conspiring against Machado, was jailed. Menegildo, too, is imprisoned, but for the wrong reason; if it is assumed that Menegildo personifies the opposition to exploitation, then this becomes the reason for his imprisonment. The love theme and Menegildo's presumed innocence spoil the plot and confuse issues. In the final analysis, he is not so much Longina's lover as America's hater. Although Carpentier details the conditions of Menegildo's prison life, the reader does not sympathize with him. He has been transformed from the stereotype of unremitting defender of Cuba into a Black knight errant, thus causing confusion of issues.

He does remain, however, a witness to the wrongs of Cuba. In this context, his initiation in *Ecué-Yamba-ó* is necessary and real. He arrives, with Antonio, on the compound of the sugar estate, and he sees a square building of red wood covered with palm leaves. The symbol of a circle and three crosses enclosing two triangles, a palm, and a snake are marked on the door to represent the supreme secrets of *ñañiguismo*. He gives Antonio the ritual black rooster he had brought, and Antonio goes into the hut, from which Menegildo has heard the sounds of drums and crying on previous occasions. Suddenly the noise inside stops. Antonio is now his *padrino*, who will

introduce him to the secrets that will alter his life. He reappears in a blindfold with yellow chalk and is now a different man, no longer part of the baseball world and the *marimbula* with which Menegildo associates him. Naturally, Menegildo is afraid, for the Antonio he sees is stripped of the popular legends with which Cuba has embellished the Black man. The time for oath taking has come.

First, Menegildo disposes of his t-shirt and leather shoes, and rolls up his pants to his knees. Antonio draws two crosses on his back, one on his forehead, one on each ankle, and two on his chest. He abruptly blindfolds Menegildo, leads him to the center of the shrine and tells him to kneel and place his elbows on the ground. Later, he is placed with other neophytes in a circle. Famballén, the guardian of ritual objects, leads them with a drum adorned with a rooster tail. The call of the rooster is heard. The magical moment begins for Menegildo when "in the heart of the palm offered [there was] the golden eye of Montoriongo, the first rooster sacrificed by the *ñañigos* from over there [in Africa]." Then he hears "Una serie de golpes secos, entrecortados de pausas bruscas. Y una voz burlona que grita:—Nazacó, acó, sacó, querembá, masangará . . . Un gorro puntiagudo, rematado por un penacho de paja, asomó a la puerta del bohío. Se ocultó. Volvió a salir. Desapareció otra vez.—Nazacó, sacó, sacó . . . Una voz gritó detrás de Menegildo:—Námalo, Arencibia, que no quiere salil" (a series of dry thumps interrupted by abrupt pauses and a mocking voice which screamed, "Nazacó, acó, sacó, querembá, masangará." A pointed hat topped with a bunch of straw appeared at the door of the hut. It hid itself. It came out again. It disappeared again: "Nazacó, sacó, sacó." A voice shouted behind Menegildo: "Call him, Arencibia; he does not want to come out" [p. 20]). A secret door is then opened for the Cuatra Fambá, and the neophytes are led into the sanctuary and made to kneel in front of the altar. A table is covered with red paper and adorned with paper flowers. A Catholic cross towers above, and in the center is a large jug covered with seashells. Four feathers—the bengué, the mogobión, the abacuá, and the manantión—embody the force of Ecué.

They hear a sound, something like the croaking of a frog, or sandpaper, or leather. The noise comes from a box covered and bound with palm leaves. Menegildo feels the Ecué and has goose bumps.

Antonio has advised him that this is all part of the ceremony, the meaningfulness of the earth. The drums sound again, and a being without a face and bearing a large triangular head on his chest comes from one of the huts. The figure has a white cross, a triangular hat, a string of bells on its ankle, and a tail. It holds a broom in its right hand and a scepter for exorcism in its left. Then comes the sound of "Yamba-ó," or "Be praised," in *ñañigo*. The figure begins to dance and to reenact the glories of the African past. A rooster is passed over the novices' heads and shoulders by the god, who then runs to the entrance and throws the sacrifice into the middle of the road.

The purification is now complete. The new members rise and are led to a hut where the *munifamba*, god of the faithful, waits for them. There is a symbolic turning, followed by dizziness, that marks their forgetting what they have witnessed. Further cleansing follows. In another hut, their heads are anointed with a special sacrificial ointment made of rooster blood, gunpowder, tobacco, pepper, alcohol, and sesame seeds.

After the ritual, the swearing in takes place, in the form of call and refrain:

> ¡Jura usté decil la verdá?
> ¡sí señol!
> ¿Pa qué viene usté a esta Potencia?
> ¡Pa socorrel a mi 'hemmanos'! (p. 126)

> Do you swear to tell the truth?
> Yes Lord!
> Why did you come to this faith?
> To help my 'brothers'!

Then Eshu speaks in *ñañigo* to them.

After the oath comes the initiation proper. As the sun begins to descend over the mountains, they have to perform a final test. They kneel around the offerings to the dead, and seven crosses are traced out with gunpowder around them. The god reappears in the form of a small man who dances to the drums. The crosses are lit and the god takes off his suit and dances in the nude. By now, they have made offerings of rum, and they are all dancing. One of the new members must take the offerings and throw them over a cliff, to appease the ancestors. Then the new members line up and return singing a lit-

urgy. Thus Africa has asserted its living presence in the New World.

Novels like *Ecué-Yamba-ó*, in which the clear embodiment of the African past is so clearly depicted, do not abound. It matters little whether this is a true and exacting ethnographical account, or one in which the author, in employing his knowledge of *ñañiguismo*, may have introduced fictitious elements. What surely matters is the vivid evocation of Africa in realistic terms. The *ñañigo* vocabulary adds to the authenticity and, indeed, to our faith in the writer's credibility. But what matters above all is that the ceremony has restored something of grandeur to the squalid life of Menegildo and those he represents. Though he physically dies, he lives on in his son, Menegildo, who now becomes the ancestor of the future.

Whether the *ñañigo* rites are dutifully reported, *Ecué-Yamba-ó* remains a most interesting document of Afro-New World experience. Ecue is the great mysterious one, and by focusing on him, Carpentier seems to imply that, through this Black mystery, Afro-New World man can take his White counterpart into the region of a new culture that will save him from complete extinction. The detail that is devoted to *ñañigo* rites and the death of Menegildo during a *ñañigo* ceremony would suggest the potency of belief and the durability of all that Menegildo stood for in a muddled world of another time.

The ceremony links him firmly with an authentic African past, not an invented fallacy. However, he is unable to go back along the path of a lost past; instead, he must use signposts of a half-remembered ritual to tell him the way in which he should direct his footsteps to a New World future. This seems to be the most valid and unquestionably affirmative indicator of the novel's worth.

II

Menegildo's revival of Africa is a combination of definite reflection and ardent invention. It serves a need; Menegildo, the outcast, finds a place in the ancestral rites of his forebears. Carpentier has worked the material of Ortiz and Cabrera into an imaginative reordering. He has not distorted it but given it greater credibility.

Similarly, "Pocomania," a poem by Philip Sherlock, takes its name from a Jamaican religious sect that is characterized by its ability to evoke the spirit within converts and thus enable them to make proph-

ecies and revelations. The second stanza intentionally has an incantatory rhythm to emphasize the ritualistic nature of the ceremony. The middle of the poem is philosophic: What, the poet asks, is the significance of all that he has described in the second stanza? There is Asia with its idea of Christ the shepherd and his flock, and Africa with its ancient gods. Then, after an injunction by someone involved in the ceremony (appropriately couched in dialect), the poem comes to a climax in lines that vigorously describe the way that the dead take control of the living.

> Grunting low and in the dark
> White of gown and circling dance
> Gone to-day and all control
> Now the dead are in control
> Power of the past returns
> Africa among the trees
> Asia with her mysteries.
>
> Black the stars, hide the sky
> Lift you' shoulder, blot the moon.
> Long Mountain rise.[5]

The final line gives the poem its final dramatic effect.

In Eric Roach's "Ballad of Canga," the treatment of the idea is different, but the intention is the same. Although a number of stories are related here about Canga, a legendary African, in reality, the poem loosely strings together an assortment of popular survivals. Basically, the poem is humorous in intent, since Roach seems more than a little skeptical of Canga's powers. Consequently, there is some intentional exaggeration. The narrative line and the etiological ending are in keeping with a certain type of West African folktale:

> When God come for the man
> And call him: "Canga, Canga."
> That old sinner tie his mouth;
> Not he, he wouldn't answer.
>
> God stretch out his crockstick:
> "Sinner, get up, go down,"
> "Lord, call me Mister Brown."

5. Philip Sherlock, "Pocomania," in O. R. Dathorne (ed.), *Caribbean Verse* (London, 1967), 66.

> God vex until he laugh in heaven;
> Pull a big chair for Canga.
> Is that why when the man dead
> You hearing so much thunder.[6]

The chief success of the poem lies in the way it debunks the power of the European and the omnipotence of God. In the end, it is Canga who triumphs.

Vera Bell, in her poem "Ancestor on the Auction Block," reevaluates her own place as a Black woman in the history of the New World. By the repetition of the phrase "ancestor on the auction block," she emphasizes the humiliation of the slave. The poem describes a dramatic reassessment of self, the third stanza marking the turning point toward the new understanding. Intentionally, the rhythm of the first two stanzas is fixed and almost harsh, and the lines contract into disappointing revelations at the end. In the last two stanzas she rebuilds her confidence in herself through the new understanding. This is why there is an expansive pattern in the line structure.

> I look you in the eyes and see
> The spirit of God eternal
> Of this only need I be ashamed
> Of blindness to the God within me
> The same God who dwelt within you
> The same eternal God
> Who shall dwell
> In generations yet unborn.
>
> Ancestor on the auction block
> Across the years
> I look
> I see you sweating, toiling, suffering
> Within your loins I see the seed
> Of multitudes
> From your labour
> Grow roads, aqueducts, cultivation
> A new country is born
> Yours was the task to clear the ground
> Mine be the task to build[7]

6. Eric Roach, "Ballad of Canga," in *ibid.*, 59.
7. Vera Bell, "Ancestor on the Auction Block," in *ibid.*, 18–19.

Finally, one is left with a deep feeling of satisfaction and awe, partly derived from an insistent belief in the future of Afro-New World man.

Harold Telemaque's "Poem" shows how the African theme is synthesized in Caribbean literature. He associates Africa not only with Egypt, the Congo, and the Guinea forest, but also with American Negro spirituals. In spite of the public nature of the utterance, the poem succeeds because Telemaque consciously uses a number of devices. For instance, the descriptions that follow *who* gather force and momentum as the poem proceeds until, in the latter part, the lines expand into a swelling rhythm.

> To those
> Who lifted into shape
> The huge stones of the pyramid;
> Who formed the Sphinx in the desert,
> And bid it
> Look down upon the centuries like yesterday;
> Who walked lithely
> On the banks of the Congo,
> And heard the deep rolling moan
> Of the Niger. . . .[8]

This poem seems pitched two or three levels above the normal level of sound. It has a swelling overture and is perfectly balanced from a rhythmical standpoint. The eulogy is contained between the words "To those," found at the beginning, and the end. The syntactical device of making the reader wait until the final line for the main verb, "hail," has the effect of exploring the full tonal properties of the last word.

These poems "revive" Africa though they are not African poems or translations of African poems or even, as with *Ecué-Yamba-ó*, a close recollection; but they do attempt to render the African past in terms of the Caribbean present. The writers are not, as M. G. Smith states, "faced with the problems of marked cultural dissimilarities within the West African regions, from which the bulk of Caribbean Negroes trace descent."[9] Indeed, few would agree now that such a

8. Harold M. Telemaque, "Poem," in *ibid.*, 73.
9. M. G. Smith, "The African Heritage in the Caribbean," in Vera Rubin (ed.), *Caribbean Studies: A Symposium* (New York, 1957).

problem could possibly exist, for a new Africa was forged out of what came to these new shores. As Leonard Barrett puts it, "Out of the despair [of slavery] the Africans began to rebuild their belief system, adapting it to the new conditions of slavery."[10] This is the way that ethnic man became African man. But Afro-New World is his name, not Africa.

III

The revival of Africa was also undertaken by White writers. Racist assertions like Philip Curtin's, that Africans might become so Europeanized as to present a Western outlook, will not constitute part of the reasoning here.[11] Instead, I will examine some attempts at White affirmation of Africa in the New World that serve two purposes: to confirm the inferiority of the Black man and to establish the stereotype that Black writers would use later on. Aphra Behn's *Oroonoko: or the Royal Slave* (1688) comes to mind. It supposedly gives an account of an African prince, Oroonoko, sold into slavery and taken to Surinam. There, he encounters his former lover, Imoinda, from whom he had been separated. Because she fears the capture and death of her lover following the failure of his attempt to lead a slave revolt, Imoinda agrees to a happy death at his hands. He is later executed when found near her body.

Oroonoko cannot be a real person. He is a mixture of mistaken notions, for his very name is part New World Indian and presumably African. He is a European invention, given to a belief in honor. He is a scholar, soldier, prince, and, above all, a gentleman. Although he was a slave, he admired the Romans, knew of the civil wars in England, and "in all points addressed himself as if his education had been in some European court."[12] His nose was Roman and his mouth different from those of the other Africans. Behn goes to a great deal of trouble to establish that Oroonoko is Black, yet not African.

The beginning of the crisis of so-called educated Afro-New World

10. Leonard E. Barrett, *Soul-Force* (New York, 1974), 60.
11. Philip D. Curtin, "African Reactions in Perspective," in Philip D. Curtin (ed.) *Africa and the West* (Madison, 1972), 232.
12. Aphra Behn, *Oroonoko: or the Royal Slave* (London, 1688), 19. Frederick M. Link, *Aphra Behn* (New York, 1968), 139–42, discusses the book.

man is clearly expounded in literature. It is obviously an invented one. As Nathan Hare bluntly puts it, "The life of a mimic is accordingly one endless duplication of White society."[13] Oroonoko is the archetypal example of this. Whatever may have been Behn's motives, and one does not doubt that she meant well, Oroonoko merely confirms the Europeans' ethnocentric view of their world.

Robert Browning's poem, "Caliban upon Setebos," continues this view. Africans, according to popular beliefs, were godless, and so Caliban *invents* the Quiet, a power supreme over Setebos. There is a certain savagery in the reflection, "He is strong and Lord," which may easily be compared with Oroonoko's reflections. But Africans (and one may assume that Caliban is one) inherit a cosmology; they do not invent it. This misconception becomes another way in which the revival of Africa is distorted. However, the linkage becomes a point of interest here, because in both cases, Europeans are doing the distorting. In other words, before Afro-New World man could adequately chart his own world, it had already been misdrawn for him. A notable pioneering work was Thomas Jefferson's *Notes on the State of Virginia* (1782), which downgraded every single Black author of that time.

If one excuses Behn and Browning on the grounds of ignorance, how does one explain Evelyn Waugh? He had visited Ethiopia in 1930 and 1935. His travel book, *Waugh in Abyssinia* (1936), welcomes the Italian invasion and expresses hope that a European influence will emerge. His novels, *Black Mischief* (1932) and *Scoop* (1938), are relevant here. One critic deduces from Waugh's satire of Emperor Haile Selassie, in *Black Mischief*, "that his people are wholly barbaric and whatever merits European ways may have in Europe they are meaningless among the savages of Azania."[14] *Scoop* contrasts Azania with Ishmaelia, which is ruled by the Jacksons, who are "innocent of progressive ambitions."[15]

The African revival is in the hands of Europeans who either do not know Africa at all or only know it cursorily. Yet they write about it,

13. Nathan Hare, *The Black Anglo Saxons* (New York, 1965), 75.
14. Christopher Hollis, *Evelyn Waugh* (London, 1958), 9.
15. *Ibid.*, 12.

and naturally, when Blacks begin to write, there is a tendency to copy not only the European form (the novel, the play, the poem), but also the European stance.

Usually, what Europeans see is observed from a balcony. Lady Nugent, the American wife of a British governor of Jamaica, keeps a journal in which she meticulously makes entries between 1801 and 1805. She is observant, almost to the point of regarding her subjects as curious objects. For instance, on one occasion, when returning from a morning ride, she observes some Ibos, recently arrived as slaves, and stops her carriage so that she "might examine their countenances as they passed."[16] This she proceeds to do, and soon notices one man with "cannibal teeth." However, she merrily concludes that they all looked happy.

Taken out of a purely African setting and transported to the New World, the Black man may have lost some of the nobility bestowed by Behn, but he is still, strangely enough, happy. We can see another extension of the European mythical revival of Africa in this. Of course, it could be little different, for if these writers were to say otherwise, they would be implying that slavery was wrong.

Because the revival by Europeans was insipid, contradictions abound. The cowardly, whining African is also described in these exhilarating terms by one writer. "It is not in the American colonies that we are to look for their bodily exertions; we should trace them in their wilds, the interminable forests of Africa, we should behold them in their native woods, their deserts and their waters; we should follow them in the chase of the lion, the tyger and the crocodile; in fatigue that would melt down an European constitution."[17] Edward Long found that the very same people "had a covering of hair like the bestial fleece instead of hair."[18] Oliver Goldsmith added that "as their persons are thus naturally deformed, their minds are equally incapable of strong exertions."[19] Then, a "liberal," toward the end of

16. Maria Nugent, *Lady Nugent's Journal; Jamaica One Hundred Years Ago . . . 1801–1815* (London, 1966), 220.
17. William Beckford, *Remarks upon the Situation of Negroes in Jamaica* (London, 1788), 86.
18. Edward Long, *History of Jamaica, or a General Survey of the Ancient and Modern State of That Island* (London, 1970 [1774]), II, 352.
19. Oliver Goldsmith, *History of the Earth and Animated Nature* (London, 1774), I, 212.

the eighteenth century, said, "It is cruel and illiberal to insinuate the least suggestion of their partaking of the brute creation."[20] Not unnaturally, in Harriet Beecher Stowe's *Uncle Tom's Cabin* (1852), the only Blacks who are comely have European features.

These confused ideas established little truth and left the field wide open for imaginative writers. Hence, in this free-for-all, Shakespeare, Behn, Browning, and Waugh were *all* right. By the nineteenth century, the false beliefs had been rationalized, and Carlyle wrote that, on a visit to Demerara (Guiana), one would see "an idle Black gentleman with his rum bottle in his hand"; for "Quashie" is a "merry-hearted, grinning, dancing, singing, affectionate kind of *creature*." (italics added)[21]

As a creature, the Afro-New World man is therefore unbelievably stupid. A plantation owner, Matthew Lewis, writing in 1815, shows that slaves are fools. Sometimes he fails to understand that the joke is directed against him. For example, when he reprints a song made up to herald a slave uprising in an entry on March 22, 1816, the leader of the uprising claims that the song was a mere hymn![22]

Whenever the English look at Afro-New World man, he is nearly always good for a laugh. This emerges especially in Michael Scott's two travel books, *Tom Cringle's Log* (1829–1833) and *The Cruise of the Midge* (1835), as well as in the anonymous book, *The Adventures of Jonathan Corncob* (1787). Michael Scott had visited the Caribbean in 1806, and he makes his chief character, Tom Cringle, draw on what are supposed to be real life experiences. Some of the comedy is simply in bad taste; John Crow, "the Black," and Jackoo, the monkey, fight a shark together near Kingston, and Snowball sings about how he was sold into slavery. Dignity is granted no one, not even the Black pilot who tells them that their way of addressing him as "Blackie is not poli'ful."[23]

Scott's prejudices are even more evident in *The Cruise of the*

20. James Bigham Moreton, *West Indian Customs and Manners* (London, 1790), 151.

21. Thomas Carlyle, *Occasional Discourse on the Nigger Question* (London, 1853), 12–14.

22. Matthew Gregory Lewis, *Journal of a West India Proprietor, 1815–17* (Boston, 1929 [1834]), entry for March 22, 1816.

23. Michael Scott, *Tom Cringle's Log* (New York, 1895 [1836]), 119.

Midge. Sergeant Quacco, an important character, displays Scott's opinions of New World Blacks. The typical sneers abound: Quacco cannot speak English well, he is ugly, and he has no respect for his compatriots. But the joke is on the narrator in the following encounter.

> At her call two tall young Mulatto fellows, with necks like cranes, and bushy heads like the long brooms used to clean staircases, without stockings or neckcloths, dressed in white duck trousers and blue coatees, and a very pretty, well-dressed brown girl, of about eighteen, presented themselves at the door of the room.
> "Pray, who are those?" said I, during a lull of the matron's paroxysm.
> "Who dem is? why your own cosin—your own flesh and blood—your oncle, God bless him—him children dem is, all—ay, every one on dem."[24]

Quacco had arrived in Montego Bay and sought lodgings from a Black woman, Sally Frenche, who he is amazed to discover is the daughter of his dead uncle. It is a sad joke that appears in the first Afro-American novel, *Clotel* (1853), by William Wells Brown (in the English edition, Clotel is described as Thomas Jefferson's daughter), and that continues into the twentieth century with the Jamaican author Herbert G. de Lisser's *Psyche* (1952) (Psyche belatedly discovers she has a Black mother).

These concerns, which might more properly belong to a full treatment of race in the New World, have to be alluded to here as a way of demonstrating the bequeathal of a distortion. Briefly put, White writers refused to see Quashie as another man in the New World; for basically examined, his sperm was that of God's: it had the power of transforming and inventing New World man. To downgrade his African ancestry and, later on, himself was to attempt to laugh off the real and significant threat. He was, as I have asserted, the New World man. Only he could fill the vacant spaces of history by a novel approach to life.

One way of saying that Quashie could not be New World man was to downplay his religion and emphasize Christianity. Vachel Lindsay's 1913 poem, "The Congo," insolently subtitled "a study of the States), the Congo, Mumbo-Jumbo (a tutelary genius of the Mandin-Negro race," confuses "Voodo" (Haitian), hoo-doo (southern United

---

24. Michael Scott, *The Cruise of the Midge* (London, 1894 [1836]), 124.

gos), various references to African music, and Afro-American dance and music. It attempts to pose a basic confrontation between the Black "witchmen" and the Apostles, "in their bright white steele." Written in memory of a missionary who had drowned in the Congo, the poem continues this confusion. Naturally, Europe wins.

> Oh, a singing wind swept the negro nation
> And on through the backwoods clearing flew:—
> "Mumbo-Jumbo is dead in the jungle . . ."

It is this death of Mumbo-Jumbo that is the death of the Black man's past in White literature. Such a death Black authors themselves celebrate but seldom mourn, time after time.

In *The Adventures of Jonathan Corncob*, another eighteenth-century travel account, Jonathan Corncob's adventures take place in Barbados. There he witnesses a whipping, and the reader is expected to laugh at the casual remark of the innkeeper who, when asked for the reason, states glibly, "It is the first day of the month, when I always make it a rule to give a few lashes to my slaves." A sorrowful farmer tells him tearfully that not only has he lost twenty slaves, but six were pregnant. One might infer that the humor is a way of exposing the callousness of slave owners, but Corncob himself is part of this very pattern. For instance, during a hurricane, he finds himself on a slave girl's back and reasons: "As my good fortune had placed me on her back, I thought proper to keep my hold, for as she was in the front, it was clear that she would first encounter any obstacle in the way, and save my bones at the expense of her own. This reasoning as she was a slave was very fair." The double standard emerges here, amusingly recounted, but nevertheless true. It is not so amusing when the reader learns that "Mr. Wynter is the father of them all. When he was young he had the mulatto woman by the white; when the mulatto was twelve years old, he took her for his mistress, and had by her the mestee. At about the same age his intimacy with the mestee produced the quadroon who had by him a few months in her arms [a White child]. This is what is called in his country washing a man's self white." [25]

Joel Chandler Harris has Uncle Remus tell the story of the pond

---

25. Jonathan Corncob [pseud.], *The Adventures of Jonathan Corncob, Loyal American, Written by Himself* (London, 1787), 145, 139, 127.

and how those who got there first became White. The second and the third Mulatto, however, remained Black except for palms and soles, because there was only enough water left so that "de morest dey could do wuz ter paddle wit der foots en dabble in it wid der han's."[26] It is a joke too, in slightly bad taste; I am concerned not only with the repetition of the joke, but the necessity for it.

Robinson Crusoe goes through the process of conquest and enslavement. After he shoots Friday's two companions, his conquest of Friday begins with smiles and signs of encouragement. Friday is accepted as a man, however, and when he speaks, his words "were the first sound of man's voice." Our illusion of his humanity is soon dispelled when Friday helps eliminate a wounded companion; and "when he had done this, he comes laughing to me in a sign of triumph." This is quite logical in the book, since we are prepared for Friday's acceptance of Crusoe as a White god. "At length he came close to me, and then he kneel'd down again, kiss'd the ground, and laid his head upon the ground, and taking me by the foot, set my foot upon his head; this it seems was in token of swearing to be my slave for ever." Crusoe is as confused about New World man as most Europeans of his time were. At one stage, Crusoe refers to Friday's companion as "the other Indian," and Crusoe's description of Friday is very much like Behn's: "He had all the sweetness and softness of a European"; "his hair was long and black, not curl'd like wool"; and "the colour of his skin was not quite black."[27]

Friday is Crusoe's creation. Naturally he is a cannibal, but with European ways. He speaks English badly and has no spiritual god. Crusoe becomes master and savior, while Friday is servant and worshiper. In one melodramatic scene, he would rather be killed than return to his own people.

The prejudices are inherited in one form or another by twentieth-century writers. Anthony Burgess' *Devil of a State* (1961) has Dunia rife with cannibalism, superstition, and bad government. Graham Greene's *A Burnt Out Case* (1961) is set in Africa merely because he

---

26. Joel Chandler Harris, *Uncle Remus* (New York, 1965 [1880]), 164. A similar account is given by Lydia Cabrera, but without the downgrading; see *Cuentos negros de Cuba* (Havana, 1940).
27. Daniel Defoe, *Robinson Crusoe* (New York, Dutton, 1945 [1719]), 149.

wished to place Query in an "inaccessible" part of the world, and his book *The Comedians* (1965) shows the emasculating effect of the European view of Africa; in it, voodoo is not to be taken seriously. Indeed, for the narrator, the dancers "to me who had been born a Catholic . . . seemed as distasteful as the ceremony of the Eucharist would have seemed performed as a ballet on Broadway."[28]

Because of the socializing process of Afro-New World writers, it is necessary for them to bypass the propagandistic prejudices of their forebears. And these forebears were White writers who had established earlier terrains wherein the victor was White, the victim was Black, and the humor was directed at the victim. The irony, for the Black writer, emerges when the victim is the writer and as such has to see himself as a buffoon.

Many of these European writers claim to be writing fact. For instance, Waugh said in *Ninety-two Days* (1934) that the macabre Mr. Todd, who forces the chief character in *A Handful of Dust* (1934) to read Dickens to him, was based on a Mr. Christie, whom he met in the Guyana jungle. In addition, Crusoe is based on Alexandre Selkirk, and Graham Greene has assiduously researched his novels. Joel Chandler Harris and Harriet Beecher Stowe claimed a personal knowledge of the South. Aphra Behn's work and Michael Scott's travel books lend further credence to the Black man's role as savage, buffoon, or European noble, for the authors claimed actual knowledge of the places they described.

With an alien eye, constantly turned inward, these authors purport to relate a world they do not understand. Their characters behave more than a trifle irrationally. They are given to constant fawning, clowning, stupidities, a belief in the incredible, and a desire for racial and physical suicide. The Reverend John Laputa in John Buchan's *Prester John* (1938) strips himself down to his leopard skin and then, finally naked, hurls himself into the gulf. Europeans are king-makers in Africa and the New World; they dominate matter and environment. The Afro-New World man is part of this.

In search of self, Henderson, the chief character of Saul Bellow's *Henderson the Rain King* (1958), goes to Africa—a strange place for

---

28. Graham Greene, *The Comedians* (New York, 1974), 205.

a White middle-class American to seek to understand himself. Before long he becomes a latter-day Crusoe. True, Henderson is bewildered, but it is a benign misunderstanding. As with Friday and Crusoe, the inevitable occurs: "After this Tamba and Beba lay on the ground and took turns in saluting me formally. Each took my foot and placed it on her head as Itelo had done to acknowledge my supremacy."[29] The very man who comes to Africa seeking, ends up by being sought. The Europeans had passed on the legacy of supremacy to White Americans.

The catalog of books containing prejudice grows endless. Ronald Firbank's "Prancing Nigger" goes back to the ugliness of Afro-New World people. In it, an English duchess expresses both her own and Firbank's prejudices, in her dislike of what she called "the parfum d'Afrique of the sooties."[30] Joyce Cary was not as crude and even believed in African independence, as he argued in *The Case for African Freedom* (1941). But this scarcely prevents his chief character in *Mr. Johnson* (1952) from being slightly oafish, childlike, and naïve. The relationship between the Englishman Rudbeck and the African Mr. Johnson is a strange one. Molly Mahood finds that Rudbeck needs Mr. Johnson's inspiration, but the truth is that for Celia, Mr. Johnson is a Wog, and even Mahood has to admit that he becomes "a sort of attendant nigger minstrel."[31]

Our conclusion has to be that few Europeans *see* Africa in truth. Perhaps this is why André Gide's *Voyage au Congo* (1927) became a new landmark, for Gide could actually see the folly in the generalization of his cultural inheritance. But he too slips; he berates his fellow Whites for stupidity but adds that Blacks are "only capable of the slightest mental development; their brains as a rule are dull and stagnant."[32] He marvels at the fact that Africans bury their dead. Of course these are not the prejudices of Firbank, Carlyle, or Goldsmith. Nor are these observations quite so blatant as Archibald's words, in Jean Genet's *Les nègres*, or *The Blacks: A Clown Show* (1958): "I order you to be black to your very veins. Let Africa circulate in them.

29. Saul Bellow, *Henderson the Rain King* (New York, 1974), 205.
30. Ronald Firbank, "Prancing Nigger," in *The Complete Ronald Firbank* (London, 1961), 632.
31. M. M. Mahood, *Joyce Cary's Africa* (London, 1964), 178, 183.
32. André Gide, *Travels in the Congo* (Berkeley, 1962), 96.

Let Negroes negrify themselves. Let them persist to the point of madness in what they're condemned to be, in their ebony, in their odor, in their yellow eyes, in their cannibal taste. Let them not be content with eating Whites, but let them cook each other as well."[33] *Les nègres* probes into the meaning of blackness. It asks two very intelligent questions: What is blackness, and how Black is a Black man? In many ways the play is ontological and concerns itself with the nature of reality.

A social interpretation of the play is only one possible commentary on it, but it is nevertheless one that concerns us. Thus the *black* masque is given for the entertainment of a *White* audience. The eight Blacks who dance around the body of a murdered White woman, are judged by five Whites—in reality, five Blacks wearing white masks. The first part of the play establishes an intentional confusion regarding the motive for this crime, and the second part is really a contest between "Black" and "White." Felicity, in her long speech, envisions a world of blackness: "Milk will be black, sugar, rice, the sky, doves, hope will be black." In a way, this is the complete inversion of images that became so necessary for the Black writer.

Perhaps this play, *Les nègres*, is the best rebuttal, for the administrators, constituting a judge, a governor, and the missionary, are all agents of the Black cultural conscription. They are all consigned to their fates. One of them had previously alluded to stages of mental indoctrination: capture, propaganda, and later the illusory freedom of the parrot. The seer is the destroyer of cultural perversion, not a pop artist such as one finds in Ernst Krenek's *Jonny speilt auf*, in which the so-called Negro, Jonny, conquers Europe with his vitality and jazz rhythms. For he would have to be condemned along with those in Genet's play who have all denied their heritage.

White writers who achieve some proximity to truth are those who wave no banners and chant few marching songs. If Joseph Conrad's *Heart of Darkness* (1902) were only about anticolonialism, it could not have been a good novel. If it were only about good Blacks, it would not have worked. It is not necessary for us to believe in Conrad's color equation to estimate his work or to laugh at his hungry

33. Jean Genet, *The Blacks: A Clown Show* (New York, 1960), 52.

"savages," whom he praises tongue-in-cheek for not eating each other or their White companions. "Black," for Conrad and Genet, is little more than a starting point, a color, a way of life, to make certain important statements about Europeans. The other writers who have been examined do not have this sense of honesty.

To some extent, Samuel Johnson did. He knew his own Black servant, Frances Barber, personally, but nowhere in *Rasselas: Prince of Abyssinia* (1759) does one get the feeling of Johnson's personal involvement. *Rasselas* is a dialogue, and the so-called Prince of Abyssinia is not so much a prince as he is Rousseau's child of nature. Without denigrating him by alluding to the noble savage, one sees in the prince a European device for measuring European values.

> In enumerating the particular comforts of life, we shall find many advantages on the side of the Europeans. They cure wounds and diseases with which we languish and perish. We suffer inclemencies of weather which they can obviate. They have engines for the dispatch of many laborious works, which we must perform by manual industry. There is such communication between distant places that one friend can hardly be said to be absent from another. Their policy removes all public inconveniences: they have roads cut through their mountains, and bridges laid upon their rivers. And, if we descend to the privacies of life, their habitations are more commodious, and their possessions are more secure.
>
> "They are surely happy," said the prince, "who have all these conveniences, of which I envy none so much as the facility with which separated friends interchange their thoughts."
>
> "The Europeans," answered Imlac, "are less unhappy than we, but they are not happy. Human life is everywhere a state in which much is to be endured, and little to be enjoyed." [34]

Therefore, through European ideas, Afro-New World man sees his world in a way that makes it possible for him to subscribe to notions of being a buffoon as well as to believing in the revival of Africa. It is to be recalled that not all detractors acted out of malevolence; many meant well, but the net effect was an accumulation of racial disjointedness, which afterwards became wholly connected in terms of the perverted logic of the European Old World. In turn, these misconceptions were exported to the New World, where they formed part of the experiences of Afro-New World man. His response was

34. Samuel Johnson, *Rasselas: Prince of Abyssinia* (London, 1886), 88.

either one of outright condemnation or eager acquiescence. In either case, it meant a revival of Africa in the New World.

For many White writers in the New World, the Black man, therefore, becomes a way of asserting kinship with Europe. Europeans condemn, and *ipso facto* New World Whites must also condemn to prove that they both may relate from a common cultural standpoint. Hence this description by one of William Faulkner's characters of "a race doomed and cursed to be forever and ever a pail of the White man's doom and curse for its sins." For this reason, New World White is forever bound in fierce but unwilling allegiance with New World Black. It is an ironic entrapment from which New World White has to free himself if he can ever claim to be a blood brother of Europeans.

It is not surprising therefore that the White world seeks redemption through the Black. Joe Christmas in Faulkner's *Light in August* (1932) is J. C. (Jesus Christ), a child found on Christmas Day. He is killed when he is thirty-three years old.[35] But one must not be led away too far by this. Faulkner believed that the White man "must teach the Negro to be responsible," and his letter to Paul Pollard refusing a donation for the NAACP amplifies this.[36] One returns to the comfortable world of Crusoe and "Boy" Friday.

Blacks are doled out a servile mentality, and with this comes a White nostalgia for servitude. Thomas Nelson Page has an "uncle" who comments about slavery. He says: "Dem (slavery days) wuz good ole times. . . . Niggers didn't had nothin' 't all to do—jes had to 'ten' to de feedin' and cleanin' de hosses, an' doin' what de marster tell 'em to do."[37] Most of his stories are told through an "uncle"; many issues are considered laudable, which, in a contemporary setting, would seem belittling. Charles Chesnutt and Paul Lawrence Dunbar are Black writers who seem to accept themselves in this role. The American "classics" confirm the Black man in this inferior position, and Nigger Jim in *The Adventures of Huckleberry Finn* (1885) gives further credence to what has been discussed. Jim is stupid, lazy,

---

35. Hugh Holman argues that Joe Christmas is *like* Christ, in *The Roots of Southern Writing* (Athens, Georgia, 1972), 151–53.

36. Charles D. Peavy, *Go Slow Now: Faulkner and the Race Question* (Eugene, 1971), 82.

37. Thomas Nelson Page, *In Ole Virginia, or Marse Chan and Other Stories* (New York, 1887), 6.

and comical (as Huck says, "You can't learn a nigger to argue").[38] The idea of the adult Jim accompanying the boy Huck on a raft, despite the apparent urgency to escape from the New Orleans slave market, is a ludicrous one that most critics have chosen to ignore. Perhaps it is as well, for it merely proves again the simplistic nature of Afro-New World man as a friend to dogs and small children. The figure of Uncle Tom pervades, sadly, not only in the literature of Whites about Blacks, but equally in that of Blacks about themselves. Only when one deals with physical confrontation is there a firm assertion of Black manhood.

Two final examples are sufficient to show the main problem of color in the imagery of White writers. In *Moby Dick* (1851), Melville closely associates blackness with evil, even though Ishmael is vaguely apprehensive of its ambiguity. For him the whale seems pregnant with meaning because of its white color, and he perceives the duality incarnate in white—brides, old age, kings, gods, a range of paraphernalia from the Greco-Roman world that indicate their positive values. However, Ishmael adds that "there yet lurks an elusive something in the innermost idea of this hue which strikes more of a panic to the soul than that redness which affrights in blood." There are polar bears and sharks, place names, albinos that are "more strangely hideous than the ugliest abortion."[39] It becomes necessary for the Afro-New World writer to be wary of this trap. It is one that Aimé Césaire, Léon Damas, and Ralph Ellison dealt with. To state what blackness did, or could stand for, becomes an important issue; the writer in the Black world must reexamine what it connotes and denotes for him in his new environment.

In Melville's "Benito Cereno" (1856), Delano wants to know what has debilitated Benito to the extent that he is unable to care about the past and the possibility of his own future. The question, almost a riddle, is "What has cast such a shadow?" and Benito's answer is "The negro." True enough, one may assert that the Black memory Benito carries with him is powerful enough to turn him into a victim of physical and mental anguish. But it is through the imagery of blackness that the languid evil of Benito is perceived by the reader.

38. Samuel Clemens, *The Adventures of Huckleberry Finn* (New York, 1885), 111.
39. Herman Melville, *Moby Dick* (New York, 1957), 185, 188.

As a result one even empathizes with Delano that Black people are "the most pleasing body servants in the world."[40] His blindness to the possibility of Black competence makes him impervious to an understanding of Benito's needs.

One of the reasons for the failure to come to terms with the power of blackness is that Black people are only seen as adjacent to the whole idea of being. They never truly seem to partake of intellectual life, as seen by these writers. They are attendants; the Black shipboy in Conrad's *Heart of Darkness* is a good example. When they do rise to lofty heights, as with Othello, there is an implied basic savagery that reduces them to subhuman levels. To say that White characters have fared little better in the hands of Afro-New World writers is not a satisfactory answer. The question still remains: Why is the Black man ugly, cowardly, and grotesque? Edward Brathwaite, the Barbadian poet, gives us a reflection of this bare, startling image.

> for we who have achieved nothing
> work
> who have built
> dream
> who have forgotten all
> dance
> and dare to remember[41]

These groping impulses constitute the art of certain illuminative basics that Afro-New World man seeks. There are no positives, no negatives; the dark landscape is slowly mapped. Answers cannot readily be forthcoming, for not only is the writer endangered by history, but he has already been trapped by the myths of another people. And he who would seek to create a novel, a poem, a play, must do so in terms that are violently opposed to him in form and content. Césaire echoes these sentiments: "Ceux qui n'ont inventé ni la poudre ni la boussole / ceux qui n'ont jamais su dompter la vapeur ni l'électricité . . ." (Those who invented neither powder nor compass / those who have never tamed steam or electricity). He recognized:

---

40. Herman Melville, "Benito Cereno," in *Herman Melville: Four Short Novels*, (New York, 1971), 114.

41. Edward Brathwaite, "Rights of Passage," in *The Arrivants: A New World Trilogy* (London, 1967), 12.

ce qui est à moi
c'est un homme seul emprisonné de
blanc
c'est un homme seul qui défie les cris
blancs de la mort blanche . . .[42]

That which is mine
is a lone man imprisoned
in white
a lone man defying
the white cries of white death.

The necessity to break out of the White trap is then the task of the colonized, ghettoized.[43] One has to move away from the curious acceptance of the Black writer as a kind of fascinating animal, *not to* wonder, as Countee Cullen did, how God could "make a poet black and bid him sing." For the Afro-New World writer cannot afford the acceptance of these structures. Instead, he has to be the agent of his own work, to witness truly hidden areas and bring his profound (because it is so different) knowledge to bear on new areas of experience. He cannot, and must not, consent to the imposition of established organs of European opinion, for they are inquisitorial, as Genet so ably demonstrated. He must seek iconic alternatives to translate the legacies of real history and discard the invented myth, to respond to the immediate and to actively assert a new presence. For the Afro-New World writer, there can be no ape-like role of imitation, but only knowledge and involvement in the creation of new Black humankind.

42. Aimé Césaire, *Cahier d'un retour au pays natal* (Paris, 1956), 68, 45.
43. Robert F. Fleissner, "Herbert's Aethiopesa and the Dark Lady: A Mannerist Parallel," *College Language Association Journal*, XIX (June, 1976), 458–67, shows how the White trap even involved Black and White in inverted roles.

5 Contact, Conflict, and Reconciliation

It is not until the arrival of the Negrista movement that one encounters the glorification of the Mulatto. Previous writers dealt instead with the meetings of alien worlds and how this conjunction brought about a necessary alteration of images. So, the White Federico and the Black Natividad in Diaz Sánchez's *Cumboto* (1959) represent the manner in which a Venezuelan writer perceives the confrontation and resolution of disparate ethnic groups. Similarly, the Uruguayan writer Eduardo Acevedo Díaz highlights the encounter between Black and White in *Soledad*. The San Salvadorean novelist, Salazar Arrué, in *El Cristo negro* (1917), utilizes the symbolism of color to explicate the spiritual clash of worlds. Through love and its unrequited state, Manuel Díaz-Rodriguéz attempts to show in *Peregrina* (1952) the imagistic manipulation of color. All these books show contact and confrontation, and the emergence of the Black man in New World literature as a unique presence.

Cumboto is a heavily structured book that takes the entire confrontation of Black and White in the New World as its theme.[1] Set in Cumboto, a rural province on the northern coast of Venezuela, incidents are recollected through Natividad, the young Black boy who is friend and servant in Don Guillermo's household. The boy is exposed to his own African world through the person of an old Black woman and also to an initial rejection of the White world through Frau Berza. There are gray elements in both worlds; Abuela Anita,

1. Ramón Diaz Sánchez, *Cumboto* (Caracas, 1969), from which page references herein are taken. The novel has been published in translation by the University of Texas Press, 1974.

133

the old Black woman, has a loyalty to Whites that disturbs Natividad. Frau Berza, the teacher, has a love affair with a Black milkman that bewilders him. *Cumboto* is therefore not only about the crisis of growth, but the adventure of discovering identity.

There is a great deal of mobility in the story, although it is set on a plantation. Incredible mental distances between characters are combined with denseness of time. Nevertheless, there is action, including two murders, within the framework of the novel.

Miriam DeCosta comments:

> *Cumboto* abounds in the worn clichés and tired archetypes of Afro-Hispanic prose: (1) the clandestine love affairs of white masters and Black servants; (2) the birth and disappearance of the mulatto child of the white mistress; (3) the mysterious appearance of the "noble mulatto"; (4) the sensual Black woman, and; (5) the old grandmother, seeress and sage. However, the novelist weaves the whole together in such a way that the characters are convincing, tension and drama are heightened and the prose is fluid and lyric without the melodrama, sentimentality and pathetic fallacies that often mar Black Southern American prose.[2]

Don Guillermo, Federico's father, seems to be a Spaniard. His wife, Doña Beatriz, is apparently a melancholic and takes her meals in her room. She lives in a fantasy world withdrawn from all reality. Gertrudis and Federico leave for Europe to study, and by that time Natividad is becoming an adult. Federico and he have also grown apart by this time. Natividad has his first sexual encounter with a mentally retarded Indian woman in the forest. In this second part, five years have gone by and Cruz María, Frau Berza's lover, is killed by Don Guillermo, who sees him darting through his house. Natividad is now asked to take his place as a servant, and there with Cervelíon, another Black servant, he begins to learn his own blackness in the tales he hears at night, in the stories of the wars in Venezuela, and in Abuela Anita's attitude that a Black man's duty is to be a loyal servant. Natividad feels different, for he envies Cruz María's daring. The polarity thus begins.

Now that he has taken over Cruz María's job, he has to work hard. He slowly manages to reorient himself into the White world, realizing that it is his also. His sojourn into the Casa Blanca is an idealis-

---

2. Miriam DeCosta, review in *Black Word*, XXIII (May, 1974), 97.

tic retreat from the realities of the deplorable condition of his Black world. He has to come to terms with the Black world around him—its legends and beliefs—and the remnants of African life impress themselves on him. Later, Natividad becomes dissatisfied with his life and thinks of the sea as a way of escape. He has witnessed an African religious ceremony, centered around Don Guillermo's death, and because of this is almost ready to accept the mysterious forces that lie outside the Casa Blanca.

The new master of the Casa Blanca is a German, Herr Gunter, who is supposedly Don Guillermo's brother. He assumes the guardianship of the estate for his nephews. These are times of despair and melancholy for Natividad, since many of the people he knew have left. Through Herr Gunter, Natividad goes back to the Casa Blanca, and both go hunting for rattlesnakes. He is able to go back to the library and to his two favorite books—one on race and *Paradise Lost*. Herr Gunter is scientific and mathematical in all he does; he wants to label everything. His attitude counterbalances the religious mystical experiences that Natividad has witnessed. He introduces another aspect of White to Natividad's blackness.

Laura Lamarca, Doña Beatriz's sister, and her daughter come to live in the Casa Blanca. When Federico returns, the *raison d'être* for the story does not cease, though Federico seems indifferent to it all. There is a kind of power struggle between the Lamarca women and Herr Gunter. Eduvige, the housekeeper, also fights for her own place. Natividad becomes part of this power play. He wants the protection and friendship of Eduvige; she is a woman of great and mysterious Black power. Both Abuela Anita and Cervilíon had feared her, and Natividad suspects that Cervilíon's sudden departure is due to her presence. Federico's return does not change things for Natividad; he is cold and treats him more as a servant than a friend. His return reasserts the presence of the White way of life, but only for a while. In his mind there still remains a memory of the Black possibility.

Now Niña Lotha, Herr Gunter's daughter arrives. Despite his wishes to see his daughter married, he is disappointed. Federico becomes so annoyed with the constant bickering between Laura Lamarca and Herr Gunter that he throws them out of the house, just before Herr Gunter tries to kill Doña Beatriz. Federico discovers a

skull in her room, and Natividad concludes that it is the skull of the Black man which Don Guillermo's shovel had touched.

Federico and Natividad now seem to become closer. They go for walks, and Federico tells Natividad that he wants to belong to the town. He too witnesses the festival of San Juan and the burning of the effigy. At the carnival they see Pascua performing a sensuous dance, which alters Federico completely. Discarding his coldness, he yearns for Pascua and goes to her house with Natividad. A Mulatto doctor visits them at Casa Blanca and tells Natividad of racial hatred. As a result, Natividad is constantly in a state of pivotal uncertainty.

Pascua and Federico begin to see each other, and Natividad becomes a kind of watchman. He waits while Federico and Pascua make love, and he begins to resent this situation. When Pascua visits, Federico is at first embarrassed, but later he becomes emboldened and orders her to dance. Once again, as at the carnival, she is portrayed as a snake. She represents the energy of the land, and he symbolizes its intellect. Natividad can identify with both of them and instinctively understands the paradox.

On one occasion when they attend church together, Pascua's ex-lover attacks them, and Natividad has to intervene. Federico has to take him home in a semiconscious state. When he recovers consciousness, Federico and Pascua have left, and Abuela Anita's trunk has arrived (she is presumably dead). In the trunk, they find old letters from Federico's mother to her Mulatto lover. It appears that Cruz María was the son of this liaison. The skull in her room was that of her dead lover.

A depressed Federico takes to his room. Meanwhile, Natividad reads about Solomon and the Queen of Sheba, and David and Bathsheba in the library. One is a love forbidden by caste; the other is denied by society. He seems to be involved in both of them.

Federico's recovery results in the formation of a new man. He takes Pascua's advice to write a melody that would blend the African and European elements of Cumboto. The last chapter of the book reverts to the first, when they are old men and Natividad walks behind Federico, as his shadow. The final irony in the novel is one that perhaps Federico did not intend. The representation of the symphony Federico wanted to compose appears in the form of a Mulatto son on horse-

back. At the end of the book we are given the impression that he is Cumboto.

The book tries to evade stereotypical views of Blacks and Whites, and succeeds at times. It succeeds best in projecting the characters in terms of a symbolic correspondence between them. However, the theme of race remains in the forefront.

From the beginning, Don Federico's father, Don Guillermo, and his mother, Doña Beatriz, are pigeonholed by their trivial dimensions. In a conversation during dinner, Don Guillermo gives his version of the establishment of Guipuzcoana Company by the king of Spain to colonize Venezuela. His version is that they were escaped slaves from the Spanish Indies who went into the jungles of Venezuela. When the Spaniards asked the slaves how they got there, they replied "con botes" (with boats). Hence the name of the province.

The principal industry of the estate is coconut farming. Among detailed descriptions of the coconuts is how they resemble the heads of Black men. The Casa Blanca, the master's house, has many fearful and sinister associations that set the stage for the story. Natividad, the young narrator, recounts how bats had made their home in the ceiling. The furniture, piano, and chairs are black. A Black servant lives there, and she sometimes sees Natividad in the huge library, absolutely fascinated with the books he could neither read nor understand. The color symbols help elucidate existing differences and pinpoint ambiguities. Black is understood with reference to White and vice versa.

The story is revealed through flashbacks. At the very beginning Don Federico is an old man, and together with Natividad, he goes for walks in the jungle and on the beach. A flashback to Don Federico's childhood is echoed later in the novel; the meaning of the Black soul, as recalled by Natividad, is one. This soul is related to trees and vegetation, and nature is equated with the Black man throughout the novel. The White man, dressed in white and walking on the beach, is contrasted with the darkness of life that is blackness. Black life is also presented as violent and happy.

> En Cumboto existen consumados maestros de esgrima a garrote y machete, y los hombres, cuando no llevan armas, antes que los puños prefieren usar sus cráneos que son duros como los cocos. (p. 47)

. . . .

Esto no obstante el negro es alegre e ingenuo como los niños. Su vida ondula en un holgorio constante, entre risas, cantos y charlas interminables. La encanta jugar. Su atmósfera es de retozo. Imita a los animales del bosque, particularmente a los pájaros por los que siente predilección. No existe un negro que no crea a pie juntillas que los animales hablan y que algunas personas poseen el secreto de su lenguaje. (p. 50)

In Cumboto there exist perfect masters of fencing with clubs and machetes, and the men when they are unarmed, before using their fists, prefer to use their heads which are as hard as coconuts.

. . . .

Regardless of this, the Black is as happy and naïve as children. His life sways constantly in frolic amid laughter, songs, and unending stories. He loves to play. His air is one of friskiness. He imitates the animals of the forest, particularly the birds for whom he feels predilection. There is no Black who exists that does not believe quite literally that the animals speak and that some persons possess the secret of their language.

Color symbols equate blackness with mystery and whiteness with Satanic impulses. War among men arises out of diabolical urges. The forest through which the young boys walk symbolizes the mystery of the land. Before the death of Cruz María, the lover of Frau Berza, Natividad thinks of the skull of an unknown Black man and a silver shovel, which represent for him all the unknown Blacks who were buried in Cumboto.

An excellent example of the underscoring of color symbols is in Cruz María's death scene. He lies in a black coffin dressed in a white linen suit. A white mantle covers the table on which the crucifix and the Virgin Mary stand. A Black girl makes an offering of black coffee and white cheese. The color manipulation is well handled and never overdone. It emphasizes the coexistence of two modes of being, and at the same time pinpoints the contrast and contradiction in Natividad's life.

Of course, the color comparison is sometimes overdone. The simplistic child of nature offends our latter-day sensibilities, but the writer uses this characterization to get at something much deeper. He is attempting to show the link between the Black man in the New World and in Africa. The common ground is the capacity for imagi-

native faith in the way that thing, animal, and man are associated in a unique oneness.

Frau Berza is the first person to introduce the element of color difference to the boys. As they play with each other, she reminds Federico that this is not the place of the Black boy; he should be cleaning floors. Her influence helps separate the children, but when she sleeps during the day, the children get together. Both Gertrudis and Natividad worry about what Frau Berza whispers to Federico. It seems that Frau Berza is in love with the Black milkman, according to a conversation that Natividad overhears. In fact, she is quite aggravated when she discovers that he knows. The boys compare notes, and it seems that Federico also knows about this. He had also witnessed the amorous embraces of Frau Berza and Cruz María. After this incident, Natividad is allowed to become a pupil. His introduction to the contradictions in his growing world has begun.

The racial issue is neatly introduced at this point. The European stands between the Creole, Don Federico, and the Black, Natividad. But even the European (the English, Dutch, French, and in this case the Spaniard) has his "secrets," because the life he pretends to lead is not the truth of his real experience. As a result, the races intermingle on all levels. Don Guillermo always embarks on his trips accompanied by a Black servant. The three children decide to make an important journey to a river for they have never seen one, and a Black servant directs them through the dark, unknown forest to Abuela Anita's house. Later, they are led by a Black granddaughter of Abuela Anita and followed, unknown to them, by the Black servant to whom they had spoken. The picture becomes clear. The Black servant is guide, leader, and defender. Whites hate him yet passionately love him. Natividad's contradictions continue.

Abuela Anita initiates the reader directly into the supernatural, and the ancient beliefs of the African. She is ninety years old and, in the African style, uses a wooden stick to clean her teeth. She also reinforces the racial element by pride in her own blackness and finds it difficult to accept one of her two sons, for "se casó con una blanca y que pa mejorá la raza" (he had married a White woman to improve the race). Here she is being extremely cynical. She is "negra retinta,

absolute" (absolutely ink black) and holds a majestic pride in her black body and her "aire de fetiche Africano" (air of African fetish). She is supposed to be Africa personified, with her flat nose, large lips, and headkerchief. Since the entire story is told by Natividad, this becomes doubly significant. She represents, in an indirect way, a goal that he aims at but can never attain. In other words, she is the contradiction in his life.

The apparent "supernatural" nature of African religion is counterbalanced with Christianity, which of course helps to elaborate Natividad's dualism. When the young boy first hears Frau Berza and her Black lover talking in the night, they remind him of souls in purgatory. When the old Black woman allows them to go through a trunk she has inherited, the photographs seem to him as if the people had been trapped in purgatory. Obviously, Natividad is fearful and uncomfortable with the torments of hellfire and with the superstitions he inherited from the European world.

Abuela Anita has numerous visions of spirits from cemeteries which possess human bodies. The tormented deceased bring chains from another world to this one, raising havoc in churches and getting into bedrooms. The worst spirit is Mandinga, according to Abuela Anita, and he is highest in the hierarchy. Some spirits possess cities, houses, living people. Then there are the Eshu, or mischievous type *duendes* who knock dishes off tables. But it should be added that this world of demons is closer to the European than the African.

There is no Shango here, no real presence of African gods. The reader does see Africa in the flesh, in the young boy and the old woman, but their beliefs are not truly African. They do not even have African religious attitudes tempered by European views. What they seem to be are "superstitious," purely within a European frame of reference.

The reason might be that, in Venezuela, the preservation of African culture was not as intensive as it was in Cuba and Brazil. Therefore, when the writer comes to relate the life of a Black man in the New World, he has to fall back on references to black magic, which is of course a European concept. If one, however, refutes what appears to be a valid argument and accepts the characters as they are, the distinctions the author is making become more manifest. On

one hand, there is the European (Spanish) world, which does not admit to magic or its possibility; on the other is the African state of being, which perpetually expresses itself in a magical interpretation of its environment. The writer does his best with what he knows. At one stage the children are looking at faded photographs with the old woman's granddaughter. There is the symbolism in the hungry dog, which Don Guillermo drives away, and Pascua's furious interjection about the dog, "¡Este fulano perro por qué no sigue a sus amos!" (That dog! Why doesn't it follow its master!), which makes Natividad question the entire resemblance between dog and servant, which was really his entire heritage. These dead White men in the photographs were masters to the old woman's grandfather, but they were surely nothing to him. Consequently, redefining the dead masters, he begins to reassess his own relationship with Federico and his new meaning of freedom.

After Federico and Gertrudis go off to Europe and Natividad takes the place of Cruz María, Don Guillermo enters a Black world. At first he despises it, but slowly he begins to understand and appreciate the stories told at night. He hears Roso reminisce with his friend about the brutality of the war of independence and the five-year civil war. The cruelty is presented in his way: men are possessed by devils. The reader is reminded of Abuela Anita's descriptions.

Don Guillermo is amused by his half-crazed wife who relives the past. Adorned in a white dress, towed by two dark mules, she had come to attend the ceremony, twenty years too late. Don Guillermo laughs at this and at the entire opening ceremony of the railroad with its look of absurdity. He makes fun of the Blacks who seem to have thought the general had come to liberate them. As he goes through his ceremonial digging with the general's silver shovel, he encounters a skull: "—¿Humana?"—preguntó Federico con ansiedad. "—No: la calavera de un negro" ("Human?" asked Federico with anxiety. "No: the skull of a Black man" [p. 92]). Natividad cannot understand why Don Guillermo constantly makes these anti-Black statements. Federico seems to him to be his protector, and later when they find the silver shovel in the library, Natividad cannot bear to look at it. For him it is an instrument of his torture. Don Guillermo's antiblackness makes Natividad in turn feel a repugnance for Whites, and he wants

to know why they behave themselves as if all of them had this terrible mark of the devil. Not so the Blacks. Venancio and Cervelíon, bird seller and basket weaver, respectively, are presented in another way. They are the simple, almost simplistic creatures of the natural world, who live happily and without neurosis. This is equally absurd.

When Natividad's reading takes him to a translation of *Paradise Lost*, he wonders about Satan's color. Was he like the Mandingo people or was he White, as the illustrations showed? Cervelíon and Venancio cannot help him, but the old woman tells him of the preponderance of White devils. Devils, Black and White, walk the earth at night. Even Frau Berza is "la diabla blanca."

As hero and narrator, Natividad passes through periods of self-depreciation. The image of the starving dog driven off by Federico's father makes him begin to question his role of dependence. Likewise, after he takes over Cruz María's job, he is looked upon indifferently, like a dog, by Cervelíon. Resented for the part he played in unwittingly hunting down Cruz María, he is likened by fellow Blacks to a hunting dog. The animal images confirm his growing awareness of his low caste in Cumboto society.

In Cervelíon's house, he discovers that

> en los cuentos se revelaban los grados de inteligencia y espiritualidad de aquellos seres. Algunos eran simplísimos, elementales; otros complicados y llenos de humor. Había narradores especializados en relatos espeluznantes, lúgubres y sobrenaturales, de aparecidos y brujerías; otros en fábulas alegres e ingeniosas, en las que bullía el sentimiento humano del valor y de la astucia encarnados en los animales del bosque. (p. 115)

> in the stories were revealed grades of intelligence and incorporeality of those beings. Some of them were very simple, fundamental; others complicated and full of humor. There were narrators who specialized in hair-raising tales, gloomy and supernatural, of ghosts and witchcraft; others in happy and ingenious fables, in which bubbled the human sentiment for the valor and astuteness incarnated in the animals of the forest.

Here he finds out, in a devious way, about the nature of his African past. The meaning of the skull, which had been mocked, and his true place in New World society are still not clear, but they begin to make more sense to him. Slowly, Natividad is acquiring a new conception of self.

Natividad recoils from the descriptions of raping and looting that Venancio and Prudencio relish. The two old men sit and reminisce about the wars in which they fought and how they had pursued White women and raped them, in churches and anywhere they could find them. Sadly, they reflected that this came to an end when General Zamora was killed and Falcón came to power. Natividad concludes that it was a time when "los diablos negros embestían contra los diablos blancos" (the Black devils were like beasts against the White devils). So war makes devils of men; circumstances become the important factors here, not skin color.

During the war of independence, Creoles and Blacks had fought side by side against Spain, but after independence there were civil wars; factions of Zamora, Simon Bolívar, José Antonio Paéz, and others fought against each other. Then the Creoles and Blacks seemed polarized in the new Venezuela. Venezuelan literature constantly mentions these wars and their brutality.

Cumboto gives no account of ideals, as Mexican or Cuban literature does. The emphasis here is on the brutality of the war and what man had done to man. There are no heroes. Abuela Anita believes that wars unleash the devils in which she profoundly believes, and she feels her own soul is doomed for a betrayal. She remembers the Black rebel, Cervelíon's brother, who takes to the mountains and cannot understand his anger. As a young girl, Abuela Anita had worked for the Arguindequi family; and she recalls with tears and bitterness how the Spaniards were destroyed, for she is obviously a monarchist.

Natividad feels great nostalgia for his past friendship with Federico; in doing so, he expresses the core of his dividedness. He experiences, at the Feast of San Juan, the meaning of the drums, the possession of women, and his instinctive relationship with all this. Thus, Natividad becomes a divided man and yearns for some escape. The sea image is powerful here, as a symbol of departure and of mysterious and fearful yearnings. Soon he is to come into contact with his lost religion. One night he awakes and sees a gathering of men and women, including Cervelíon. He observes a ceremony in which there are lit candles and incantations. There is a fire in the middle; a woman has a rattlesnake in a basket, and she seems to play with it. He hears the

voice of Don Guillermo; later Don Guillermo dies, bitten by a snake.

Of course, this increases Natividad's conflict. From the beginning of the book, he had heard of these rites from the old woman, Abuela Anita, but they had not touched him as they now do. Now, he is unable to explain the meaningfulness of his African religion. But the reality, which he cannot deny, is the death of Don Guillermo. When his ghost appears, they all agree that he seems very White and feminine. This is almost a direct inversion of what Zeus, (Don Guillermo's family name) was. Natividad's conflicts at first become external, highlighting his desperate desire for self-comprehension.

Herr Gunter helps Natividad, unwittingly, to discover part of what he is. Doña Beatriz appears to him almost in a ghost-like form and entreats his help. She summons her son home, but when Federico comes, he is cold and distant. Naturally, this disturbs Natividad, for he is treated almost like a servant—another reminder to him that he is an outsider. Earlier on he had realized just how different he is.

> Federico debía conocer esta tradición que los negros festejan por junio. Alguna vez oiría desde las ventanas de la Casa Blanca, en el silencio mercurial de la noche, llevados y traídos por las brisas del Este, el ritmo apretado y sexual del tambor y el herido grito de las mujeres que invocan al Santo. Sín embargo, no habría visto, como yo las veía ahora, estas sombras que tejen las sombras con el canto y el pujido que les brota por los poros del cuerpo. A ratos sentía yo el deseo de seguirlas, de internarme también en la oscuridad y saturar mi espíritu de su vago olor sulfuroso, pero sentía miedo. Por otra parte, deseaba estar solo. (p. 158)

> Federico should have known this tradition of Blacks to feast around June. Sometimes he would hear from the windows of the Casa Blanca, in the mercurial silence of the night, carried and brought by the breezes of the East, the tight and sexual rhythm of the drum and the loud cry of the women who invoke the Saint. However, he might not have seen, as I am seeing now, these shadows that weave the shadows with the chant and the violent desire that runs through the pores of the body. At times, I felt the desire to follow them, to go deeply also into the darkness and to saturate my spirit with its sulphuric odor, but I felt afraid. On the other hand, I wanted to be alone.

The desire for European individuality and aloneness is contrasted with mass involvement. Natividad is a man caught in the middle,

unable to take either way. He is entranced as he listens to the women singing to the saint and the drums sounding out "Cumboto! Cumboto!"

They sing of their ancient freedom in the forests before the Spaniards came. The drums tell that the sound "Cumboto" arose from a Spanish misunderstanding. Natividad feels that he has been misunderstood, and that he, in turn, misunderstands. His memory of Frau Berza and her unhappy love affair with Cruz María confirms his confusion, for he recalls the way in which Cruz María smelled like a cow and how Frau Berza had seduced him with her perfumes in her neat room. How and why, he asks himself.

To believe, or not to believe, in his Africanness becomes an important decision for Natividad. The tension is "como un pantano lleno de miasmas en el cual debatíase la pequeña y débil forma blanca de mis anhelos de superación" (like a swamp full of miasmas in which my weak and little white wishes of conquest were arguing). The white wishes are the European side of his education, and the swamp the larger African side. Natividad thinks that Federico abandoned him in this swamp. But later, one learns about "un pantano blanco o de los blancos" (a white swamp or one for White men). Not even his European side can explain the numerous appearances of Don Guillermo. True, he tries to avoid having to explain this, as he does the coming of Herr Gunter and Laura Lamarca and her daughter, by adopting a standoffish attitude, much as other Blacks seem to do.

It is to him that Laura Lamarca has to turn in her desire for approval from Blacks. He becomes a go-between, again representing this lost middle figure, for Laura Lamarca and Herr Gunter. He still does not find his place when Federico returns, for his former playmate has grown up. Ironically, his first impressions of the new Federico do not differ from his own inner concerns: Federico is a man also of two worlds, now returning from old Europe to the New World. His recognition of Federico brings about a sad and ironic difference, and a very visible one, that lies between them. He now reflects on his mistaken dog-like devotion to Doña Beatriz after she had said that he and Federico were like brothers.

The real understanding of Cumboto, of being Black, and of being Venezuelan is not found in Federico or Natividad. It lies in the off-

spring of the union between Pascua and Federico. The nameless Mulatto who arrives at the end of the novel as the heir to Casa Blanca is the truth of Cumboto. It may be said, therefore, that the discovery of blackness is surely in the social acclimatization of Natividad, that is, in his acceptance of the new role of having a Black (really Mulatto) master. Natividad, despite his failure to resolve the struggling elements of his personality, is the receptacle of the experiences of the New World Black man. He is dog, slave, servant, seer; he is the soul of Cumboto, which awaits the body of the Mulatto.

"Camina" (walk, grow, experience) is the advice that Natividad had once given to a confused Federico, and the novel is indeed a movement not only in historical terms, but also in the acquisition of cultural values, the experience that was to relieve both of them. Natividad's advice could be applied to himself as well, for he has to get out of the swamp. Both of them lack an understanding of the land, and Natividad's role as Federico's shadow is to help him "penetrar en la entraña viviente de este universo" (penetrate into the living entrails of this universe), so that he might acquire "una segunda conciencia, una conciencia Negra" (a second conscience, a Black conscience). To help him, Natividad seems to acquire special spiritual powers in assuming the role of guide and leader. Since he himself has problems with identification, his aid is very limited. However, he does help Federico to see the image of Christ with *black* blood, the sorrowing Virgin with a *black* mantle, and San Juan "brujo y parrendero" (Black god and trickster) dressed in the manner of Shango. Natividad's impression is chaotic and contradictory. Perhaps he resolves the enigma of being for Federico, but not for himself.

In the mountain town of Goaiguaza Natividad first sees the figure of a Mulatto striding through it—an image, he says, that will remain with him. It is one that the reader will soon reencounter, in the Mulatto doctor and in Abuela Anita's grandson, Fernando Arguindequi, and finally, in the embodiment of the shadow (which was Natividad), which is seen in the person of the new heir to the Casa Blanca. The initial meeting with the nameless Mulatto prepares the reader for the chance encounter with Pascua, which will finally seal the interrogative.

The Mulatto, in the person of Abuela Anita's grandson, Fernando,

wishes that he could, "volver lo negro blanco, transformar la noche en día" (turn black into white, transform night into day). He, however, is not going to remain in Cumboto. His vindications of the servile mentality of his compatriots strike the core of Natividad's being. He is a bitter man, resentful of all that he has experienced. He personifies the hidden truths of Venezuela, but he is so bitter that he cannot represent the being of Cumboto. His presence is the chaos of Natividad's dream in which a Black queen has White slaves. Fernando would simply invert the hatred of the world, and when Natividad wakes up, he does so in realizing that "era una sombra" (it was a shadow [p. 199]).

The knowledge that Doña Beatriz had slept with a Black man disturbs both Natividad and Federico. The man had been murdered and the child of their union, Cruz María, had been shot by Doña Beatriz's husband. This makes the reality even more difficult for them to bear, for it is compounded with violence. The irony is further confirmed by the appearance of Federico's Mulatto son at the end of the book. Natividad suggests at one stage that being a Mulatto is really an impossible state, for as the drunken Federico tries to compose on the piano, Natividad reflects that "el sexo de la pantera no correspondía al del albatros" (the sex of the panther does not correspond with that of the albatross [p. 214]). The more meaningful comment is that being Mulatto cannot really exist, either in terms of spirit or in terms of mentality. The suggestion must remain that just as Federico fails in his composition, likewise the Mulatto who plays the piano and who comes to inherit Casa Blanca, will also fail. The novel's answers are left wide open at the end; the reader is not told what possibilities for order exist. We have been warned before of the impossibility of a Mulatto culture, and we have seen the futile striving of Whites to assert a European state of being and of Natividad to attempt to assert blackness. This powerful novel, which so ably captures some of our concerns, leaves the reader with a meaningful interrogative at the end.

II

It is not the task of the writer to give the reader pat solutions, and the author of *Cumboto* does not attempt this. Instead, we are opened

up to the varieties and complex cultures of New World man. There is a confrontation of the spirit in Federico and Natividad. As old men, they still cannot arrive at an answer to explain a collective history. The author has penetrated a situation—almost a riddle—to confront a continent. For there are, *Cumboto* suggests, ramifications that lie beyond ethnic realities and involve cultural apprehension.

European man is seemingly incarcerated in a European context. *Cumboto* warns of a similar danger in which African man can likewise be imprisoned. How, the novel asks, can one have some coherent insight into complex patterns? Surely not by isolating one or the other. History has many perspectives, and the New World author has to engage in a dialogue of being if he is to attempt to bear witness. Instead of a one-sided utterance, *Cumboto* gives us a far-reaching type of art.

When describing the politics of confrontation, a writer must tread warily. Like William Blake ("I am black, but O! my soul is white"), Luis Cané's "Romance de la Niña Negra" is equally absurd. This Argentinian poet is only satisfied when, after suffering a lifetime of discrimination, the little Black girl goes to heaven.

> Dios la mira dulcemente,
> le acaricia la cabeza
> y un lindo par de alas blancas
> a sus espaldas sujeta.
> Los dientes de mazamorra
> brillan a la niña negra.
> Dios llama a todos los ángeles
> y dice: "Jugad con ella!"[3]
>
> God looks at her sweetly,
> he caresses her head
> and a beautiful pair of white wings
> spring from her back.
> Her teeth like bread crumbs
> shining on the Black girl.
> God calls all of the angels
> and says, "Play with her."

Presumably, the Almighty could agree to these frolics in Heaven be-

3. Luis Cané, "Romance de la Niña Negra," in D. Augustin del Saz (ed.), *Antología de la poesía Argentina* (Buenos Aires, 1959), 609–10.

cause the Black girl had white wings and white teeth. This is perhaps the supreme example of distortion and of racist propaganda. The poet reduces the Black girl in our eyes by imprisoning her in a European, ethnocentric content and, therefore, fails to lead us through the gateway manifestations of *Cumboto*.

One does not seek any absolute solution when a New World writer deals with confrontation in the New World. It would be far better to have variations of aspects of reality, rather than a definite answer lacking in creative dimension. Salazar Arrué's *El Cristo negro* has a multitudinous number of sustaining images; the clues in the novel, like those in *Cumboto*, play on Black and White. In this case the racial issue is restricted to the confrontation between Indian and White ethnic groups. What is more interesting in the work is the delicate and poetic use of color symbolism and the manner in which the theme is projected.

A major interest in *El Cristo negro* is in the dialogue that Salazar Arrué establishes. There is metaphorical equality between blackness and evil. The story, which is set in Guatemala, is an account of Uraco, a mestizo of Indian and White parentage. His father, Argo de la Selba, had worked for the governor-general, and his mother, Txinke, was Indian. One day, Argo is punished for an alleged wrongdoing and is killed by the governor-general. Txinke (in the original her name is also spelled Txinque) is a supernatural figure who tries to assassinate her husband's murderer. She is killed, and Uraco seeks refuge in a monastery where he is taught Spanish and Christianity.

Uraco grows up to become such a fervent Christian that the other priests in the monastery begin to doubt his intentions and to distrust him. He leads a holy life and visits the slaves, teaching them the Bible. Some priests believe that he has an illegitimate son and a mistress.

Actually, they are right. He had heard the confessions of a mestizo woman who had said she was a virgin and that her master's son was making advances to her. Father Uraco tells her that temptation is bad and then puts the burden of evil on himself. He seduces the mestizo so that the master's son does not commit evil. He is, therefore, like an inverted Christ figure. He commits evil to prevent others from doing so. First, he takes the Indian woman away from the house

and makes her his mistress. By treating their son as cruelly as possible, he further adds to his sins.

Speculation grows in the monastery about Father Uraco. One day he sees thieves about to break into the monastery to steal gold and he steals it from them. He escapes to the mountains, where he leads a life of suffering—living in caves, praying, and meditating. He has many visions; in one, a Black angel appears to him with a Black crucifix. He does not know whether the message is from Satan or God, and so he continues his penance. The Black angel reassures him of his actions, stating that his apparent evil has really brought about good. But he is still not sure of the moral quality of his acts, since he questions the appearance of a Black angel.

He is discovered in a village and taken to the town. Orlando, the blacksmith son of a freed slave woman, intercedes for him, saying that the priest was out of his mind. The burden is, therefore, shifted to Orlando, who takes the priest to his house. He shares everything with Father Uraco, refusing to allow him to help him in his work. The priest spends the time mending his vestments.

One day, a group of important government officials stop by. The wife of one of them has been hit with a poisoned arrow. They seek a local doctor to help them. Orlando is unable to assist, but Father Uraco says he can if he sucks the wound. The priest's clothes are in tatters, and at first his offer is taken as an insult. But soon he cures the woman and then enjoins her to get up in the name of the Devil. The two are advised to leave town, but Father Uraco is caught and condemned to death by flogging. No one will consent to flog him, and during the week of the Passion he kills Orlando. His motives are consistent; he has killed because Orlando's life was in jeopardy and because he wishes to be the bearer of still another sin. Father Uraco becomes his own executioner, since no one will kill him. He perceives this mission as a way of redeeming men by preventing them from committing evil.

The color equation is interesting, for as the priest becomes more and more involved in evil, he becomes darker and darker. Criminals consult him and he carries out their wishes. His only regret is that he cannot take on the sins of the entire world. On one occasion, a group of Indians attacks him because they wish to reinstate Mayan

government, culture, and religion. They are going to desecrate the church and, of course, Father Uraco does it for them. The crucifix he tears down is seen as a fitting instrument for his death. He protests, arguing that he is not worthy of crucifixion. A sculptor, Quirio Cataño, is commissioned to make another crucifix. He is sent to Jutiapa, where the plot of the novel is set, and he witnesses the crucifixion. Out of pity, the sculptor tries to help the priest with his cross as he walks up the hill, and he attempts to give him water. By the time of his crucifixion, the priest has turned completely Black.

In this novel, Salazar Arrué has obviously reversed the biblical equivalent. His Christ is dark, a man who took on the evils of the world and whose intense passion cost him his life. The plot follows the events of Christ's life and the crucifixion, and at the end, we are presented not with a madman, but with a Black saint. While Quirio Cataño paints a portrait of the dying man, he asks himself:

> Pero: ¿por qué es de color oscuro aquél Cristo? La sangre bermeja que goteaba de las heridas, o corría en regueros por el rostro, el pecho, las piernas y espaldas, a penas se destacaba sus rosas en las carnes oscuras. De la llaga del costada, veíase escurrir la sangre, que se iba coagulando en la cintura y sobre el taparrabo indígena y un último grumo de coágulo, quedábase en la herida misma.[4]

> But why was that Christ so dark a color? The bright reddish blood which dropped out of his wounds ran in circles from his face to his chest to his legs and his back. You could barely see the roses in his dark flesh. From the wounds on the side one could see the blood flow; it was coagulating on his waist and over the indigenous loin cloth; the last drop of coagulation remained in the wound itself.

Cataño recognizes in Father Uraco the true Christ. His face is humble, he has a dark beard, and above him there is a halo of saintliness. Cataño paints with fervor, for he recognizes all the details. At the end, he is "medio loco de jubilo" (half-crazed with joy) about what he has witnessed.[5] At the end of the episode, night falls and blackbirds descend on the cross.

The novel is a fantastic manipulation of black images. The writer inverts the usual connotations of good with white, and evil with

4. Salazar Arrué, *El Cristo negro* (San Salvador, 1936), 90.
5. *Ibid.*, 91.

black. The priest is not a lunatic but a person determined to rid the world of the stereotypes it accepts. Of course, he cannot be a real man; he is a legendary figure moving in the twilight shadows of right and wrong. His crucifixion is society's estimate of him; he has become not just the good White Christ, but a dark god who had truly borne the casualties of the world. The metaphorical potentialities of blackness have been extended.

III

Contact and confrontation between Black and White in literature does not only appear in the form of the color equation. In the poetry of Miguel Barnet, there is emphasis on African gods within the context of Cuban history. In L. N. Calvo's work, attention is paid to dance. The Venezuelan writer, Manuel Díaz-Rodríguez, shows in *Peregrina* (1952) that the contrast is between town and country. The town is European and the country African, though this is not wholly so.

Miguel Barnet's *La sagrada familia* (1967) is a collection of poems that utilizes a personal note to state matters of a public nature.[6] The author goes back repeatedly to the Afro-Cuban past for Cuban identification, not in a romantic manner, but in a realistic one, to show its active presence in the White world. He has researched his material well; mention is made of *al ba hanca* which is a medicine used in *brujería* for purging evil spirits and in connection with Chango (Shango) and Ifa. The link with community, love for mother, and loyalty for island are blended here.

> Ya tengo casa
> ventana
> ojos para entregar profecías
> Amigos como todo el mundo
> y madre
> madre que caliente mi cuerpo
> Ya tengo ísla a lo largo del verano
> Noche
> Viento que me anuncie la muerte
> Vida

6. Miguel Barnet, *La sagrada familia* (Havana, 1967), from which page references herein are taken.

Ya tengo signo de amor
según Orula
Vamos a ver cómo acaban las cosas
Son las dos de la tarde todavía. (p. 125)

I already have a house
a window
eyes to hand over prophecies
Friends like everyone else
and a mother
mother who warms my body
I have an island through the length of the summer
Night
Wind which announces death to me
Life
I already have a sign of love
according to Orula
Let us see how things turn out
It is still two o'clock in the afternoon.

So far from restricting the writer, the 1959 Cuban Revolution has forced him back to his land and his relationship with it. This is not the wild incestuous relationship in the writings of the Negrista poets, but a sober, restrained, and dedicated one.

The Ifa poems in the book reveal an ability for imagistic inventiveness, utilizing the basic metaphor of the African past. Here it is a rallying cry for unity:

Abre esa puerta dijó Ifa
Hay tiempo todavía
Ábrela (p. 151)

Open that door said Ifa
There is still time
Open it.

Barnet's style is not an obvious one. The symbols are subtle and the important messages in the poems never obtrude. The nearest that Barnet comes to the Negrista style is in his poem, "El Monte," dedicated to Guillén. There are the unfamiliar words, the sacrifice of a goat, a mysterious "woman of ashes," and the wild construction of a delirious set of images.

"Dice Ifa" (Ifa says) is closer to the African context and is, at the

same time, a beautiful re-creation of the blend of African past and European present. The poem begins with a reversion of images; the black bird that ascends into the sky represents "los amores del día" (the loves of the day). This is what the oracle says and what the poet affirms. The god of the paths reminds one that the way of the West is not necessarily the truth; Afro-Cubanism is one possible truth, and indeed it might be *the* truth. Certainly, the old African style of writing is ornamentative.

> una creencia
> en medio de un error
> como si todo fuera imaginar la vida
> a ciertas horas del café en la calle. (p. 189)

> A belief
> in the midst of an error
> as if everything could be imagined in life
> at certain hours from the café in the street.

Barnet uses the African past to communicate with his people. It is particularly interesting that he should do this in Cuba, where the majority of people are White. He seems to suggest that prerevolutionary poets lacked the ability to establish a dialogue and so he interprets their forgotten words as art. To resuscitate artistic vitality, he turns to Ifa, the Yoruba oracle and Afro-New World god, and converts Ifa in the manner that New World man should—into a patron of poetry. Thus Ifa becomes a reminder and verification of his role.[7]

Lydia Cabrera familiarized Cubans with many Black accounts. Some of these were negative; in *Cuentos negros de Cuba*, God overhears a short Black man saying, "I don't want to be dark but as light as the day." Olofi, or Olodumare, the creator god, created him White, made one brother Mulatto, and left the other Black. The White enslaved the Black, the myth goes, and only the Devil felt any compassion for him.[8] So in Afro-Cuban myth, blackness still carried slave status and the association of kinship with the Devil. By returning to the primary source of these accounts and to the Lucumí people them-

7. William Bascom, *Shango in the New World* (Austin, 1972), has an interesting section on Cuba and Yoruba worship, pp. 13–15.
8. Cabrera, *Cuentos negros de Cuba* (Havana, 1940), 11–15.

selves, Barnet manages to give them a more positive connotation. Hence, he can praise in poetry the Black Yoruba cosmology.

Not unnaturally, other Cuban writers turned to Africa for affirmation of faith in the New World. In L. N. Calvo's *Pedro Blanco* (1940), there are references to slavery and the plight of the enslaved and the slave master. A part of the action of this novel takes place in Africa, another on the slave ships, and another in Cuba. From this viewpoint, it is a very ambitious undertaking.

Calvo uses dance, not for its own sake, but to express the fierce latent energies of the Black slaves. They are planning to run away, and the music brings all together in a fierce bond of union, in an identification that unites them against the Whites. On their side is the *monte*, the environment with which they are one.

> Entonces comenzó la verdadera danza. El tan-tán, rabioso por el contacto con el fuego, comenzó a retumbar, dominando al bongó. Los negros comenzaron a danzar en torno a la hoguera, deteniéndose ante el guardiero, que los mojaba las bembas. Los tambores emitran ya un aullido largo y cavernario, y todos (hombres, mujeres, mulecónas y mulecónes) se habían incorporado a la danza. Sólo Mina permanecía erguido, pero, sus ojos se íban enconando por la música, y las cosas íban cobrando en derredor de la manigua el color de la hoguera. Pedro tuvo la sensación de que allí occuría algo anormal. Mina terminó por unirse al baile. Los tambores íban cobrando un eco bélico y los negros, incluso el contramayoral, iban como torbellinos sobre las percusiónes. Pero los doce conjurados se veían cabalgando más alto en las notas. La rebeldía conjurada que tenían en si comenzaba a hablarles dentro, y el tan-tán respondía cada vez más violentamente a aquél flúido magnético que embargaba a la negrada.[9]

> Then the real dance started. The furious tam-tam, in contact with the fire, began to vibrate, dominating the bongo. The Blacks began to dance and turn around the fire, hesitating in front of the guards, who wet their mouths. The drum already had emitted a long and cavernous howl, and all the men and women, slave girls and boys, had been incorporated into the dance. Only Mina remained erect, eyes turning to the sound of the music. Things began to take on the feeling of the wilderness in the heat of the great fire. Pedro had the sensation of something abnormal. Mina ended up by being united with the dance. The drums took on a bellicose sound, and the Blacks, even the supervisor, were going like cyclones over

9. L. N. Calvo, *Pedro Blanco* (Madrid, 1955).

the percussion. But the twelve conspirators saw themselves moving higher with the notes. The conspired rebellion that they had within themselves began to speak to them and the tam-tam responded each time more violently to the magnetic fluid that enveloped the Black mass.

Black music and dance can liberate, as Pedro, the outsider, discovers in his desire to be free from the plantation. The Blacks go to the wilderness, having overpowered the guards, and the beautiful Spanish sounds in the passage capture the African war dance. Its meaning is confrontation in its most violent sense.

IV

Díaz-Rodríguez's *Peregrina* brings us back into the world of European fantasy.[10] Although there are Blacks in the four parts that make up this book, they are not always genuine, nor do their actions seem to have any meaningful significance in terms of the reality of Africa. True enough, color is used to extend the basic meaning, but the author seems to rely too heavily on European ideas of Africa. The four parts of *Peregrina* are completely independent of each other. They are like four long short stories, and the first is the longest and lends its name to the book.

Some of Díaz-Rodríguez's basic concerns emerge in this book. He is an important Venezuelan writer who has been of tremendous importance to other writers. As with most Venezuelan literature, there is a great emphasis on the geographical location and natural settings. Mountainous areas are populated, and the valleys remain unknown. The narrative setting here is the valley area surrounding Caracas. The city of Caracas remains distant from the lives and events of people in this book. It is almost like a foreign country, associated in the sensibilities of the characters with Europe.

The first section, "Peregrina o el pozo encantado" is easily understood. Peregrina suffers from sloppily handled, unfulfilled love. After her excursions with Bruno, she becomes pregnant, and when he refuses to marry her, she attempts suicide. Before she dies, she prevails on Bruno to make peace with his half brother, Amaro.

Our chief interest in this story is not in the slow and sentimental

10. Manuel Díaz-Rodríguez, *Peregrina ó el pozo encantado* (Madrid, 1952), from which page references herein are taken.

plot outline, but in the assembly of images as they operate in people. Characters relate the larger realities of the world in which they live, in microscopic perspective.

Race and color are imagistically manipulated. Most of the characters are Black, Mulatto, or White. The handling is subtle, and the author gets away from crude equations. Whiteness is associated with the moon, especially in the first section, and with something ghostly and with the town. Blackness, also mysterious and unknown, is linked with the countryside. One is back in *Cumboto* territory. So blackness becomes a capacity for vision.

The names of characters are significant; for instance, Don Vincente Blanco is the owner of the coffee plantation, and Peregrina, meaning "pilgrim," is a Mulatto. But there are complications; "obscure in skin and origin, they bear white surnames" (p. 13). Other names are used either within an ironical framework or to give some indication of character.

The rural and urban issues correspond with the racial themes. Caracas is evil and corrupt; but corruption is not contained there, for it seems to overflow into the rural areas. Symbols of roads, railroads, and polluted rivers confirm this. In contrast with these connecting lines are the forests, the plains, the mountains, and the savannas, which are natural barriers and which erect fortifications against the city.

Characters typify this distancing, this attempt to move away from the clutch of the city. There is a double irony here, for not only is it almost impossible for them to do this, but in attempting this they distance themselves from the sea, the symbol of purity. This irony forms the basis of the author's complex use of imagery. In the rural areas there is an emphasis on the Black presence and all that this involves on the symbolic level. The Mulatto is mentally dominated by the Black presence in the country areas, where the Black man feels the surge of the power of the earth. For Díaz-Rodríguez, the differences between rural and urban are between Black and White. But this is an oversimplification. The logic of its symbols suggests an overflow of images associated with the Mulatto.

Peregrina is the eldest of Feliciano's seven children. Felix, the only son, is a sickly child. Feliciano, a widower, is a ranch hand on the

Avila coffee plantation owned by Don Vincente Blanco. Peregrina is the whitest of all the children. Juan Francisco is an important link with Africa; he is the inheritor of the magic of Africa and informs Peregrina at an early stage of protective measures against witches. When Felix becomes ill, he turns to Juan Francisco for help. Peregrina usually fetches water from an enchanted well, from which voices can be heard.

The half brothers, Amaro and Bruno, are figures similar to Cain and Abel. Amaro, a peasant, is a man of the earth, plowing the soil with his oxen. He had fought during the Civil War but had deserted. The war is recalled as a destroyer of the land, and the soil is glorified in the novel. During the war, Amaro's family had died, and his ranch was destroyed. He dreams of returning to it. Bruno, his half brother is, like Amaro, in love with Peregrina. This is a closely guarded secret. Amaro's father, Zoilo, is a taciturn man who cuts away the branches that cast dark shadows on the coffee trees. He suddenly falls and dies one day.

Ursula, Zoilo's widow, remarries and bears Bruno. Her husband is the captain of a schooner. He is kind to his wife, but he suddenly disappears. Bruno, an adventurer like his father, escapes the army recruiters and hides in the forests, dodging the workers and patrols during the day. The white rocky hills provide shelter, but one day, he and his fellow runaways are discovered. He escapes and turns to picking and selling wild orchids for a living. Peregrina is concerned about him, and Bruno, in turn, is worried about his half brother's potential jealousy. Even after the war, he continues his existence, despite Peregrina's pleas that he should settle down. Matters are complicated by the fact that Garzón, one of Don Vincente's sons, is also in love with her.

Don Vincente had abandoned his family in Caracas and left for the interior, to become a ranch owner. His business prospers as his morals decline. When he realizes that a Black woman is stealing his chickens and fruits, he stands guard. Eventually he catches Higinia, but the lengths to which he goes in order to do so are ridiculed by the author. The woman is of slave descent and is from a nearby Black village. The author comments that these Blacks had copied, in a sim-

plistic manner, the life-style of their former masters. She is the truth of Don Vincente's own past.

Throughout the novel, color is emphasized in the landscape. There is contrast between the wild and the fallow land. Vegetation is circumscribed by water—a river, a well, a stream. There are descriptions of water sounds and wild flowers. The insects that abound are described in terms of the sound they make. At times, the author inverts his images; for example, with the coming of rains, white is equated with germination and beauty, and black with death and drought. "La negra llaga de las nozas" (the black scar of the stubbles of grass). Sometimes landscape can be frightening. Feliciano has to tell the women that the shadow they fear is only a cambur plant. The leaves of the banana trees are like "un fantasma que llamase con signos de misterio" (a phantom that calls to them with mysterious signs). All these are ways in which the author associates race and landscape.

José de Jesús is a poor, Black man who dresses in white; he dreams of possessing great wealth and hunts after treasures hidden during the war, especially the great treasures of Caracas that were buried in 1814. Other men on the ranch are also interested in acquiring this treasure, but José de Jesús believes it is buried under an enormous tree near the house. He and some others decide to dig up the tree, but their plan is overheard. Because it is believed that the tree is sacred, they get drunk before they go.

Bruno's friend Felipe tells him about the plan, and Bruno, who has fabricated most of the stories about buried treasure, decides to scare them off by dressing in a white sheet. Thereafter the men become the subject of humorous stories.

Finally, Bruno moves back to the ranch and becomes the harvest supervisor. When Peregrina learns that he has played this practical joke, she fears the repercussions from Juan Francisco, the magician, and José de Jesús himself. Since she and Bruno used to make love under the tree, she feels that she will be found out. Bruno does not want to marry her but agrees to it when she becomes pregnant. He soon misses his free life and runs off before they marry.

When Feliciano discovers Peregrina's pregnancy, he is enraged and

tells Amaro to tell his brother to marry Peregrina. When Amaro discovers Bruno, his brother refuses, and Amaro almost kills him. Peregrina falls into the river and is rescued by Amaro; her child dies and her own life is in jeopardy. Bruno now returns to marry her, but she refuses him, asking that the brothers make peace before she dies.

Obviously, this is a very sentimental story, but the account is important because it represents another aspect of Black contact and immersion in the New World. Although the writer is a White Venezuelan, he shows certain important aspects of culture in the account.

It can be argued that this book is a concoction of Spanish superstitions. True enough, Juan Francisco knows of herbs, but the references to ghosts in white sheets and an enchanted well fit more securely into the European world. The author probably intends us to see the characters as carrying on an African heritage, but he does not always succeed in this.

The characters are afraid of the moonlight as it falls on the banana fronds. They are convinced that they have seen a fantastic apparition, but it is only Pedrito and a companion dressed in white. Garzón, one of Don Vincente's sons, thinks he sees the image of Death. Ramon, the eldest son, sees a kind of Black giant smoking a pipe. Occasionally they see a peasant near the well. The level of water seems to rise, and they hear the music of harps and violins coming from the well—hardly the music of Africa!

In summary, it all seems terribly silly. The Blanco family is always drunk, and out of their alcoholic stupor come the weird phantoms of their own perverted selves. This is of no social importance, except as an indication of family feelings.

Some account of slavery is given. After the abolition of slavery, Black men had abandoned the land to the new immigrants and had taken up jobs that brought them more money, for example, bricklaying and carpentry. While they idled, they made their women work. Ironically, it is as a result of Spanish superstition that the old woman, Higinia, is able to steal. While the Whites lock themselves up in fear every night, she becomes "una noche dentro de la noche" (a night within the night [p. 155]).

She is presented as an avenger of the postslavery lot of Black men after independence. They could not obtain the jobs they wanted and

therefore resorted to drinking and gambling. Higinia is the Black ghost that haunts the Spaniards for their misdeeds. She can be contrasted with the immaculate White woman that Bruno makes love to at the well.

Life and death are seen in the change of scenery. They are also present in the struggles of the civil war, in Peregrina's death, and in the strange twilight world that ghosts and humans inhabit. The end of the story is not the termination of the constant changes in life, for these are part of the landscape and will continue.

> Nada se volvió a decir del encanto del pozo, y todos terminaron por no creer en tan claro prodígio, a pesar de la ciencia incuestionable del Brujo. Pero algún día volverán a creer en el encanto, porque el encanto se renovará. Las mozas de los contornos oirán de nuevo resonar en el seno del agua la misma vieja y suave música de aspas y violines. Bastará que una de ellas, flor de belleza rústica, se mire en el trémulo cristal del pozo, conturbada por la música y el recóudito misterio de ciertas palabras. Bastará que alrededor de una de ellas, flor de belleza rústica, empiecen a tejer su ronda, eterna y mágica, los dos hermanos gemelos e invencibles:El Amor y la Muerte. (p. 172)

> Nothing was ever again said of that enchanted well, and everyone ended up by not believing in such a clear miracle, despite the unquestionable science of the *brujo*. But someday they would once again believe in the enchantment, because the enchantment would once again be renewed. The young girls of the surroundings will once more hear the new sounds in the breasts of the water, in that same old and soft music of harps and violins. It is enough that one of them, flower of rustic beauty, would look at herself trembling in the mirror of the well, perplexed by the music and the hidden mystery of certain words. It is enough that there would be woven around one of them, flower of rustic beauty, the eternity and magic of the two twin brothers who are invincible, Love and Death.

At the end, the writer pinpoints the themes. The last paragraph is a brutal summary of what he has stated so well. Amaro, symbol of life, and Bruno, suggestive of death, are every person's experiences. Peregrina dies at the moment when the season of life is coming, and the entire burden of bearing life ends in death. Only African magic, in the form of the *brujo*, seems real. The Spaniards suffer through fear, and the color contrast accentuates this suffering.

"The Sheep and the Roses of Father Seraphim" shows some correlation. As with the other stories the setting is the same. The charac-

ter of Higinia adds continuity to this. A stranger has bewitched her son, Saturno, and then accidentally kills him. When they try to catch Saturno's killer, his hair turns into mice and he escapes. The search party pursues him through the coffee plantation and finally catches him near a well. He is taken back to town.

Despite the stranger's protests with regard to his innocence, the mob is determined to get him. An insipid town priest, though, convinced that the man cannot be a *brujo*, comes to his defense. As they leave the church together, someone stabs the killer; an old woman thinking that he is still alive, cuts off his sexual organs. The priest leaves in disgust and seeks refuge in the mountains. When they find him, three live roses have grown from his body.

The priest and the stranger share a mutual denominator of faith in Black mystery (magic), and, therefore, perhaps without realizing this, the priest comes to the rescue of his kin, the stranger. He cannot save his life but he does retain a miracle that enriches his own. As a result, the Black prisoner and the Spanish priest have an alliance of hope through the story.

Higinia's cry of anguish is like a dirge. The landscape echoes the color and meaning of the action, as it did in the previous story: "Los búcares floridos, en su perenne despojarse de flor, fugazmente esmaltaban de sangre la nieve, o el ébano lustroso, o la canela oscura de los cuerpos" (The blossoming shade trees in their perennial loss of flowers fleetingly embellished the snow with blood, or the lustrous ebony, or the dark cinnamon of their bodies [p. 174]). During the chase for the murderer, coffee plants brush against their skin, causing them to bleed. The colors, red and white, allude to Christian symbols. The White Spanish priest and the Black *brujo* are firmly yoked together in the color imagery. Later on, when the victim cries out for water, as Christ did, the priest warns the mob that they might be harming Christ himself in the person of their victim. But they reply scoffingly, asking whether Christ was Black.

The last two narratives, "Ecologues of Summer" and "Barbaric Music," are extensions of the interplay of color and religion. In "Ecologues of Summer," Sandalio's wife, Justa, tells him of the unwelcome attention she is getting from a Black man who works in a sugarcane

plantation. At first, Sandalio cannot believe this, but eventually his wife kills the man. Sandalio and Justa are Mulattoes, and from the description, she falls into the category of the sensuous Mulatto with "netas y precisas" features. In this account, the Black man is no martyr, but a villain. Justa (Justice) is meant to typify the leveling force in the society.

The chief character of "Barbaric Music" is the blind, Black Benito, who is poor. Like Higinia, he is a night within a night. In this section also, Caracas is seen as evil and corrupt; the roads and railways from the main town destroy a way of life. When the protagonist dies, it is as a result of so-called modern civilization. He is blind because he is oblivious to change. The barbaric music is the sound of the railroad; the protagonist cannot alter this, and so he becomes a victim of contemporary progress.

All the stories contain individuals who are in conflict with the basic values of their societies—Peregrina, the *brujo* in the second story, Justa's admirer. Blacks do not marry Mulattoes. Benito is the supreme individual who attempts to resist change. Like other characters, he follows a dream, but those who seek to upset the order of things are themselves destroyed. There are no rebels who survive in *Peregrina*. Life is a Mulatto, and he who pursues the extreme paths of blackness or whiteness is doomed.

V

Certainly, one admits to a confusion in these accounts. But what is of main interest is how color symbols are utilized in these novels and poems. *Cumboto* is the best example, in that every element and character has a color tag. The novel begins with the exploration of race through the persons of Federico and Natividad; Cruz María is the Mulatto symbol that at first suggests despair. Toward the end of the novel, the Mulatto is not only inheritor of the Casa Blanca but the custodian of its values. The Mulatto figure will be featured more prominently in Negrista poetry but in some instances will be reduced to a figure of dance, rhythm, and swaying buttocks. In the four stories of *Peregrina*, the Mulatto is representative of New World norms— values that incidentally reconcile Black and White.

The religious element, especially present in the figures of the priests, Father Uraco and Father Seraphim, are meant to contrast vividly with their African equivalents and they do. Both priests empathize and take on the color (and ostensibly the world) of Africa. One turns Black; the other recognizes a Black Christ figure. If these novelists seek answers, then they seem to be saying that true identity in the New World is discovered by retracing the Black man's history. If out of this the Mulatto emerges, then he must stand, not for conflict, but for reconciliation. Herskovits' point is then applicable not only to the Black incorporation of White mores, but also to White absorption of Black culture. When referring to West Africa he stated: "It was common for both conquerors and conquered to take over one another's gods and . . . in the course of a man's everyday experience, it was deemed more advantageous for him to give way to a point of view against which he could not prevail than to persist in his attitude, however firmly he might hold an opinion."[11] Africa had seemingly taught the New World about the pliability of tradition and the need for involvement in a new anthropological quest in the grand restoration of the cleavage between past and present. The African world, because it was involved with the spirit, had to make constant adjustments. The New World experience for Afro-New World man was such a multicultural one that out of a dynamic disorder was created the basic logic for a new cultural voice. Writings in English, French, and Dutch all confirm this. An additional voice, that of Plácido, the nineteenth-century Cuban Mulatto poet, reveals the extent to which art and life are frequently one. Out of the disorder of his time and his own life, he left a lasting tribute to a new synthetic faith.

Plácido was born on March 18, 1809, and died a young man at thirty-five years of age. He was a Cuban poet, an *octavón* (one-eighth Black). His father, Diego Ferrer Matoso, was a *cuarterón* (one-quarter Black), whereas his mother, Concepción Vasquez, was a White Spanish dancer at Liceo, the principal theater in Havana at the time.

When Plácido was born, he was taken to La Real Casa Cuna, where he was cared for along with other children. He was named after the

11. Melville J. Herskovits, *The Myth of the Negro Past* (Boston, 1958), 141.

founder, Jerónimo Valdés y Sierra, and was baptized on the day he arrived at the house. The baptismal certificate stated that he appeared to be White, but probably had Black blood.[12]

At the time Plácido was born, the total Black and Mulatto population of Cuba was 326,000 and approximately 212,000 of these were slaves. Plácido was born a free man, because his father was a hairdresser. Most of the free men lived in the cities, and the largest population of them lived in Havana.[13] Some Mulattoes were well off and owned their own horses and carriages and homes.

After two months in Casa Cuna, Plácido was removed. It was considered an advantage for him to be considered White, but the presence of his father obviously showed that he was not. His father, Diego, was doing well at the time, and the young boy was taken to live with his blind Mulatto grandmother. She reared him, but he did not begin school until he was ten. One of his first teachers was Don Pedro J. del Sol, a poet. He briefly attended the Colegio Belen, a Catholic school of some repute, and then went to El Angel, which was under the supervision of Don Francisco Bandaran, a noted educator. Between the ages of ten and twelve, therefore, he had been to three schools. It is necessary to give details of Plácido's life, because in his poems there are references to events of importance in his life, to people who influenced him, and to women with whom he came into contact.

The early pattern of mobility is reflected in his later life. After El Angel, he sought a job. He tried carpentry for a short time. With the help of a mentor, the Mulatto painter, Don Vicente Escovar, Plácido learned pencil drawing. Escovar was well known for his drawings of the Cuban countryside; he was also a calligrapher, and he taught his young student the art of calligraphy. According to Itzahk Bar-Lewaw: "El famoso pintor, bueno por naturaleza, le acogió como su propio hijo, enseñandole pintura y preferemente el dibujo. En sus momentos libres, lee todo lo que encuentra en la casa del maestro que viajaba por Europe y tenía en su biblioteca varios libros españoles y

---

12. Itzahk Bar-Lewaw, *Plácido* (Mexico City, 1960), 11.
13. M. García Garófalo y Mesa, *Plácido: poeta y martir* (Mexico, 1938), 114, 115. There is a breakdown by Garófalo of where the free men lived—which towns and provinces.

franceses."[14] (The famous painter was very good natured, and he treated Plácido like his son, teaching him painting and particularly sketching. In his spare time Plácido read all the books he could find in his mentor's home, for he had been through Europe and had in his library Spanish and French books.) The name Plácido had been taken from a novel by Countess de Jenlis, entitled *Plácido y Blanca*.

At the age of fourteen Plácido became an apprentice in typography under Don José Severino Bolona. Bolona was a writer, a poet, and the author of many *decimas*, stanzas with ten octosyllabic lines. Plácido was to utilize this stanzaic form later on in his own works. Many of Bolona's *decimas* celebrated local events, as did Plácido's poems. Through Bolona, he met many of the leading intellectuals of Havana. When he was sixteen years old, he decided to become a *peineta* maker, constructing large combs to decorate the heads of Spanish women.

It seems his life was always one of poverty, and he commented on this in "Mi casa."

> De pantalónes, ni indicios;
> Porque el uno esta de guardia
> y es centinela perpetuo
> Mientras el otro se lava.[15]

> Of pants not a sight,
> for one stands as a guard
> and is a perpetual sentinel
> while the other one is being washed.

Here he refers, in a crisp and witty manner, to his poverty. He states in the poem that the loaves of bread are like bullets because they are so hard. He feels that some unwary mouse wandered into his house and, finding nothing, left three teeth behind. Plácido does not feel sorry for himself; he mocks his poverty and relates how his neighbor lends him her broom and asks him for a sonnet in exchange.

Plácido was a working poet, constantly being asked for poems to celebrate birthdays and weddings. He did not like this, but he always acquiesced. In one poem, "A mi cumpleaños" ("To My Birthday"), he speaks with muted bitterness of how he seeks no special

14. Bar-Lewaw, *Plácido*, 21.
15. Gabriel de la Concepción Valdés, *Musa cubana* (Paris, 1868), 78.

favors for his birthday, not even a kiss from his passionate lover, "Flora."

> Ni que mueva mi voz los trances rudos
> ni que alaben mis obras los discretos,
> ni en la guerra ganar bandas y escudos.

> Nor that my voice would move the rude trances
> Nor that my accomplishments be praised by the discreet
> Nor in war win ribbons and shields.

Instead, he states:

> Todos mis gozos quedaran completos.
> con que se vuelvan ciegos, mancos, mudos
> cuantos piensen mandarme hacer sonetos.[16]

> All my satisfactions will be complete if
> they would turn blind, armless, and dumb
> all who think about making me write sonnets.

This clearly shows that he did not take everything he wrote very seriously. His poems were often experiments in the trite and the commonplace, done for friends, existing for a single moment, and having little universal significance.

Plácido's life was centered around the strangers he met. He had little to do with his mother, although his biographers say that she attempted to write a poem in his style after his death; and his father died in Mexico when he was still young. His entire life, therefore, evolved around the artists he met and his grandmother. He was a self-made man in many ways.

The meeting with Bolona brought out his spontaneity and his ability with language. His apprenticeship as a *peineta* maker was important in that he utilized his father's craft as a hairdresser while fashioning women's headwear. It should come as no surprise that his love life encompassed a variety of women. He uses pseudonyms for them in his poetry. One is called "Iguana" because she is brash; another is named "Lesbia," and still another "Delia." The latter was a beautiful woman from Matanzas, where he set up a shop to make *peinetas*. Along with his poetry (which he sold) and his calligraphy

16. Jorge Casals (ed.), *Plácido como poeta cubano* (Havana, 1944), 54.

(which he did for commercial houses in Havana), he managed to make some sort of living.

His relationships with women were always tragic. He experienced with "Filena" (María Josefa) disloyalty and infidelity. After that love affair he almost committed suicide.[17] "Iguana" was an ignorant girl, but he writes wryly of how she applauded his poetry without understanding a single word. He had met "Lesbia" at eighteen and "Filena" at twenty-two. His next love was "Fela," a woman in whom he found all the qualities of warmth and kindness. But this love was doomed as well.

> Cuando contemplo el rostro
> de una gallarda ninfa,
> Mi eternidad es ella
> y el mundo se me olvida.
> Entonces como un angel
> de la región Empirea
> présentamela siempre
> mi ardienta fantasía:
> mas a tocar llegando
> la realidad divina,
> encuentro un ser humano,
> que la ilusión me quita.[18]

> When I contemplate the face
> of a high-spirited nymph
> my eternity is her
> and I forget the world
> then, like an angel,
> of the divine region
> present her to me always
> my ardent fantasy:
> in touching reaching
> the divine reality
> I find a human being
> who takes my illusion away.

This sums the problem. The poet is aware of his own ideals and how they differ from those of other human beings. The tragedy of his women, all Mulattoes (with the exception of "Celia," who was White)

17. Bar-Lewaw, *Plácido*, 41.
18. *Ibid.*, 44.

is surely this; Plácido perhaps sought in these women the very perfection that his mother lacked and which he obtained, momentarily,
in creating the *peineta*. But because a woman is real, his illusions
were shattered. "Fela" died of cholera, much like his first love, but
their love was also plagued by problems. She had had another lover,
and when Plácido wrote "El muerto de Fela", he mentions him (Pilar),
hoping that since he also mourns her passing, their sorrow will make
them friends. Her death was particularly traumatic for Plácido, because he saw her body being taken away.

"Celia" gets pregnant and tries to convince him that the child is
his. When he learns the truth, he is very hurt. Again, he writes about
his poverty, his loyalty to her, how he maintained her, and how he
was deceived, thus coming across as a kind of puritan. He accuses
her of being a liar and flatly denounces her because of her infidelity.
He sees her as a wretched woman who is carrying a doomed child
and who refuses to face the truth. Elements of color are present here,
for Plácido points out that "Celia" knew that the real father did not
want to recognize the child as his own.

Two years before his death, Plácido married a Black woman, María
Gil Morales. According to Bar-Lewaw, he felt that marriage was a
mistake. Plácido says that when he got married, he was half-converted
to a belief in marriage. María came from a stable home, and Plácido
enjoyed this, because in some measure it made up for his own lack
of home life. María was faithful and a good housewife to Plácido, but
he was not in love with her. He was a well-known man in intellectual circles but regarded as dangerous by the Spanish authorities.
They viewed him with suspicion because of the problems they had
encountered in putting down slave revolts on plantations.

Although some of his works were patently superficial, others were
quite revolutionary. His constant movement between Matanzas and
Havana created suspicion. Two of his Mulatto friends, Don Nicolás
Bota and Ponce de León, were intellectual revolutionaries who lived
in Matanzas, the hotbed of Black unrest. Damaso García was also a
Mulatto who introduced Plácido to other Mulattoes in Matanzas.
Afterwards, the Spanish authorities accused Plácido and his Mulatto
friends of being involved with plotting the "Escalera," a planned uprising against the White population. Basing their accusations on the

confessions of tortured slaves, the Spanish authorities accused Plácido of being the leader of the revolution. He was detained in Villaclara for six months, but his White friends from Havana interceded on his behalf.

The evidence continued to build against him. By winning a poetry prize in 1834 (at twenty-five), he had unwittingly become an object of suspicion, for the prize had been awarded in honor of Francisco Martinez de la Rosa, a liberal Spanish writer who had been exiled by King Fernando VII, and whose efforts had brought some measure of political reform to Cuba. Plácido's contribution had been "Siempre-viva" ("Always Alive"), in which La Rosa is referred to as "el cisne de Granada" (the swan of Granada)—a statement considered revolutionary at the time.

Plácido was becoming more and more popular and increasingly suspect. He founded the periodical *El eco de Villa-Clara* in December 1831, and published his poetry there.[19] It was aimed at the White and Mulatto middle classes and ensured that Plácido was a force to be reckoned with. He had written extensively for *L'Aurora de Matanzas*, and in 1836, he was asked by the editor to write poems eulogizing the Spanish monarchy. He complied but still continued to write his revolutionary poems. He published his powerful verse, "A Polonia" ("To Poland"), which was then being overrun by the Czar, and "A Grecia" ("To Greece"), which was in conflict with Turkey. Clearly antiimperialist in tone, these were meant to show the similarities of the plight of those victims of invasion and conquest. A poem he had written earlier commemorating the anniversary of Napoleon's death and the poem "La rosa inglesa" clearly show his admiration for the English and the French in their antislavery efforts. His very use of the word *liberated* was revolutionary in itself, for the word was prohibited in Cuba.

The true revolutionary fervor emerges in "A Polonia," in which he writes that "a thousand nations had been oppressors." The oppressors themselves, he argues, become the victims. He exclaims:

> Exclamarán a su enemiga aliada
> "esas son las cadenas que me diste
> tuyas son, te las vuelvo, estoy vengado."

19. Garófalo, *Plácido: poeta y martir*, 34.

> They will shout at your allied enemy,
> "These are the chains you gave me;
> they are yours, I am giving them back,
> I am avenged."

The history of war, he says, suggests that former enemies became allies, forgot their own serfdom, and wrested new kingdoms from former allies. This idea is continued in "A Grecia," in which the powerful image of the waves introduces the idea of liberty.

> Como las olas de la mar sombría,
> tal es la libertad, pues por un lado
> un pueblo cubre, y deja abandonado
> otro pueblo a la horrenda tiranía
>
> Like the waves of the somber sea,
> so is liberty because, on one hand,
> a nation protects and abandons
> another nation to horrendous tyranny.

Poland and Greece are used as symbols to describe the consequences of aggression. The point could not escape the readers of the poem; there is a universal suffering, for "Canto la Grecia el himno de victoria / pasaron a Polonia sus cadenas" (Greece sings it hymn of libtery / and to Poland passes its chains).[20]

After a six-month detention he was freed, but despite requests from a friend to go to Mexico, he remained in Cuba. He was a suspect man, and General Tacón, the authoritarian Spanish general, was taking vicious steps to counteract the upcoming revolution. Soon the authorities accused Plácido along with forty other free men and slaves. After a mock trial, he was found guilty of being the leader of the uprising that never was. Some of his former friends turned against him. In jail he continued writing—this time poems of farewell to his mother, to writing, to friends, and to "Flora," his present love. He even wrote a poem on the prison wall and recited lines of his poetry as he was being led to the firing squad. He was executed June 28, 1844. Fifty-four years later Cuba was finally free from Spanish rule, but Plácido, the lover and the warrior, had been in the vanguard of the revolution.

20. Casals, *Plácido como poeta cubano*, 63.

6 Afro-New World Movements: Harlem Renaissance, Negrista, and Négritude

The Harlem Renaissance was the midwife to a host of Black literary movements throughout the Black pluriverse. Why these movements should have occurred when they did, in the early part of the present century, and what indeed caused them, help us see the Black literary world in clearer perspective.

These movements asserted the positive nature of blackness and attempted to chart a new practical mythology. The ancient legends were debunked, and frequently new ones were concocted. But they represented a group sense of feeling, identification, oneness.

It would be foolhardy to suggest that the movements were all one. Obviously, different impulses could be credited with giving birth to any one movement in the specific geographical area. It might be said that Harlem became a Black city that drew Africans, Afro-Americans, and Caribbeans to it, and that within their search for a common understanding, the Harlem Renaissance grew. But this is only part of the truth.

It might also be argued that the Blacks living in France who launched the Négritude movement had for the first time seen the splintering of Europe and the repercussions this had for the powers that had agreed to the Berlin Conference. Colonialism had proven itself wrong and, in the free-for-all, the Blacks opted for no cultural or intellectual control. Négritude was a new kind of autonomy.

With Negrista one may infer that White writers in Cuba and Puerto Rico had come to seek a tryst with their environment. The wars against Spain had clearly demonstrated the need for a new faith. Negrista was conceivably the answer.

172

But these responses tell us little about the common territory these literary movements shared. In the first place, they operated independent of the larger White cultures—American, French, Spanish. They represented a proclamation, not only of faith, but of firm belief. Second, they confirmed that the creature known as the African only inhabited the New World, for in Africa there were only separate nations. The blood-soaked soil of the New World was the cradle of a new culture, related to a past one, but distinctive, because the new African was the radical sperm of transformation. Therefore, these movements focus a great deal of attention on the Mulatto because he is representative in many ways of a genesis that had not previously taken place. The Black and the White had made him, but such was the contradiction, he chose to be Black, or at least non-White.

In the final analysis, this becomes a question of aesthetics, not genetics. The physical makeup of the New World was culturally slanted in the direction of this new man. He wrote, and was written about. New stereotypes were developed about him, but through all this he survived. There is a type of pollution of Old World dogma from which he seemingly frees himself and is recycled into the liberating pattern of an elastic symbol. Many of the writers of the Harlem Renaissance were physically Mulattoes; still others were "cultural Mulattoes," as Léopold Senghor the Black African Négritude poet was later to call himself. Léon Damas, who wrote in French, and Nicolás Guillén who composed in Spanish, were Mulattoes. The major emphasis of the twenties, in what we will term the Afro-New World Movement, was to locate, describe, and even idealize the Mulatto.

I

Alain Locke, an important thinker of the North American aspect of the movement, had edited the March, 1925, issue of the Harlem number of *Survey Graphic*. Later on, he expanded this into an influential volume, *The New Negro* (1925). In his own essay, he dismissed the stereotype of the "old Negro." He argued that the "New Negro" was getting rid of "the psychology of implied inferiority." Thus he would seem to infer that this new Black man was reacting to the stereotypes in which the nineteenth century had bound him. James Wel-

don Johnson adds, in *Black Manhattan*, that radical papers such as the *Emancipator*, the *Voice, Challenge*, the *Crusader*, and the *Messenger* contributed to this reaction.

Along with Johnson and Locke, W. E. B. Du Bois and Marcus Garvey must be mentioned. Although Pan-Africanism does not necessarily advocate a return to Africa, the rhetoric is not dissimilar, for whether Garvey and Du Bois realized it, they were debating the same issue.

Allusion has been made to the European deculturation of the Black. Here it would be more appropriate to add a few nineteenth-century American examples, which provided the immediate need for the Afro-American literary movement. John H. Van Evrie in *White Supremacy and Negro Subordination* (1867) had found it necessary to show that an educated Black man would be one who would be incapable of walking upright; the law of gravity would pull him toward the earth. C. C. H. Hassgarl, not to be outdone, pointed out in *The Missing Link* that the Black man entered the ark as a beast. Charles Caroll, in *The Negro as Beast* (1900), inferred that the Black man had been created "that he may be of service to the white man"; and Josiah Nott's *Types of Mankind* (1854) claimed that there had never been a Black culture of any value. Frederick Hoffman in *Race Traits and Tendencies of the American Negro* (1869) attempted to show that certain endemic diseases would shortly end the Black race in any event. S. P. Fullinwider adds:

> Thus, as the 20th century approached, the spokesmen for the Negro race in America found themselves fighting a swelling tide of racism ranging from those of pretentious erudition to the crudities of the red-neck demagogue. Energies that might have been turned to constructive channels were dissipated in a futile attempt to bring a modicum of reason into the picture. In defense of their race, Negro writers produced works that ranged from admixtures of biblical scholarship and doubtful anthropology to what was, in one case, quite respectable history. Always it was defensive, but usually it struck a note of faith, both in God and in the ultimate victory of reason. This was the season of hope.[1]

1. S. P. Fullinwider, *The Mind and Mood of Black America* (Homewood, Ill., 1967), 3–4.

II

The heaviest concentration of interest in the Black world came not from Englishmen, Frenchmen, or White Americans, but from Whites in the Spanish-speaking New World. The movement, which was a spin-off from the Harlem Renaissance, sought a symbol for Caribbean man. The wars against Spain for independence meant that the European was not acceptable as a figure of unity, but the African was; therefore, the physical product of Africa and Europe—Mulatto and Mulatta—became for these writers the emblem of New World experience.

In many ways, Negrista was a perversion, for in their frenzy to exalt, these poets and novelists distorted the reality of the Black experience. It may be argued that they were themselves unfamiliar with this experience and hence they needed to invent. Whatever the circumstances, Cuba was the central point of an important way of seeing which lasted until the beginning of World War II. It spread throughout Central and South America and was particularly noticeable in Mexico, Brazil, Argentina, the Dominican Republic, and Puerto Rico. Federico García Lorca visited Cuba and wrote two poems in this vein, giving the movement a kind of European stamp of approval. Negrista poems were also written by writers in Columbia, Costa Rica, Chile, Guatemala, Honduras, Nicaragua, Panama, Peru, El Salvador, Uruguay, and Venezuela.

The literature was Mulatto, which these writers perceived as truly Caribbean. The vestiges of Africa were invested with fanciful notions. The Mulatta was sensuous, happy, and dancing. Emilio Ballagas' María Chacón is an excellent made-to-order recipe of such a person. Che Encarnación is her male embodiment, as seen in José Zacarias Tallet's poem "La Rumba."[2] Parrots, snakes, roosters, drums, rum, the sun, dancing, and music permeate this poetry. A list of names might sometimes suffice to give an apparently African note to the poetry.

This does not emerge from a vacuum. The Cubans were showing

2. See "María Belén Chacón," in Hortensia Ruiz del Vizo (ed.), *Black Poetry of the Americas* (Miami, 1972), 30, 31. Also see "La Rumba," in Ruiz del Vizo (ed.), *Poesía negra del Caribe* (Miami, 1972) 43–45. The poem is a good example of Negrista verse. It makes use of *jitanjáfora*, dance, music, sensuous Mulattoes, a suggestion of sex.

Europeans such as Picasso and Gide that homemade images could conjure up an African world in the Caribbean. As one critic said: "El rasgo característico de la poesía afrocubana actual es el mestizaje. Es un arte de relación: poesía negra con referencia al blanco, al mulato y al negro mismo; poesía escrita por blancos que abordan el tema negro. Por eso se llama con razón poesía mulata." (The characteristic feature of Afro-Cuban poetry is actually the Mestizaje. It is an art of relation: Black poetry with reference to the White, to the Mulatto and the Negro himself. Poetry written by Whites which borders on the Negro theme. For this, it is rightly called Mulatto poetry.) Later on he adds, "Our Afro-Creole poetry is an echo of the Black European style."[3] And from Europe came news of the 1904 African Art Exhibition in Paris, the massive works of the German scholar-explorer Leo Frobenius, especially *Der schwarze Dekameron* (1894), Blaise Cendrar's *Anthologie nègre* (1921), translated into Spanish by 1930, and Maurice Delafosse's *Les noirs de l'Afrique* (1921).[4] Several other minor figures are there, but, more important, René Maran's *Batouala* was translated and published in Spanish the same year it originally appeared in French. Africa was in. A Spanish emigré, Alfonso Camín, wrote his "Elogio de la negra"; Ramón Guirao followed and developed a deep, vibrant poetry; Nicolás Guillén wrote his *Sóngoro consongo*, first published in a Cuban newspaper, Luís Palés Matos heard the singing of Eusebia Cosme and turned to his own brand of Black poetry in Puerto Rico, publishing "Pueblo negro" in a San Juan periodical. The movement—or rather the spasmodic assembly of ideas—spread to Colombia, Costa Rica, the Dominican Republic, Panama, and Venezuela.

Alfonso Camín, the Spaniard, wanted first place for himself. He wrote:

> Negro: no olvides mañana
> que yo fuí el primer pregón
> negro en la tierra antillana.[5]

3. Oscar Fernández de la Vega and Alberto N. Pamies, *Iniciación a la poesía afroamericana* (Miami, 1973), 84, 96.
4. Oscar Fernández de la Vega disagrees and points out in "Medio siglo de la poesía negra," in *Cubanacan* Vol. I, No. 74, p. 65, that Froebenius, Cendars, Maran, and Delafosse never reached a mass public in Spanish America.
5. Vizo, *Black Poetry*, 22.

Black man, tomorrow don't forget
that I was the first spokesman
for Blacks in the Caribbean.

But his place is contested by Ramón Guirao, who brought into his poems the rhumba, the *guaguancó*, dance, laughter, and the serpent (of ritualistic significance in Arara rites of the Dahomey). Camín precedes him by some two years, for he had published *Carteles* in Madrid in 1926, a collection of four poems dealing with Black themes.[6] Other early writers of the movement were José Zacarias Tallet, a Cuban who only wrote two poems in the Negrista vein; Ildefonso Pereda Valdés, a Uruguayan who published *Raza negra* in 1929; Emilio Ballagas, a Cuban who first published his "Elegía de María Belén Chacón" in *Revista de avanse* (1930) in Havana; Nicolás Guillén, who had two books out: *Motivos de son* (1930) and *Sóngoro consongo* (1931). Also, the Dominican Manuel de Cabral published *12 Poemas negros* in Santo Domingo in 1932. By 1934, Guirao, Vicente Gómez Kemp, Guillén, and Ballagas had produced books of poetry. The journal, *Athenea*, of the University of Puerto Rico, obviously thought the movement important enough to devote a literary section to it.

Naturally it would be impossible for such diverse writers to agree on given themes. Folkloristic elements are there, frequently becoming no less than picturesque adornments. The rhythms, dance, and music, which frequently expressed a sexual theme, were quite popular. Rosa E. Valdés Cruz sees a distinction. "Los primeros temas son los predominantes en los poetas representativos de las Antillas, Centro y Suramérica pero el tema racial y economico va a ser tratado mayormente por poetas de habla inglesa y francesa, como Langston Hughes, Charles [sic] McKay y L.G. Damas."[7] (The two main themes are predominant in the representative poets of the Caribbean, Central and South America, but the racial and economic themes are only going to be used primarily by poets of English and French, as with

6. I exclude Felipe Pichardo Moya, who published a carnival poem, "La Comparsa," in his *La ciudad de los espejos* (Camaguey, 1923). The poem only seems Negrista by hindsight, but it had appeared before in the Havana review *Grafitico*, in 1916.
7. Rosa E. Valdés Cruz, "Tres poemas representativos de la poesía Afro-antillana," in *Hispania*, LIV (March, 1971), 39.

Langston Hughes, Charles [Claude] McKay and L. G. Damas.) She
implies that the racial concerns were handled by writers of the Harlem Renaissance and the Négritude movement, leaving the more
fanciful aspects to be dealt with by the Negrista writers. This is only
partly true, for the Negrista poets were frequently so taken with the
Mulatta that they even exalted her poverty.

The Negrista poets invent words, utilize African words, use local
expressions, and make use of Spanish words that help give sound effect to the rhythm they attempt to describe (for instance, words such
as *bacha*, an Afro-Cuban word for a frantic party, and *sandunga*,
Cuban Spanish slang for a sexually suggestive walk). References to
musical instruments abound; apart from allusions to the rhumba
and son, there are references to *chocas*, used by Afro-Cubans, and
gongo for the Spanish *tambor*, or drum. In a *sexteta* in Cuba, one of
the instruments would be a *tres*, or small guitar.

References to other Afro-New World cultures abound; for instance,
poets are fond of itemizing place names as well as making references
to ceremonies such as the *candomblé* in Brazil and the *macumba*.
These words sound strange and mysterious in Spanish and lend an
air of authority to the poem. Of course, writers are restricted by their
geography. So Luís Palés Matos would use *bambula* for an Afro-
Puerto Rican dance, whereas Cuban writers would prefer the word
calendos. Allusions to local fruits are there as well—the *güira*, which
is used for maraccas and *melado* (really *melao*), or molasses, and
zafra, the sugarcane harvest. The references frequently made to sweet
fruits are quite intentional.

Often, the Negrista poets dropped parts of a word in conformity
with Black Spanish. So *María Isabel* became *Mari Sabel* in José Antonio Portuondo's well-known poem of that name, and *Jesus* became
Sus. In some instances Afro-Cuban poets dropped the final *s* (*lo* for
los, *do* for *dos*). Sometimes, the internal *s* is lost, and *diste* becomes
dite, or *desarmaste* changes to *desalmate*. Often an *l* is preferred in
Afro-Cuban Spanish to an *r* and so the poets write *ayel* instead of
ayer, or *resolte*, instead of *resorte*. It should be emphasized that the
writers are not inventing words but are making use of local, especially Afro-Cuban, words, which add to the special effect they attempt to create.[8]

8. *Ibid.*, 42.

III

Camín's "Elogio de la negra" appeared in 1925, the same year that Felipe Pichardo Moya published his book of poems, *La ciudad de los espejos*, which contained two poems that were to be known afterwards as Afro-Cuban verse. For Camín, this poem was therefore a breakthrough, an original. The color *negra* took on a freshness that had been lacking in Spanish.

> Negra que tienes la dentadura
> fresca y carnal como el coco de agua,
> y la sedosa piel oscura
> como las "brevas" de Cumanayagua;
> la boca, como dulce raspadura,
> gruesa y morena como amor cubano,
> que dan de ñapa o que se vende en yagua
> en la tienda de table y de guano.[9]

> Black woman your teeth
> are fresh and carnal like coconut water,
> and your silky dark skin
> like the cigar leaves of Cumanayagua;
> Your mouth like brown sugar,
> thick and dark like Cuban love,
> given as *ñapa* or sold like palm leaves
> in the store made of wood and leaves.

Already we see the beginnings of a style that will be copied later. This is the poem that adores the Black woman and compares her with local things. Place names are mentioned, for instance, Cumanayagua, which is famous for its cigar leaves, and Cuba, which is to be given more specificity by later writers. Cuban Spanish abounds; *ñapa* is an Oriente word in which a gift would follow a sale. The practice goes back to West African market economy in which the "dash" formed part of normal buying; the purchaser received a gift after his transaction. Camín prefers the local word *yagua*, a type of palm leaf. Later on *nambisa* (the Cuban patriots during the War of Independence) are associated with the woman's virtue. In this poem, like the others that followed, the Black woman is still happy even on Sunday, when she still has to work. As the poem advances, one sees the

9. Vizo, *Poesía negra*, 26.

manipulation of blackness. Black is Mulatto and Cuba; Black is tobacco and the Cuban flag.

Gastón Baquero feels that Camín was very important in launching a racial awareness. Though Camín was Spanish, he was able to give a proud, sensuous image of the Black. The Black Antillian was reborn in him, and for sensuousness, the Black woman was invented. Baquero relates that Camín was responding to the myth of the invisible Black woman and her apparent absence of charms when he wrote "Elogio de la negra." He praises him for being able to cut through the undergrowth of racial prejudice in doing this.[10]

Guirao was wary; he was afraid of what he termed "negrofilia," and therefore he claimed that the purpose of his poetry was different. But his actual implementation of Negrista was no different from Camín's, and certainly it has a great deal in common with Tallet, Ballagas, and Guillén. His 1928 poem, "Bailadora de rumba," has the women at the center. *O* and *a* sounds glide the rhythm of the poem forward.

> Bailadora de guaguancó,
> piel negra,
> tersura de bongó.
> Agita la maraca de su risa
> con los dedos de leche
> de sus dientes.
> Pañuelo rojo
> —seda—,
> bata blanca
> —almidón—,
> recorren el trayecto
> de una cuerda
> en un ritmo afrocubano
> de
>   guitarra,
>   clave
>   y cajón
> "¡arriba, María Antonia,
> alabao sea Dio!"
> Las serpientes de sus brazos

10. "Alfonso Camín y la poesía Afrocubana," in Gaston Baquero, *Darió Cernuda y otros temas poéticos* (Madrid, 1969), 220, 231.

van soltando las cuentas
de un collar de jabón.

Woman, dancer of guaguancó
black skin,
tenseness of the bongo
Shake the maraca of her laughter
with her fingers of milk
and her teeth.
Red handkerchief
—silk—
White dress
—starch—
run the journey
of another chord
in the Afro-Cuban rhythm
of
   guitar
   pitch
   and drums
"Forward María Antonia
praise be God!"
The serpents of your arms
release the beads
of a necklace of soap.

The poem is reproduced because it ably demonstrates, at this early stage, what the later interests of the Negrista poets would be. As many subsequent poems demonstrate, the dancing woman becomes the music; hence, the poem alludes to "la maraca de su risa." In the confusion of the dance, all seemingly become one—her black skin and her white teeth, the serpents and her arms; the music and her clothing.[11]

It is of course absurd to think of Mulattas as constantly dancing to Afro-Cuban rhythms. But no poet pretended that these were realistic sketches of everyday life. Guirao and those who followed were capable of a healthy excess. In his "Canto negro de ronda," mention is made of the Oriente, of the king of the Congo, of a little Black boy, of Babayú-ayé. Seemingly, the poem deals in structures of rhythm,

11. Guirao, *Orbita*, 38, 55.

not in any cold, everyday meaning. The focal point is a rooster, and "Quíquiriquiri" occurs five times in a brief poem of twenty-eight short lines. Forced rhymes are allowed, so long as they contribute to the towering effect. So "mi puchunguito" is used with "Jongolo-jongolojongo / del Rey Congo."[12] These are not genuine *santería* references but are made-up words—*jitanjáfora*. Use is also made of Spanish words that bring out the musical buildup of the poem and of African place names.

Once the movement develops force and popularity, the minor excesses of Camín and Guirao seem like virtues. The dance to which Tallet alludes in "La rumba" and which has strong sexual overtones begins with *jitanjáfora* that suggest the drum, and end with those that suggest a flute.

> Zumba mamá, la rumba y tambó
> mabimba, mabomba, bomba, y bombó
> Zumba mamá, la rumba y tambó,
> mabimba, mabomba, nomba, y bombó
> Chachi, chaqui, chaqui, charaqui.
> Chaqui, chaqui, chaqui, charaqui.

In the same poem, when they continue to dance, they become creatures who smell of the jungle—of the urban *solar* (tenement). When their two heads become dry coconuts, the point of disparate absurdity is achieved.

Tallet disproves the critic who would only seek out childish fantasies. In "Negro ripiero," he comes to the later Guillén theme of social statement. Here, a Black man walks with bowed head, because time and time again he has been duped by Cuban politicians. The poet almost turns Negrista against itself in suggesting that the fallen state was because "te guta rumbia de vera" (you really like to rhumba).[13] Ironically, the rhumba, so lauded by the Negrista poets, is partly at fault!

In Tallet, we begin to see the forerunner of Guillén. The politics of Cuban life are all here. For instance, this entire poem is in Black Spanish, which makes it much more authentic than Camín. "Negro

---

12. *Ibid.*, 63.
13. Vizo, *Poesía negra*, 47.

ripiero" is untranslatable, but later references are meaningful, especially for Cubans. The word *liberal* in the second line refers to the
Liberal party and *machadistos* are supporters of the Machado dictatorship (1925–1933). Other references are to Grao San Martin of the
Auténtico party and to the 50 percent law which discriminated
against Spaniards in favor of Cubans and which had to be repealed.
The cornet yells a political slogan.

The references to the rhumba, to the solar, to making love, to the
large mouth, and the onomatopoeic sounds *Mongo* and *Congo* will
all be utilized by later poets. But it is to be emphasized that several
of these writers simply make music out of these words, whereas
Tallet is conscious of the music as well as the possibilities for social
statement.

Although Cuban poets led the movement, others such as the Uruguayan writer Idelfonso Pereda Valdés were also important. Though
White, he expressed the uniqueness of Black culture and introduced
not only Afro-American spirituals to the Spanish-speaking world,
but also the works of Black poets themselves.[14] His poems, like "El
buque negro," "La guitarra de los negros," and "El condombré," display a nostalgic glance back to an Africa he did not know. "El buque
negro" is a slave ship; the Black man has exchanged his ornamentative collar for the slave collar. For him this is the symbol of the ex-
termination of a race.

This harsh notion of resentment is absent from a great deal of the
work of Cuban poets. For Valdés, his Negrista could be no mere adoration; it had to be a straightforward, fierce identity: "Nuestros abuelos
vieron el candombé / entre faroles rojos junto a la ciudadela . . ." (Our
grandfathers enjoyed the candombé / among red lamp-posts near
the fortress). Obviously Valdés is a more sensitive poet than either
Guirao or Tallet. He is not content merely with the ornamentation
of Negrista—its sights and sounds—but he seeks its spirit as well.
Even when he describes in music the suffering of Blacks, he does it
with restraint, as in "La guitarra de los negros." There are no artificial aids that mock the men as they sing and weep. Here one feels
real, deep tragedy.

14. See E. Anderson Imbert, *Historia de la literatura hispanoamericana* (Mexico,
1967), 128.

> Dos negros con dos guitarras
> Tocan y cantan llorando.
> Tienen labios de alboroto . . .[15]
>
> Two Black men with two guitars
> play and sing crying.
> They have lips of noise . . .

The dignity of the subject matter would not allow the poet to slip into some of the absurdities of the Cuban Negrista writers. Why he does not must surely lie in artistic ability, for he did not have the advantages (if indeed they can be so termed) of the Cuban poets. The Black population in Uruguay is minute.

Ballagas, the creator of María Belén Chacón, recognized the simplicity and "realism" in Afro-Cuban poetry, but he felt that there were many missing artistic elements.

> La forma sencilla, el tono familiar y el realismo son otros atractivos de la poesía negra: elementos que la hacen agradable tanto al hombre culto como el hombre iletrado. Da ahí su immensa popularidad. Popularidad no quiere decir ímportancia. Una cosa puede ser muy interesante para el público y sin embargo faltarle el valor artístico. No es este el caso de la poesía afrocubana, pero queremos aclarar que aunque no le faltan del todo los valores artísticos, el valor social y la curiosidad o la moda, priman sobre su calidad como arte.[16]

> The simple form, the familiar tone and the realism are other charming characteristics of Black poetry: elements that make it appealing to the cultured man, as well as the illiterate. Its immense popularity comes from this. Popularity does not imply importance. Something can be very interesting for the public and nevertheless lack artistic value. This is not the case with Afro-Cuban poetry, but we want to clarify that although it is not entirely without artistic values, the social value and novelty or style, are more outstanding than its value as an art form.

Ballagas affirmed that he knew the limitations of the uninformed writing about something of which they knew so little. But ironically he too wrote his carnival poems, his rhumba poems, and his drum Negrista poetry.

He did move further away and achieved a new dimension of thought. His "Comparsa habenera" is not about just any carnival but one in

15. Vizo, *Poesía negra*, 163, 136.
16. Valdés-Cruz, "Tres poemas representativos," 11.

which the dead of the sugar plantations begin to appear. In other words, the culmination of the lay dance is the liturgical evocation of ancestry. This is, and is not, genuinely African. It is in that African ritual addresses itself to the propitiation and exhortation of the ancestors. It is not in that African masquerade tends to be more earthy, utilizing satire and fun. Ballagas is, therefore, inventing a New World form. Often, as in "Elegía de María Belén Chacón," the invocation is to the cross and the Virgin of Charity. In "Rumba," the invocation is to the Yoruba God, Shango.

> El ombligo de la negra
> en la sandunga se abrió
> fijó como un ojo impar
> para mirar a Changó

> The navel of the Black woman
> opened up in the sensuous walk
> fixed like an odd eye
> to watch Shango.

I am not suggesting that Ballagas was not capable of his excesses. There is constant mention of blood, rum, fire; he too makes use of *a* and *o* sounds and is fond of words like *rembombiando, remomba,* and *ronda que rondando,* which emphasize the dance as well as the rolling sound of the drums. On the other hand, he is capable at times of completely assuming the mask of a Black man. Irony blends in these lines, for instance, in which the Black man complains of racism, even as he dances:

> Compañero?
> ¿Compañero yo con un blanco?
> Lo dudo . . .[17]

> Comrade?
> Comrade I, with a White man?
> I doubt it . . .

IV

The poet who managed to effectively combine song, dance, and laughter with the mistaken excesses of mirth and the piety of reli-

17. Guirao, *Orbita,* 109, 122.

gion, as well as the true ache of wounded feelings, was Nicolás Guillén. His anthologists say as much: "While it has always been plain to the point of commonplace that Cuba is a lively protean synthesis, so to speak, of the White Spanish thesis and the Black African antithesis, no one before Guillén had affirmed such a bold affirmation of the latter."[18] They find that Guillén's eight *son* poems achieve an insider's view. What, in effect, he repeats in *Motivos de son* is that people are hungry, do not easily identify with their own blackness, and live in moral squalor. He moved away from this to a fiercer, better poetry in which the harsh hammer of Marxism was hurled against the imperialism he saw in Cuba.[19]

Guillén's advantage was that he wrote in *Motivos de son* authoritative monologues that, while utilizing the *son* much as the Negrista poets had, sought to focus on life in the slums of Havana. Robert Márquez comments:

> The total effect of the collection is comic and picturesque. The poet's vision of the world of his creations is a mixture of roguishness and sympathetic amusement. He also focuses on the sensual and frivolous features of that world, and though he faithfully transmits the names and subtleties of popular Black speech, he highlights the entertaining characteristics of its linguistic distortions of the normative language. Yet the book contains an implicit, compassionate critique of life in Havana's Black slums—a social dimension almost entirely lacking in earlier negrista poetry.[20]

Motivos de son (1930) and *Sóngoro consongo* (1931) constitute the real Guillén input into the Negrista movement, although it is possible to see a continuation of concerns and techniques in later volumes: *West Indies Ltd* (1934), *El son entero* (1947), and *El gran zoo* (1967).

As early as 1930, one hears in "Bucate plate" of the search for essentials. A woman's voice speaks for her poverty and how she has to

---

18. Robert Márquez and David McMurray (eds.), *Guillén: Man-making Words: Selected Poems of Nicolás Guillén* (Amherst, 1972), xi.

19. For a complete treatment of Guillén's biographical background and its effect on his poetry, see his *Nicolás Guillén: Notas para un estudio biográfico-crítico* (Santa Clara, I [1962], and II [1964]). It covers Guillén's life from 1902 to 1948.

20. Nicolás Guillén, *Patria o muerte: The Great Zoo and Other Poems*, ed. and trans. Robert Márquez (New York, 1972), 18–19.

eat crackers. She will run off soon if matters do not improve. The world of *Motivos de son* is one of pimps, whores, and poor people, who wistfully desire the appearance of wealth. "Negro bembón" is about a small-time pimp who achieves fanciful desires; the irony is that all he seeks and gets is a white suit, two-tone shoes, and a life free of the doldrum of work. But, as Guillén reminds us, in the refrain throughout the poem, he is still "Negro bembón" (nigger lips).

Motivos de son was reissued with eight new poems as *Sóngoro consongo*. The title itself was clearly a *jitanjáfora*, meant to conjure up Africa, although Guillén himself had described this as "Mulatto" poetry. Some of the poetry is remarkably modern; for instance, the Black woman's praise could have been done by Haki R. Madhubuti or Imamu Baraka in the United States.

> Con el circulo ecuatorial
> ceñido a la cintura como a un pequeño mundo
> la negra, mujer nueva
> avanza en su ligera bata de serpiente[21]

> With the circle of the equator
> tied round her waist like a small world
> the Black woman, the New Woman
> advances in her airy morning serpent gown.

Certainly there is exaggeration; the movement, the serpent, and even the circle, suggesting the procession, are elements from the earlier Negrista poetry of Tallet and Guirao. But there is a different feeling here—of discovery. The stereotyping is no longer part of the poetry, though conceivably it may well be argued that the Black woman is stereotyped. Guillén radiates a freshness. He says in *Sóngoro consongo* that "the word comes to us humid from the forests," and perhaps this is what is occurring in the poetry. Sometimes he falls back into the Negrista morass, as in "Canto negro," which is full of *a* and *o* sounds, *jitanjáfora*, and drum and dance sounds. "Tamba, tamba, tamba, tamba, tamba del negro que tumba"—the happy Black man is dancing again. Here Guillén stops, for he handles neither the favorite *comparsa* theme nor the violent sweaty lovemaking of dancing Blacks. From these early poems he recog-

21. *Ibid.*, 140.

nized the absurdity of distortion. Sometimes the terseness of the statement makes the criticism even sharper. "Caña" is a short, early poem.

> El negro
> junto al cañaveral
> El yanqui
> sobre el cañaveral.
> La tierra
> bajo el cañaveral
> ¡Sangre
> que se nos va![22]

> The Black man
> next to the sugarcane field.
> The Yankee
> over the sugarcane field.
> The earth
> under the sugarcane field.
> The blood
> which we are losing!

Lemuel Johnson alluded to the "tightlipped, barely controlled violence of the poem," and Márquez sees the poem as one in which "the reader is given a terse glimpse of the antiimperialist feelings which are to become one of the major preoccupations of Guillén's later poetry." And Baquero writes, "Del negro pasó al hombre oprimido en general."[23] (The Black man became the oppressed man in general.) Negrista was for Guillén a corridor through which his poetic genius passed. Although it led him to other considerations of the oppressed, his flirtation with Negrista did help the movement make some realistic adjustments.

Guillén's sound in his first two volumes is that of a jeer. It is directed at the self, for allowing the dreadful visitation of poverty and American overlordship and for turning the other cheek. Biblical references, absent in later poetry, are found here and there. The poetry is still seeking an authentic voice. One sees the duality in *West In-*

22. *Ibid.,* 150.
23. Lemuel Johnson, *The Devil, the Gargoyle and the Buffoon* (Port Washington, 1969), 136; Introduction, in Guillén, *Patria o muerte,* 19–20; Baquero, *Darió Cernuda,* 234.

dies Ltd, epitomized in the well-known "Balada de los dos abuelos," wherein the African past becomes a point of tension.[24] Who is Afro-New World man, the poem asks. Should he harken to the lighter or the darker side? No pat solution is given; the poem recites the dilemma.

Guillén saw the connections in the Black world of the thirties and the manner in which Blacks in Cuba and the United States were related. He was a friend of Langston Hughes and had read his poetry. *West Indies Ltd* expanded his concerns beyond Cuba to the entire Caribbean. He did not join the Communist party until 1937, and it is fair to see *West Indies Ltd* as both a swan song and a new start. In the long poem from which *West Indies Ltd* takes its name, several tones may be noted. The West Indies is berated, partly as Aimé Césaire does in his *Cahier d'un retour au pays natal* (1939), and equally the West Indies is laughed at, as Palés Matos does in "Elegía del Duque de la Mermelada." But it is praised and commended.

Overall the tone is one of irony and bitterness, unlike *Motivos de son*. Here the poet seemingly speaks with his own voice and on behalf of a wider group. The Cuban dictator, Machado, had been deposed in 1933, and the laissez faire conditions that predated his downfall must have struck deeply at Guillén. But it is certainly not a Negrista poem about Cuba; indeed there are no *jitanjáfora* or Negrista jargon, but only one harsh repetition. Instead, familiar images from Guillén's two previous books are given a new significance. The reference to "un oscuro pueblo sonriente" (a smiling dark populace) is meant to be as harsh as it sounds. There are no good points given here for laughing, since life is always tragic.

No dignity is awarded to the laborer—Black, White, Chinese, or Mulatto. The past is shameful, for "bajo el relampagueante traje de dril/andamos todavía con taparrabos" (beneath the dazzling white drill of our clothes we still wear loincloths). The reference here is interesting if only to show how far Guillén had departed from the romantic notions of his Negrista peers. This is the beginning of the criticism of a downgraded people, and he refers to "puertos que hablan un inglés que empieza en *yes* y acaba en *yes*" (ports in which

24. Nicolás Guillén, *West Indies Ltd* (Havana: Úcar, García, 1934).

they speak a type of English which begins with yes and ends with yes [p. 34]).

The image of the fist reappears. Previously the Black man had been enjoined to use his fist to shape a new world. Here the fist is helpless, for the Black man does not recognize his own self-worth and is therefore incapable of destroying the negative images of himself.

Sugarcane is the real villain, and it is mentioned implicitly in the poem. In addition to this it takes on a larger dimension. Just as the laborers burn the fields before cutting the cane, so must a revolution erupt in order to get rid of the large landowners. The music of the cha-cha is not the docile sound of Mulattoes dancing. So when he writes, "Cortar cabezas coma cañas / ¡chas, chas, chas, chas!" (Cut down heads like cane / cha, cha, cha, cha!), this is no musical adornment in the manner of Guirao or Tallet. And when he adds, "Arder las cañas y cabezas" (Burn both canes and heads), he achieves a violent climax in which images and message are superbly fused in poetry that reveals the depth of his anguish and a reminder of slavery, past and present, in the criticism of a poor people who seem to seek nothing. The child who plays at killing another child is an injunction to act, to do away with weak conformity. The end is superb and triumphant with the reappearance of fire, palms, sugar, coffee, and the American exploitation of the West Indies. Then once again the image of "un puño vengativo" (a vengeful fist) appears, followed by "son de esperanza estalla en tierra y oceano" (the *son* of hope bursting over land and ocean). The year was 1934; Guillén had anticipated the Castro revolution by a quarter of a century.

V

Guillén's importance underscores the Negrista movement. What he emphasized was surely this: there had been no past models for him or the poets who were his contemporaries. There was folklore and, when not distorted, Mama Inéz, a kind of earth mother who appeared with monotonous regularity, to link the poets more firmly to their roots. The two Black writers in Cuba who had preceded Guillén—Juan Francisco Manzano and Gabriel de la Concepción Valdés (or Plácido)—wanted "to 'bleach out' any strains of a darker sensibil-

ity."[25] They cannot be faulted for this, since in large measure, they were products of a Spanish mind. The leaders of the Negrista movement—Camín, Guirao, Tallet, Valdés, and Ballagas—saw the Black experience in a fanciful and exotic manner. Guillén's task was to alter their oversweet simplifications and show the complications of blackness, not just for Cuba, but for the entire Caribbean.

Manuel del Cabral, a Dominican poet who joined the movement at a later date, followed Guillén. His first book of Black poems did not appear until 1935. His importance must surely lie in this: he had no easy props to glorify blackness, especially when one considers the current temper of anti-Haitian sentiment in the Dominican Republic at that time. There was no opportunity for warbling, sickly, sweet sentimentalities. His grimness is surely that of Guillén's, and the tenseness of his lines also conveys something of Guillen's impatience.[26] A hatred of imperialism and a love for land are implicit, for instance, in these lines.

> Juguetes de geografía
> con que juega el huracán . . .
> Islas del Mar del Caribe:
> no parece que fué Dios
> quien las puso en ese Mar.
> Hoy algo pasa en el aire
> Telegramas, y algo más
> (Por el aire de Manhattan
> se ven las islas pasar). (p. 22)

> Toys of geography
> with which the hurricane plays . . .
> Islands of the Caribbean Sea:
> it does not appear as if it were God
> who put them in that sea.
> Today something is happening in the air
> Telegrams and something more
> (Through the air of Manhattan
> you see the islands go by).

25. Márquez and McMurray (eds.), *Guillén*, xi.
26. Manuel del Cabral, *Trópico negro* (Buenos Aires, 1941), from which page references herein are taken.

The Black boy is at the very center of this poem, "Islas de azucar amarga." He recognizes the paradox that makes the sugar of the islands bitter. The Black boy "remoto y blanco" is the least common denominator, and so he is able to feel the agony of where he lives. His life, the poet says, offers him little, but his song—symbolic of the island's hope—should be sung, for with it the island can come to a new reckoning. Cabral had obviously read Guillén.

He also experimented with the Mulatto theme in "Mulatta." There is the music and the drunkenness, but the poem moves away from being purely descriptive to making firm statements about life of the Caribbean. The girl here symbolizes more than mere sensuality, particularly as she is alluded to in the lines "roncos ruidos arrancas / para las tempestades de tus ancas" (hoarse sounds rip up / to make the storm of your buttocks [p. 32]). So the Mulatta is no longer portrayed as an erotic figure of fun and warmth, but as a potential for revolution.

Cabral is able to use the subject of the Negrista poets to affirm strong statements of protest. "A la guitarra de un negro" is such an example; the guitar is anonymous, for it seems to come from nowhere and to belong to no one, and yet the feeble efforts of its strings proclaim the meaning of the land and its people.

Some of Cabral's Spanish does come across to the reader as being very European. There are words in the poems that are foreign to Caribbean Spanish, for instance *señoritos* for an unmarried man and *terruño* for native land. They seem odd coming from a writer who has such close Caribbean affinities. But his forte is surely in his images.

Cabral, unlike the poets of the Negrista movement, recognized his own limitations as a White man. He wrote of his inability to feel the Black experience. "Quiero llegar a ti, pero llego lo mismo que el río llega al mar. . . . De tus ojos, a veces, salen tristes oceanos que en el cuerpo te caben, pero que en ti no caben" (I want to reach you, but I reach in the same way that the river reaches the sea . . . from your eyes, sometimes, sad oceans rise which are contained in your body but not in you [p. 115]).

Unlike the early Negrista poems of Cuba, not all of Cabral's poems are laudatory. His "Negro manso" shows how the Black man has

been tamed like a beast. He is useless, the poet comments, and "Negro siempre" enforces this.

> ¿Que hará contigo el hombre
> tú que tienes
> la herida abierta como un surco inútil? (p. 119)

> What shall the man
> do with you
> you with the open wound like a useless canal?

Of course, toward the end of most of these poems, the symbol of the Black man is vindicated, as in Guillén. Constant references are made to the way in which the White can "clean" himself by contact with the Black. By doing this, the poet not only invests what is considered to be everyday Western logic but also attacks the very concept on which the great Mulatto society of the Caribbean was supposedly founded—that of the Black man cleaning out his race. Guillén would have agreed that Black/White contact produced a great Mulatto society.

It would seem, therefore, that the movement started by White Cubans saw its zenith in the work of two non-Cubans, Valdés and Cabral, and one Cuban Mulatto, Guillén. To say this is to admit that these poets understood their own need to search. The early Negrista poets, and even later writers such as José Antonio Portuondo and Marcelino Arozarena, were confused. One suspects that this is because of the large Black population in Cuba and the tendency to generalize half-understood notions. So Portuondo (like Langston Hughes, in "The Negro Speaks of Rivers") can make statements of a sweeping nature.

> Cuatro lunas de hojalata
> velan tu carne abrasada;
> congos verdes de los mapas,
> Tanganika, Djibutí,
> Nyasa, Niger y Sudán
> bailan con sus cataratas,
> sus selvas y su terror,
> en el fondo de la rumba
> que esta rugiendo el bongo.[27]

27. Guirao, *Orbita*, 139.

Four moons of leaves
watch your brazen flesh;
green congos of the map,
Tanganyika, Djibuti
Nyasa, Niger and Sudan,
dance with their waterfalls,
their jungles and their terror,
in the depths of the rhumba
which is sounding in the bongo.

African countries and ethnic groups become mere place names. The terror must surely be the poet's, and he finds nothing odd in throwing in the rhumba and bongo for good measure. Nor was Arozarena to be outdone. As the Mulatta dances, there is "la epilepsia rimbombante que revuelve sus entrañas" (the resounding epilepsy that stirs her innermost recesses). Here is another instance in which the snake dance becomes truly ridiculous.

Vamo a be:
"Alaalá-a-la
alaalá-a-láaa"
Otra be:
"Alaalá-a-lá
alaalá-a-láaa"
saca la cabeza,
guélbela a sacá
qu' aquí viene rebala . . .
—¡Ah!
no sigas bailando má.[28]

Let us see:
"Alaalá-a-lá
alaalá-a-láaa"
Once again:
"Alaalá-a-lá
alaalá-a-láaa"
take your head out
take it out again
here she comes sliding . . .
—Ah!
do not dance any more!

28. Marcelino Arozarena, *Canción negra sin color* (Havana, 1956), 34.

More important, here and elsewhere, is that the writers are trying to represent a reality. But it is not one they fully understand. The snake here is a demon figure, but the *maja* in Cuba is a black, non-poisonous snake whose appearance is attributed to Obatala, Ogún, and Yemayá. Its appearance is sacred and could never be construed by *santero* worshipers as anything else. The point that one is tempted to make is this—that proximity to the Blacks imprisoned White Cuban writers in a straitjacket. Their compositions enabled other writers to break out, because they were not restricted by this second-hand and slightly oppressive misunderstanding. And since none could claim, like Camín, that they were mouthpieces for the Caribbean, they were better at the individual reordering of the group emotion that Cuban writers so inelegantly tossed on paper.

A Puerto Rican, Luís Palés Matos, remains an excellent example of how distance can frequently enhance the poetic object. Like Guillén, he had few models before him. Luís Lloréns Torres (1878–1944) published *Sonetos sinfónicos* as early as 1914, and in this volume, two poems "Negro" and "La Negra" are especially worthy of consideration. The latter, for instance, is a praise poem to the Black woman long before she became a poetic commodity.

> Bajo el manto de sombras de la primera noche,
> la mano de Elohim, agita en el derroche
> de la bíblica luz del fiat omnifulgente,
> te amasó con la piel hosca de la serpiente.
>
> Puso en tú tez la tinta del cuero de moroco
> y en tus dientes la espuma de la leche del coco
> Dió a tu seno prestigios de montañeza fuente
> y a tus muslos textura de caoba incrujiente.
>
> Vírgen, cuando la carne te tiembla en la cadera
> remedas la potranca que piafa en la pradera.
> Madre, el divino chorro que tu pecho desgarra,
> rueda como un guarismo de luz en la pizarra.
> ¡Oh, tú, digna de aquél ebrio de inspiración
> cántico de los cánticos del rey Salomón . . . ![29]
>
> Under the cape of shadows of the first night,
> the hand of Elohim, agitates the drenching

29. Luís Lloréns Torres, *Sonetos sinfónicos* (San Juan, 1914), 93–94.

of biblical light, of omnifulgent fate,
he piled on you the rough skin of the serpent.

He put in the color of your skin the ink of moroccan leather
and in your teeth the foam of coconut milk.
He gave to your prestigious breasts the mountainous fountain
and in your loins the texture of inflexible mahogany.

Virgin, when your flesh trembles in the hips,
you imitate the hips of a small horse kicking in the fields.
Mother, the divine stream which is ripped out of your breast,
rolls down in a festival of light on the wall.
O you worthy of that inspiration
song of songs of the King of Solomon.

Here the formal structure of the sonnet is disarranged quite intentionally. These are themes that will become commonplace in the
twenties, and this poem, published in 1914, is in many ways a har-
binger. Note for instance, the association of the Black woman with
the Dahomean snake, a theme that Negrista poets overworked later
on. The emphasis on things African should also be mentioned—the
reference to Morocco and the association with the Queen of Sheba
through reference to Solomon. One aspect here which is, at base, the
form of the poem and which will not be taken up by Negrista poets is
the attempt at idealizing the Black woman in the manner of the Bible.
Here she stands at the very center of creation, but it is a very biblical
creation, reinforced by references to the Virgin and Solomon. The
very strong way in which the woman is associated with the land and
with the New World will be used by later poets including Palés
Matos. Coconuts and mahogany are the visible images here, and
other New World poets will invent larger associations for the Mulatta, the Black woman, and indeed the entire New World.

VI

Luís Palés Matos, the most exciting Negrista writer from Puerto
Rico, does not deal with anything Black until *Pueblo negro* (1925).
It is important to note that he did not exist in a vacuum and that he
had a history of Spanish and Puerto Rican tradition behind him. With
José de Diego, a critic, he formed a movement that did not last long
—Diepalismo. Basically their ideas were to be taken over and utilized

by the Cubans. Although Palés Matos did not travel much, he met José Antonio Portuondo in New York, and in this way the ideas of these two movements complemented each other and later became fused.

Palés Matos had come from a family of poets. When he was only fourteen he compiled a volume of his verse. "Danzarina africana" was his first poem in the Afro-Hispanic vein. Although it might sound trite to assert that the poem is basically a description of the Black woman's projection of lust and beauty as she dances, it predates the poems with similar themes, which have already been examined.

Wilfred Cartey said that with Palés Matos, Black "music and dance is projected out from his folklore."[30] But what Palés Matos puts forward is an invention, not only of music and dance, but of a gross, cannibalistic "African" world, which the poet somehow positively associates with a glorious past. Examination of specific poems will reveal the extent of the distortion and the element of controlled craftsmanship.

Palés Matos was born in 1898. He died in 1959. Although he seemed to take instinctive delight in Black life (what could be seen of it in Puerto Rico), he had to rely on his imagination (essentially a European nineteenth-century one) to invent most of it. His virtue is that he translated negative European stereotypes of "dark" Africa into positive ones; his vice is that he understood little of what he actually saw, and the references in his poems may therefore be insulting to the modern reader.

With great sincerity Palés Matos uses the names of Black gods and kings like Bombo, Papa Ogún, and "El gran rey del caimán" (the immortal king of the crocodiles). Puerto Rico is the central design of the poetry of *Tuntún de pasa y grifería* (1937), and the Caribbean and Africa are the two semicircles that surround it.[31] But Puerto Rico remains an island of his own invention.

In one example, something of how the use of positive and negative features works against Palés Matos may be seen. He wishes his reader to come away despising the protagonist, but does he succeed?

30. Wilfred G. Cartey, *Black Images* (New York, 1970), 85.
31. Luís Palés Matos, *Tuntún de pasa y grifería* (San Juan, 1937), from which page references herein are taken.

¡Oh mi fino, mi melado Duque de la Mermelada!
Dónde están tus caimánes en el lejano aduar del Pongo,
Y la sombra azul y redonda de tus baobabs africanos,
Y tus quince mujeres olorosas a selva y a fango? (p. 85)

Oh my fine, my sweet Duke of Marmelade!
Where are your alligators in the distant settlement of the Pongo
And the blue and round shadow of your African baobabs
And your fifteen aromatic women with the smell of jungle and mud?

This is the opening stanza of a mock elegy, "Elegía del Duque de la Mermelada," in which the poet berates the Black man who allows European fashion to change him. There is something most affected in the way in which the Duke of Marmelade turns his back on his African heritage and becomes a laughable, effeminate creature.

Palés Matos at times is most insulting; he is so eager to write about the beautiful primitive savagery of the Black man that he does not take careful stock of what he says. So the duke has women who "smell of jungle and mud," which certainly cannot be considered to be in keeping with proper hygienic habits. The argument against foppish imitation is also spoiled in this poem by references, which are supposedly to be taken as nostalgic, to the eating of monkeys. Madama de Cafole, the Duke's companion, is intended to be a ridiculous figure, and one feels relieved that like has found like. Also, the African nights that Palés Matos describes seem too frightful.

Neither Palés Matos nor any of the Negrista poets saw themselves as lending absurdity to racist propaganda. Perhaps one is more prone to read them now from the polarized point of view of the 1980s. But even when this is taken into consideration, the poetry still seems lopsided; the arguments are the wrong ones for the right reasons.

Because Puerto Rico has a limited Black population, Palés Matos borrowed *candomblé* from Brazil and, like other Negrista poets, used place names from Africa and the Caribbean. Often, line upon line of his poetry would simply make use of the connotation of place names.

¿Por qué ahora la palabra Kalahari?
Ha surgído de pronto, inexplicablemente . . .
¡Kalahari! Kalahari! Kalahari!
¿De dónde habrá surgído esta palabra? . . . (p. 68)

Why now the word Kalahari?
It rises up suddenly and inexplicably . . .
Kalahari! Kalahari! Kalahari!
From where has this word come?

Of course it is absurd, but the poetry set a trend with its reference to Africa, dance, drums, music, and beautiful Black women; it was part of the Negrista culture.

At times, Palés Matos' poetry sounds like parody. For instance, in "Lepromonida," he is dealing with vanished Indian races, but the symbol he uses of the queen ruler is not very flattering. It represents the very benevolent excess of which Palés Matos is frequently guilty and which he bequeathed to inferior poets.

Lepromonida es reina de vastas tribus rojas
Sobre un cráneo diseco tiende la mano rígida.
Tened, oh capitánes del agua y de la tierra,
Tened un grande y largo miedo a Lepromonida!

Lepromonida vive rodeada de silencio,
Sobre su trono negro un buho gris habita,
Y una enorme serpiente luminosa se alarga
En sigilo a los blancos piés de Lepromonida.

Lepromonida, araña de la sombra, profunda
Araña de los sueños y de las pesadillas;
—Incendios, pestes, gritas, narcóticos azules,
Venenos, horcas, fetos, muertes: Lepromonida! (p. 105)

Lepromonida is queen of vast red tribes;
She extends her rigid hand over a dissected skull.
Oh captains of land and sea
Have great and long fear of Lepromonida!

Lepromonida lives surrounded in silence;
on her black throne a gray owl lives,
and an enormous luminous serpent extends itself
secretly on the white feet of Lepromonida.

Lepromonida, spider of the shadows, profound
spider of dreams of nightmares;
—fires, plagues, screams, blue narcotics,
venoms, gallows, fetus, deaths: Lepromonida!

Note that Lepromonida is to be feared because of certain associations—a skull, a gray owl, a serpent, a spider. The last two lines of the third stanza almost explode into a verbal orgy of sounds. The references seem more Spanish than African.

"Ron" ("Rum") is little different; the Black women dance "with watermelon mouths." The scene has shifted, but the ungainly Black person yet remains. For Palés Matos, Black people seem to have the fascination of the horrible.

> Los negros con antorchas encendidas
> Bailando en tí
> Las negras—grandes bocas de sandía—
> Riendo en tí
> Los mil gallos de Kingston, a la aurora
> Cantando en tí,
> —Eh, timonel, proa a tierra:
> Estamos en Jamaica! (p. 109)

> The Blacks with lit torches
> are dancing in you.
> The Black women—great watermelon mouths—
> are laughing in you.
> The thousand roosters of Kingston, at dawn,
> are singing in you.
> —Hey, helmsman, take us ashore:
> We are in Jamaica!

All that Palés Matos lacks is restraint, but he does achieve some balance in poems such as "Majestad negra" and "Mulata-Antilla."

Some of the excesses remain even in "Mulata-Antilla." In the first publication of *Tuntún*, the poem established the Mulatta as representative of the Caribbean. It concludes:

> ¡Oh Cuba! O Puerto Rico!
> Fogosas tierras líricas . . .
>   ¡Oh los rones calientes de Jamaica!
>   ¡Oh el aguacate de Santo Domingo,
> Y el caldo denso de la Martinica!
> Ahora eres, mulata,
> Glorioso despertar en mis antillas. (p. 39)

> Oh Cuba! Oh Puerto Rico!
> Fiery lyrical lands . . .

> Oh the warm rums of Jamaica!
> Oh avocado of Santo Domingo,
> And the thick stews of Martinique.
> You are now, Mulata,
> the glorious awakening of my Antilles.

The 1950 publication of this poem had been revised for the worse.[32] The central idea is still present, but the itemizing becomes a drawback.

> Cuba, Santo Domingo, Puerto Rico
> fogasas y sensuales tierras mías
> ¡Oh los rones calientes de Jamaica!
> ¡Oh fiero calalú de Martinica!
> ¡Oh noche fermentada de tambores
> del Haiti impenetrable y voduísta!
> Dominica, Tortola, Guadelupe,
> ¡Antillas, mis Antillas! (p. 40)

> Cuba, Santo Domingo, Puerto Rico
> Impetuous and sensual lands of mine.
> Oh warm rums of Jamaica!
> Oh furious vegetable stew of Martinique!
> Oh night fermented with drums
> of the impenetrable Haiti of voodoo!
> Dominica, Tortola, Guadeloupe,
> Caribbean, my Caribbean!

The additions seem unnecessary; the point had already been made earlier in the poem, and the recital of islands with epithets tagged onto them does little to enhance the poem.

In "Majestad negra," the poet attempts to speak with the voice of a Black man and to show how an outsider could be made to see anew. The women are sensual and the men have rhythm; the White poet admires the Black woman. *Jitanjáfora* is used in sounds like "tembandumba de la Quimbamba." The poem simply describes a Black woman walking; she is a "flor de Tortola, rosa de Uganda" (flower of Tortola and rose of Uganda). It concludes with the heavy rhythmic sound: "Rumba, macumba, candombé, bámbula— / ve Tembanduma de la Quimbamba" (p. 53). Sugarcane and molasses are blended in

---

32. Luís Palés Matos, *Tuntún de pasa y grifería*, intr. Jaime Benitez (San Juan, 1950), from which page references herein are taken.

her walk, which grinds out a rhythm that turns the drums into rivers of sweat.

Had Palés Matos written more poems like "Pueblo," verses that describe the lethargic life of poverty in the manner of Guillén and show his own concern for his country, he would have been a greater spokesman for the movement. The words are short and the lines long, reinforcing an intense feeling. The Black theme is not in the forefront here. But when in "Ñam-Ñam" Palés Matos also protests, he protests too much. The Black theme is overdone and Africa made absurd.

> Ñam-ñam. Africa mastica
> En el silencio—ñam-ñam,
> Su cena de exploradores
> y misioneros—ñam-ñam. (p. 77)

> Ñam-ñam. Africa chews
> in the silence—ñam-ñam,
> Its evening meal of explorers
> and missionaries—ñam-ñam.

Throughout the poem, ñam-ñam, presumably representing the sound of an African chewing, reinforces the physical cannibalistic nature of what Palés Matos fondly imagines to be the African past. But it is not meant to be insulting; this is indeed the tragedy. For instance, note how the poem ends.

> Asia sueña su nirvana
> América baila el jazz.
> Europe juega y teoriza
> Africa gruñe—ñam-ñam.

> Asia dreams its nirvana.
> America dances its jazz.
> Europe plays and theorizes.
> Africa grunts—ñam-ñam. (p. 53)

This shows that everyone seems to be engaged in a positive human endeavor, except Africa, which grunts.

Balance is, in large measure, maintained in "Pueblo negro." There are still coconut trees and a singing Black woman, but the setting is a dark village. Written in a grand manner, the smells and sounds

come to light in the darkness. There are detailed descriptions in this poem of people, animals, and things. Of course, the village does not actually exist, for the poet tells us it can be anywhere, but it is "un pueblo de sueño" (a dream town). Besides some exaggeration concerning the symbolic Black woman, the poem displays a verisimilitude that is apparently African; man, tree, and animal come together as one.

The poem expresses the myth of lazing, easygoing Blacks living among the palms. But this should not unduly disturb the reader. Palés Matos takes great care with words; his slow, rhythmic incantation and evocation of sharp, clear symbol—the Black woman who relates back to an earth figure—mark the success of the poem. She *is* the village, the source of all life, and Palés Matos convinces this reader that such a conclusion is not absurd.

Jitanjáfora come into their own in poems like "Falsa canción de Baquine" ("False Song of Baquine"). The opening of the poem prepares us for the magic of its evocative language.

> Ohé, nené!
> Ohé, nené!
> Adombé gangá mondé,
> Adombé.
> Candombé del baquiné,
> Candombé. (p. 77)

This is a poem without a statement. Strange words are used to evoke a mood, and within their context these words seem most appropriate. The poem, a type of praise poem to Papa Ogun and a birth song, hopes that a newborn child will have the qualities of a warrior like Ogun. Palés Matos is not merely writing a poem, but re-creating the idiom of an indigenous African song that would be geared to a specific occasion—here birth—and would thus seek certain concessions from the *orisha*.

Similarly, the sound element is present in "Canción festiva para ser llorado" ("Festive Song To Be Cried"). Opening refrains make use of itemizing, *jitanjáfora*, and local words from the African idiom.

> Cuba—ñañigo y bachata—
> Haití—vodú y calabanza—
> Puerto Rico—Burundanga—

The poem utilizes quaint words like *tinaja* (a ceramic pot associated with Guadeloupe), *tortos* (a type of cake), *do* (probably meaning two, or the stale smell of liquor), as well as other words. The first three lines are repeated in the middle of the poem. Couched in the metaphor of food and eating, the poem has no translatable meaning; it is an encyclopedia of sound with various ideas juxtaposed within the context of Caribbean geography. The opening lines recur, and suddenly there are the strange lines "the ñañigo will catch you," followed by "the ñañigo isn't going to catch me." Suddenly there is a switch to Haiti, accompanied by associations with the zombie, the toad, Dessalines, and L'Ouverture. Then once again it returns to the refrain. There are references to ceremonies, sugar refining, the *dril*, or a white linen "plantation suit" (p. 63). The poem has no "sense" in a direct, literal manner, but it communicates its ideas through the use of evocative and exotic Spanish words and concludes with the primary triplet. It is the very quintessence of *jitanjáfora*, achieved by a poet with a remarkable sense of verbal discretion.

Palés Matos always takes us from the outer circle of the Caribbean and Africa back to the core of Puerto Rico. The poem, "Placeres" ("Pleasures"), illustrates this well.

> El pabellón francés entra en el puerto,
> Abrid vuestros prostíbulos, rameras.
> La bandera británica ha llegado,
> Limpiad de vagos las tabernas.
> El oriflama yanki . . .
> Prepared el negrito y la palmera.
>
> Puta, ron, negro. Delicia
> De las tres grandes potencias
> En la Antilla. (p. 101)
>
> The French fleet enters the port;
> Open your brothels, whores.
> The British flag has arrived;
> rid the taverns of vagabonds.
> The Yankee flag . . .
> Prepare the black boy and the palm tree.
>
> Whore, rum, black. Delight
> of the three great powers
> in the Antilles.

This marks a shift from senseless verse to poems of protest. The tone here is sharp, direct, and ironical, and the subject matter is one that can appeal on a mass level. Its terseness accounts for the wry, direct attack and a dull feeling of sadness. As Palés Matos said more directly in "Topografía," "Esta es la tierra estéril y madrasta" (This land is sterile and stepmothered). Palés Matos, in the final analysis, used Afro-New World themes to make important statements about relationships in the Black world. If at times he seems rude or frankly offensive in his expressions, he still remains one of the forerunners of Afro-New World Black poetry in Spanish.

VII

Because Palés Matos, Guillén, Valdés, and Cabral managed to escape the iron grip of secondhand folklore, and because they were far enough removed from the reality of *santería* that they could reshape the African's world, their poetry works through a type of reinvention. They invested Spanish words with new meanings and began to adopt quite seriously the task that faced all writers in the New World—that of naming things. They were aided in this endeavor by the band of Negrista poets who, despite their distortions, sought to fuse music, dance, and words. This was obviously easier in the tonal languages of West Africa, and hence their accomplishment must lie in the alteration of the Spanish tongue to suit new experiences that had never been part of European culture, and in their relentless struggle to reject the Spanish mold and proclaim a new role and identity for themselves. Now they were New World men who happened to write in Spanish and who just happened to be White.

VIII

Négritude is not unlike Negrista or the Harlem Renaissance movement. It too sought a resurgence of Black pride. Unlike Negrista, Négritude was not homebased, for its writers were in exile, like the Harlem Renaissance artists. The only difference was that the Négritude writer was only seldom a novelist and nearly always a poet, like his Negrista counterpart.[33]

33. Two recommended anthologies are: Marie Collins (ed.), *Black Poets in French: A Collection of Caribbean and African Poets* (Totowa, 1972); and Norman Shapiro

One element that they all have in common—Négritude, Negrista, and Harlem Renaissance artists—is that they were all *évolué* artists who addressed themselves to a public that was largely a patronizing bourgeoisie and that in two cases was a different ethnic group. Few Blacks read any of the works of such writers at the time, for although the authors spoke of a specific need for being, they found that food, clothing, and shelter were much nearer the needs of Blacks.

All of these works represent a literature of disenchantment with colonial values, alien cultural affinity, and an artificial oneness. The writers in English, French, and Spanish, to a greater extent, wish to go outside the society in which they find themselves, whether it be in the United States, France, or Cuba. A new symbol for the outsider had to be found, and for it these adventurers nearly always turned to Africa—an Africa more imagined than real. Thus creatively there is a nostalgic reflection out of which Négritude (like Negrista and the Harlem Renaissance) is born.

Léopold Sédar Senghor of Senegal, Aimé Césaire of Martinique, and Léon Damas of French Guyana were students in Paris in the 1930s. They met Langston Hughes, were familiar with the work of the Haitian Price-Mars, and knew Claude McKay's *Home to Harlem* (1928) and *Banjo* (1929). Damas explained to me in a taped interview that they were familiar with English and met as a group to discuss these works; consequently, it was in a Paris apartment that Négritude was born.[34]

The immediate forerunner of Négritude was *Légitime Défense*, which had appeared in June, 1932, in Paris. Published by French-speaking students from Martinique and Guadeloupe, this single issue of a manifesto still lacked what the Négritude journal was to fulfill—namely, a cosmopolitan contribution from the Black world. *L'Etudiant noir* had the work not only of New World Blacks, but also of Senghor, Birago Diop, and Ousmane Socé from Senegal. The journal arose out of the Sunday meetings of a group they formed and named the Association of Black Students, which included member-

---

(ed.), *Négritude: Black Poetry from Africa and the Caribbean* (New York, 1970).
34. Léon Damas, taped interview by author, April, 1977, in *Journal of Caribbean Studies*, I (July, 1979).

ship of Caribbean and Malagasy students.[35] By the time Damas' *Poètes d'expression française* (1947) and Senghor's *Anthologie de la nouvelle poésie nègre et malgache de langue française* (1948) appeared, they reflected the two-dimensional aspects (Caribbean and African) of the Black world. *Présence Africaine*, which was first published in October, 1947, was a further extension, which encompassed the Black United States. Négritude had completed its triangle.

In the meantime, the pioneers turned out individual work. Césaire first published his *Cahier d'un retour au pays natal* in *Volontés* in August, 1939; Damas wrote *Pigments* (1937); and Senghor produced *Chants d'ombre* (1945). René Maran, an important pioneer from Martinique, produced two novels: *Batouala* (1921) and *Djouina* (1927).

In large measure, the Caribbean writers were the leaders because they were more familiar with the Africanist work being produced in Haiti. This was a direct result of Haitian nationalism that dates back to the American occupation, which lasted from 1915–1930. There was a great deal of opposition, which began with guerrilla warfare and caused definite ill-feeling from among the Haitian *évolué*. The literati expressed their hostility in the newspapers and in a literary movement, which by 1927 was in full bloom.[36] One such journal, *La revue de la ligue de la jeunesse Haitienne* appeared in 1916, but to a large extent this was a half-measure. Haitian nationalism was still associated with France, and it took a group of younger men who founded *La nouvelle ronde* in 1925 to seek out true originality in their analysis of the Haitian soul. *La trouée* and *La revue indigène* likewise enunciated what was to be the role of literature; as the first issue of *La trouée* notes, literature "is the cry of a people which wants to express something boiling inside"; equally emphatically, the first issue of *La revue indigène* adds that literature "gives the infallible expression of the soul of a people."

35. Léopold Sédar Senghor, "Négritude and Marxism," in O. R. Dathorne and Willfried Feuser (eds.), *Africa in Prose* (Harmondsworth, 1969), 340–41.
36. For a fairly good study of periods leading up to this and some description of the Haitian opposition, see Carolyn Fowler, "Haitian Literature: A Case Study in National and Race Consciousness," C.A.A.S. Occasional Paper No. 19, Atlanta University, cyclostyled, n.d. The translations that follow are hers. For a comprehensive treatment of Haitian poetry, consult Garret, *The Renaissance of Haitian Poetry*.

These viewpoints were hardly ones with which African writers could have quarreled. From time immemorial, the African oral artist was spokesman for his own group. The group gave his work substance and form and lent it credibility. The word was peculiar to the group's world, and a living manifestation of their daily experience. These Haitian journals went back to folklore, to the tom-tom and the conch shell, and in the process found that they had to return to Africa for verification of the past. Price-Mars' *Ainsi parla l'oncle*, which appeared in 1928, reflects this. For him, the return to Africa was necessary to legitimize the concept of Haiti. By 1934, a group calling itself Les Griots, after the Senegalese praise singers, published a journal with the same name. The slave triangle of Négritude had now twice drawn itself; the first instance was found in the metropolitan center of France, where New World Blacks and Africans were linked in a new chain; the second occurred in Haiti, where New World Blacks reached out to an albeit mythical Africa in an effort to proclaim the truth of their identity. In their search for information about their African past . . . common causes had been found with American Negroes.[37]

Not unnaturally, Aimé Césaire returned to Haiti in *Cahier*, in describing his own predicament as a Black Frenchman. Toussaint L'Ouverture, the liberator of Haiti, was "a man alone imprisoned in white"; this distortion of racial identity was similar to that of all early Négritude writers, who were completely denied their blackness in the fervent pursuit of a French education.[38] Damas was to state the case much more bitterly and wittily.

> Taisez-vous
> Vous ai-je ou non dit qu'il vous fallait parler français
> le français de France
> le français du français
> le français français[39]

> Quiet
> Pray have I told you or not that you must speak French
> The French of France

37. Garret, *The Renaissance of Haitian Poetry*, 84.
38. Césaire, *Cahier d'un retour au pays natal*, 45.
39. Damas, *Pigments*, 35.

The French of French people
French, French.

Therefore, not only did Négritude turn away from France, but in this very rebuttal, it attempted an alliance with Africa. Although the association might have been purely mythical or might have been through Haiti, it was there. It was with this association of Africa that Négritude linked itself firmly to Negrista and the Harlem Renaissance.

Therein lies the problem; for the "Africa" that was reconstructed by Négritude poets from the Caribbean was found to be different from the reality of any known Africa. Surprisingly, however, the Africans wrote in like manner; so that Négritude, at least in its early stages, was a no-man's land that Sartre referred to as "Africa beyond reach, imaginary continent."[40] Certainly, this idea is present in Senghor's poems; for instance, he remembers "bitter and sweet scents" in a Senegalese village and recalls the ancestors. But the references are so broad that Senghor does not seem to be remembering the childhood of any specific locality; these are broad references which seem to have little to do with any remembered fact. The writers from the Antilles had exported their phantoms.

Nowhere is the Black presence clearer, in its widest sense, than in the Négritude movement. For these writers utilized the work of Harlem Renaissance artists and Haitian poets, and according to Price-Mars, through the Latin interests of the Haitians, they included even the Negrista movement. Négritude was then truly in Senghor's words, "the sum total of the cultural values of the Black world."[41]

40. Jean Paul Sartre, "L'art nègre," in L. S. Senghor (ed.), *Anthologie de la nouvelle poésie nègre et malgache de langue française* (Paris, 1948), ix–xliv.
41. Senghor, "Négritude and Marxism," 341.

7 The Black Pluriverse

In the multifaceted Afro New World there is really no distinctive black coloration; instead there is a shade of gray. Afro-New World man inhabits the shadows of this invention, a synthetic reordering of Europe and Africa. The myth becomes more complex than Franz Fanon would have us believe when he alludes to the clear-cut stands that colonialism established. These positions were divided with the African on one side, and the European and West Indian on the other.[1] For the Afro-Caribbean man is not European, nor indeed is he African.

A Guyanese writer, E. R. Braithwaite, relates, in *A Kind of Homecoming* (1963), the travails he experienced in Africa. He argues that the European in Africa is frequently accorded a better reception than a Black man. But he does seek a union and petulantly asks himself, "Was there part of me which remained African after all these years?"[2] Of course, the answer at one level is a happy and desperate affirmative, but on another level, the response must be a dismal negative.

The argument continues not only in imaginative fiction but in articles such as Mervyn Morris' "On Afro West Indian Thinking," in which he claims, "We are a people basically of African stock whether we want to accept it or not. . . . But it is no direct fault of ours that we, a black people, are European in orientation."[3] This is the very crux of the problem, one that I sought to come to terms with in the novel

1. See Franz Fanon, "West Indians and Africans," in *The Aftermath of Sovereignty*, one of 4 vols., in David Lowenthal and Lambros Comitas (eds.), *West Indian Perspectives* (Garden City, 1973), 269.
2. E. R. Braithwaite, *A Kind of Homecoming* (London, 1963), 49.
3. Mervyn Morris, "On Afro-West Indian Thinking," in Lowenthal and Comitas (eds.), *The Aftermath of Sovereignty*, 277.

The Scholar Man (1963), and one that is extremely difficult to apprehend in a direct way. At the end of the novel, my understanding is that Adam Questus is just as confused as when he began. True, he mates with a half-demented African woman, but Africa had already rejected him, and it is to the understandable Europe and to Helen that he thinks he belongs.

One agrees with Ngugi, the Kenyan writer, when he argues that Afro-New World man was "denied language and a common culture" and that Africa became anathema.[4] But how does this explain the search of the Barbadian poet, Edward Brathwaite, for assurance from Africa?

> in comes
> this shout
> comes
> this song.[5]

Note that the memory of Brathwaite is loud—a shout.

This, one might argue, is the institutionalizing of a memory. Blackness becomes a totality, an affirmation of plural being. In addition, the cultural requirements of a non-White being played no part in the prevalent system of White identity. Out of this negation arose the group man of the New World—an invention out of necessity.

For whom does he transcribe his experience? Obviously, there must be an experience of mutual understanding between writer and reader, but this hybrid, Afro-New World man can no longer write in a language that Africa understands and no longer shares the experiences that Europe recognizes. Ralph Ellison claimed that in writing *Invisible Man* (1952), "my minority status rendered all such [commonly held] assumptions questionable."[6] In other words, the Afro-New World writer has to assume that he cannot be seen or heard; hence he has to shout and display his anger. This allows him, in large measure, to witness for all Black people. It is for the group then that this individual writes. But this is a new assortment of displaced persons. The artist is not sanctified; no one has invested him with the

4. Ngugi wa Thiongo, *Homecoming* (New York, 1972), 49.
5. Edward Brathwaite, *The Arrivants: A New World Trilogy* (London, 1973), 90.
6. Ralph Ellison, *Shadow and Act* (New York, 1964), 112.

African power to create. I have, therefore, referred to him as a usurper in another context.

Ibo masquerade verse, Ngoni funeral songs, Yoruba *oriki* (praise poems), and Ewe dirges are examples of this sanction.[7] They were only required on specific occasions and no one man invented them. They evolved from the group cosmos and were given life by its reaction. So the Yoruba praise song to Obatala, the god of creation, shows clearly the authority vested in it by an anonymous creator.

> I delivered my child in toil and tribulation,
> yes, mother Poruwaa
> Komfunko, child of wealth
> I would have performed your puberty rites,
> were it not because of Death
> Death! Death! Death![8]

Here the *I* is plural. The African writer faces the same problem when writing in English, French, Portuguese, or any foreign language, even indigenous ones. On whose behalf does he speak? Who has conferred the authority of artist on him? If the answer is necessity, then one must quickly add that an African aesthetic *demands* an allegiance to what lies beyond a mere *I*.

Let us return to the predicament of the New World writer by examining Winthrop Jordan's statement, "Still another curious phenomenon tended to confirm the widespread feeling that black was not a natural color for a human being. For just when Europeans had become adjusted to the fact that some men were black, reports sifted in from Africa and America that some black men were white."[9] This is not the predicament of the artist alone, but of all human beings entrapped in the New World. They were adventurers who had been thrown together without any ceremony or historical introduction. Stanley Elkins, in referring to Blacks, alludes to this entire coming together as one in which "the new adjustment, to absolute power in a closed system, involved infantilization."[10] One may infer that, for

---

7. Many of these oral verses have been reproduced in Dathorne, *African Poetry, passim.*
8. *Ibid.,* 37.
9. Jordan, *White Over Black,* 249.
10. Stanley M. Elkins, *Slavery: A Problem in American Institutional and Intellectual Life* (Chicago, 1959), 88.

the artist in the home society in Africa, this was even more acute. Still, he maintained some kind of allegiance to his ethnic group. Lorenzo Turner has revealed Africanisms, and Blassingame has shown the similarity between a Louisiana tale and a Senegalese one. In addition, the Ewe tale of a hare that escapes is not unlike the Tar Baby stories.[11] Jordan also illustrates actual African word retention in songs from New Orleans. Africa was always remembered.

Turner points out a number of survivals. Examples of these survivals were the five West African languages spoken in Brazil, the folk literature that prevails throughout the Black New World, and the religion, art, dance, and music that managed to survive and thrive until the present.[12] But, and this takes us back to our original concerns, "'the black apostles,' as they have been described, find themselves obliged to 'edit their gospel' of liberation in the language of the oppressor."[13] In this way a curious irony immediately presents itself. Colonizer and colonized become yoked in an attempt at understanding self. Part of the condition of the colonized is the constant need to react to the colonizer, or as Albert Memmi puts it, "The colonized must rise above his colonized being."[14]

Accomplishment of this objective requires not only a backward glance to an African past, but a clear and positive assertiveness where the present is concerned. St. Clair Drake speaks of the sense of communion and the power of myth making as positive asserted values that still prevail in the Black church of the United States.[15] However, he sees the Europeanization of the Black man as inevitable. William Demby, in his book *Beetlecreek* (1950), implies that cultural merging must result when the White recluse, Bill Trap, accepts the friendship of a young Black, Johnny. In both of Ishmael Reed's novels, *The Free-Lance Pallbearers* (1967) and *Yellow-Back Radio Broke Down* (1969), he uses satire to assault a society that is cruelly

11. John Blassingame, *The Slave Community: Plantation Life in the Antebellum South* (New York, 1972), 26.

12. Lorenzo Turner, "African Survivals in the New World with Special Emphasis on the Arts," in *Africa Seen by American Negroes* (Paris, 1958), 154.

13. Samuel Allen, "Tendencies in African Poetry," in *Africa Seen by American Negroes*, 180.

14. Albert Memmi, *The Colonizer and the Colonized* (Boston, 1965), 151.

15. St. Clair Drake, "Hide my Face? The Literary Renaissance," in Okot Edet Uya (ed.), *Black Brotherhood* (Boston, 1971), 202.

alienated. William Melvin Kelly's *A Different Drummer* (1962) has Tucker Caliban wrestling with the weight of his ancestry. This brings about the destruction of his farm, the shooting of his animals, and finally his departure from the town with his wife and child. How, they all ask, is this New World man to be secure amid insecurity? How does he find home away from home? We will return to this in the final chapter.

II

In Brazil, the so-called Lei Aúrea (Golden Law) abolished slavery in 1888. In addition to the absence of provisions to accommodate the new freedmen, their position was worsened by competing immigrants from Europe. When the runaway slave was welcomed, it was because he could be paid a small token for his labor and kept on the fringes of a White family. The history of the New World is notoriously repetitive where the history of Black people is concerned.

The Frente Negra Brasileira was founded in 1931 to advance the work of the conservative publication, *Clarim da Alvorada*, which first appeared in 1924. The search began for cohesiveness; slavery had provided a camaraderie of sorts but had not prepared Black Brazilians for any type of unity. By 1937, the group had broken up in dissension, and its activities ended with Getulio Vargas' regime and his Estado Nôvo, or New State. According to Florestán Fernándes, "Never again was it possible to raise up an organization of such proportions."[16]

Group loyalty remained uppermost in the family unit. The diary of María Carolina de Jesús reveals that, despite the constant problems that the family faced, a sense of African group instinct held it together. Again in reaction to the status quo, the denial of family life gave a positive affirmation to the importance of its perpetuation—a fact that was part of the racial memory.

Machado de Assis' *Memorias Posthumas de Braz Cubas* (1880), translated under the title *Epitaph of a Small-Time Winner*, can best be understood in the context of the failure of Blacks to unite and of Whites to convince Blacks that they were part of a new family.[17] As

16. Florestán Fernándes, *The Negro in Brazilian Society* (New York, 1969), 221.
17. Joaquim María Machado de Assis, *Epitaph of a Small-Time Winner*, trans. m William Grossman (New York, 1952).

Braz Cubas recalls his life from the grave, what is emphasized is his father's wish for a family. His father had told him, "You have to continue our name, continue it and make it even more illustrious."[18] He fails to do this, for he makes Virgilia, the woman his father wishes him to marry, his mistress. His life is a collection of failures. The supreme irony, according to Lorna Williams, is that "he had no children, and therefore did not transmit to any of his progeny the legacy of human misery."[19]

Gilberto Freyre's continuous semisociological themes of the happiness of Brazilian Blacks among Whites have come to be taken for granted. Blackness, he claims, can have no place in Brazil, since Brazil is itself a mixture of ethnic groups living in a "hybrid culture."[20] However, many of Freyre's theories do not emerge in the truth of literature. Instead, there is a poetry that is born of the tension of knowing. Therefore, Mário de Andrade refuses to collaborate with the ancestors.

> Não volta oferecer-me a tua
> esperança corajosa
> Nem me pedir para os teus sonhos
> a con formação de Terra![21]
>
> Do not come again to offer me your
> courageous hope
> Nor ask me for your dreams, the
> confirmation of earth!

As early as the nineteenth century, Castro Alves had protested in "The Slave Ship" against the indignities of slavery and one of its consequences, the subsequent destruction of group life. Although João da Cruz e Souza was a symbolist, he too attempted to show his own value of color and his loss of family. The slave poet, Luis Gonzanga Pinto de Gama, bemoaned the fact that Blacks "their Negro race are hastily forgetting." And even in the present century, White Brazilians

18. *Ibid.*, 78.
19. Lorna Williams, "Perspective in the *Memorias Posthumas de Braz Cubas* by Machado de Assis," *College Language Association Journal*, X (June, 1955) 501–506.
20. Anani Dzidzienyo disagrees with Gilberto Freyre, in *The Position of Blacks in Brazilian Society* (London, 1971). See also Freyre, *The Masters and the Slaves* and his *New World in the Tropics: The Culture of Modern Brazil* (New York, 1959).
21. Elizabeth Bishop and Emmanuel Brasil (eds.), *An Anthology of Twentieth Century Brazilian Poetry* (Middletown, 1972), 20–21. Translations are by the editors.

constantly refer to the images of blackness that haunted their youths: "Coffee blacker than the black woman"[22] or "my grandmother / betrayed among the slave girls."[23] The poets seem to speak with a greater truth than does Freyre. I am not suggesting that this kind of backward glance is any more genuine for Brazilians that it is for the Cubans, but I do maintain that Brazilians were unique in the New World in that they kept the original forms closer to them. If they moved away, they did so because they wished to state their case more forcefully, or because they were influenced by the writings of Blacks in other parts of the world.

Such an example is Jorge Amado's *Teresa Batista* (1975), because the chief character is half-White and half-Indian, and because she ought not to have been subjected to the problems of the tragic Mulatto. At age 13 she is sold to the monstrous Captain Justo, whom she murders. After leaving jail she finds herself in a brothel and falls in love with an old plantation farmer. Then, not unexpectedly, her death occurs. She could very well be a representative of the character mentioned by Richard Ligon in the *History of Barbados*, passed down later on as the Inkle-Yarico legend. It is the tale of a young Black woman torn apart in having to adapt herself to New World conditions.

To find the roots of African presence in Brazil, as well as in the rest of the Black world, we must look into the communal activities of dance and song, of storytelling and myth making, of languages and cooking. Among the figures contained in the Afro-Brazilian folklore are the one-legged Saci; the papa-figo; Quibuango; and Jabati, the trickster turtle. On the religious level, Ogun, Shango, and Yemayá survive in the rituals. We have already demonstrated how the *pae de santo* and the *mae de santo* correspond to the priest and priestess of standard Yoruba worship.[24]

In 1850, the Queiroz law abolished the African slave trade in Brazil. In 1885, all slaves over sixty were freed, and finally, on May 13, 1888,

22. *Ibid.*, 87.
23. *Ibid.*, 50. Both poems are by Carlos Drummond de Andrade.
24. Courtenay Malcolm Batchelor, *Stories and Storytellers of Brazil*, I, 23–33, 172–77.

a decree abolishing slavery without compensation to slave owners was signed by Princess Regent Isabel. Dorothy Porter shows that Afro-Brazilians had worked toward their own emancipation; particularly, she cites Luis Gonzaga Pinto de Gama and José Carlos de Patrocíno.[25]

Naturally, slavery and its ramifications dominate the cultural landscape of Brazilian literature of both Whites and Blacks. Rollie Poppino points out that travel accounts specify the extent to which "statistical data on commerce, slavery, and the slave trade" predominate until the eve of the nineteenth century.[26] What should interest us more than accounts of Frenchmen, Dutchmen, Spaniards, Portuguese, and Germans on Brazil is the lesson of social hierarchy that had been reinforced by European colonialism, but which was in effect part of the cultural assertiveness of Africa. Many of the masquerade verses and songs refer to kings and queens; and, although royalty was the natural extension of the African cultural landscapes, it became more marked in Brazil because royalty patterns from Portugal reinforced it.

Rei de Congo was only one of the many surviving African kings who is commemorated in public theater. The combination of Carlos Mango and God in the character of Rei Congo is no surprise; he is perhaps the finest example available of the emergence of secondary synthesism in the New World. Yet this African king has all the African attributes. He is powerful and demonstrates the extent of his physical ability by having his secretary and his general in attendance. When the secretary speaks, he enunciates the *oriki* of a typical Yoruba praise singer. There is no contradiction here—only the finely tuned merger of one culture with another.[27]

No wonder Freyre sees this as a blending of race and culture. While the conclusions of neither the *Masters And the Slaves* (1946) nor *The Mansions And the Shanties* (1962) are acceptable from the point of view of the smooth fusion that Freyre sees, the works neverthe-

25. Dorothy B. Porter, *Afro-Braziliana: A Working Bibliography* (Boston, 1978), xiv.
26. Rollie E. Poppino, *Brazil: The Land and People* (New York, 1973), 343.
27. Araújo, *Folclore nacional*, I, especially 216–38, 245, 258, 387–91.

less contain a great deal of erudite scholarship. A careful reading of
Freyre's work reveals that the true Afro-Brazilian culture had reached
a perfect unity with all its former ethnic variations.

The apparent merger between the African and European consciousness. This may still be found in the social layers that are part of the
Yoruba religion indigenous to Brazil. Both the objects of worship
entiation between the familiar *tu* and the formal *vos*; this tended to
stress a pattern of norms that had been institutionalized in language.
Yoruba and Hausa could equally respond to the emphasis that placed
a distance of formality between the immediate family and perfect
strangers. In a way, therefore, the Portuguese language reinforced a
pattern of hierarchy that was embedded in the African consciousness. This may still be found in the social layers that are part of the
Yoruba religion indigenous to Brazil. Both the objects of worship
and the instruments through which they are worshiped demonstrate
this hierarchical pattern. The *mae de santo* has her *filhas*, or hand-
maidens, and her *feitichra*, or a lesser priest. The high God, Olorun,
was not worshiped; but Oxala (Christ), Omolu (Saint Lazaras), Ogun
(Saint Anthony), and Shango (Saint Jerome) were worshiped in varying degrees within the religious strata of the pantheon.

One way of viewing the reverence found in *macumba* is to see it
as an African aspect of devotion demonstrating the ability of the
Afro-Brazilian to worship in a kind of verbal prostration.

> Mestre Carlos, grande mestre
> Due-me o saber sem me
> ensinar . . . Dios dias
> Ficou deitado; E quando se
> levantou Em curandeiro
> tinha-se tornado[28]

> Mestre Carlos, powerful
> mestre you gave me
> knowledge without teaching
> me. For two days you
> remain dormant and
> then you awoke.
> With the power of a healer.

28. Roger Bastide, *Brasil: terra de contrastes* (São Paulo, 1964), 73.

Note that the figure of adoration is given extremely important qualities. Observe the manner in which the repetition of *mestre* freezes the poem in a single moment, similar to the way in which an African praise poem is contained in a moment of time. The most important quality, which also harks back to an African origin, is the human-God motif that is part of the imaginative expression.

An examination of some of the works of Afro-Brazilian writers reveals a certain commonality. For example, with Gil Vicente, the overriding theme is the manner in which his characters attempt to relate to their world. As a result of an inability to embrace the African past, his characters find themselves in a quandary. Vicente's Black characters have "an amusing half unintelligible speech." The Mulatto writer, Alfonso Alvares, sees the situation in distressingly similar and profoundly more pointed terms. God, in creating the Mulatto, does not make him a "pure" African; he is, by a curious twisted logic on Alvares' part, an illegitimate man:

> Estes são os mulatos,
> que procedem de malicia . . .
> e viven com seus biocatos,
> porque nascem da immundicia. [29]

> These are the types of Mulattoes
> who act out of evil . . .
> and are always thinking of evil
> because they are products of filth.

This is the type of statement that belies the simplicity of Freyre. Obviously, this tormented soul does not see life in exactly those glowing terms. The races do not come together in Freyre's idyllic manner; and throughout Alvares' poetry, plays, and novels, the lack of achievement of a secondary synthesis is paramount.

The noble Negro theme is presented as in the case of José Basílio de Gamas' *Quitubia*. Sayers describes him as "probably the first African Prince to appear in Portuguese poetry." [30] Inkle, Yarico, and Oroonoko are there again.

The artificial African of the New World is brave and heroic, but he

29. Raymond S. Sayers, *The Negro in Brazilian Literature* (New York, 1956), 23.
30. *Ibid.*, 59.

is still incredible. For instance, Manuel Ignacio da Silva Alvarenga and Domingos Caldas Barbosa were both eighteenth-century Mulatto poets who had experienced Black life but chose classical European forms and equations for their lyrics and sonnets. They did not seem to have been interested in anything relating to the African presence in Brazil, though there was certainly a challenge for them to express their blackness in poetry.

The Black man only ceases to be a shadow and becomes substantial when Afro-Brazilian writers are able to grasp the meaning of their material and are better able to apprehend and utilize their world. Neither Tobias Barreto nor the earlier Castro Alves dealt with the immediate. Barreto, for example, was not very concerned with the problem of slavery and emancipation, although Blacks were actively participating on a political level.

Some of these writers succumbed to the common clichés. The Black woman was "Morena e sublime / Como a hara do sol posto" (Dark skinned lady / like the hours of sunset).[31] This could have represented an evocation in the manner of the later Négritude and Negrista poets, except that Barreto died in 1889. These pious effusions lasted throughout the nineteenth century and continued into the twentieth. Some poets with an acute sense of history and a responsible commitment to realism returned to the Republic of Palmares, as exemplified by Silvio Romero's "Cantos do Fim do Seculo." For him the republic is a lesson in order and an example for further generations.

> Como em appello aos seculos futuros
> Floresce ao sol d'America a Republica
> Pela primeira vez . . .
>
> Cresce O Estado. Jorram valentias
> N'aurea idade em que os povos são ousados
> A lei é justa; triumphante e bela
> A Igualdade contra os seus soldados . . .[32]
>
> As an appeal to the future centuries
> The Republic flourishes in the sun of America

31. Tobias Barreto, *Obras completas* (Rio de Janeiro, 1926), I, 171.
32. Silvio Romero, "Os Palmares," *A Revista brasileira*, X (October–December, 1881), 332, 315.

for the first time. . .

The state grows, bravery rises
at the peak of the age where the people are most daring.
The law is fair triumphant and beautiful,
Equality against its soldiers . . .

Palmares had appeared before in poetry throughout the eighteenth century. *Quilombo* poetry, in which Zumbi is idealized, appears constantly. After all, Palmares did withstand Dutch and British attacks from 1630 throughout 1695. But whenever White Brazilians describe Palmares, they are far removed from it in time and in the threat that it had posed. Therefore, this poetry must not be seen as a real response to a situation but as a delayed reaction to a historical reality.

The abolitionist verse of Luis Gonzanga Pinto de Gama celebrated the freedom of the *quilombo* and the right of Black men everywhere to overthrow their masters. His writing was based on his own experience. He not only glorified the Black woman, but he also downgraded the White woman. The poem "Junto a estatua" is about a green-eyed, blonde-haired woman who turns into a cold marble statue. What these Afro-Brazilian writers emphasize repeatedly is that whether they dealt with skin coloration, race, prejudice, slavery, or the attendant problems that occurred before Blacks were in the process of becoming part of the larger society, there is a unique thread of continuity that links them socially to all New World Blacks. They disprove Freyre and even latter-day hopefuls like Pierre Verger, who wrote of the harmonious Brazilian mixture of elements from diverse countries, *and* their ready acceptance and integration without shock or prejudice. He speaks of "how all the descendants of Africans now living in Brazil have become good Brazilians, their social status is improving all the time. . . . What is more they are very firmly attached to their native land [Brazil]."[33]

It would be tempting to see Brazil in these terms, and even now, Brazilians have tended to envision Brazil as a racially ideal society. So the Uruguayan writer Gaston Figueira, in giving an evaluation of contemporary Brazilian poetry, feels that the beauty of Brazilian

33. Pierre Verger, "Nigeria, Brazil and Cuba," in *Nigeria* (October, 1960), 168, 177.

verse is in the diversity of the race and the physical differences in landscape.[34] But imaginative writers do not give such lush, synthetic projections as Figueira's. Instead, because there is syncretism on the religious level, the Black-White contact is even more impossible to achieve. Note this exchange among six women over the death of a boy.

> SENHORA–Um menino tão forte e tão lindo!
> SENHORA–De repente morreu!
> SENHORA–Moreninho, moreninho!
> SENHORA–Moreno, não. Não era moreno!
> SENHORA–Mulatinho disfarçado!
> SENHORA–Prêto!
> SENHORA–Moreno!
> SENHORA–Mulato!
> SENHORA–May Deus do Céu, tenho mêdo de prêto?[35]

> WOMAN: Such a strong and beautiful boy!
> WOMAN: He died suddenly!
> WOMAN: Little colored boy! Little colored boy!
> WOMAN: Not colored. He was not colored!
> WOMAN: Disguised Mulatto!
> WOMAN: Black!
> WOMAN: Colored!
> WOMAN: Mulatto!
> WOMAN: My God, why such a fear of being Black?

As the drama unfolds, we learn that it is the funeral of a boy who committed suicide. The reason for his death is seen as one over which he was powerless. His father was Black and his mother White, which further confounds his situation.

An examination of the oral literature reveals a similar conflict. "A Festa dos Matos" ("Festivities for the Dead") shows that the rituals were divided into three distinct sections: prayer, sacrifice, and dancing. Prayer was chanted to the beat of instruments and would last until daybreak. The chief wore a long white costume with a white hat. There was a sacrifice of a sheep on the second night, which entailed a solemn ceremony and the distribution of food. On the third

34. Gastón Figueira (ed.), *Poesía brasileña contemporanea, 1920–1968* (Montevideo, 1969), 10.

35. Abdias do Nascimento (ed.), *Dramas para negros e prólogo para brancos* (Rio de Janeiro, 1961), 311–12.

night, after the chanting and dancing, drums would invoke the dead.[36]
I suggest that the preservation of the dead—a distinctly African phenomenon—was the purpose for this and was the manner in which
African culture was retained and perpetuated. The collision course
between African and European mores that has been observed in
imaginative literature is demonstrated quite clearly in the performance of oral literature.

The instances can be multiplied in José Lima's "A festa de egun."
One reads of the total commitment of Bahian Blacks to an African
way of life. The beads and rosaries that are sold are as African as those
employed for the *candomblé* ritual. Work loads are carefully divided;
only the daughters of Ochala can sell products made of coconut, but
the daughters of Ogun and Shango are the true sellers. The Mulattoes
sell foods that are related to the sects of their grandmothers. Observe
how the African penchant for hierarchy is blended with the New
World preoccupation with color. There is no contradiction for the
Afro-Brazilian when he sings praise songs to Saint Rita the Impossible. As the prayer to cure jealousy avers:

> Deus quer
> Deus pode
> Deus faz
> E Deus Desfaz
> Assim como as estrêlas
> Andam astraz da lua
> E a lua atraz
> De Deus Senhor Jesus Cristo.[37]

> God wants
> God can
> God ties
> and God unties
> Just as the stars
> Go behind the moon
> and the moon
> Behind our Lord, Jesus Christ.

The Christian God exhibits elastic properties and therefore becomes
the earthy, human-related God of the Africans.

One does not need to seek too far into Brazilian oral literature,

36. See Mello Moraes Filho, *Festas e tradiçōnes* (Rio de Janeiro, 1946).
37. José Lima, *A festa de Egun e quatros ensarios* (Rio de Janeiro, 1955), 102.

whether ritualistic or spontaneous, religious or lay, to see the equivalents of an African assertion. On the popular level of folklore, self-criticism is paramount, as it is among all peoples; but here the laughter is directed at the predicament of man because of the whimsy of color. The Black man lags behind the White man and the Indian in reaching the stream. Therefore, there is only enough water for him to wash the palms of his hands and the soles of his feet.[38] Perhaps this tells us more about the Portuguese presence in Africa and the New World than it does about the African presence, because a similar story appears among the people of Angola and has also been translated into Portuguese. The account links African mythical etiology with Afro-New World man's legendary adaptability.

Saci-pererê is another case in point. He is a one-legged Black boy born of pure fantasy, who pursues travelers and sets traps for them. He is, in a larger sense, the Afro-Brazilian equivalent of the Sierra Leonean Creole Wan Foot Jumbie and serves the same purpose. Both warn against assuming that the New World landscape can be taken for granted. The written imaginative literature points this out repeatedly, since the writer is responding to the reality that he knows. Therefore, in a way, Saci-pererê is not just one man's fantasy but is the symbolic nightmare of a group. This is not farfetched, since Sayers points out that in Portuguese literature about Blacks there is a "lyric purporting to be a speech by the King of Sierra Leone, newly arrived from his distant country [who] speaks in a kind of gibberish."[39] Saci-pererê may well have traveled from Africa to the New World and back again to Africa.

In all ways, Afro-Brazilian oral literature provides the firm complement to its written counterpart, because it confirms the subtle discomforts in ethnic relationships and thus mitigates the importance of Freyre's sociological belief. The most cursory glance at works of nonfiction, like Oliveira Vianna's *Evoluçao de povo brasileiro* (1933), shows the great gulf that slavery had created between victor and victim. Vianna points out issues that are common denomina-

---

38. Compare the African version in Castro Soromenho, *A marvilhosa viagem dos exploradores portugueses* (Lisbon, 1956), 359. The Afro-Brazilian version appears in Lindolfo Gomes (ed.), *Cantos populares brasileiros* (São Paulo, 1931), 164.
39. Sayers, *The Negro in Brazilian Literature*, 18.

tors of the regions we have examined: African slavery, and the dominance of sugarcane and its need for a large labor force. C. R. Boxer, in *The Golden Age of Brazil, 1695–1750*, makes the same point, that in Brazil the social patterns were founded on a slave base.[40] As a result of slavery itself, a host of associated occupations sprang up. Blacksmiths, masons, stoneworkers, carpenters and cobblers—all became part of the autonomous plantation. It is because of this great chasm in Brazilian society, not despite it, that Freyre can allude to the *quilombos* as being "isolated in space and backward in time."[41] The greatest tragedy of any multiethnic society is when it would deny its own ethnicity, as is seen in the words of the man who candidly said, "I have no prejudice," and admitted to having a Black grandmother. But he could not logically see his own Black features. The conundrum exists in Brazilian life, enacts itself in oral literature, and appears in written creative literature; yet it is repeatedly denied by the sociologists of the Freyre school.

Up until 1925, according to Richard Pattee, the Black man in Afro-Brazilian letters was picturesque, frequently confused with the Indian, and thus a decided problem as regards the understanding and investigation of relevant areas of his Black experience.[42] In a later paper, Pattee found that the "pendulum [had] swung to the opposite extreme in which only that which was traceable direct to Africa was worthy of repetition."[43] I have avoided any such implication since what I have described is both "African" and "Afro-Brazilian" as derived from retention, invention, and alteration. The *quilombo* forced the retention of African communal forms and perpetuated the literature that it needed to function. New life in the cities and on the plantations forced the alteration of new myths (Saci-pererê is a case in point). And the invention is clearly demonstrated in the praise songs to Saint Rita the Impossible, or in the way the new hierarchy was applied to color. We may term this a reapplication of the body

40. C. R. Boxer, *The Golden Age of Brazil, 1695–1750: Growing Pains of a Colonial Society* (Berkeley, 1962), 1–2, 11, 45, 305–306.

41. *Comissão nacional de folclore de Instituto Brasileiro de Edução, Ciêncla e Cultura* (Rio de Janeiro, 1948), folklore seminar (August 22, 1948), 23.

42. Richard Pattee, "Negro Studies in Latin America," in *Bulletin No. 32*, American Council of Learned Societies (September, 1941).

43. Richard Pattee, "Barriers to Latin American Negro Studies," *Crisis*, LVII (1940), 255–57.

myth, which at its worst appears in Alberto Rangel's "Terra caída."[44] There the main character, Possidônio, is a combination of stock Indian and stereotyped African, as he performs a snake act and recites his prayers for a young girl.

One is constantly reminded of just how wary any approach must be to Brazilian literature and how impossible at times it becomes to view Brazil from any preconceived angle.

> Dejando a un lado la modinha, de tiempos ya lejanos, y en la que sin-duda son demasiado visibles las influencias europeas, podemos nombrar, como per tenecientes a la música genuinamenta brasileña: el lundú, el marācatú, el catereté, el coco, el bātuque, el samba, el macumba, el jongo. De carácter indígena algunas—por ejemplo, el catereté—otras, afrobra-sileñas—el bātuqua, la macumba—todas ellas en la multiplicidad de sus matices musicales forman una orquestración en que se reconoce la brasili-dad con sus elementos inseparables: el indígena, el africano, el luso.[45]

> Leaving aside the *modinha* of past years, in which undoubtedly the European influences are readily visible, we can name a pure Brazilian music: the *lundu*, the *maracatu*, the *catereté*, the *coco*, the *batuque*, the *samba*, the *macumba*, the *jongo*. Some of the indigenous characteristics, for example, occur in the *caterete* and in others characteristic of Afro-Brazilian, such as in the *batuque* and the *macumba*. All of them, in the multiplicity of musical color, make one orchestra that one recognizes as the inseparable Brazilian elements: the indigenous, the African, and the mixed.

Here again, the craving for unity is present; but there is also another point—a signpost warning that the investigator must be wary of making too many rash generalizations that, although applicable in most instances to the New World, might have no meaningful relevance in the Brazilian context.

Alfonso Alvares is therefore no blacker than Castro Alves; nor are Gonçalves Dias and his "noble savage" any less relevant in the total Brazilian context. Of course, we are happy when we encounter the work of Cruz e Sousa, the modern symbolist, and Mário de Andrade, a contemporary poet who uses Brazilian folklore and popular music. But Andrade's interests are matched by a White contemporary, Jorge

44. Alberto Rangel, "Terra caída," in Pinto de Aguiar (ed.), *Contos regionais bra-sileiros* (Salvador-Bahia, 1957), 32.
45. Figueira, *Poesía brasileña contemporanea*, 10–11.

Mateus de Lima. This is clearly demonstrated in de Lima's "A Mão Enorme," with its reference to the slave ship and the destiny of the slaves. He writes with authority.

> . . . Acima dela
> que mão é essa maior que o mar?
> Mão de pilôto
> Mão de quem é?
> A nau mergulha
> o mar é escuro,
> o tempo passa . . .[46]

> Above this ship
> what hand is that more huge even than the sea?
> Hand of the pilot?
> Whose hand?
> The caravel plunges,
> the sea stands dark,
> time moves.

This passage is no less moving or accurate than one by the Mulatto poet, Mário de Andrade, who breaks every rule in the relationship we have sought to establish in this dirge to a dead boy: "Oh, depart, for I no longer know you!"[47] The African need to preserve the dead is certainly not present here; instead, Andrade's attitude towards his environment (the new object) is one that emphasizes utilization, destruction, and ultimate replacement. African Old World replenishment is not there.

How then can Afro-New World man change his world and free it so that out of a new type of liberation he may be able to speak? It calls for a different approach to literature. For instance, in Machado de Assis' novel *Braz Cubas* (translated as *Epitaph of a Small-Time Winner*) the chief character reminisces on his life, summarizing it as a "series of negatives."[48] He ought to have affirmed the truth of his ethnicity, for the legislation of Alfonso Arinos' law had made racial practices illegal. Various Black organizations, such as the Centro Civico de Palmares (in 1927), the Frente Negra Brasileira (in 1931),

---

46. Bishop and Brasil (eds.), *Anthology of Twentieth Century Brazilian Poetry*, 18–19.
47. *Ibid.*, 22–23.
48. Machado de Assis, *Epitaph of a Small-Time Winner*, 72.

which became a political party in 1936, and numerous others, were formed to push for civil rights. *Clarim de alvorada* (beginning in January, 1924) and *A Voz de raca* were politically oriented media organized around a racial theme.[49] The full expression of the racial dilemma varies, from Luis Gama's realistic cry that belittles his slave self as "negro o bode" (Black or goat) to the folk verse we have examined.[50]

III

Today, in Haiti, there has been a revival of folk forms. Creole was always the language of the people and the communication between rich and poor. Now the formerly solid stratification is apparently being slowly shaken as Creole is given more and more cultural authority.

In a small way, François Duvalier's death contributed to this liberation. On the literary level, the revival of Creole is seen in Frank Etienne's play *Pèlin-Têt*, which, despite government opposition, is still being performed in theaters. Due to a similar breakdown of the old order in places like Jamaica, reggae music shows not only the expulsion of the colonial, but also the destruction of all "Babylon." In Haiti, the mood is not as explosive as in Jamaica, but it is there, and the sentiments of the new writers would be similar to this Jamaican reggae:

> Eh Mister Wicked Man how long will you reign
> Robbing of the poor
> Of what is his for sure.
> I Rasta tell you
> It's all in Jah-Jah's plan.

According to Ras Michael, who wrote it, this is not just a song but a statement of fact that goes along with the *ankh* (the key of life), the red, green, and gold "colors of civilization," and the assertion of the "dread" as a political force in Jamaica.

Jamaican reggae is sharp, pugilistic music punctuated with a kind of gunshot rhythm. In recent years it has spread throughout the

49. Fernandes, *The Negro in Brazilian Society, passim.*
50. Ildefonso Pereda Valdés, *Antología de la poesía negra americana* (Montevideo, 1953), has a good selection of early Black writers.

Caribbean to America and England. The down home proverbs, biblical interpretations, and fierce godliness might seem to be foreign to the young. But it is to the rhythms of Bunny Wailer, Rita Marley, Peter Tosh, and the inimitable Bob Marley and Ras Michael that the followers pay homage. The tribute is not to the music alone, for who could miss the clear references to the relationship between evil and good and the obvious path of righteousness? If you believe, you can accept that the Jews were originally from Ethiopia, that Abraham and Jacob were born in Africa, and that Christ and the late emperor, Haile Selassie, are manifestations of God. Beware of the "screwface" (the capitalist) and the unrighteous. As Bob Marley said in an interview, "Me just want Black consciousness to unite all Black people."[51] A man must be strong, not cut off his "locks," and always abstain from pork. Marijuana is a liberating influence.

Whatever confusions may appear, it is evident that the sound and words of Jamaican reggae have altered the life of the English-speaking Caribbean. The extent of this alteration is still unknown, but this new sound has touched, *more than any other single art medium*, the consciousness of the people of this region. In other words, they have been able to see, feel, and hear their own inner needs expressed in art. This fundamental tie binds the mini-revolt in Haiti to the larger revolts of Cuba, Guyana, and Jamaica.

The pre-Négritude movement in Haiti brought the contributors of *Les griots*, *La revue indigène*, and *Optique* to the public eye. These writers were the Marcelin brothers, Philippe Thoby and Pierre; Jean Brièrre, Roussan Camille, René Belance, and, of course, Jacques Roumain. They were a late reaction to Price-Mars and the true Négritude movement, but perhaps the contemporary literature in Haiti is heralding a reaction such as was seen with reggae. It is a response that has not yet exploded in all its power, but this new literature could not have existed without the older writers.

The American occupation of Haiti, according to Louis Morpeau, could be seen in this way.

L'occupation apporte un bienfait—de provoquer une reviviscence de l'idée de Patrie, de nous forcer à opérer un reclassement de nos valeurs

51. Bob Marley. Reprinted from an interview in the New York *Amsterdam News* in program literature to accompany Bob Marley on tour in 1978.

morales, intellectuelles, sociales, de nous forcer à comprendre combien et comment nous avions péché envers le pays et envers la race, et combien nos hérédités gallo-noires, nos affinités afro-latines, notre culture française se trouvaient à l'opposé du frustre pragmatisme, du rude néo-saxonnisme nord-américain, dédaigneux des nuances, ignorants de la finesse et persuadés que toute civilisation est d'abord matérielle.[52]

The occupation brings a benefit—to encourage a renewal of national pride and bring about a reclassification of moral, intellectual, and social values. It forces us to understand how we had sinned against the country and against our race; and how our Black-Gallic, Afro-Latin, and French cultures were at odds with the crude pragmatism of the unrefined neo-Saxonism of North America, unaware of shades, devoid of all polish, and convinced that all civilization is above all material.

The critic Naomi Garret as well as the writers Oswald Durand, Jacques Roumain, Jean Brièrre, and René Depestre concur.

Durand tells his readers something of his cultural predicament: "And my mother was white, as white as Lisa." But Lisa scorns him and his world, and he has to resign himself to the rejection. In another poem, in *Rires et pleurs* (1869), a mother sees death as the only way out of grinding poverty. The note there is anticipatory.[53] Durand is very good, yet atrociously bad in some ways. He commits all the sins of the romantics but manages to remain a poet with a distinctly Haitian sensibility. With his sonnets, odes, and elegies he shows that it is possible to write about the Haitian landscape in French; he Creolizes it.

Jacques Roumain was cofounder of the *Revue Indigène* with Jean Price-Mars, and Naomi Garret feels that he was the leader of these younger poets. "Bois d'ébène" is a long piece that shows his disgust for exploitation of Blacks, whether "strangled by iron collars" or dying at the hands of the "sower of death" (the slave master). The poetry of protest had begun to make itself heard; the year was 1928.

Roumain's *Gouverneurs de la rosée* (1944) was translated into English as *Masters of the Dew*. In it he moved even closer to the culture of his own people. The men hoed the fields to the tune of a Creole song, and Creole was paramount in the voodoo ceremony that was described. Roumain is a true grandsire of the modern Haitians who

52. Quoted by Garret, *Renaissance of Haitian Poetry*, 61.
53. Oswald Durand, *Rires et pleurs* (2 vols.; Corbeil, 1896).

use the language as a liberating tool. Both Jean Brièrre and René Dépestre had sought a different type of liberation. This was not possible under the Duvalier regime, with the result that Brièrre went to
Senegal, and Dépestre to Paris and later Cuba, where he now lives.
Brièrre (like Roumain) had been imprisoned. His poetry is a response
to his condition as man, and it is not surprising that he admired this
very quality in Price-Mars and writes, "Vous avez orienté les con-
sciences haïtiennes vers la découverte de leur essence ethnique"
(You have oriented Haitian thinking towards the discovery of its
ethnic essence).[54] His first volume appeared in 1934 and showed few
of the later concerns of *La source* (1956), which exhibits a total preoccupation with Haitian life and culture.

Depestre is more explosive than Brièrre, and he is similar to Césaire in manner. A classic poem, *Minerai noir* (1956), demonstrates
the great concern with the suffering of Blacks. He uses a historical
approach to show Indian labor and the later introduction of Black
slaves. His lyrical ability saves the poems from being mere tracts
against racism.

> Dans tous les lieux du monde
> on les reconnaît
> au lait qui coule de leurs rires
>
> On les reconnaît
> à leur coeur rompu
> à leurs muscles sans repos . . .
>
> Dans tous les lieux du monde
> Nègres de triste saison.[55]
>
> Everywhere in the world
> they are recognized
> by the milk which flows from their laughter
>
> They are recognized
> by their broken heart
> by their tired muscles. . .
>
> Everywhere in the world
> the sad state of Blacks.

Obviously, the poem lacks the subtlety of Césaire, but it does point

54. Jean Brièrre, *La source* (Buenos Aires, 1956), 8.
55. René Depestre, *Minerai noir* (Paris, 1956).

to the issues that troubled the poets of the era between the 1930s and the 1950s.

Before the contemporary interest arose in exploring folk forms in depth and in using Creole, poets like Marie-Ange Jolicoeur depended on relating individual experience, a blanket acceptance of Christianity, and a limited amount of social protest. To some extent poets like Jean Dieudonné Garçon took refuge in images, but his Creole language is at times blunt and outspoken.

> Nèg rinmin san
> Nèg rinmin cassé-brisé
> Pi bonnè çe grand matin
> jou fèye boi tombé nan d'leau
> Ce pa jou li pourri
> Si çe pou ouè na ouè
> Nèg conn goût bouche li.[56]

> The Black man loves blood
> The Black man likes to destroy
> The earlier the better
> The day when the leaf falls into the water
> Is not the day when it dies
> We'll see what we'll see
> The Black man knows the taste of his own mouth.

Observe the way in which proverbs are neatly blended into the Creole syntax. The obvious is stated; the day is coming when the apparently dead Black peasant will rise up and do something about his condition. Note how well folk belief may be similarly incorporated by Dépestre.

> Je suis Alegba-Papa
> Le dieu de vos portes
> Ce soir c'est moi
> Le maître de vos lagons
> Et de vos carrefours de blancs . . .[57]

> I am Alegba-Papa
> The god of your doors
> Tonight I am

---

56. Jean Dieudonné Garçon, *Poemes pour trois continents* (Paris, 1972), 62.
57. René Dépestre, *A Rainbow for the Christian West*, trans. Joan Dayan (Amherst, 1977), 122, 123.

> The master of your small paths
> And of your white man's crossroads . . .

The search for Africa has prevented writers from dealing with the immediate problems of Haiti. As we have noted, the African presence is very real and cannot be ignored. But the tragedy of the present cannot be obscured, and it is to this that many writers are now turning, even more vocally than before. Josaphat Large's collection of poems *Nerfs du vent* (1975) is one of the best examples encountered.

Large's images create an international discordance. The protagonist cannot be certain of the past.

> moi
> assis sur tes cheveux en confectionneur de
>   boules de nerfs
> le vent rompu dans nos poches dans nos mains
>   et dans nos coeurs[58]
>
> me
> seated on your hair to make balls of nerves
> the wind broken in our pockets, our hands and hearts

The protagonist says, "I am my own victim," and the images of the fetish woman and chaos, demonstrated in the lines above, show that indeed, at this stage, there can be no compromise with the present. Saint-John Perse's early poetry may be read in this same manner.

Other young poets testify to this. Soucougnan, in *La troisième île*, speaks of "les mots tombent comme des pierres" (words falling like stones), and how these very stones are going to be used to rebuild the past. The new exercise in reassembly is interesting; one moves back from the present. The past cannot be taken for granted, for "je viens chercher ma vie" (I am looking for my own life).[59] The poem is "Lonesome Road," and it reminds us of Sterling Brown and Langston Hughes. However, it is not a poem of celebration, but one of quest; it does not glorify the past, but seeks assurances in the present. Elie Stephenson's "A ma mère" concludes that the green bamboo, corn, and bananas will grow again, once it is realized that, "l'ennemi est sur nos rives" (the enemy is on our shore).[60]

58. Josaphat Large, *Nerfs du vent* (Paris, 1975), 25.
59. Soucougnan [pseud.], *La troisième île* (Paris, 1973), 25.
60. Elie Stephenson, *Une flèche pour le pays à l'encan* (Paris, 1975), 12.

These new writers publish their works in Paris. Those who continue to publish in Haiti (with the exception of Frank Etienne) steer clear of such obvious charges against the government. What is amazing is just how versatile these new poets are. In *Négociations*, Jean Claude Charles uses a surrealistic scene to contrast two cannibals—technological and traditional man. The blame is laid squarely on Haiti, which has brought about the destruction; the *loas* are massacred and Baron Samedi has even lost his power over death. The reason, stated simply and yet profoundly, is as follows.

> Je suis né dans un pays où le soleil joue à
>   cache-cache avec le
> pain et l'eau courante[61]
>
> I was born in a country where the sun plays hide
> and seek with bread and running water.

References to a napalm cigarette and the peasant who should have his chicken but slaughters it with a tommy gun show the direction of these poets and their definite striving for a new sense of order. Africa is no longer a blanket that covers the social inequalities; the true patriotism becomes no patriotism at all. As early as 1969, Joseph Polius wrote that Haiti was like the other side of misery: "Comme deux aiguilles bien sûr / Qui depuis trois siècles marquent la même heure" (Like two clock hands / which for three centuries show the same time).[62] It is, not unlike Martinique, "a broken crumb waiting for its birth." There is no reversal here, as with Césaire, and no piling up of negatives that point to an affirmative. The statement is a grim one, and the poet does not retract it.

Rodolphe Moïse sees George Jackson as a Black hero of the Haitian revolution. Again, a departure should be noted here. Earlier references to Black Americans in Haitian poetry nearly always saw them as pawns and victims in American society. Moïse turns all our understanding inside out. "Munich 72" shows that the games are leading to serious issues, to the end of the games; in "Au pays," the world is like a whorehouse with "les proxénètes, la corruption et le dollar" (pimps, corruption, the dollar).[63] Haiti is like Greece at that time;

---

61. Jean Claude Charles, *Négociations* (Paris, 1972), 37.
62. Joseph Polius, *Bonheur de poche* (Paris, 1968), 13.
63. Rodolphe Moïse, *Aux armes guerilleros* (Paris, 1975), 26.

both share a common tyrant and the desire of people to be free.

The new Haitian writing is the beginning of a breakdown of an artificial social order. The apologists do not seem relevant anymore. Facts are reinterpreted and translated, and the poets do not seem to seek any self-sufficient status. Almost unintentionally, they have reverted to the ancestral role of traditional artist and town crier. It is ironical that they accomplish their best when they are least conscious of it. The new writers see Roumain, Brièrre, and Depestre as godfathers, not ancestors; but it is extremely debatable whether they could have written as well had they not been liberated by these writers. The earlier poets had freed them from any slavish imitation of empire and, in this way, made them realize how an entire alien civilization had been transported lock, stock, and barrel to Haiti, how the agents of this new order and its victims became intertwined in a curious paradoxical relationship, and how the dismantling of the French cultural empire called for a secondary synthesis.

IV

Two of the most important poets of the contemporary English-speaking Caribbean are Derek Walcott and Edward Brathwaite, both born in 1930. They write in English and are products of the University of the West Indies. Both have lived in Jamaica and England for extensive periods. However, they are different in important ways: on the surface the work of Derek Walcott, born in Saint Lucia, shows some of the influences of his having grown up there, such as its patois, its geographical place names, and the entire autobiographical elements of a childhood there. On the other hand, since Brathwaite did not publish his first volume until he was thirty-seven, his boyhood experience in the Caribbean has been underscored by his sojourn in Ghana. Both experiences have given a different meaning to his contemporary life. Brathwaite seems more at home with a style that he has himself invented; Walcott, still struggling for a style, once remarked a trifle sardonically that "as long as I write in the West Indies, I will always seem to be a visible imitator."[64] One feels that Walcott's voice is the more interesting of the two, although Brath-

64. Derek Walcott, "Leaving School," *London Magazine,* V (September, 1965), 4–14.

waite is more strident. Brathwaite handles dialect with ease, whereas Walcott is extremely cautious in his use of Caribbean English.

If there is a resolution in their poetry, then Walcott's is a tentative one, poised almost on a precarious negative: "I began with no memory / I began with no future."[65] This Brathwaite would not assent to, or if he seems to, then it is balanced on the ranting side of a positive.

> To hell
> with Af-
> Rica
> To hell
> with Eu-
> rope too,
> just call my blue
> black bloody spade
> a spade.[66]

One statement comes quite early in Brathwaite's career as a poet, and the other relatively recently in Walcott's. But we should not oversimplify the issue by asserting that Brathwaite has seemingly found answers and Walcott has not. Both poets attempt to show a constant inward search for answers, and the questions they ask are these: Who is Caribbean man? What is his origin, his language, and his religion? Who are his heroes?

These poets first attempt to look at their origin. If we are only concerned with the factual nature of poetry, then Brathwaite the historian has an obvious head start. Walcott has pointed out that "the African revival is escape to another dignity, but one understands the glamour of its simplifications." The poet has, he continues, to go about "his father's business. . . . Both fathers."[67] This Walcott does in his poetry, for he cannot opt for any one ancestor; the choice would seem too easy for him. Tradition, as Wilson Harris the poet-novelist says, is not dogma, and the writer does not have to be committed to causes.[68]

---

65. Derek Walcott, "Names," in *Sea Grapes* (London, 1976), 40.
66. Edward Brathwaite, "Prelude," in *Rights of Passage* (London, 1967), 27.
67. Derek Walcott, "What the Twilight Says," introduction to *Dream on Monkey Mountain and Other Plays* (New York, 1973), 9.
68. Wilson Harris, *Tradition and the Writer in West Indian Society* (London, 1967), 31.

In the search for origin, Walcott's world is hazy and unsure, but his poetry derives its greatest interest from this lack of certainty. On the other hand, Brathwaite's world is secure, even with its uncertainties, as in *Islands*.

> The Word becomes
> again a god and walks among us
> look, here are his rags,
> here is his crutch and his satchel
> of dreams, here is his love and his
> rude implements
> on this ground
> on this broken ground.[69]

Not until the last line do we hear *broken*; we seem fairly sure that the "nommo" (word, or poetry), by transforming itself, will survive, but Brathwaite implies that it has to be religiously motivated in the New World. The figure described is probably that of Babaluayé, the Yoruba god of illness.

Both Walcott and Brathwaite are occupied with the nature of the word. Brathwaite puts it this way, again in *Islands*:

> I
> must be given words to shape my name . . .
> I
> must be given words to refashion futures . . .[70]

The section concludes with the positive assurances of a Haitian mass, with its suggestion of syncretism. It blends Catholicism and African religion, and seems to present the world of the future. But always present is the trickster Papa Legba, like Eshu, a god of the crossroads.

Here again we thread through large cycles of the poem with the reassurances of the repetitive *I* and end with the Creole equivalent of "broken ground." Walcott rather testily rejects this, for "no one whose one God is advertised as dead can believe in innumerable gods of another life."[71]

If the writer's duty is to "first break out of the existing mold of frozen conventional preconceptions," then he must decide on any

69. Edward Brathwaite, *Islands* (London, 1969), 109.
70. *Ibid.*, 66–67.
71. Walcott, "What the Twilight Says," 8.

one of a number of ways to do this.[72] Walcott chooses first to recognize it, then to manufacture his poetry out of the need for breaking out. He never resolves his issues; they are constantly presented. The early poems, which dealt with death, growing up, looking toward the future, friends, landscape, and local events, as well as the later ones, which explore larger paradoxical issues such as those that emerge in his extended metaphors, show Walcott always as an inquirer. To resolve would end the drama of intellectual and sensual interaction; to state a preference would be to dodge the debate altogether.

Walcott utilizes all kinds of sources to substantiate his argument; Brathwaite has seemingly found his answer in the exercise of Afro-New World religions and in Akan songs, especially dirges. Since he would have had to read the latter in English, and since J. H. Kwabena Nketia has been the sole translator of these, some of Nketia's remarks, such as the following, are relevant to an understanding of Brathwaite's poetry. "In dealing with the Akan dirge then, we are dealing in the main with traditional expression stored up in the minds of individuals and re-created by them in appropriate contexts, traditional expressions cast in forms which individuals learnt to handle because society expects them to use them in the situation of the funeral."[73] The main point is this: Akan oral verse (like all African verse) is group oriented. The singer is a group spokesman who is allowed little room to maneuver and develop his own individuality. This brings us to the second major difference between the work of Brathwaite and Walcott. Brathwaite is not, and cannot be, an individual; his art is on behalf of a group, and he views himself as the spokesman for this group. Walcott, on the other hand, admits to ignorance about any such group. If such a group did exist, it did not offer security: "My generation had looked at life with black skins and blue eyes."[74]

Secure in the confines of his group, Brathwaite is able to criticize,

72. Joyce Sparer, "The Art of Wilson Harris," in John La Rose (ed.), *New Beacon Reviews* (London, 1968), 22–30.

73. J. H. Kwabena Nketia, *Funeral Dirges of the Akan People* (Achimota, 1955), 3.

74. Walcott, "What the Twilight Says," 9.

mock, condemn, and vilify. He has to look around in his search for a group, for he well knows that the ancient formations have lost their unit status. Akan, Yoruba, and Hausa had been altered in the crucible of history. They had undergone primary synthesis during the slave passage, when the old groups of Africa broke down, and a man could then proclaim, as one of Alex Haley's characters does in *Roots*: "We are now one big village." Therefore, Brathwaite's poem includes the entire Caribbean as well as the Black world.

> Demerara bleeds
> Anguilla bleeds
> Kingston breeds felonies[75]

In "The Journeys" in *Rights of Passage*, twenty-three place names throughout the world appear in the space of two pages, and Brathwaite adds the following, speaking for his group of Afro-New World persons.

> Never seen
> a man
> travel more
> seen more
> lands
> than this poor
> path-
> less harbour
> less spade[76]

This kind of journeying is necessary to establish, for Brathwaite, the new group concept. The old tranquility had been shattered with Columbus' coming.

> Now he was sure
> he heard soft voices mocking in the leaves
> what did this journey mean, this
> new world mean: dis-
> covery? Or a return to terrors
> he had sailed from, known before?
>
> I watched him pause.

75. Brathwaite, "Trade-Winds," in *Islands*, 9.
76. Brathwaite, "The Journeys," in *Rights of Passage*, 39.

> Then he went splashing silence.
> Crabs snapped their claws
> and scattered as he walked towards our shore.[77]

The proprietorial *our* confirms the reader's belief in Brathwaite's view of the poet as group seer. Walcott sees Columbus' coming quite differently. Walcott's Columbus is represented in his play *Drums and Colors*, and in his poetry Crusoe and Columbus are one. Crusoe-Columbus is a master craftsman and, as such, a poet.

> . . . even the bare necessities
> of style are turned to use,
> like those plain tools he salvages
> from shipwreck, having a prose
> as odorous as raw wood to the daze,
> but of such timbers
> came our first book, our profane Genesis
> whose Adam speaks that prose
> which, blessing some sea-rock startles itself
> with poetry's surprise . . .[78]

In Walcott's poetry, Adam-Columbus-Crusoe do not disrupt the world. They bring speech, literature, and books. They are not disturbers of the pastoral peace, but liberators. Walcott sees this symbol as the first challenge to the writers of the New World, for all become altered as a result of the new presence. As a result the writer undergoes a metamorphosis

> into good Fridays who recite His praise
> parroting our master's
> Style and voice, we make his language ours.[79]

The master is primordial; because of him a major theme persists in Walcott—the individual "wrenched by two styles."[80]

The artist secure in the world of the group has no such problems. This is surely Kenneth Ramchand's misunderstanding when he says that "In *Rights* the poet Brathwaite's relationship to his material and to his readers is personal; by the time he comes to *Islands*, the

77. *Ibid.*, 52.
78. Derek Walcott, "Crusoe's Journal," in *In a Green Night: Poems, 1948–1960* (London, 1962), 51.
79. *Ibid.*
80. Walcott, "Codicil," in *In a Green Night*, 61.

poet has become authoritative."[81] The tone (personal or authoritative), the pronouns *I* or *he* can never have any subjective significance in the oral poetry of Brathwaite. And it is equally ridiculous to argue, as Edward Baugh does, that "Brathwaite has nothing new or especially illuminating to say about the condition of the Negro in the West."[82] His sociological works do this; his vocation as a poet is to develop the plain style that Walcott speaks of but never quite achieves.

It is to be hoped that one is not caught up in the "myth" to which Baugh alludes in another article. "The myth persists. It is used, for instance, to play off Brathwaite against Walcott, the former being supposedly the vigorous, optimistic and truly West Indian one, the latter the pessimistic, too-introspective, too 'Eurocentric' one."[83] There may be some obvious truths in this so-called myth, but it contains no conclusions regarding who is the better craftsman. Both strive in their own way for the perfection of an art that both visualize as life itself.

Michael Gilkes writes, "The integrity of the personality is almost always the subject, and its establishment and preservation most frequently the main theme."[84] He adds that "Walcott therefore regards his ambivalent heritage as a poetic strength."[85] For Denis Williams, the lack of "the assurance of the undwelling racial ancestor" is the reason Walcott can state, "Mongrel as I am, something prickles in me when I see the word Ashanti as with the word Warwickshire, both separately intimating my grandfather's roots, birth, both baptising this neither proud nor ashamed bastard, this hybrid, this West Indian." Walcott further states that "pastoralists of the African revival should know that what is needed is not new names for old things, or old names for old things."[86] Therefore, Brathwaite has been set a new task; he has to be not only the expert joiner, the re-

81. Kenneth Ramchand, *An Introduction to the Study of West Indian Literature* (Kingston, 1976), 135.

82. Edward Baugh, review in *Bim*, XII (July–December, 1967), 20.

83. Edward Baugh, *A Brief Account of West Indian Poetry* (Kingston, 1977), 17.

84. Michael Gilkes, *Racial Identity and Individual Consciousness in the Caribbean Novel* (Georgetown, 1975), 43.

85. *Ibid.*

86. Denis Williams, *Image and Idea in the Arts of Guyana* (Georgetown, 1969), 10; Walcott, "What the Twilight Says," 10.

fashioner, but also the inventor of a mythical past. Despite what Walcott says, such a task is similar yet at the same time very unlike the craft of the African oral spokesman. For instance, Wole Soyinka, the African Yoruba poet and playwright, confidently asserts that "history is not the history of primal becoming but of racial origin which is historically dated."[87] This is a statement that he can make because he is secure in group enclaves. Walcott pointed out the impossibility of producing Soyinka's play *The Road*, because Ogun "was an exotic for us, not a force" and "the naming of the god estranged him."[88] For Brathwaite this has to be a problem, but he has chosen to do, not what Walcott implies—follow a beaten track—but instead to carve out new territory.

We are back with the Word. The Word can be named in the New World, but according to Walcott it has lost its energy to compel. But Brathwaite's repetitious puns, linguistic twists, and evocations of African tag words do suggest power. In addition, there is a real quest for an answer beyond these superficialities.

> I travelled to a distant town
> I could not find my mother
> I could not find my father
> I could not hear the drum
>
> Whose ancestor am I?[89]

Not surprisingly, Walcott is also concerned with the question of origin:

> We left
> somewhere a life we never found
> customs and gods that are not born again
> some crib, some grill of light
> clanged shut on us in bondage, and withheld
> us from that world below us and beyond
> and in its swaddling cerements we're still bound.[90]

The paradox of terms such as *life, grill of light,* and *swaddling* leaves us with some suggestion that there exists the possibility of

---

87. Wole Soyinka, *Myth, Literature and the African World* (Cambridge, England, 1976), 9.
88. Walcott, "What the Twilight Says," 8.
89. Brathwaite, "Trade-Winds," 9.
90. Derek Walcott, "Laventille," in *Castaway* (London, 1969), 35.

the birth of a new culture (not a resurrected one), which will embrace the static old ones of the Caribbean. It seems that Brathwaite is part of the process of the invention of this new culture (the second synthesis), whereas Walcott is still very wary of the merging. For Walcott it seems that poetry will remain a fashionable literary ailment, voluntarily contracted.

V

If the writers whom we have examined are cognizant of their peculiar time in history, and if they even partly understand the issues at stake, then they become group spokesmen for their time. What an Afro-Cuban, Afro-Brazilian, Afro-Caribbean, or Afro-American writer utters at any given time is important to this study, in relationship to the developing patterns of that time. Therefore, to seek modern radical thought in Phyllis Wheatley (eighteenth-century America), Juan Latino (sixteenth-century Spain), Plácido (nineteenth-century Cuba), or Luis da Gama (nineteenth-century Brazil) would be tantamount to requiring them to be modern men. If we have shown that some of these writers were aware of the burdens of history and related them, then surely their task as group men would have been fulfilled. The real relationship they have in common with each other and more recent writers is that they contributed to an understanding of involvement in a primary synthesis and to an awareness of how close they are to an absorption within a secondary synthesis.

This will have to remain a question of hypothetical nature, though worthy of continued investigation. Primary synthesis, as we have seen, involves an understanding of self, of the irony of "tribe" that has been part of New World culture for both Blacks and Whites. It means an acceptance of a new nation and almost the creation of a new state of mind; and coming to terms with this, New World Man is able to deal realistically with the fundamental problem of his relationship to his neighbor, who has undergone a similar experience. The beginning of the secondary synthesis is when these alien people regard themselves in a new light, as being part of a new world. But, and here the irony of history is clearest, there is a constant struggle for a backward glance to a preprimary synthesis when the world was different. This accounts for three distinct aspects to our literature: a

polarity that arises out of tension, a conformity (which is part an artificial acquiescence), and the interrogative of the pendulum that swings between the polarity and conformity. The latter is basically at work in the poetry of Walcott and Brathwaite. We turn to their work to complete our examination of the various degrees of synthesism.

8 Towards Synthesis: An Opinion

I hesitate to call this chapter a conclusion because there is little of which one can be certain or about which specific indications are shown. Time has obscured the evidence; the important witnesses are either dead or too old to testify. We inhabit lands with few ruins, and all that can be truly asserted must be painstakingly formed from present conception.

The present demonstrates that there have obviously been two syntheses, the second of which is still taking place. The first, which I have termed the primary synthesis, is the reorganization of the Old World groups from Africa and Europe. The effect of this was two-fold, having repercussions on both peoples. The Hausa, Ibo, Yoruba, or Ashanti who came to the New World was, by the very nature of his passage, no longer Hausa, Ibo, Yoruba, or Ashanti. He was nigger, negro, Negro, Colored, Quashie, African, Black.

Similarly, for the Whites the differences in language, norms, and cultural appurtenances were just as real; the Spaniard, Englishman, Dutchman, Portuguese, and Frenchman were of alien "tribal" backgrounds. They had fought wars over their kings and religion and had for centuries sought to usurp each other's power. Only in the New World did Black and White undergo the rich and unique experience involved in the process of primary synthesis. The result was the formation of large categories of persons no longer constrained by petty boundaries and the caprice of language. The New World has become for them an agent of release, allowing them to participate more fully in the role of humans with a destiny toward a mutual goal.

Herein, however, lies an enormous obstacle to the complete liber-

ation of the human spirit. The time is past when humans could perceive themselves as belonging to the same family because of a common environment and common destiny. Even after the liberation from the petty constraints of the serfdom, the mind was still tethered. The mind of the White European, like the mind of the Black African Negro, was unable to make the final leap that New World living entailed. It was a precarious jump into a hitherto unknown forging of interests that spanned continents. Once the extensions of the national boundaries had become a reality, the mind boggled at the idea of a union of continents. The New World became a trap, a vast echo chamber wherein people not only heard about their own past, but also the discordant note of what they could barely tolerate and the cacophony of what they could never understand.

The secondary synthesis during which Black meets White is still occurring. One should wonder as to why this is taking so long. The visible presence of racism in the Ku Klux Klan, the Bakke decision, the last vestiges of private clubs and schools, and police brutality against the minority are open manifestations of an incomplete union. But one can take consolation in the fact that it is only here in the New World that the human being has been given such an enormous challenge—one that dwarfs the problems of ancient Europe and Africa.

The problem becomes a challenge for living, since the uniqueness of our situation makes us both an example and a scapegoat for the whole world. No one can prophesy whether a secondary synthesis will take place—one in which attributes from all groups will become intrinsic parts of a large supergroup. Should the synthesis take place in that magnificent sense, no one would deny that it would be a fulfilling experience for conqueror and conquered—White and Black, rich and poor. It would represent a shared experience out of the common bounty of humanity and a necessary activity in the business of living in the New World.

I

The various African and European retentions may be observed on three levels. We have concerned ourselves only with African retentions because they seem to be significant links for all New World

persons. But this does not deny the presence of European norms, and indeed such norms represent a sine qua non of the secondary synthetic process.

The various African retentions are both material and nonmaterial in nature. In order to examine them more closely it is convenient to divide them into physical, intellectual, and emotional manifestations. On the physical level we can observe the preservation of what I shall term ancestral function. Since it was important to the Africans that the ancient gods continue to exist and be summoned with appropriate ceremony, it is not difficult to see life itself as that ceremony, and birth as a summoning. The physical retentions become the material reminders of the presence of the gods. At the same time, the adaptability of the gods to survive, not as owners of the world, but as guests is an important transformation.

For instance, in *santería*, a tureen is employed for the mud bowls that would normally contain the essence of the gods. Not everything physical is elastic or levels itself in adaptation. Often physical survivals, as in the case of place names, survive intact because of the refusal (not the inability) of the incarnate deity to alter. I do not refer here to adaptations of African culture or to reaffirmations of the presence of Africa as seen in translations of place names in European tongues. This is the difference between the adapting of a semisounding African name and the wholesale lifting of an African place name.

An example of transplantation is a neo-African place name like *Oyatunji*, a village founded by Black Americans in South Carolina. An adaptation of an African word with a mixture of Dutch is the word *Betervawagtin*, a place on the east coast of Guyana. *Cuffy Gully* in Jamaica derives from an authentic African slave name modified in the New World. All of these represent other extensions of the physical presence of Africa in the New World.

The preparation and naming of food and the manner in which it is eaten also shows the persistence of an African presence. In some areas of the Caribbean pounded food is still called *fu-fu*, is still eaten with the fingers, and is served communally from a large dish. There are certain rites associated with eating and drinking, such as the placation of the ancestors before drinking by giving them an offering; this is usually done by pouring a libation on the floor and may

be observed in Haiti, Cuba, and Jamaica. This book has attempted to show not only the presence but the function of the dead ancestor who, unacknowledged or not, continues to exist in day-to-day activities. So far, examples have been selected from creative literature, but other disciplines are equally pertinent to this investigation.

When Haitian women carry fruits to market on their heads, and when farther south we find a replica of this among Trinidad women—in both cases the folk—we can readily assert that this non-European characteristic represents the physical presence of the African ancestor. In Europe the head was the place where the mind was, and it seemed important to keep the head "free." Africans, however, regarded the cranium as comfortable for carrying objects and enabling movement of hands; in West Africa we can observe this very activity as well as other cultural parallels, such as the mother positioning her baby on her back, which would again keep the hands free. Thus we see a survival, however unimportant, persisting to this day among the Gullah people in the United States.

It was important to free the hands for more practical purposes such as defense, greetings, and work. This was carried over to the New World not only as a pragmatic way of dealing with a similar environment but, in a Jungian sense, as a remembrance of the race. For a people who came without passport or baggage, the one visible sign of the acknowledgment of humanity in an alien latitude was surely the group memory.

Such a muted recollection of a group past meant, above all, that people would continue to live in organizations with which they were familiar. A new kind of social patterning took place. Slavery removed the landscape and kinship ties and altered the gods, but the social organizations traveled in a kind of memory bank. When they were changed as a result of the adaptability of African culture, new African-type gods were made in man's image. In the New World the physical nature of the landscape combined with the work and living conditions of slaves caused some adaptability, change, and even complete eradication of mores.

Adaptability is perceived in the persistence of the extended family. Slavery forced the mother to exist apart from the father and emphasized the strong matriarchal ties with the old country. In addi-

tion, slavery underscored a new communal living style unrelated to the nuclear family structure of the master; this acted as a catalyst for continuity. Because the style of the master (even when it was "proper" and did not involve too many excursions into the slave cabins) could not be copied, slaves fell back on what had been preserved in the mind of the group. The propensity for the matriarchal concept and the extended family continues today, and surely this is not just for "economic" reasons. It is a large legacy from the African homeland, converted into a practical tool for immediate use.

The handling of money changed very little. The Haitian "coumbite," the Dominican Republic "sociedad," the Jamaican "susu," and the Eastern Caribbean "box" are good examples of how African economies survived in the New World. The logic, which seems disarmingly simple now, is that by using many "hands" (payments from others) one person could amass a large sum in a given time frame. It is only today in more sophisticated times that we inquire about interest and worry about the honesty of brokers. It is interesting to note that dishonest brokers who acquire several contributions in a given week may find themselves in trouble with new laws that have recognized this form of banking.

The economic ways of saving, family patterns, work habits in groups, adherence to a fairly conservative model of having a central leader, and an advisory council are manifestations of the indwelling African ancestor in these societies. Africa has prevailed, and the communal emphasis with its insistence on the group rather than the individual, whether it be in work or play, eating or dancing, singing or performing religious exercises, has remained paramount.

The physical level of African retentions are the most apparent. There is, however, the second type of survival—the intellectual— which may be demonstrated but is not always as easily proven as the first. Specifically, we refer here to the manner of exportation of a *Weltanschauung* and, more important, the manifestation of the *Weltanschauung* in the survival of the creative thought of cultural Africa. Its adaptation occurs in the new social clime, and in some cases, an "invention" hearkens back, however vaguely, to Africa.

Thus we find a preponderance of African folktales in the general cultural milieu. The creative accounts of the origin of man and the

world, the actions of the gods, and the etiological reasons why important events took place in the drama of human evolution were in large measure substituted for the ready-made answers that Christianity provided. In important instances Christianity was either partially altered, as in the case of *santería*, supplanted, as in the case of voodoo, or rejected outright, as with *brujería* and *obeah*. One might infer that *brujería* and *obeah* were retained because neither Christianity nor any syncretic blend provided the power to invoke the god and bid him carry out harm to another person. One should also note that the new religion often proved inadequate. There were insufficient symbols or a specific notation of properties associated with the god, and thus, syncretism (as in voodoo and *santería*) emphasized that with god substitution and attribute substitution the deity was not just being transplanted, but was taking on new and distinct characteristics.

Anancy, the spider god, exists in the New World, but he is only seldom a spider and never a god. Among the Jamaican folk, he is a cunning human who outwits all others, and in Bahamian folklore, although he is sometimes outwitted and laughed at, he is certainly not to be despised. In the New World then, the trickster was the embodiment of the Black man's ability to transcend obstacles, to come to terms with the new social environment, and to "get over." This was the reason for the change from his merely being acted upon to his being an actor. The New World trickster does not simply react to a given situation (hunger, dishonesty, lies, and challenges) as he does in Africa, but he frequently creates both the problem and the solution.

This is why the Signifying Monkey initiates the antagonism between Lion and Elephant, makes them fight, and laughs at Lion's defeat. In the African folktale, the fight would already have taken place, and his function would have been to react to it by using some ruse. The Signifying Monkey begins the ruse when he "signifies" to Lion that the Elephant had been less than charitable in his remarks about Lion's mother. This role is made even clearer in tales about High John when it is understood that his master is not described as being a wicked man. In most of the accounts, High John acts out some piece of antagonism directed against the master. The heroes in Black folktales, unlike African folktales, are intensely aware of color and

social stratification. The actions they initiate are a means of attempting to bring about social change.

When Africans came to the New World, they left their ethnic heroes behind. New names were made up around new situations. A single pattern persists in the hero tales: the hero's adventures are only valid if they renew the life of the New World group. No accounts survive that simply restate the virtues of an individual unless that individual detects, measures, records, and transmits the values of his people, and in so doing can initiate change. John Henry with his hammer, Stagolee the badman, and Shine, the lone survivor from the *Titanic* disaster, are examples of men who act on behalf of the group. Through them the group expresses itself, measures its feelings and its failings, and prepares prescriptions for its maladies.

The third level in which we perceive both the old and the new forms of survival is the emotional. By the emotional is meant the nonintellectual responses to the world. One hates to resurrect an old corpse, but the oversexed Black is indeed this. Far from being passionate lovers, Blacks seem by and large to be rather conventional in the European sense. Throughout the Black world for instance, oral sex is taboo. In parts of Africa, everything except the most formal aspects of mating is frowned upon. Calypsos in the Caribbean repeat the laughter with which any type of sexual deviation is treated, be it homosexuality, anal or oral sex, or even undue pleasure on the woman's part. This attitude is also found among Blacks in the United States; and although these are broad statements unsupported by the painstaking data of the sociologist, they are mentioned tentatively, because they show a link with Africa.

Dance and music seem to be more obvious examples, but a problem arises when one is asked to prove that. There is no way of showing that John Travolta wriggles any better than the Pointer Sisters. What does matter is that John Travolta and Elvis Presley learned to wriggle because they lived in a society where Blacks danced in a certain manner. I am not implying that the monopoly of "wriggling" belongs to the Black race. I am suggesting that certain rhythms (the *son*, the *guaguancó*, jazz, the calypso, reggae) have more in common with indigenous African music than with the European fox-trot. I am also suggesting that the manner in which Blacks respond to

music is part of a racial memory and that the preponderance of the drums in this music helps emphasize the remembrance. Furthermore, Whites in the New World have obviously benefited from this.

I am wary about venturing into fields such as laughter and tears, because I feel ill-equipped to deal with them, and I can merely indicate some observations that may (and perhaps should) be refuted by my critics. Laughter and tears in Africa are responses to specific emotional states. Perhaps we were all like this when the world was not so complex. A White characteristic is that a person may cry from joy and laugh because he is angry. He also smiles or laughs to greet people and, like Blacks, nods, says a greeting, or uses the hands; but the display of teeth as a greeting belongs, not to an African, but to a European culture. In large measure, Blacks have tended to preserve these folkways in the New World, especially in areas where there has been a minimum of European contact and penetration.

These elements point to one indisputable fact. Blacks have tended to preserve African mores when they were geographically removed from too much contact with Whites. The Black Caribs of Saint Vincent, the Djuka of Surinam, the Haitian *paysans*, the Gullah people, and Blacks of the Oriente Province in Cuba and of Bahia in Brazil were able to preserve aspects of their own language in varying degrees, because of their isolation and because the language could function. Since the expression of African life, be it artistic or mundane, tended to resolve itself around function, one readily sees how African emotion (if the creature exists) would tend to be more paramount in areas where cultures were enclosed, self-governing, and removed —in other words, where an African of the New World had been created and preserved in an almost fossil state.

When Birago Diop, the Senegalese poet, speaks of "the dead who are never truly dead," we see an idea that manifests itself in two important ways in the Black New World. People here, as in Africa, speak to the dead, address the dead at funerals, speak to the dead at their graves, and claim that the dead are physically present in dreams. Just as the African dirge seeks to show that close link between the present and the ever-living past, so do the wakes among the Gullah and Caribbean people. This link with past and present is established in songs that "speak" to the dead as if they were living.

II

I do not wish to show that Africa merely survives in the writing of the Black man, since this is a given, but I hope I have illustrated the extent to which, despite cultural erosion (a nonactive process) and cultural rejection (one for which the individual is responsible), Africa nevertheless positively persists. Countee Cullen, a product of the Harlem Renaissance, was bewildered at the apparent paradox of a "curious thing" in which God was said "To make a poet black / And bid him sing." For Cullen saw himself in Keatsian terms. But apart from his dismissal of the African past in "What Is Africa to Me?" he perceives that "Ten thousand years of jungle clues / Alone shaped feet like these." [1]

I don't think we need be sidetracked here by Arthur Davis' true assessment that Cullen "knew little or nothing about the real Africa." [2] We know this because Africa represented a savage place for him, where people were forever dancing naked to the rhythm of the tom-toms. The truth is that the poet, middle-class and Westernized, has sought out Africa. Why? The answer has to be found in preceding arguments. He was an unwilling inheritor of its culture, and for Cullen as well as for some of the writers discussed in this study, Africa was a convenient way of understanding the trauma of their society. "Exotic Africa served a distinct purpose. History to the Negro was not a national pageant of exploration, settlement, independence, western expansion, and wars to preserve freedom, but a story of bondage, physical freedom and Jim Crow." [3] We therefore return to the earlier assertion that Africa, a meaningless word, served a very functional purpose. Whether Cullen and others knew it, they had inherited an enormous archetype, and their art was the expression of this. Therefore, he associated Africa with the Black woman and with the acceptance of Christianity, especially in his poems "Pagan Prayer" and "Black Christ," much as Andrew Salkey has a character say in *A Quality of Violence* (1959): "Make me tell you something. I bigger

---

1. Countee Cullen, *Color* (New York, 1925), 39.
2. Arthur P. Davis, "The Alien and Exile Theme in Countee Cullen's Racial Poems," in *Phylon*, XVI (1953), 400.
3. Stephen A. Bronz, *Roots of Racial Consciousness: The 1920's: Three Harlem Renaissance Authors* (New York, 1964), 50–51.

than everybody here tonight! Bigger than any drought! I'm you' conqueror. And you know why? Because Africa is me."[4] These are no intense searches for origins, as Alex Haley makes in *Roots* (1976) and Edward Brathwaite in *The Arrivants* (1973). These are the gateway manifestations wherein, suddenly and inexplicably to the writer, one suspects, Africa becomes the panacea.

One might view this differently and see instead that the writers are seeking a lost mask. In Chinua Achebe's *Arrow of God*, the chief priest, Ezeulu, is quite specific when he says to one of his sons: "The world is like a mask dancing. If you want to see it well you do not stand in one place."[5] The wisdom of this has been inherited by writers in the New World. There have been occasions when one had to don the mask, thus making it an enforcing agent of African tradition.

The mask may be introduced by Black New World writers as a way of challenging the status quo. Manuel, in Jacques Roumain's novel *Masters of the Dew*, returns from Cuba and patches up the warring factions of his group. Beneatha, in *A Raisin in the Sun*, searches for the mask to help overcome the hostilities in her own family; she is interested in her African culture and actively cultivates the friendship of a rather stereotyped African. Both works show Manuel and Beneatha as insiders within a group that is slowly splitting apart. They have to act to rectify the situation, but their action is on behalf of their group. When Manuel finds water for his drought-striken people and is murdered, he is both liberator and martyr; and when Beneatha discovers a thorough understanding of communal living, she has done it for Walter, Mama, and Ruth.

Apparently, African acceptance can mean total rejection by the seeker. Du Bois' little-known *The World and Africa* (1947) dealt not only with the Black man in Africa but also a strong indictment of the White race. Hence another factor emerges: Africa may frequently become the means through which Garvey-like Blacks in the New World seek for apartness in order to define a unique sense of being. I am not sure of how much the little boy understood from Uncle Remus' narration, but Uncle Remus repeatedly attempts to establish just this kind of identity. He does this in the manner of a mask

4. Andrew Salkey, *A Quality of Violence* (London, 1959), 127.
5. Chinua Achebe, *Arrow of God* (London, 1964), 55.

wearer: "'Jamaica!' exclaimed the little boy. 'But if dat the way dey talk, I hope de lord spare me from ever gwine dar.'"[6] In this little aside he dons the mask of complete folly in order to state the realization that Uncle Remus understood so well. Both he and Jimps shared something in common, namely, the ability to create a new language. In the popular (and misunderstood) "Tar Baby Story," Uncle Remus puts on the mask again when the boy asks if the fox ate the rabbit: "Dat's all de fur de tale goes." He never reveals his true African self. Nor does he link the fox with an African trickster figure transported to the New World—a fox who is not just wily but a dangerous Black man bent on vengeance.

One might say that this inability or unwillingness to establish that direct link with Africa is a manifestation of earlier Black art. Nowadays, Margaret Danner could write of "Etta Moten's Attic," full as it was of African paraphernalia, and conclude that it was "quickening and charming till we felt the bloom / of veldt and jungle flow through the room."[7] This is not Cullen's "jungle boys and girls"; the jungle has become a welcome extension into the European building, and the poet can state this with ease and precision. There is no need to conceal it, as Dunbar might have done, or even romanticize it, as Cullen did. Still, it must be noted that Africa is apprehended in large geographical terms. In other words, the correct assumption here on Margaret Danner's part is that the primary synthesis has taken place. John Higham's *Strangers in a Land* and Nathaniel Glazer and Daniel Moynihan's *Beyond the Melting Pot* have one common statement: A melting pot does not include Blacks, and even the assimilation of White has only been partial in New World society. The positive side to this is that Black ethnic consciousness and identity remained a thing apart that developed unassociated, to a large extent, with New World mainstream culture.

Apprehending Africa in these large terms has meant, as with Negrista, that the writer is capable of great absurdity. Waring Cuney's "No Images" and McKay's "Harlem Dancer" are not unlike the Negrista poems that followed them. The female symbol was reduced to

6. Thomas R. English (ed.), *Seven Tales of Uncle Remus* (Atlanta, 1948), 16.
7. Margaret Danner, "Far from Africa: Four Poems," in Barksdale and Kinnamon (eds.), *Black Writers of America*, 817.

its lowest mythical denominator—nakedness. The woman was beautiful because she seemed naked, not because she was. This is part of the disparity that Derek Walcott recognizes in his poetry when he refuses to take sides.

Obviously, race has scarred the New World imaginative output or, put differently, the Afro-New World writer may utilize racial pros and cons as never-ending points of an eternal see-saw. If our examples at this stage have tended to be predominantly Black American, this is due to the fact that in the United States the drama of race consciousness has been, and is being, played to its fullest. Both Baraka's play *The Slave* (1946) and John Williams' *Sons of Darkness, Sons of Light* (1969) clearly indicate this. The race war in both of these works, though a distressingly convincing issue, is subsumed into the larger issue of racial integrity. The writers assume that chaos cannot be avoided, and its very inevitability is part of the process towards the secondary synthesis. The works are troubling reflections on the mandate that any group writer sees as his: to state and solve the problem of dual identity in a culture that denies its own Mulatto quality.

In these works and in others examined before, the indigenous African from Africa and the New World Afro man become a mythopoetic fusion. It matters little whether the reality of Africa brings out the negativity of Richard Wright's *Black Power* (1954), in which the writer's presence in Ghana conjures up "an odd kind of at-homeness." Wright was perceiving in Africa the true reality of his own predicament—the moral and psychological weakness that had come about because of an unwary acceptance of the condition of serf. If Wright had read his own works, he would have observed the curious juxtaposition between his quandary in Ghana and his revulsion toward Black life in the United States, which he saw as "bleak and barren" as early as 1945 in *Black Boy*. I am suggesting, therefore, that Africa is not just a mirror, not even a distorting one, but a crucial agent of age. In the enormous manner in which New World writers apprehend it, speaking as they do from the trap of a monocultural synthesis, Africa becomes a permanent reminder of a repressed unconscious. The slave's prayer states it in even more climatic terms that point to chaos. "Oh Lawd, gib him [the White man] de eye ob de eagle, dat he may spy out sin afar off, weave his hands to de gospel plow, tie his

tongue to de limb ob truth, nail his ear to the South pole. . . . Noint him wid de kerosene oil of salvation and set him on fire."[8] The drama of synthesism assumes archetypal proportions and may be well seen in Douglas Turner Ward's play, *Day of Absence* (1968), when all the Blacks leave town, or in William Melvin Kelley's *A Different Drummer* (1962), when Tucker-Caliban destroys the fertility of the earth with salt, shoots his farm animals, and leaves the state with his wife and baby. Ward was awakened to the possibilities of a renewal of life and, although no such crude solution as a return to Africa is presented in its Garveyite fancy, the departure of all the other Blacks from town is a clear symbol of the exercising of an option and establishing of a wall of respect.

An obvious irony here is that the potential for erecting that wall was always there, even in relatively well-assimilated group structures such as those in the Afro-American hollers, which supplanted the talking drums and were the means by which Black slaves identified each other; work songs were altered from those sung Africa but were still sung. The rural blues developed from the hollers, and later on, the spirituals evolved, with their hidden meanings, as well as the "sermonette," during which early ministers began their preaching with a chant. Plantation slaves danced, although the drum was prohibited in America, for the very slave ships that brought them encouraged dance as a form of exercise. In Cuba, as John Storm Roberts points out, rhumba dancing "took the common form of a couple (or solo) dance inside a ring of singer watchers"; in the Dominican Republic, the Afro-Dominican forms had solo call melodies, a chorus, and drumming. Roberts also notes that the call and response is present in calypso.[9] These patterns of music indicate that wherever these songs were sung or the dances performed they were communal activities, not merely displays of the dexterity of a single performer. Again, the New World African emphasized this new group of disparate beings, for the anonymous artists saw the dire need to forge a common past.

Taban lo Liyong's conclusion in *The Last Word* (1969) is not easy to agree with, for he says that "the Negroes [New World Blacks] are

8. J. Mason Brewer (ed.), *American Negro Folklore* (Chicago, 1968), 140.
9. John Storm Roberts, *Black Music of Two Worlds* (New York, 1972), 96.

only Africa's cousins and nephews in a patriarchal world: Europe, settled in America, dominates the landscape."[10] We have noted that although this might be the case superficially, there is the lurking soul of the African ancestor beneath the cracks and crevices. We can understand Taban's weariness, however, in the imaginary letter from "Uncle Africa," which points out that the African is no guiding spirit in America; he is a guest. Taban is alluding, though, to today's African; he is speaking of a future in which Afro-New World man did not partake, that is, the present Africa. We are speaking of the common past we all shared and that we recall in differing ways.

III

Whatever is said at this juncture must be hypothetical and pragmatic in the sense that it awaits fulfillment or denial at a time in the near future. The Black writer's search, his trading on agony, is in Fanon's words, "the fight for national existence [that] sets culture moving and opens to it the doors of creation."[11] I have suggested that it also opens a vista on the probability of the occurrence of a secondary synthesism. In this way, Négritude and Negrista become, not the signals for open warfare, but manifestos of group accomplishment.

Ellison's narrator in *Invisible Man* (despite Ellison's remarks to the contrary) is the classic African legendary hero bent on quest, except that his journey is undertaken for the recognition of a negative —the Black man's own absurd position within the American cultural framework. And though Ellison in private claims that his novel is one in the tradition of the European picaresque, the journey does involve the symbolic points of departure—initiation and return— and the travelers are very much like Wilson Harris' stereotype figures in *Palace of the Peacock* (1960) and Amos Tutuola's *persona* in *Palm-Wine Drinkard* (1952). None of these fellow travelers is individual; all perform group acts intended to illuminate our understanding of group identity and move us toward some kind of goal. In Ellison's novel, the basement with electric lights; in Harris', the peacock sym-

---

10. Taban lo Liyong, *The Last Word* (Nairobi, 1969), 88.
11. Philip J. Staundenraus, *The African Colonization Movement, 1816–1865* (New York, 1961), 17–30, 50–66.

bol at the end of the book; in Tutuola's, the acquisition of a symbolic egg, are group fortifications.

Tutuola is Nigerian, Harris is Guyanese, and Ellison is an Afro-American. The latter two cannot admit to the positive qualities of their environments, since they do not partake in it. The difference is that Tutuola's African world is more certain. The similarity in the novels is the need for the journeys and the African archetypal experience that gave rise to them.

On one level all the protagonists seek the same object. They wish to understand the environment and model it so that others can partake in it. But the object is not material, since it is the environment —physical, spiritual, and intellectual—that has dwarfed man's understanding. Afro-New World man attaches qualities that are frequently not part of this object in his need for self-realization. He invests his psyche in an automobile or an art work. Therefore, soulless man, with his penchant for superlatives, simply mistakes the shadow for the substance. That is why, when Eulalie, an Afro-American woman, marries Ato, a Ghanaian, and returns home, in Ama Ata Aidoo's *Dilemma of a Ghost* (1965), she finds it so difficult to relate to a new group. Her relations to one group are evident from her recollections of her mother and of her youth in America, but the mores of African life are alien to her. Therefore she insists on not having a family. This is a personal, individual right, she thinks, but in reality she has locked off the life flow.

If I seem to be suggesting a lackluster conformity in communalism, then perhaps my rebuttal must be that it is inevitable in old and new groupings. What *Dilemma of a Ghost* brings out more poignantly than Wright's work is the inability of a person (on the verge of attaining secondary synthesis) to return to former group formations before primary synthesis has taken place. Eulalie's new group is Afro, not Twi or Ga or Ewe. The conflict is not between a Westernized woman and a "prehistoric" man, but between someone on the verge of individuality and another who conforms to the proprieties of group sense. In several ways, the twilight zone of the merging of the two syntheses results in an extreme isolation, such as Eulalie deeply feels.

Miti experiences such a loneliness when he comes to America in Seruma Enriko's *The Experience* (1970), and this is shared by the narrator of Cheikh Amidou Kane's *Ambiguous Adventure* (1963). The confrontation with the Western world illustrates how these Africans are ill equipped to deal with two of the givens of primary synthesism—the investure of the material object with sacred qualities and the intense need to possess, utilize, and eventually discard it. Again, the similarities between the American car and Western craftmanship are apparent. Both are creations of individuals and both are revered, not for any latent function intrinsic to them, but for a very pragmatic consideration—money. Both must be owned to be enjoyed and utilized (displayed, loaned, or used for collateral), and both may be, indeed must be, discarded at some future time. This demonstrates an awareness of the differences between New World Blacks and Africans. We seek to dominate a material reality, while Africans wish to be possessed by a spiritual essence.

This example leads us to the point where both Afro man and African realize that they do share a vested interest, first, in the object and, second, in its renewal. Therefore, though masks and costumes of last year's carnival are discarded in Trinidad and retained in Nigeria, this suggests an attitude that is on one hand liberal and on the other conservative. It shows that both Afro-New World Blacks and Africans seek to renew an acquaintanceship with the object in ritual at set times. The automobile and the art work may be disposed of during a sale, and likewise, the African mask, though never discarded, reappears at a given time when the spirits market their own essences. Seemingly, then, we are bogged down in semantics. Members of both cultures respect the object and have agreed rituals for its display. Thus the characters in the works of Enriko and Kane, Africans adrift in the Western world, must learn the difference between *sale* and *market*. They are corrupted in the process and return home. Their cycle seems so easy, for there is somewhere to go. Not so with the Black man of the New World.

Historically, he attempted to resettle with successful results. The Creoles of Liberia, Gambia, and Sierra Leone are not Africans in that they have no African tongue, and even now, their very dependence on the Western world for cultural fodder suggests that they are still

to reconquer the African environment, to move away from their group formations in the New World to the older ones in Africa. The London-based Committee for the Black Poor had dispatched 411 passengers to Sierra Leone in 1787 and another set in 1791. The American Society for Colonizing the Free People of Color in the United States, later the American Colonization Society, dispatched 86 in 1820 to Sierra Leone, and by 1823 there were 150 colonists in what was now called Liberia. But could these people reclaim a lost ethnical affinity? Their sheer reliance on England and America for provisions, combined with their inability to deal with local conditions and lack of understanding of African group life, still leaves them in a quandary. They are Afro-New World persons adrift in the Old World.

In understanding Afro man in the New World it becomes necessary to see how these first attempts at resettling worked. More than a hundred years after, we can identify a people who (a) share a common identity, (b) live apart from the indigenous African groups, (c) have modified the English language into new Creoles, and most important, (d) do not consider themselves men of the group. If one had to single out *individuals* (apart from the so-called elite) who live in Africa, it would have to be these people. Their failure to come to terms with the surrounding ethnic groups is not their fault alone. It was one that Wright realized when he alluded to the "fortuity of birth."

The real life situation of Richard Wright and the African Creole people, as well as the fictionalized account of Eulalie and Miti, indicate that they are all confused by the nature of the object, the properties that should and should not be vested in it, their apprehension of it, and, consequently, their ill usage. They all have an extremely dismal encounter with what is alien to them. The reason is simple; out of their isolation they confront the object in barren cultural territory, as semi-individuals. But they do not have the autonomy to do this, for they live only on the periphery of a possible entry into the circle of secondary synthesism. The African landscape cannot respond for them. Wright merely sees (like Cullen, like the Négritude and Negrista writers, like Ellison's chief character, like McKay's dancer) "jungle, nudity, mudhuts." He writes: "As the bus rolled swiftly forward I waited irrationally for these fantastic scenes to fade;

I had the foolish feeling that I had but to turn my head and I'd see the ordered, clothed streets of Paris. . . . But the string of mud villages stretched out without end. My protest was not against Africa or its people; it was directed against the unsettled feeling engendered by the strangeness of a completely different order of life."[12]

What we term *exotic* in Black New World writing may very often be just this, the misunderstanding of the object, the fear it engenders, and our wish for its renewal. Wright goes home, and the settlers remain on African soil but are a thing apart; and Miti returns to Africa. All are imprisoned by a history that is not of their own making but which gives them a common attribute that, wherever they go, they must seek a restoration of their group identity.

This paradox of being alien to oneself would be an interesting conjecture for its own sake; for us it becomes even more so when we realize that all literature of the Black New World is a variation on this theme. Black writers may gloss over the alienation, may debate it with various degrees of assuredness, may reject it for another type of fiction by embracing the false gods of Europe, or may present it in their art from a set of hypothetical viewpoints. It is no real concern whether there is a right or a wrong approach. What seems important is the study of all the literature, aesthetically good or bad, in order to form some judgment regarding what writers have made of their pact of renewal in the vested properties of the object. Ann Cook gave the aforementioned true account of the man she had met in Brazil, who placidly said to her that his grandmother was Black but refused to accept the fact that he had Black features. She called him a creature of a "twilight zone," and in this respect, our logic for studying the Mulatto is that he becomes representative of Afro-New World man on the periphery of a changing group consciousness.[13] The Mulatto is symbolic of both a desire to achieve full role acceptance within the secondary synthesis and at the same time to proudly assert his oneness with patterns contained inside the primary synthesis. He experiences the second step, of discarding the object. For

12. Richard Wright, *Black Power* (New York, 1954), 37.
13. Ann Cook, "Black Pride—Some Contradictions," in *Negro Digest*, VII (February, 1970) 36–42, 59–63.

when a society declares itself to be Mulatto, (as with past and contemporary Cuba, Brazil, and the Caribbean), it avoids the final secondary synthesis when Black and White cease to exist. Instead, a new type of fraud is created—one in which White standards become operative. John Clytus in *Black Man in Red Cuba* (1970), admittedly a propagandistic account, shows that much. *Sab* (1841) and *Cecilia Valdés* (1839) do not really contradict the inferiority of Blacks, although they claim to; instead they reinforce patterns of ethnocentrism. Negrista, alas, must also come into this category. It is the poetry of the absurd, dealing with superlatives and acquiring, utilizing, and discarding the object (the Black man) but never coming to the point of renewal when Afro-New World man is seen within the context of his own real and meaningful group domain.

In literature, when we look throughout the Afro-New World of Dutch, French, Spanish, English, and Creole peoples, we seek, for our new aesthetic, ways in which the cultural environment, if fulfilled, becomes complete through renewal. We see clear examples of this in the works of writers in Spanish. On the linguistic level, we recognize that a mosaic is not a fusion. Afro-Venezuelan Spanish is used in Diaz Sánchez's *Cumboto* (1972) and, although not used by Natividad, it is utilized by Abuela Anita, who directs the religious outlook of the growing boy. Gip, the nurse who speaks Afro-Caribbean English, is also a guide, in Geoffrey Drayton's *Christopher* (1959). These women are not just language devices but important educators; they discourse on religion, their understanding of the world, man's place in the universe, and the existence of good and evil. The fact that this can be done in Black Spanish and Black English is a firm indicator of the success of primary synthesis. Seemingly, it has reached perfection in Surinam, where the recent anthology *Creole Drum* (1975) demonstrates the versatility with which Dutch, English, Portuguese, and African words combine to form Srantongo. Henny F. Zeil's poetry shows how well this works:

mi go—m'e kon	I've been gone, I am back.
sowtwatra bradi.	The sea is wide
tak wan mofo,	Utter something
ala mi mati,	All my friends,

tak wan mofo	Utter something.
m'go	I've been gone,
m'e kon.	I am back.[14]

This is an example of the definite completion of the circle of primary synthesis. Like the culture in general, the languages can only exhibit this autonomy when they are physically required to function, and in no way are they considered inferior. In Mervyn C. Alleyne's words:

> I can find no convincing linguistic evidence that Creole languages are deficient or pathological or simplified, or that they ever were. They appear to be reduced or simplified only when juxtaposed to European languages of the same lexical base—and when these European languages are viewed as the norm. They are considered deficient because it is impossible to participate in, and manipulate the norm culture using Creole language. And therefore Creole languages are deficient only to the extent that their speakers wish to or are expected to participate in and manipulate this norm culture.[15]

In language and literature we find our closest affinities. Enough work has not been done to establish how the world corpus of related Black literatures, languages, Creoles, and dialects share a commonality that would establish the oneness of a unique and surviving culture beyond doubt. The "Creolese" I knew as a boy in Guyana is not unlike the pidgin English I spoke in Nigeria, or the Krio I learned in Sierra Leone. Even without historical and geographical evidence or the lack of pointers to the obvious similarity or norms, Afro-New World language and literature, with its resurrection of the ancient memories of the group, display, not the mouthings of a noble savage, but the missing link in our evolutionary process from the group man of Old World traditions to the individual Afro-New World man of our present inheritance. There is a marked shift in allegiance to a given clan, but no severance from our loyalty to the embracing archetype of a common ancestral past. In observing this we may well come to an understanding of how the renewal of the object is the ritualistic

14. Jan Voorhoeve and Ursy M. Lichtveld (eds.), *Creole Drum* (New Haven, 1975), 205. Translation by editors.
15. Mervyn C. Alleyne, "The Linguistic Continuity of Africa in the Caribbean," in *Black Academy Review*, I (Winter, 1970), 10.

conclusion of the first synthesis, and how its fulfillment will be realized in the grand and unique possibilities of the second. At the moment, this must remain our fervent wish for the direction of New World society. Its completion would be the acceptance of our entire past and a total commitment to our present and future experiences as New World persons.

Bibliography

1. Bibliographies

Bissainthe, Max. *Dictionnaire de bibliographie haïtienne*. Metuchen: Grolier, 1973.

Comitas, Lambros. *The Complete Caribbeana: A Bibliographical Guide to the Scholarly Literature, 1900–1975*. 3 Vols. Milwood: K.T.O. Press, 1977.

Jahn, Janheinz. *A Bibliography of Neo-African Literature from Africa, America and the Caribbean*. New York: Praeger, 1965.

Miami, University of. *Catalog of the Cuban and Caribbean Library*. 6 Vols. Boston: G. K. Hall, 1977.

Porter, Dorothy. *Afro-Braziliana: A Working Bibliography*. Boston: G. K. Hall, 1978.

Turner, Darwin. *Afro American Writers*. New York: Appleton-Century-Crofts, 1970.

2. Background

Africa Seen by American Negroes. Paris: Présence Africaine, n.d.

Almeida, Renato. *História da música brasileira*. Rio de Janeiro: F. Briguiete, 1942.

Andrade, Mário de. *Compendio de história de música*. São Paulo: n.p., 1933.

Aptheker, Herbert. *Nat Turner's Slave Rebellion*. New York: Humanities Press, 1966.

Barrett, Leonard E. *Soul-Force*. New York: Anchor Press, 1974.

Bascom, William. *Shango in the New World*. Austin: University of Texas Press, 1972.

Bastide, Roger. *Brasil: terra de contrastes*. São Paulo: Difusão Européia do Livro, 1964.

Beckford, William. *Remarks upon the Situation of Negroes in Jamaica*. London: T & J Egerton, 1788.

Beier, Ulli. *Sacred Wood Carvings from One Small Yoruba Town*. Lagos: Ministry of Education, 1957.

Blassingame, John W. *Black New Orleans*. Chicago: University of Chicago Press, 1973.

———. *The Slave Community: Plantation Life in the Antebellum South*. New York: Oxford University Press, 1972.

Boxer, Charles Ralph. *The Golden Age of Brazil: 1695–1750*. Berkeley: University of California Press, 1962.

Braithwaite, E. R. *A Kind of Homecoming*. London: Muller, 1963.

Bronz, Stephen A. *Roots of Racial Consciousness: the 1920's: Three Harlem Renaissance Authors*. New York: Libra, 1964.

Burton, Richard Francis. *Explorations of the Highlands of Brazil*. New York: Greenwood Press, 1869.

Butcher, Margaret Just. *The Negro in American Culture*. New York: Knopf, 1956.

Cabrera, Lydia. *Anago, vocabulario Lucumí*. Miami: C. R. Publications, 1970.

———. *El Monte*. Originally published in Havana, 1954. Miami: Colección del Chicherekú, 1971.

———. *La sociedad secreta Abakuá*. Originally published in Havana, 1959. Miami: C. R. Publications, 1970.

Carlyle, Thomas. *Occasional Discourse on the Nigger Question*. (Reprinted with additions from *Fraser's Magazine*). London: Thomas Bosworth, 1853.

Chametzky, Jules, and Sidney Kaplan. *Black and White in American Culture*. Amherst: University of Massachusetts Press, 1969.

Courlander, Harold. *The Drum and the Hoe: Life and Lore of the Haitian People*. Berkeley: University of California Press, 1960.

Crummell, Alexander. *Africa and America*. Miami: Mnemosyne, 1969.

Curtin, Philip D., ed. *Africa and the West*. Madison: University of Wisconsin Press, 1972.

———. *The Atlantic Slave Trade: A Census*. Madison: University of Wisconsin Press, 1969.

Eugene D. Genovese and Laura Foner, eds. *Slavery in the New World: A Reader in Comparative History*. Englewood Cliffs: Prentice Hall, 1969.

Delany, Martin. *The Condition, Elevation, Emigration and Destiny of the Colored People of the United States Politically Considered*. Originally published in Philadelphia, 1852. New York: Arno Press, 1968.

Dickson, Donald. *Negroes in Brazil*. Chicago: University of Chicago Press, 1942.

Duberman, Martin B. *The Anti-Slavery Vanguard*. Princeton: Princeton University Press, 1965.

Du Bois, W. E. B. *The Negro*. Originally published in New York, 1915. London: Oxford University Press, 1970.

——. *The Souls of Black Folk*. New York: Washington Square Press, 1970.

Dzidzienyo, Anani. *The Position of Blacks in Brazilian Society*. London: Minority Rights Group, 1971.

Elkins, Stanley M. *Slavery: A Problem in American Institutional and Intellectual Life*. Chicago: University of Chicago Press, 1959.

Fanon, Franz. *The Wretched of the Earth*. New York: Grove Press, 1963.

Fernándes, Florestán. *The Negro in Brazilian Society*. New York: Columbia University Press, 1969.

Franklin, John Hope. *From Slavery to Freedom*. New York: Vantage Books, 1969.

Freyre, Gilberto. *The Masters and the Slaves*. New York: Knopf, 1946.

——. *New World in the Tropics: The Culture of Modern Brazil*. New York, 1959.

——. *The Position of Blacks in Brazilian Society*. London: Minority Rights Group, 1971.

Froude, J. A. *The English and the West Indies*. London: Longmans, 1888.

Fullinwider, S. P. *The Mind and Mood of Black America*. Homewood: Dorsey Press, 1967.

Genovese, Eugene D. *The World the Slaveholders Made*. New York: Vintage Books, 1971.

Gide, André. *Travels in the Congo*. (trans. of *Voyage au Congo*, 1927). Berkeley: University of California Press, 1962.

Goldsmith, Oliver. *History of the Earth and Animated Nature*. Vol. I. London: A. Fullarton, 1774.

Hare, Nathan. *The Black Anglo Saxons*. New York: MacMillan, 1965.

Haskins, James. *Witchcraft, Mysticism and Magic in the New World*. New York: Doubleday, 1974.

Herskovits, Melville J. *Life in a Haitian Valley*. Originally published 1937. Garden City: Anchor Books, 1971.

——. *The Myth of the Negro Past*. Boston: Beacon Press, 1958.

——. *Trinidad Village*. New York: Knopf, 1947.

Idowu, E. Bolaji. *Olódúmaré: God in Yoruba Belief*. London: Longmans, 1962.

Jahn, Janheinz. *Muntu: An Outline of Neo-African Culture*. New York: Grove Press, 1961.

——. *Neo-African Literature: History of Black Writing*. New York: Grove Press, 1969.

Jordan, Winthrop. *White Over Black*. Chapel Hill: University of North Carolina Press, 1968.

Kemble, Frances Anne. *Journal of a Residence on a Georgia Plantation in 1838–1839*. New York: Knopf, 1961.

Lewis, Matthew Gregory. *Journal of a West India Proprietor, 1815–17*. Originally published in London, 1834. Boston: Houghton Mifflin, 1929.

Long, Edward. *History of Jamaica, or a General Survey of the Ancient and*

Modern State of That Island. Originally published in London, 1774. 3 Vols. London: Frank Cass, 1970.

Lowenthal, David and Lambros Comitas, eds. *West Indian Perspectives.* 4 Vols. Garden City: Anchor Press, 1973.

Memmi, Albert. *The Colonizer and the Colonized.* Boston: Beacon Press, 1965.

Moreton, James Bigham. *West Indian Customs and Manners.* Originally published in 1853. London, 1970.

Nketia, J. H. Kwabena. *Funeral Dirges of the Akan People.* Achimota: privately published, 1955.

Nugent, Maria. *Lady Nugent's Journal; Jamaica One Hundred Years Ago . . . 1801–1815.* Originally published in 1907. London: Institute of Jamaica, 1966.

Ortiz, Fernándo. *La africanía de la música folclorica de Cuba.* Havana: Editoria Universitaria, 1965.

———. *Los negros brujos.* Originally published in Havana, 1906. Miami: Ediciónes Universal, 1963.

Pattee, Richard. "Barriers to Latin American Negro Studies." *Crisis.* LVII (1940), 255–57.

———. "Negro Studies in Latin America." *Bulletin No. 32.* American Council of Learned Societies (September, 1941). Originally presented as a paper at the Conference on Negro Studies, Howard University, March 29–30, 1940.

Pierson, Donald. *Negroes in Brazil.* Chicago: University of Chicago Press, 1939.

Poppino, Rollie E. *Brazil: The Land and People.* New York: Oxford University Press, 1973.

Ramos, Arthur. *The Negro in Brazil.* Washington, D.C.: Associated Publishers, 1939.

Roberts, John Storm. *Black Music of Two Worlds.* New York: Praeger, 1972.

Rodrigues, Nina. *Os Africanos no Brasil.* São Paulo: Compania Editora Nacional, 1932.

Rubin, Vera, ed. *Caribbean Studies: A Symposium.* New York: Program for the Study of Man in the Tropics, Columbia University, 1957.

Saco, José Antonio. *Historia de la esclavitud de la raza Africana en el nuevo mundo y en especial en los países Americano-Hispanos.* Havana: Colección de Libros Cubanos, 1938.

Soromenho, Castro. *A maravilhosa viagem dos exploradores portugueses.* Lisbon, 1956.

Southern, Eileen. *The Music of Black Americans.* New York: Norton, 1971.

Staundenraus, Philip J. *The African Colonization Movement, 1816–1865.* New York: Columbia University Press, 1961.

Taban lo Liyong. *The Last Word.* Nairobi: East African Publishing House, 1969.

Uya, Okon Edet. *Black Brotherhood*. Boston: D. C. Heath, 1971.

Williams, Eric. *British Historians and the West Indies*. New York: Africana, 1964.

Wright, Richard. *Black Power*. New York: Harper & Brothers, 1954.

Young, William. *A History of the Black Caribs in St. Vincent*. London, n.p., 1795.

3. Critical Commentary: Articles

Alleyne, Mervyn C. "The Linguistic Continuity of Africa in the Caribbean." *Black Academy Review*, I (Winter, 1970), 10.

Baquero, Gastón. *Darió, Cernuda y otros temas poéticos*. Madrid: Editora Naciónal, 1969.

Barreda-Tomás, Pedro M. "Alejo Carpentier: Dos visiones del negro, dos conceptos de la novela." *Hispania*, LV (March, 1972).

Cook, Ann. "Black Pride: Some Contradictions." *Negro Digest*, VII (February, 1970), 36–42 and 59–63.

Davis, Arthur P. "The Alien-and-Exile Theme in Countee Cullen's Racial Poems." *Phylon*, XIV (1953), 390–400.

De Costa, Miriam. Review, in *Black Word*, XXIII (May, 1974), 97.

Fernández, Oscar de la Vega. "Medio siglo de poesía negra." *Cubanacan*, Vol. I, No. 4, p. 65.

Fleissner, Robert F. "Herbert's Aethiopesa and the Dark Lady: a Mannerist Parallel." *College Language Association Journal*, XIX (June, 1976), 458–67.

Haslam, Gerald. "American Oral Literature: Our Forgotten Heritage." *English Journal*, LX (September, 1971), 718.

Sartre, Jean-Paul. "L'art nègre," in L.S. Senghor, ed. *Anthologie de la nouvelle poésie nègre et malgache de langue française*. Paris: Presses Universitaires, 1948, ix–xliv.

Valdés-Cruz, Rosa E. "Tres poemas representativos de la poesía afroantillana." *Hispania*, LIV (March, 1971).

Verger, Pierre. "Nigeria, Brazil and Cuba." *Nigeria*, (October, 1960), 168–77.

Walcott, Derek. "Leaving School." *London Magazine*, V (September, 1965), 4–14.

———. "What the Twilight Says." Introduction to *Dream on Monkey Mountain and Other Plays*. New York: Farrar, Strauss and Giroux, 1973.

Warner, Maureen. "Africans in Nineteenth-Century Trinidad." *African Studies Association of the West Indies Bulletin*, No. 5, n.d., 30.

Williams, Lorna. "Perspective in the *Memorias posthumas de Braz Cubas* by Machado de Assis." *College Language Association Journal*, X (June, 1955).

4. Critical Commentary: Books

Bar-Lewaw, Itzahk. *Plácido*. Mexico: Impresora Juan Pablos, 1960.

Baugh, Edward. *A Brief Account of West Indian Poetry*. Kingston: Savacou Publications, 1977.

Bontemps, Arna. *The Harlem Renaissance Remembered*. New York: Dodd, Mead, 1972.

Cartey, Wilfred G. *Black Images*. New York: Teachers College Press, 1970.

Casals, Jorge. *Plácido como poeta cubano*. Havana: Ministerio de Educación, 1944.

Dathorne, O. R., and Willfried Feuser, eds. *Africa in Prose*. Harmondsworth: Penguin, 1969.

Ellison, Ralph. *Shadow and Act*. New York: Signet Books, 1964.

Fowler, Carolyn. "Haitian Literature: A Case Study in National and Race Consciousness." Center for African and Afro American Studies Occasional Paper No. 19, Atlanta University, cyclostyled, n.d.

Garófalo, M. García y Mesa. *Plácido: poeta y martir*. Mexico: Ediciónes Botas-Mexico, 1938.

Garret, Naomi. *The Renaissance of Haitian Poetry*. Paris: Présence Africaine, 1963.

Gilkes, Michael. *Racial Identity and Individual Consciousness in the Caribbean Novel*. Edgar Mittelholzer Memorial Lectures. Georgetown: Ministry of Information and Culture, 1975.

Guillén, Nicolás. *Nicolás Guillén: Notas para un estudio biográfico-crítico*. Santa Clara: Universidad de Las Villas, 1962 and 1964.

Harris, Wilson. *Tradition and the West Indian Novel*. London: West Indian Student Union, 1965.

————. *Tradition and the Writer in West Indian Society*. London: New Beacon Publications, 1967.

Hollis, Christopher. *Evelyn Waugh*. London: Longmans Green, 1958.

Imbert, E. Anderson. *Historia de la literatura hispanoamericana*. Mexico: Fondo de Cultura Económica, 1967.

Johnson, Lemuel. *The Devil, the Gargoyle and the Buffoon*. Port Washington: Kennikat Press, 1969.

La Rose, John, ed. *New Beacon Reviews*. London: New Beacon Books, 1968.

Link, Frederick M. *Aphra Behn*. New York: Twayne, 1968.

Márquez, Robert, and David M. Murray, eds. *Guillén: Man-making Words: Selected Poems of Nicolás Guillén*. Amherst: University of Massachusetts Press, 1972.

Ngugi wa Thiongo. *Homecoming*. New York: Lawrence Hill, 1972.

Peavy, Charles D. *Go Slow Now: Faulkner and the Race Question*. Eugene: University of Oregon Press, 1971.

Ramchand, Kenneth. *An Introduction to the Study of West Indian Literature*. Kingston: Nelson Caribbean, 1976.

Rosa-Nieves, Cesareo. *La poesía en Puerto Rico*. San Juan: Editoria Edil, 1969.

Sayers, Raymond. *The Negro in Brazilian Literature*. New York: Hispanic Institute in the United States, 1956.

Shapiro, Norman, ed. *Négritude: Black Poetry from Africa and the Caribbean*. New York: October House, 1970.

Soyinka, Wole. *Myth Literature and the African World*. Cambridge: Cambridge University Press, 1976.

Valdés, Gabriel de la Concepción. *Musa cubana*. Paris: Casa Editorial, 1868.

Vega, Oscar Fernandez de la, and Alberto N. Pamies. *Iniciación a la poesía afro-americana*. Miami: Ediciónes Universal, 1973.

Williams, Denis. *Image and Idea in the Arts of Guyana*. Edgar Mittelholzer Memorial Lectures. Georgetown: Ministry of Information and Culture, 1969.

5. Anthologies

Barksdale, Richard, and Keneth Kinnamon, eds. *Black Writers of America*. New York: Macmillan, 1972.

Bishop, Elizabeth, and Emmanuel Brasil, eds. *An Anthology of Twentieth-Century Brazilian Poetry*. Middletown: Wesleyan University Press, 1972.

Bontemps, Arna, and Langston Hughes, eds. *The Book of Negro Folklore*. New York: Dodd, Mead, 1958.

Collins, Marie, ed. *Black Poets in French: A Collection of Caribbean and African Poets*. Totowa: Scribner's & Sons, 1972.

Dathorne, O. R., ed. *African Poetry*. London: MacMillan, 1969.

———, ed. *Caribbean Narrative*. London: Heinemann Educational Books, 1966.

———, ed. *Caribbean Verse*. London: Heinemann Educational Books, 1967.

Dathorne, O. R. and Willfried Feuser, eds. *Africa in Prose*. Harmondsworth: Penguin, 1969.

Figueira, Gaston, ed. *Poesía brasileña contemporanea, 1920–1968*. Montevideo, Uruguay: Instituto de Cultura Uruguayo-Brazileño, 1960.

Guirao, Ramón, ed. *Antología de la poesía de la poesía afrocubana*. Havana, 1928.

———, ed. *Orbita de la poesía afrocubana 1928–1937*. Havana: Ucar García, 1938.

Lima, José Lezama, ed. *Antología de la poesía cubana*. Vols. I–III. Havana: Editorial del Consejo Nacional de Cultura, 1965.

Saz, D. Augustin del, ed. *Antología de la poesía Argentina*. Buenos Aires: Editorial Bruguera, 1959.

Senghor, L. S., ed. *Anthologie de la nouvelle poésie nègre et malgache de langue française*. Paris: Presses Universitaires, 1948.

Shapiro, Norman R., ed. *Négritude: Black Poetry from Africa and the Caribbean*. New York: October House, 1970.

Valdes, Ildefonso Pereda. *Antología de la poesía negra americana*. Montevideo: Biblioteca Uruguaya de Autores, 1953.

Vizo, Hortensia Ruiz del, ed. *Black Poetry of the Americas*. Miami: Ediciónes Universal, 1972.

Voorhoeve, Jan, and Ursy M. Lichtveld, eds. *Creole Drum*. New Haven: Yale University Press, 1975.

6. Folk Literature

Abrahams, Roger. *Deep Down in the Jungle*. Chicago: Aldine, 1970.

Aguiar, Pinto de. *Contos regionais brasileiros*. Salvador-Bahia: Imprensa Vitória, 1957.

Araújo, Alceu Maynard. *Folclore nacional*. São Paulo: Edicões Melhoramentos, 1964.

Batchelor, Courtenay Malcolm. *Stories and Storytellers of Brazil*. Vol. I. Havana: Imp. Talleres de Úcar García, 1933.

Bell, Henry H. *Obeah: Witchcraft in the West Indies*. Originally published in 1889. Westport: Negro University Press, 1970.

Bontemps, Arna, and Langston Hughes. *The Book of Negro Folklore*. New York: Dodd Mead, 1958.

Brewer, J. Mason, ed. *American Negro Folklore*. Chicago: Quadrangle, 1968.

Cabrera, Lydia. *Ayapá*. Miami: Ediciónes Universal, 1971.

———. *Cuentos negros de Cuba*. Havana, 1940.

———. *Refránes de negros viejos*. 2nd ed. Miami: C. R. Publications, 1970.

Comissão nacional de folclore de Instituto Brasileiro de Edução, Ciêncla e Cultura. Rio de Janeiro, 1948.

Dundes, Alan, ed. *Mother Wit from the Laughing Barrel*. Englewood Cliffs: Prentice-Hall, 1973.

English, Thomas R., ed. *Seven Tales of Uncle Remus*. Atlanta: Emory University Publications, 1948.

Feijóo, Samuel, ed. *Cuentos populares cubanos*. Havana: Universidad Central de las Villas, 1962.

Filho, Mello Moraes. *Festas e tradiçónes*. Rio de Janeiro: H. Garnier, 1946.

Franco, José. *Folklore criollo y afro-cubana*. Havana: Publicaciónes de la Junta Nacional de Arqueología y Etnología, 1959.

Gallop, Rodney. *Portugal: A Book of Folkways*. Cambridge: Cambridge University Press, 1936.

Gomes, Lindolfo, ed. *Cantos populares brasileiros*. Saõ Paulo: Edições Melhoramentos, 1931.

Guirao, Ramón, ed. *Cuentos y leyendas negras de Cuba*. Havana: Ediciónes "Mirador," 1943.

Harris, Joel Chandler. *Uncle Remus, His Songs and Sayings*. Originally published in New York, 1880. New York: Schocken, 1965.

Herskovits, Melville J., and Frances S. Herskovits. *Suriname Folklore*. New York: Columbia University Press, 1936.

Hurston, Zora Neale. *Mules and Men*. Philadelphia: Lippincott, 1938.

Lester, Julius. *Black Folktales*. New York: Grove Press, 1969.

Lima, José. *A festa de Egun e quatros ensarios*. Rio de Janeiro: Spivak & Kersner, 1955.

Nascimento, Abdias do, ed. *Dramas para negros e prólogo para brancos*. Rio de Janeiro: Edição de Teatro Experimental do Negro, 1961.

Ortiz, Fernándo. *Los bailes y el teatro de los negros en el folklore de Cuba*. Havana, 1951.

Owen, Mari L. *Voodoo Tales as Told Among the Negroes of the South West*. New York: Putnam, 1893.

Page, Thomas Nelson. *In Ole Virginia, or Marse Chan and Other Stories*. New York: Charles Scribner's Sons, 1887.

Price-Mars, Jean. *Ainsi parla l'oncle: essais d'ethnographie*. Originally published in 1928. New York: Parapsychology Foundation, 1954.

Salkey, Andrew, ed. *Anancy's Score*. London: Bogle L'Ouverture, 1973.

7. Prose

Achebe, Chinua. *Arrow of God*. London: Heinemann, 1964.

Arrúé, Salazar. *El Cristo negro*. Originally published in 1917. San Salvador: Ediciónes de Biblioteca Nacional, 1936.

Behn, Aphra. *Oroonoko: Or the Royal Slave. A True History*. London: Will Channing, 1688.

Bellow, Saul. *Henderson the Rain King*. New York: Fawcett World, 1974.

Calvo, L. N. *Pedro Blanco*. Originally published in 1940. Madrid: Colección Austral, 1955.

Carpentier, Alejo. *Ecué-Yamba-ó*. Montevideo, Uruguay: Santino, 1973.

Clemens, Samuel. *The Adventures of Huckleberry Finn*. New York: Harper, 1885.

Corncob, Jonathan [pseud.]. *The Adventures of Jonathan Corncob, Loyal American, Written by Himself*. London: printed for the author, 1787.

Cugoano, Ottobah. *Thoughts and Sentiments on the Evil and Wicked Traffic of the Slavery and Commerce of the Human Species, Humbly Submitted to the Inhabitants of Great Britain*. Originally published in London, 1787. New York: Africana Publishing Corporation, 1969.

Defoe, Daniel. *Robinson Crusoe*. Originally published 1719. New York: Dutton, 1945.

DeLisser, H. G. *The White Witch of Rosehall*. London: Benn, 1929.

Díaz-Rodríguez, Manuel. *Peregrina ó el pozo encantado*. Madrid: Biblioteca Nueva, 1952.

Diaz Sánchez, Ramón. *Cumboto*. Caracas: Ediciónes Populares Venezolanas C. A., 1959.

Douglass, Frederick. *Narrative of the Life of Frederick Douglass, an American Slave*. Originally published in Boston, 1845. Cambridge: Harvard University Press, 1960.

Du Bois, W. E. B. *Dusk of Dawn*. Originally published in 1940. New York: Schocken, 1968.

Equiano, Olaudah. *The Interesting Narrative of the Life of Olaudah Equiano, or Gustavus Vassa, the African*. Originally published in London, 1789. London: Dawsons, 1969.

Eyma, Xavier, "O Jornal de Recife." *Jornal Semanal*, III (January 19, 1861).

Firbank, Ronald. *The Complete Ronald Firbank*. London: Duckworth, 1961.

Greene, Graham. *The Comedians*. New York: Viking Press, 1970.

Johnson, Samuel. *Rasselas: Prince of Abyssinia*. London: Ginn, 1886.

Machado de Assis, Joaquim María. *Memorias posthumas de Braz Cubas*. Rio de Janeiro: W. M. Jackson Editores, 1944. Translated by William Grossman as *Epitaph of a Small-Time Winner*. New York: Noonday Press, 1952.

Melville, Herman. "Benito Cereno." *Herman Melville: Four Short Novels*. New York: Bantam Books, 1971.

———. *Moby Dick*. New York: Holt, Rinehart and Winston, 1957.

Salkey, Andrew. *A Quality of Violence*. London: Hutchinson, New Authors, 1959.

Scott, Michael. *The Cruise of the Midge*. Originally published in 1836. London: Gibbings, 1894.

———. *Tom Cringle's Log*. Originally published in 1836. New York: Macmillan, 1895.

Toomer, Jean. *Cane*. Originally published in 1923. New York: Liveright, 1975.

Walker, David. *Walker's Appeal in Four Articles with a Preamble to the Colored Citizens of the World but in Particular and Very Expressly for Those of the United States of America*. Originally published in Boston, 1830. Edited by Herbert Aptheker. New York: Humanities Press, 1965.

8. Poetry

Arozarena, Marcelino. *Canción negra sin color*. Havana: Cuadernos Unión, 1956.

Barnet, Miguel. *La sagrada familia*. Havana: U.N.E.A.C. 1967.

Barreto, Tobias. *Obras completas*. Rio de Janeiro: Pongetti, 1926.

Brathwaite, Edward. *The Arrivants: A New World Trilogy*. London: Oxford University Press, 1973.

Brièrre, Jean. *La source*. Buenos Aires: Collection du Jubilé du Docteur Jean Price-Mars, 1956.

Cabral, Manuel del. *Trópico negro*. Buenos Aires: Editorial Sopena Argentina, 1941.

Césaire, Aimé. *Cahier d'un retour au pays natal*. Paris: Présence Africaine, 1968.

Charles, Jean Claude. *Négociations*. Paris: Oswald, 1972.

Cullen, Countee. *Color*. New York: Harper and Brothers, 1925.

Damas, Léon Gontran. *Pigments*. Originally published in 1937. Paris: Présence Africaine, 1962. "Poems from *Pigments*," translated by Ellen Conroy Kennedy, in *Black World*. XXI (January, 1972) 13–28.

Depestre, René. *A Rainbow for the Christian West*. Translated by Joan Dayan. Amherst: University of Massachusetts Press, 1977.

———. *Minerai noir*. Paris: Présence Africaine, 1956.

Garçon, Jean Dieudonné. *Poèmes pour trois continents*. Paris: Oswald, 1972.

Guillén, Nicolás. *Guillén: Man-Making Words: Selected Poems of Nicolás Guillén*. Edited by Robert Márquez and David Arthur McMurray. Amherst: University of Massachusetts Press, 1972.

———. *Patria o muerte: The Great Zoo and Other Poems*. Edited and translated by Robert Márquez. New York: Monthly Review Press, 1972.

Large, Josaphat. *Nerfs du vent*. Paris: Oswald, 1975.

Moïse, Rodolphe. *Aux armes guerilleros*. Paris: Oswald, 1975.

Moya, Felipe Pichardo. *La ciudad de los espejos*. Camagüey, 1923.

Palés Matos, Luís. *Tuntún de pasa y grifería*. San Juan: Biblioteca de autores Puertoriqueños, 1937.

Polius, Joseph. *Bonheur de poche*. Paris: Oswald, 1968.

Romero, Silvio. "Os Palmares." *A Revista brasileira*, X (October–December, 1881).

Soucougnan [pseud.] *La troisième île*. Paris: Oswald, 1973.

Stephenson, Elie. *Une flèche pour le pays à l'encan*. Paris: Oswald, 1975.

Torres, Luís Lloréns. *Sonetos sinfónicos*. San Juan, 1914.

Valdés, Gabriel de la Concepción. *Poesías completas de Plácido*. Paris, 1857.

Walcott, Derek. *The Castaway and Other Poems*. London: Cape, 1965.

———. *In a Green Night: Poems, 1948–1960*. London: Cape, 1962.

———. *Sea Grapes*. New York: Farrar, Strauss and Giroux, 1976.

9. Drama

Genet, Jean. *The Blacks: A Clown Show*. New York: Grove Press, 1960.

Walcott, Derek. *Dream on Monkey Mountain and Other Plays*. New York: Farrar, Strauss and Giroux, 1973.

10. Periodicals

The Beacon. Port-au-Spain, Trinidad, 1931–1939.

Bim. Ed. Frank Collymore, St. Michael, Barbados. Twice yearly, 1942–1973. 1974–

Black Orpheus. Mbari Publications, Ibadan, Nigeria. Irregular 1957–1968. 2 issues from University of Lagos, Nigeria, 1969–

Caribbean Quarterly. Extra-Mural Department, University of the West Indies, Mona, Jamaica. Quarterly, 1949–1965; 1966–1972.

Etudiant noir. Paris, 1934–1935. 10 nos.

Flambeau. Kingston, St. Vincent. 1965–1968.

Focus. Mona, Jamaica. 1943, 1948, 1956, and 1960.

Les griots. Port-au-Prince, Haiti. 1932–1940.

Haiti Journal. Port-au-Prince, Haiti. Editions spéciales de Noel 1945 et 1946.

Journal of Caribbean Studies. Association of Caribbean Studies, P.O. Box 248231, Coral Gables, Fla. 33124. Three times per year. 1980–

Kaie. History and Arts Council, Georgetown, Guyana. Irregular. 1965.

Kyk-over-al. Georgetown, Guyana. 1945–1961.

New World Quarterly. Kingston, Jamaica. 1963–1972. Two special issues in 1966; *New World: Guyana Independence Issue* (1966) and *New World: Barbados Independence Issue* (1966).

Présence Africaine. 25 bis, rue des Ecoles, Paris 5e. Quarterly. 1947–

La relève. Port-au-Prince, Haiti. 1932–1939.

A Review of International English Literature. (ARIEL). The University of Calgary, Alberta, Canada, Quarterly. 1970–1977.

Revista Cubana. Havana, Cuba. 1885–1895. Then 1935–1957. Followed by *Nueva Revista Cubana*. 1959–1960 and 1962.

La revue indigène. Port-au-Prince, Haiti. 1927–1928.

Savacou. Department of History, University of the West Indies, Mona, Jamaica. Irregular. 1970–

World Literature Written in English. Department of English, University of Texas, Arlington, Texas. Biannual. 1962–

Index

Abolitionism: in United States, 65–66, 83–86, 94–95; in Brazil, 214, 216–17, 220–21. *See also* Slaves

Abrahams, Roger, 43

Achebe, Chinua, 254

Adventures of Jonathan Corncob, The, 122, 123

Africa: influence in New World, 6, 15–19, 63–65, 140, 247–52; and Afro-New World man, 12–16, 30, 54, 63–67, 95, 258; in works by Whites, 31, 61, 118–32, 176; and Brazil, 32, 37, 40, 54, 140, 213, 216–20, 223–26; folktales, 34–40, 106, 249–51; oral literature, 41–44, 53–56, 59–60, 68–70, 106; drama, 49–52; music and dance, 57–59, 72–77, 251–52; Blacks' return to, 62–66, 85, 91, 92, 174, 257, 260–61; games, 80–83; New World view of, 87–88, 175; in fiction and poetry, 96–104, 112–18, 138–39, 183, 185, 187, 189, 194, 195, 197–204, 206–209, 225, 226, 233–34, 236–39, 242, 253–58; and Afro-New World writers, 210–13, 256, 261–62; and primary synthesis, 245, 246; matriarchy, 248–49; communal living, 249, 259; sex, 251. *See also* names of specific countries

African languages, 20, 35–40, 55, 64, 213, 263

African religion: description of, 6, 10, 18–26, 48–49, 64–65, 211, 216–19, 223, 247; and Christianity, 10, 18–30, 56, 122–23, 140, 164, 250; in poetry and fiction, 135, 139–40, 143–44, 146, 213, 237, 238. See also Brazil; *Brujería;* Christianity; Devil; Gods; Priests; *Santería;* Voodoo

Africans: characteristics, 2–7; versus Afro-New World man, 7, 8, 17, 64, 66, 118, 245, 246, 256, 260

Afro-Brazilian writers, 214–28, 243

Afro-Cubanism, 18–26, 107–14, 152–55, 176–83, 243. *See also* Cuba

Afro-New World man: and Africa, 1–3, 59–60, 64, 66, 258; characteristics of, 1–4, 15–16, 243–45, 255, 264–65; and Europe, 2–4, 59–60, 213, 258; compared with Africans, 7, 8, 17, 64, 66, 118, 245, 246, 256, 260; West Indian versus Afro-American, 61–62. *See also* Blacks; Creoles; Mulattoes; Negroes; Nigger

Afro-New World writers, 49, 62, 210–14, 243. *See also* Black writers; White writers; names of specific countries and authors

Aidoo, Ama Ata, 259

Akan, 70, 82, 238, 239

Alleyn, Mervyn C., 264

Alvares, Alfonso, 219, 226

Alvarez, Paulina, 58

Alves, Castro, 215, 220, 226

Amado, Jorge, 216

Anancy, 25, 43–44, 56, 68, 250

Andrade, Mário de, 215, 226–27

Angola, 48, 224

Animals in folklore, 16–17, 43, 48, 68–69, 105–106, 213, 216, 250. *See also* Lion in folklore; Monkey in folklore; Uncle Remus stories

279

DATE DUE

DEC 1996			
SEP 0 9 1999			
GAYLORD			PRINTED IN U.S.A.